ACCESS YOUR ONLINE RESOURCES

DON'T MISS OUT ON THE ONLINE RESOURCES INCLUDED WITH YOUR PURCHASE!

Your purchase of this product unlocks access to our Online Resources page. Elevate your study experience with our **interactive practice test interface**, along with all of the additional resources that we couldn't include in this book.

Flip to the Online Resources section at the end of this book to find the link and a QR code to get started!

TExES

Mathematics 4-8 (115)

Secrets

Study Guide

Your Key to Exam Success

Mometrix

TEST PREPARATION

Written and edited by Matthew Bowling

Printed in the United States of America

This paper meets the requirements of ANSI/NISO Z39.48-1992 (Permanence of Paper).

Paperback
ISBN 13: 978-1-61072-937-6
ISBN 10: 1-61072-937-4

Ebook
ISBN 13: 978-1-5167-0446-0
ISBN 10: 1-5167-0446-0

DEAR FUTURE EXAM SUCCESS STORY

First of all, **THANK YOU** for purchasing Mometrix study materials!

Second, congratulations! You are one of the few determined test-takers who are committed to doing whatever it takes to excel on your exam. **You have come to the right place.** We developed these study materials with one goal in mind: to deliver you the information you need in a format that's concise and easy to use.

In addition to optimizing your guide for the content of the test, we've outlined our recommended steps for breaking down the preparation process into small, attainable goals so you can make sure you stay on track.

We've also analyzed the entire test-taking process, identifying the most common pitfalls and showing how you can overcome them and be ready for any curveball the test throws you.

Standardized testing is one of the biggest obstacles on your road to success, which only increases the importance of doing well in the high-pressure, high-stakes environment of test day. Your results on this test could have a significant impact on your future, and this guide provides the information and practical advice to help you achieve your full potential on test day.

Your success is our success

We would love to hear from you! If you would like to share the story of your exam success or if you have any questions or comments in regard to our products, please contact us at **800-673-8175** or **support@mometrix.com**.

Thanks again for your business and we wish you continued success!

Sincerely,
The Mometrix Test Preparation Team

TABLE OF CONTENTS

Introduction

Thank you for purchasing this resource! You have made the choice to prepare yourself for a test that could have a huge impact on your future, and this guide is designed to help you be fully ready for test day. Obviously, it's important to have a solid understanding of the test material, but you also need to be prepared for the unique environment and stressors of the test, so that you can perform to the best of your abilities.

For this purpose, the first section that appears in this guide is the **Secret Keys**. We've devoted countless hours to meticulously researching what works and what doesn't, and we've boiled down our findings to the five most impactful steps you can take to improve your performance on the test. We start at the beginning with study planning and move through the preparation process, all the way to the testing strategies that will help you get the most out of what you know when you're finally sitting in front of the test.

We recommend that you start preparing for your test as far in advance as possible. However, if you've bought this guide as a last-minute study resource and only have a few days before your test, we recommend that you skip over the first two Secret Keys since they address a long-term study plan.

If you struggle with **test anxiety**, we strongly encourage you to check out our recommendations for how you can overcome it. Test anxiety is a formidable foe, but it can be beaten, and we want to make sure you have the tools you need to defeat it.

Secret Key #1 – Plan Big, Study Small

There's a lot riding on your performance. If you want to ace this test, you're going to need to keep your skills sharp and the material fresh in your mind. You need a plan that lets you review everything you need to know while still fitting in your schedule. We'll break this strategy down into three categories.

Information Organization

Start with the information you already have: the official test outline. From this, you can make a complete list of all the concepts you need to cover before the test. Organize these concepts into groups that can be studied together, and create a list of any related vocabulary you need to learn so you can brush up on any difficult terms. You'll want to keep this vocabulary list handy once you actually start studying since you may need to add to it along the way.

Time Management

Once you have your set of study concepts, decide how to spread them out over the time you have left before the test. Break your study plan into small, clear goals so you have a manageable task for each day and know exactly what you're doing. Then just focus on one small step at a time. When you manage your time this way, you don't need to spend hours at a time studying. Studying a small block of content for a short period each day helps you retain information better and avoid stressing over how much you have left to do. You can relax knowing that you have a plan to cover everything in time. In order for this strategy to be effective though, you have to start studying early and stick to your schedule. Avoid the exhaustion and futility that comes from last-minute cramming!

Study Environment

The environment you study in has a big impact on your learning. Studying in a coffee shop, while probably more enjoyable, is not likely to be as fruitful as studying in a quiet room. It's important to keep distractions to a minimum. You're only planning to study for a short block of time, so make the most of it. Don't pause to check your phone or get up to find a snack. It's also important to **avoid multitasking**. Research has consistently shown that multitasking will make your studying dramatically less effective. Your study area should also be comfortable and well-lit so you don't have the distraction of straining your eyes or sitting on an uncomfortable chair.

The time of day you study is also important. You want to be rested and alert. Don't wait until just before bedtime. Study when you'll be most likely to comprehend and remember. Even better, if you know what time of day your test will be, set that time aside for study. That way your brain will be used to working on that subject at that specific time and you'll have a better chance of recalling information.

Finally, it can be helpful to team up with others who are studying for the same test. Your actual studying should be done in as isolated an environment as possible, but the work of organizing the information and setting up the study plan can be divided up. In between study sessions, you can discuss with your teammates the concepts that you're all studying and quiz each other on the details. Just be sure that your teammates are as serious about the test as you are. If you find that your study time is being replaced with social time, you might need to find a new team.

Secret Key #2 – Make Your Studying Count

You're devoting a lot of time and effort to preparing for this test, so you want to be absolutely certain it will pay off. This means doing more than just reading the content and hoping you can remember it on test day. It's important to make every minute of study count. There are two main areas you can focus on to make your studying count.

Retention

It doesn't matter how much time you study if you can't remember the material. You need to make sure you are retaining the concepts. To check your retention of the information you're learning, try recalling it at later times with minimal prompting. Try carrying around flashcards and glance at one or two from time to time or ask a friend who's also studying for the test to quiz you.

To enhance your retention, look for ways to put the information into practice so that you can apply it rather than simply recalling it. If you're using the information in practical ways, it will be much easier to remember. Similarly, it helps to solidify a concept in your mind if you're not only reading it to yourself but also explaining it to someone else. Ask a friend to let you teach them about a concept you're a little shaky on (or speak aloud to an imaginary audience if necessary). As you try to summarize, define, give examples, and answer your friend's questions, you'll understand the concepts better and they will stay with you longer. Finally, step back for a big picture view and ask yourself how each piece of information fits with the whole subject. When you link the different concepts together and see them working together as a whole, it's easier to remember the individual components.

Finally, practice showing your work on any multi-step problems, even if you're just studying. Writing out each step you take to solve a problem will help solidify the process in your mind, and you'll be more likely to remember it during the test.

Modality

Modality simply refers to the means or method by which you study. Choosing a study modality that fits your own individual learning style is crucial. No two people learn best in exactly the same way, so it's important to know your strengths and use them to your advantage.

For example, if you learn best by visualization, focus on visualizing a concept in your mind and draw an image or a diagram. Try color-coding your notes, illustrating them, or creating symbols that will trigger your mind to recall a learned concept. If you learn best by hearing or discussing information, find a study partner who learns the same way or read aloud to yourself. Think about how to put the information in your own words. Imagine that you are giving a lecture on the topic and record yourself so you can listen to it later.

For any learning style, flashcards can be helpful. Organize the information so you can take advantage of spare moments to review. Underline key words or phrases. Use different colors for different categories. Mnemonic devices (such as creating a short list in which every item starts with the same letter) can also help with retention. Find what works best for you and use it to store the information in your mind most effectively and easily.

Secret Key #3 – Practice the Right Way

Your success on test day depends not only on how many hours you put into preparing, but also on whether you prepared the right way. It's good to check along the way to see if your studying is paying off. One of the most effective ways to do this is by taking practice tests to evaluate your progress. Practice tests are useful because they show exactly where you need to improve. Every time you take a practice test, pay special attention to these three groups of questions:

- The questions you got wrong
- The questions you had to guess on, even if you guessed right
- The questions you found difficult or slow to work through

This will show you exactly what your weak areas are, and where you need to devote more study time. Ask yourself why each of these questions gave you trouble. Was it because you didn't understand the material? Was it because you didn't remember the vocabulary? Do you need more repetitions on this type of question to build speed and confidence? Dig into those questions and figure out how you can strengthen your weak areas as you go back to review the material.

Additionally, many practice tests have a section explaining the answer choices. It can be tempting to read the explanation and think that you now have a good understanding of the concept. However, an explanation likely only covers part of the question's broader context. Even if the explanation makes perfect sense, **go back and investigate** every concept related to the question until you're positive you have a thorough understanding.

As you go along, keep in mind that the practice test is just that: practice. Memorizing these questions and answers will not be very helpful on the actual test because it is unlikely to have any of the same exact questions. If you only know the right answers to the sample questions, you won't be prepared for the real thing. **Study the concepts** until you understand them fully, and then you'll be able to answer any question that shows up on the test.

It's important to wait on the practice tests until you're ready. If you take a test on your first day of study, you may be overwhelmed by the amount of material covered and how much you need to learn. Work up to it gradually.

On test day, you'll need to be prepared for answering questions, managing your time, and using the test-taking strategies you've learned. It's a lot to balance, like a mental marathon that will have a big impact on your future. Like training for a marathon, you'll need to start slowly and work your way up. When test day arrives, you'll be ready.

Start with the strategies you've read in the first two Secret Keys—plan your course and study in the way that works best for you. If you have time, consider using multiple study resources to get different approaches to the same concepts. It can be helpful to see difficult concepts from more than one angle. Then find a good source for practice tests. Many times, the test website will suggest potential study resources or provide sample tests.

Practice Test Strategy

If you're able to find at least three practice tests, we recommend this strategy:

Untimed and Open-Book Practice

Take the first test with no time constraints and with your notes and study guide handy. Take your time and focus on applying the strategies you've learned.

Timed and Open-Book Practice

Take the second practice test open-book as well, but set a timer and practice pacing yourself to finish in time.

Timed and Closed-Book Practice

Take any other practice tests as if it were test day. Set a timer and put away your study materials. Sit at a table or desk in a quiet room, imagine yourself at the testing center, and answer questions as quickly and accurately as possible.

Keep repeating timed and closed-book tests on a regular basis until you run out of practice tests or it's time for the actual test. Your mind will be ready for the schedule and stress of test day, and you'll be able to focus on recalling the material you've learned.

Secret Key #4 – Pace Yourself

Once you're fully prepared for the material on the test, your biggest challenge on test day will be managing your time. Just knowing that the clock is ticking can make you panic even if you have plenty of time left. Work on pacing yourself so you can build confidence against the time constraints of the exam. Pacing is a difficult skill to master, especially in a high-pressure environment, so **practice is vital**.

Set time expectations for your pace based on how much time is available. For example, if a section has 60 questions and the time limit is 30 minutes, you know you have to average 30 seconds or less per question in order to answer them all. Although 30 seconds is the hard limit, set 25 seconds per question as your goal, so you reserve extra time to spend on harder questions. When you budget extra time for the harder questions, you no longer have any reason to stress when those questions take longer to answer.

Don't let this time expectation distract you from working through the test at a calm, steady pace, but keep it in mind so you don't spend too much time on any one question. Recognize that taking extra time on one question you don't understand may keep you from answering two that you do understand later in the test. If your time limit for a question is up and you're still not sure of the answer, mark it and move on, and come back to it later if the time and the test format allow. If the testing format doesn't allow you to return to earlier questions, just make an educated guess; then put it out of your mind and move on.

On the easier questions, be careful not to rush. It may seem wise to hurry through them so you have more time for the challenging ones, but it's not worth missing one if you know the concept and just didn't take the time to read the question fully. Work efficiently but make sure you understand the question and have looked at all of the answer choices, since more than one may seem right at first.

Even if you're paying attention to the time, you may find yourself a little behind at some point. You should speed up to get back on track, but do so wisely. Don't panic; just take a few seconds less on each question until you're caught up. Don't guess without thinking, but do look through the answer choices and eliminate any you know are wrong. If you can get down to two choices, it is often worthwhile to guess from those. Once you've chosen an answer, move on and don't dwell on any that you skipped or had to hurry through. If a question was taking too long, chances are it was one of the harder ones, so you weren't as likely to get it right anyway.

On the other hand, if you find yourself getting ahead of schedule, it may be beneficial to slow down a little. The more quickly you work, the more likely you are to make a careless mistake that will affect your score. You've budgeted time for each question, so don't be afraid to spend that time. Practice an efficient but careful pace to get the most out of the time you have.

Secret Key #5 – Have a Plan for Guessing

When you're taking the test, you may find yourself stuck on a question. Some of the answer choices seem better than others, but you don't see the one answer choice that is obviously correct. What do you do?

The scenario described above is very common, yet most test takers have not effectively prepared for it. Developing and practicing a plan for guessing may be one of the single most effective uses of your time as you get ready for the exam.

In developing your plan for guessing, there are three questions to address:

- When should you start the guessing process?
- How should you narrow down the choices?
- Which answer should you choose?

When to Start the Guessing Process

Unless your plan for guessing is to select C every time (which, despite its merits, is not what we recommend), you need to leave yourself enough time to apply your answer elimination strategies. Since you have a limited amount of time for each question, that means that if you're going to give yourself the best shot at guessing correctly, you have to decide quickly whether or not you will guess.

Of course, the best-case scenario is that you don't have to guess at all, so first, see if you can answer the question based on your knowledge of the subject and basic reasoning skills. Focus on the key words in the question and try to jog your memory of related topics. Give yourself a chance to bring the knowledge to mind, but once you realize that you don't have (or you can't access) the knowledge you need to answer the question, it's time to start the guessing process.

It's almost always better to start the guessing process too early than too late. It only takes a few seconds to remember something and answer the question from knowledge. Carefully eliminating wrong answer choices takes longer. Plus, going through the process of eliminating answer choices can actually help jog your memory.

Summary: Start the guessing process as soon as you decide that you can't answer the question based on your knowledge.

How to Narrow Down the Choices

The next chapter in this book (**Test-Taking Strategies**) includes a wide range of strategies for how to approach questions and how to look for answer choices to eliminate. You will definitely want to read those carefully, practice them, and figure out which ones work best for you. Here though, we're going to address a mindset rather than a particular strategy.

Your odds of guessing an answer correctly depend on how many options you are choosing from.

Number of options left	5	4	3	2	1
Odds of guessing correctly	20%	25%	33%	50%	100%

You can see from this chart just how valuable it is to be able to eliminate incorrect answers and make an educated guess, but there are two things that many test takers do that cause them to miss out on the benefits of guessing:

- Accidentally eliminating the correct answer
- Selecting an answer based on an impression

We'll look at the first one here, and the second one in the next section.

To avoid accidentally eliminating the correct answer, we recommend a thought exercise called **the $5 challenge**. In this challenge, you only eliminate an answer choice from contention if you are willing to bet $5 on it being wrong. Why $5? Five dollars is a small but not insignificant amount of money. It's an amount you could afford to lose but wouldn't want to throw away. And while losing $5 once might not hurt too much, doing it twenty times will set you back $100. In the same way, each small decision you make—eliminating a choice here, guessing on a question there—won't by itself impact your score very much, but when you put them all together, they can make a big difference. By holding each answer choice elimination decision to a higher standard, you can reduce the risk of accidentally eliminating the correct answer.

The $5 challenge can also be applied in a positive sense: If you are willing to bet $5 that an answer choice *is* correct, go ahead and mark it as correct.

Summary: Only eliminate an answer choice if you are willing to bet $5 that it is wrong.

Which Answer to Choose

You're taking the test. You've run into a hard question and decided you'll have to guess. You've eliminated all the answer choices you're willing to bet $5 on. Now you have to pick an answer. Why do we even need to talk about this? Why can't you just pick whichever one you feel like when the time comes?

The answer to these questions is that if you don't come into the test with a plan, you'll rely on your impression to select an answer choice, and if you do that, you risk falling into a trap. The test writers know that everyone who takes their test will be guessing on some of the questions, so they intentionally write wrong answer choices to seem plausible. You still have to pick an answer though, and if the wrong answer choices are designed to look right, how can you ever be sure that you're not falling for their trap? The best solution we've found to this dilemma is to take the decision out of your hands entirely. Here is the process we recommend:

Once you've eliminated any choices that you are confident (willing to bet $5) are wrong, select the first remaining choice as your answer.

Whether you choose to select the first remaining choice, the second, or the last, the important thing is that you use some preselected standard. Using this approach guarantees that you will not be enticed into selecting an answer choice that looks right, because you are not basing your decision on how the answer choices look.

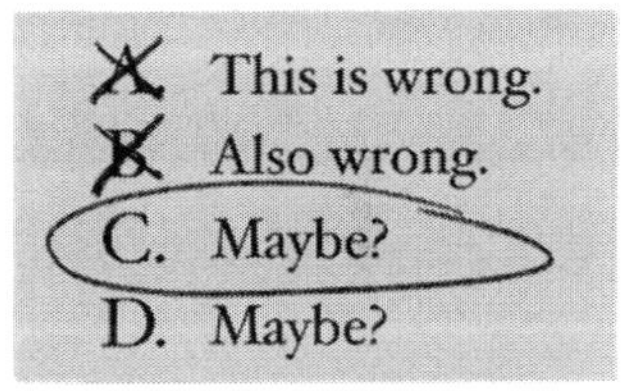

This is not meant to make you question your knowledge. Instead, it is to help you recognize the difference between your knowledge and your impressions. There's a huge difference between thinking an answer is right because of what you know, and thinking an answer is right because it looks or sounds like it should be right.

Summary: To ensure that your selection is appropriately random, make a predetermined selection from among all answer choices you have not eliminated.

Test-Taking Strategies

This section contains a list of test-taking strategies that you may find helpful as you work through the test. By taking what you know and applying logical thought, you can maximize your chances of answering any question correctly!

It is very important to realize that every question is different and every person is different: no single strategy will work on every question, and no single strategy will work for every person. That's why we've included all of them here, so you can try them out and determine which ones work best for different types of questions and which ones work best for you.

Question Strategies

☑ Read Carefully

Read the question and the answer choices carefully. Don't miss the question because you misread the terms. You have plenty of time to read each question thoroughly and make sure you understand what is being asked. Yet a happy medium must be attained, so don't waste too much time. You must read carefully and efficiently.

☑ Contextual Clues

Look for contextual clues. If the question includes a word you are not familiar with, look at the immediate context for some indication of what the word might mean. Contextual clues can often give you all the information you need to decipher the meaning of an unfamiliar word. Even if you can't determine the meaning, you may be able to narrow down the possibilities enough to make a solid guess at the answer to the question.

☑ Prefixes

If you're having trouble with a word in the question or answer choices, try dissecting it. Take advantage of every clue that the word might include. Prefixes can be a huge help. Usually, they allow you to determine a basic meaning. *Pre-* means before, *post-* means after, *pro-* is positive, *de-* is negative. From prefixes, you can get an idea of the general meaning of the word and try to put it into context.

☑ Hedge Words

Watch out for critical hedge words, such as *likely, may, can, often, almost, mostly, usually, generally, rarely,* and *sometimes.* Question writers insert these hedge phrases to cover every possibility. Often an answer choice will be wrong simply because it leaves no room for exception. Be on guard for answer choices that have definitive words such as *exactly* and *always.*

☑ Switchback Words

Stay alert for *switchbacks.* These are the words and phrases frequently used to alert you to shifts in thought. The most common switchback words are *but, although,* and *however.* Others include *nevertheless, on the other hand, even though, while, in spite of, despite,* and *regardless of.* Switchback words are important to catch because they can change the direction of the question or an answer choice.

☑ Face Value

When in doubt, use common sense. Accept the situation in the problem at face value. Don't read too much into it. These problems will not require you to make wild assumptions. If you have to go beyond creativity and warp time or space in order to have an answer choice fit the question, then you should move on and consider the other answer choices. These are normal problems rooted in reality. The applicable relationship or explanation may not be readily apparent, but it is there for you to figure out. Use your common sense to interpret anything that isn't clear.

Answer Choice Strategies

☑ Answer Selection

The most thorough way to pick an answer choice is to identify and eliminate wrong answers until only one is left, then confirm it is the correct answer. Sometimes an answer choice may immediately seem right, but be careful. The test writers will usually put more than one reasonable answer choice on each question, so take a second to read all of them and make sure that the other choices are not equally obvious. As long as you have time left, it is better to read every answer choice than to pick the first one that looks right without checking the others.

☑ Answer Choice Families

An answer choice family consists of two (in rare cases, three) answer choices that are very similar in construction and cannot all be true at the same time. If you see two answer choices that are direct opposites or parallels, one of them is usually the correct answer. For instance, if one answer choice says that quantity x increases and another either says that quantity x decreases (opposite) or says that quantity y increases (parallel), then those answer choices would fall into the same family. An answer choice that doesn't match the construction of the answer choice family is more likely to be incorrect. Most questions will not have answer choice families, but when they do appear, you should be prepared to recognize them.

☑ Eliminate Answers

Eliminate answer choices as soon as you realize they are wrong, but make sure you consider all possibilities. If you are eliminating answer choices and realize that the last one you are left with is also wrong, don't panic. Start over and consider each choice again. There may be something you missed the first time that you will realize on the second pass.

☑ Avoid Fact Traps

Don't be distracted by an answer choice that is factually true but doesn't answer the question. You are looking for the choice that answers the question. Stay focused on what the question is asking for so you don't accidentally pick an answer that is true but incorrect. Always go back to the question and make sure the answer choice you've selected actually answers the question and is not merely a true statement.

☑ Extreme Statements

In general, you should avoid answers that put forth extreme actions as standard practice or proclaim controversial ideas as established fact. An answer choice that states the "process should be used in certain situations, if..." is much more likely to be correct than one that states the "process should be discontinued completely." The first is a calm rational statement and doesn't even make a definitive, uncompromising stance, using a hedge word *if* to provide wiggle room, whereas the second choice is far more extreme.

✅ Benchmark

As you read through the answer choices and you come across one that seems to answer the question well, mentally select that answer choice. This is not your final answer, but it's the one that will help you evaluate the other answer choices. The one that you selected is your benchmark or standard for judging each of the other answer choices. Every other answer choice must be compared to your benchmark. That choice is correct until proven otherwise by another answer choice beating it. If you find a better answer, then that one becomes your new benchmark. Once you've decided that no other choice answers the question as well as your benchmark, you have your final answer.

✅ Predict the Answer

Before you even start looking at the answer choices, it is often best to try to predict the answer. When you come up with the answer on your own, it is easier to avoid distractions and traps because you will know exactly what to look for. The right answer choice is unlikely to be word-for-word what you came up with, but it should be a close match. Even if you are confident that you have the right answer, you should still take the time to read each option before moving on.

General Strategies

✅ Tough Questions

If you are stumped on a problem or it appears too hard or too difficult, don't waste time. Move on! Remember though, if you can quickly check for obviously incorrect answer choices, your chances of guessing correctly are greatly improved. Before you completely give up, at least try to knock out a couple of possible answers. Eliminate what you can and then guess at the remaining answer choices before moving on.

✅ Check Your Work

Since you will probably not know every term listed and the answer to every question, it is important that you get credit for the ones that you do know. Don't miss any questions through careless mistakes. If at all possible, try to take a second to look back over your answer selection and make sure you've selected the correct answer choice and haven't made a costly careless mistake (such as marking an answer choice that you didn't mean to mark). This quick double check should more than pay for itself in caught mistakes for the time it costs.

✅ Pace Yourself

It's easy to be overwhelmed when you're looking at a page full of questions; your mind is confused and full of random thoughts, and the clock is ticking down faster than you would like. Calm down and maintain the pace that you have set for yourself. Especially as you get down to the last few minutes of the test, don't let the small numbers on the clock make you panic. As long as you are on track by monitoring your pace, you are guaranteed to have time for each question.

✅ Don't Rush

It is very easy to make errors when you are in a hurry. Maintaining a fast pace in answering questions is pointless if it makes you miss questions that you would have gotten right otherwise. Test writers like to include distracting information and wrong answers that seem right. Taking a little extra time to avoid careless mistakes can make all the difference in your test score. Find a pace that allows you to be confident in the answers that you select.

✓ Keep Moving

Panicking will not help you pass the test, so do your best to stay calm and keep moving. Taking deep breaths and going through the answer elimination steps you practiced can help to break through a stress barrier and keep your pace.

Final Notes

The combination of a solid foundation of content knowledge and the confidence that comes from practicing your plan for applying that knowledge is the key to maximizing your performance on test day. As your foundation of content knowledge is built up and strengthened, you'll find that the strategies included in this chapter become more and more effective in helping you quickly sift through the distractions and traps of the test to isolate the correct answer.

Now that you're preparing to move forward into the test content chapters of this book, be sure to keep your goal in mind. As you read, think about how you will be able to apply this information on the test. If you've already seen sample questions for the test and you have an idea of the question format and style, try to come up with questions of your own that you can answer based on what you're reading. This will give you valuable practice applying your knowledge in the same ways you can expect to on test day.

Good luck and good studying!

Number Concepts

Number Basics

Classifications of Numbers

Numbers are the basic building blocks of mathematics. Specific features of numbers are identified by the following terms:

Integer – any positive or negative whole number, including zero. Integers do not include fractions $\left(\frac{1}{3}\right)$, decimals (0.56), or mixed numbers $\left(7\frac{3}{4}\right)$.

Prime number – any whole number greater than 1 that has only two factors, itself and 1; that is, a number that can be divided evenly only by 1 and itself.

Composite number – any whole number greater than 1 that has more than two different factors; in other words, any whole number that is not a prime number. For example: The composite number 8 has the factors of 1, 2, 4, and 8.

Even number – any integer that can be divided by 2 without leaving a remainder. For example: 2, 4, 6, 8, and so on.

Odd number – any integer that cannot be divided evenly by 2. For example: 3, 5, 7, 9, and so on.

Decimal number – any number that uses a decimal point to show the part of the number that is less than one. Example: 1.234.

Decimal point – a symbol used to separate the ones place from the tenths place in decimals or dollars from cents in currency.

Decimal place – the position of a number to the right of the decimal point. In the decimal 0.123, the 1 is in the first place to the right of the decimal point, indicating tenths; the 2 is in the second place, indicating hundredths; and the 3 is in the third place, indicating thousandths.

The **decimal**, or base 10, system is a number system that uses ten different digits (0, 1, 2, 3, 4, 5, 6, 7, 8, 9). An example of a number system that uses something other than ten digits is the **binary**, or base 2, number system, used by computers, which uses only the numbers 0 and 1. It is thought that the decimal system originated because people had only their 10 fingers for counting.

Rational numbers include all integers, decimals, and fractions. Any terminating or repeating decimal number is a rational number.

Irrational numbers cannot be written as fractions or decimals because the number of decimal places is infinite and there is no recurring pattern of digits within the number. For example, pi (π) begins with 3.141592 and continues without terminating or repeating, so pi is an irrational number.

Real numbers are the set of all rational and irrational numbers.

> **Review Video: Classification of Numbers**
> Visit mometrix.com/academy and enter code: 461071
>
> **Review Video: Prime and Composite Numbers**
> Visit mometrix.com/academy and enter code: 565581

NUMBERS IN WORD FORM AND PLACE VALUE

When writing numbers out in word form or translating word form to numbers, it is essential to understand how a place value system works. In the decimal or base-10 system, each digit of a number represents how many of the corresponding place value—a specific factor of 10—are contained in the number being represented. To make reading numbers easier, every three digits to the left of the decimal place is preceded by a comma. The following table demonstrates some of the place values:

Power of 10	10^3	10^2	10^1	10^0	10^{-1}	10^{-2}	10^{-3}
Value	1,000	100	10	1	0.1	0.01	0.001
Place	thousands	hundreds	tens	ones	tenths	hundredths	thousandths

For example, consider the number 4,546.09, which can be separated into each place value like this:

4: thousands
5: hundreds
4: tens
6: ones
0: tenths
9: hundredths

This number in word form would be *four thousand five hundred forty-six and nine hundredths.*

> **Review Video: Place Value**
> Visit mometrix.com/academy and enter code: 205433

Number Lines

A number line is a graph to see the distance between numbers. Basically, this graph shows the relationship between numbers. So a number line may have a point for zero and may show negative numbers on the left side of the line. Any positive numbers are placed on the right side of the line. For example, consider the points labeled on the following number line:

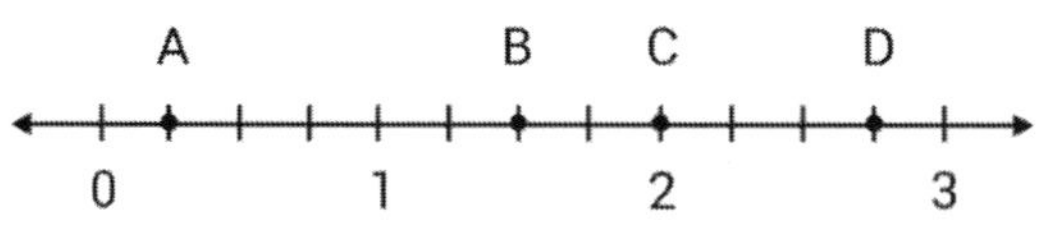

We can use the dashed lines on the number line to identify each point. Each dashed line between two whole numbers is $\frac{1}{4}$. The line halfway between two numbers is $\frac{1}{2}$.

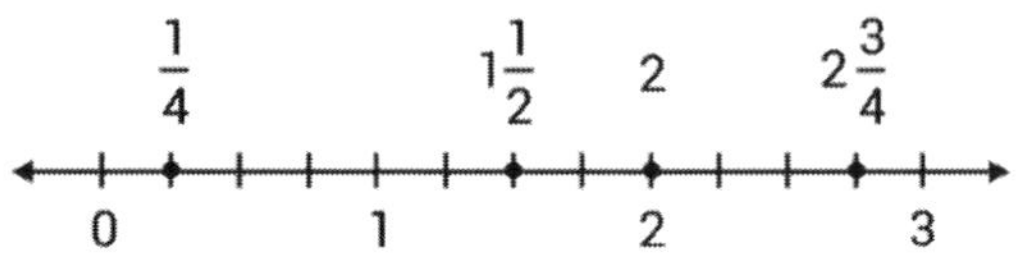

Review Video: The Number Line
Visit mometrix.com/academy and enter code: 816439

Comparing Numbers

Inequality Notation

The symbols $<$ and $>$ mean "is less than" and "is greater than," respectively. For instance, $3 < 5$ means "3 is less than 5," and $7 > 4$ means "7 is greater than 4." Statements like $3 < 5$ and $7 > 4$ are **inequalities**, and the symbols $<$ and $>$ are **inequality symbols**.

Whole Numbers and Decimal Numbers

To compare whole or decimal numbers, we look at the most significant place (the leftmost digit) at which they differ. The number with the larger digit in that place is larger. For instance, $0.3\underline{8}74$ and $0.3\underline{9}$ differ in the hundredths place (underlined). Since 8 is smaller than 9, we see $0.3874 < 0.39$. This is clearer if we make the decimals equal in length by writing extra zeroes: $0.3874 < 0.3900$. Similarly, $2\underline{3}.984 < 2\underline{5}.112$ because 3 is smaller than 5, or 23 is smaller than 25.

Fractions

If fractions have the same denominator, the fraction with the larger numerator is larger. For instance, $\frac{2}{7} < \frac{5}{7}$ since $2 < 5$. We compare fractions with different denominators by finding a common denominator. When comparing the fractions with a common denominator we only compare the numerator, so as a shortcut, we can multiply each numerator by the denominator of the other fraction. The numerator that produces the larger product belongs to the larger fraction. For example, to compare $\frac{7}{8}$ and $\frac{5}{6}$, we note that $7 \cdot 6 = 42$ is larger than $5 \cdot 8 = 40$. Since the numerator 7 produces the larger product, we see $\frac{7}{8} > \frac{5}{6}$. We can also compare fractions by converting them to decimals. For instance, since $\frac{3}{4} = 0.75$ and $\frac{4}{5} = 0.8$ and $0.75 < 0.8$, we conclude $\frac{3}{4} < \frac{4}{5}$.

Mixed Numbers

To compare mixed numbers we compare their whole number parts. If those are equal, then we compare their fractional parts. For instance, $5\frac{3}{8} > 4\frac{7}{8}$ because $5 > 4$, but $3\frac{5}{9} < 3\frac{8}{9}$ because $\frac{5}{9} < \frac{8}{9}$.

Square Roots

To compare square roots, we convert them to decimals, usually with a calculator. To compare two square roots, we compare their radicands. For instance, $\sqrt{11} < \sqrt{14}$ because $11 < 14$.

NEGATIVE NUMBERS

A negative number is always less than a positive number. Two negative numbers compare in the reverse order of their opposites. For instance, $-6 < -2$ (that is, -6 is smaller, more negative, than -2) because $6 > 2$.

Absolute Value

A precursor to working with negative numbers is understanding what **absolute values** are. A number's absolute value is simply the distance away from zero a number is on the number line. The absolute value of a number is always positive and is written $|x|$. For example, the absolute value of 3, written as $|3|$, is 3 because the distance between 0 and 3 on a number line is three units. Likewise, the absolute value of -3, written as $|-3|$, is 3 because the distance between 0 and -3 on a number line is three units. So $|3| = |-3|$.

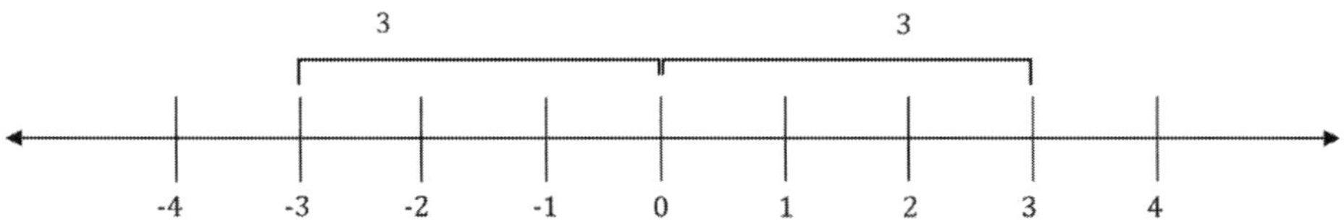

Review Video: Absolute Value
Visit mometrix.com/academy and enter code: 314669

Operations

An **operation** is simply a mathematical process that takes some value(s) as input(s) and produces an output. Elementary operations are often written in the following form: *value operation value*. For instance, in the expression $1 + 2$ the values are 1 and 2 and the operation is addition. Performing the operation gives the output of 3. In this way we can say that $1 + 2$ and 3 are equal, or $1 + 2 = 3$.

ADDITION

Addition increases the value of one quantity by the value of another quantity (both called **addends**). Example: $2 + 4 = 6$ or $8 + 9 = 17$. The result is called the **sum**. With addition, the order does not matter, $4 + 2 = 2 + 4$.

When adding signed numbers, if the signs are the same simply add the absolute values of the addends and apply the original sign to the sum. For example, $(+4) + (+8) = +12$ and $(-4) + (-8) = -12$. When the original signs are different, take the absolute values of the addends and subtract the smaller value from the larger value, then apply the original sign of the larger value to the difference. Example: $(+4) + (-8) = -4$ and $(-4) + (+8) = +4$.

SUBTRACTION

Subtraction is the opposite operation to addition; it decreases the value of one quantity (the **minuend**) by the value of another quantity (the **subtrahend**). For example, $6 - 4 = 2$ or $17 - 8 = 9$. The result is called the **difference**. Note that with subtraction, the order does matter, $6 - 4 \neq 4 - 6$.

For subtracting signed numbers, change the sign of the subtrahend and then follow the same rules used for addition. Example: $(+4) - (+8) = (+4) + (-8) = -4$

Multiplication

Multiplication can be thought of as repeated addition. One number (the **multiplier**) indicates how many times to add the other number (the **multiplicand**) to itself. Example: $3 \times 2 = 2 + 2 + 2 = 6$. With multiplication, the order does not matter, $2 \times 3 = 3 \times 2$ or $3 + 3 = 2 + 2 + 2$, either way the result (the **product**) is the same.

If the signs are the same, the product is positive when multiplying signed numbers. Example: $(+4) \times (+8) = +32$ and $(-4) \times (-8) = +32$. If the signs are opposite, the product is negative. Example: $(+4) \times (-8) = -32$ and $(-4) \times (+8) = -32$. When more than two factors are multiplied together, the sign of the product is determined by how many negative factors are present. If there are an odd number of negative factors then the product is negative, whereas an even number of negative factors indicates a positive product. Example: $(+4) \times (-8) \times (-2) = +64$ and $(-4) \times (-8) \times (-2) = -64$.

Division

Division is the opposite operation to multiplication; one number (the **divisor**) tells us how many parts to divide the other number (the **dividend**) into. The result of division is called the **quotient**. Example: $20 \div 4 = 5$. If 20 is split into 4 equal parts, each part is 5. With division, the order of the numbers does matter, $20 \div 4 \neq 4 \div 20$.

The rules for dividing signed numbers are similar to multiplying signed numbers. If the dividend and divisor have the same sign, the quotient is positive. If the dividend and divisor have opposite signs, the quotient is negative. Example: $(-4) \div (+8) = -0.5$.

Review Video: Mathematical Operations
Visit mometrix.com/academy and enter code: 208095

Parentheses

Parentheses are used to designate which operations should be done first when there are multiple operations. Example: $4 - (2 + 1) = 1$; the parentheses tell us that we must add 2 and 1, and then subtract the sum from 4, rather than subtracting 2 from 4 and then adding 1 (this would give us an answer of 3).

Review Video: Mathematical Parentheses
Visit mometrix.com/academy and enter code: 978600

Exponents

An **exponent** is a superscript number placed next to another number at the top right. It indicates how many times the base number is to be multiplied by itself. Exponents provide a shorthand way to write what would be a longer mathematical expression. Example: $2^4 = 2 \times 2 \times 2 \times 2$. A number with an exponent of 2 is said to be "squared," while a number with an exponent of 3 is said to be "cubed." The value of a number raised to an exponent is called its power. So 8^4 is read as "8 to the 4th power," or "8 raised to the power of 4."

Review Video: Exponents
Visit mometrix.com/academy and enter code: 600998

Roots

A **root**, such as a square root, is another way of writing a fractional exponent. Instead of using a superscript, roots use the radical symbol ($\sqrt{\ }$) to indicate the operation. A radical will have a number underneath the bar, and may sometimes have a number in the upper left: $\sqrt[n]{a}$, read as "the nth root of a." The relationship between radical notation and exponent notation can be described by this equation:

$$\sqrt[n]{a} = a^{\frac{1}{n}}$$

The two special cases of $n = 2$ and $n = 3$ are called square roots and cube roots. If there is no number to the upper left, the radical is understood to be a square root ($n = 2$). Nearly all of the roots you encounter will be square roots. A square root is the same as a number raised to the one-half power. When we say that a is the square root of b ($a = \sqrt{b}$), we mean that a multiplied by itself equals b: ($a \times a = b$).

A **perfect square** is a number that has an integer for its square root. There are 10 perfect squares from 1 to 100: 1, 4, 9, 16, 25, 36, 49, 64, 81, 100 (the squares of integers 1 through 10).

Review Video: Roots
Visit mometrix.com/academy and enter code: 795655

Review Video: Perfect Squares and Square Roots
Visit mometrix.com/academy and enter code: 648063

Word Problems and Mathematical Symbols

When working on word problems, you must be able to translate verbal expressions or "math words" into math symbols. This chart contains several "math words" and their appropriate symbols:

Phrase	Symbol
equal, is, was, will be, has, costs, gets to, is the same as, becomes	$=$
times, of, multiplied by, product of, twice, doubles, halves, triples	$\times$
divided by, per, ratio of/to, out of	$\div$
plus, added to, sum, combined, and, more than, totals of	$+$
subtracted from, less than, decreased by, minus, difference between	$-$
what, how much, original value, how many, a number, a variable	x, n, etc.

Review Video: Understanding Word Problems
Visit mometrix.com/academy and enter code: 499199

Examples of Translated Mathematical Phrases

- The phrase four more than twice a number can be written algebraically as $2x + 4$.
- The phrase half a number decreased by six can be written algebraically as $\frac{1}{2}x - 6$.
- The phrase the sum of a number and the product of five and that number can be written algebraically as $x + 5x$.

- You may see a test question that says, "Olivia is constructing a bookcase from seven boards. Two of them are for vertical supports and five are for shelves. The height of the bookcase is twice the width of the bookcase. If the seven boards total 36 feet in length, what will be the height of Olivia's bookcase?" You would need to make a sketch and then create the equation to determine the width of the shelves. The height can be represented as double the width. (If x represents the width of the shelves in feet, then the height of the bookcase is $2x$. Since the seven boards total 36 feet, $2x + 2x + x + x + x + x + x = 36$ or $9x = 36$; $x = 4$. The height is twice the width, or 8 feet.)

Subtraction with Regrouping

A great way to make use of some of the features built into the decimal system would be regrouping when attempting longform subtraction operations. When subtracting within a place value, sometimes the minuend is smaller than the subtrahend; **regrouping** enables you to 'borrow' a unit from a place value to the left in order to get a positive difference. For example, consider subtracting 189 from 525 with regrouping.

First, set up the subtraction problem in vertical form:

	525
-	189

Notice that the numbers in the ones and tens columns of 525 are smaller than the numbers in the ones and tens columns of 189. This means you will need to use regrouping to perform subtraction:

	5	2	5
-	1	8	9

To subtract 9 from 5 in the ones column you will need to borrow from the 2 in the tens column:

	5	1	15
-	1	8	9
			6

Next, to subtract 8 from 1 in the tens column you will need to borrow from the 5 in the hundreds column:

	4	11	15
-	1	8	9
		3	6

Last, subtract the 1 from the 4 in the hundreds column:

	4	11	15
-	1	8	9
	3	3	6

Review Video: Subtracting Large Numbers
Visit mometrix.com/academy and enter code: 603350

Order of Operations

The **order of operations** is a set of rules that dictates the order in which we must perform each operation in an expression so that we will evaluate it accurately. If we have an expression that includes multiple different operations, the order of operations tells us which operations to do first. The most common mnemonic for the order of operations is **PEMDAS**, or "Please Excuse My Dear Aunt Sally." PEMDAS stands for parentheses, exponents, multiplication, division, addition, and subtraction. It is important to understand that multiplication and division have equal precedence, as do addition and subtraction, so those pairs of operations are simply worked from left to right in order.

For example, evaluating the expression $5 + 20 \div 4 \times (2 + 3)^2 - 6$ using the correct order of operations would be done like this:

- **P:** Perform the operations inside the parentheses: $(2 + 3) = 5$
- **E:** Simplify the exponents: $(5)^2 = 5 \times 5 = 25$
    - The expression now looks like this: $5 + 20 \div 4 \times 25 - 6$
- **MD:** Perform multiplication and division from left to right: $20 \div 4 = 5$; then $5 \times 25 = 125$
    - The expression now looks like this: $5 + 125 - 6$
- **AS:** Perform addition and subtraction from left to right: $5 + 125 = 130$; then $130 - 6 = 124$

Review Video: Order of Operations
Visit mometrix.com/academy and enter code: 259675

Properties of Operations

The Commutative Property

The commutative property applies to addition and multiplication and states that these operations can be completed in any order. The **commutative property of addition** states that numbers and terms can be added together in any order to still get the same value. For example, $3 + 4 = 7$ and $4 + 3 = 7$. Also, we can use the commutative property of addition to show that $3x + 4 + 2^2$ is equivalent to $4 + 3x + 2^2$ and $2^2 + 4 + 3x$. When adding terms, you can add in any order and get the same value.

The **commutative property of multiplication** states that numbers and terms can be multiplied in any order to get the same value. For example, 12×3 is equivalent to 3×12. Additionally, we can use the commutative property of multiplication to assume that $(5 + 3) \times (36 - 6)$ is equivalent to $(36 - 6) \times (5 + 3)$. You can multiply terms in any order and still get the same value.

The Associative Property

The **associative property of addition** states that if three or more terms are being added together, the value is the same regardless of the groupings.

For example, given the expression $3 + 4 + 6$, these terms can be grouped and added in any form. $3 + 4 + 6$ is equivalent to $(3 + 4) + 6$ and is also equivalent to $3 + (4 + 6)$. This can be applied to write equivalent expressions in a variety of ways.

For example, suppose we are given the expression $5 + (y + 2) + 4$. We can generate equivalent expressions knowing the associative property. Knowing that when three or more terms are added, the grouping is irrelevant, we can say that this expression is equivalent to $5 + y + (2 + 4)$, and it is equivalent to $(5 + y) + (2 + 4)$. It is even equivalent to $5 + y + 2 + 4$.

The **associative property of multiplication** states that if three or more terms are being multiplied together, the value is the same regardless of the grouping. We can use this property to identify and generate equivalent expressions.

For example, given the expression $2 \times 7 \times 3$, these terms can be grouped in any way and still get the same value. $2 \times 7 \times 3$ is equivalent to $(2 \times 7) \times 3$ or $2 \times (7 \times 3)$.

THE IDENTITY PROPERTY

The **identity property of multiplication** states that when a number is multiplied by 1, you get the same number. That is, anything multiplied by 1 is itself. For example, $2 \times 1 = 2$, or $1 \times -36 = -36$. Using the identity property of multiplication, we can identify and generate equivalent expressions. Let's say that we are given the expression $15 - (3 \times 4)$. We can generate equivalent expressions using the identity property. One equivalent expression example would be $(15 \times 1) - (3 \times 4)$. Another example would be $15 - (1 \times 3 \times 4)$. We can say these expressions are equivalent because the identity property of multiplication states that we can multiply any portion of an expression by 1 to get the same value.

The **identity property of addition** states that when 0 is added to a number, you get the same number. For example, $2 + 0 = 2$, or $0 + -3 = -3$. We can also use this property to identify and generate equivalent expressions. For example, if we are given the expression $2 \times (1 + 2)$, we could write the equivalent expressions $2 \times (0 + 1 + 2)$ or $(2 + 0) \times (1 + 2)$.

THE INVERSE PROPERTY

The **inverse property of addition** states that the sum of a number and its opposite is always equal to 0. Remember, the opposite of a number is a number that is opposite on the number line from zero, or the same number with the opposite sign. For example, -4 is opposite to 4, and 1,726.9 is opposite to $-1{,}726.9$. So, the inverse property of addition states that if you add opposite numbers, their sum is zero. For example, $5 + (-5) = 0$ and $-5 + 5 = 0$.

The **inverse property of multiplication** states that a number multiplied by its reciprocal is always equal to 1. The **reciprocal** of a number is its "flipped" fraction. For example, the reciprocal of 5 is $\frac{1}{5}$, or the reciprocal of $\frac{2}{3}$ is $\frac{3}{2}$. The inverse property of multiplication can be applied for these values, $5 \times \frac{1}{5} = 1$ and $\frac{2}{3} \times \frac{3}{2} = 1$. This is because when you multiply across, you get a fraction that is equal to 1.

$$\frac{2}{3} \times \frac{3}{2} = \frac{6}{6} = 1$$

THE DISTRIBUTIVE PROPERTY

The **distributive property** explains how multiplication and addition interact. It says that when multiplying one number by the sum of two other numbers, the same result can also be obtained by multiplying the one number by each of the numbers individually and then adding the products. For example, to multiply 2 by the sum of 7 and 3, the direct approach says, "the sum of 7 and 3 is 10, and 2 times 10 is 20." This would be expressed as $2 \times (7 + 3) = 2 \times 10 = 20$. On the other hand, the distributive property states that the same answer can be achieved by multiplying each number inside the parentheses and adding the products. That is, "the product of 2 and 7 is 14, the product of

2 and 3 is 6, and the sum of 14 and 6 is 20." This would be expressed as $2 \times (7 + 3) = 2 \times 7 + 2 \times 3 = 14 + 6 = 20$, and it is demonstrated below.

$$2 \times (7 + 3) = 2 \times 7 + 2 \times 3$$

This same concept can be used when multiplying a number by the difference of two numbers. For example, $5 \times (10 - 4) = 5 \times 10 - 5 \times 4$. Since $5 \times 10 = 50$ and $5 \times 4 = 20$, the result is $50 - 20 = 30$. This answer can be checked by subtracting inside the parentheses first and then multiplying: $5 \times (10 - 4) = 5 \times 6 = 30$.

Review Video: Commutative, Associative, and Distributive Properties
Visit mometrix.com/academy and enter code: 483176

Properties of Exponents

The properties of exponents are as follows:

Property	Description
$a^1 = a$	Any number to the power of 1 is equal to itself
$1^n = 1$	The number 1 raised to any power is equal to 1
$a^0 = 1$	Any number raised to the power of 0 is equal to 1
$a^n \times a^m = a^{n+m}$	Add exponents to multiply powers of the same base number
$a^n \div a^m = a^{n-m}$	Subtract exponents to divide powers of the same base number
$(a^n)^m = a^{n \times m}$	When a power is raised to a power, the exponents are multiplied
$(a \times b)^n = a^n \times b^n$ $(a \div b)^n = a^n \div b^n$	Multiplication and division operations inside parentheses can be raised to a power. This is the same as each term being raised to that power.
$a^{-n} = \frac{1}{a^n}$	A negative exponent is the same as the reciprocal of a positive exponent

Note that exponents do not have to be integers. Fractional or decimal exponents follow all the rules above as well. Example: $5^{\frac{1}{4}} \times 5^{\frac{3}{4}} = 5^{\frac{1}{4}+\frac{3}{4}} = 5^1 = 5$.

Review Video: Properties of Exponents
Visit mometrix.com/academy and enter code: 532558

Factors and Multiples

Factors and Greatest Common Factor

A whole number a is a **factor** (or **divisor**) of a whole number b if a divides b evenly. In other words, a is a factor of b if the quotient $b \div a$ is a whole number with a remainder of 0. For instance, 3 is a factor of 12 because $12 \div 3 = 4$ with no remainder. Another way to say this is that a is a factor of b if we can multiply a by another whole number to get b. So, we can also show that 3 is a factor of 12 by noting that $3 \times 4 = 12$.

Every positive whole number has 1 and itself as factors. If a whole number greater than one has *only* 1 and itself as factors, we call it a **prime number**. For instance, 5 is a prime number because its only factors are 1 and 5. The first several prime numbers are 2, 3, 5, 7, 11, and 13.

If a whole number greater than 1 is not prime—that is, if it has factors besides 1 and itself—then it is a **composite number.** For instance, 10 is a composite number because it has factors 2 and 5 in addition to 1 and 10. The first several composite numbers are 4, 6, 8, 9, 10, 12, 14, and 15.

A **prime factor** of a whole number is a factor that is also a prime number. For example, the prime factors of 12 are 2 and 3. The prime factors of 15 are 3 and 5.

A **common factor** of two (or more) whole numbers is a number that is a factor of both (or all) of them. For example, the factors of 12 are <u>1</u>, 2, <u>3</u>, 4, 6, and 12, while the factors of 15 are <u>1</u>, <u>3</u>, 5, and 15. The common factors (underlined) of 12 and 15 are 1 and 3.

The **greatest common factor** (**GCF**) of two (or more) whole numbers is the largest number that is a factor of both (or all) of them. For example, the factors of 15 are <u>1</u>, 3, <u>5</u>, and 15; the factors of 35 are <u>1</u>, <u>5</u>, 7, and 35. Therefore, the greatest common factor of 15 and 35 is 5.

Review Video: Factors
Visit mometrix.com/academy and enter code: 920086

Review Video: Prime Numbers and Factorization
Visit mometrix.com/academy and enter code: 760669

MULTIPLES AND LEAST COMMON MULTIPLE

A whole number b is a **multiple** of a whole number a when a is a factor of b. This means that b is the product of a and another whole number. For example, the multiples of 7 are $0 \times 7 = 0, 1 \times 7 = 7, 2 \times 7 = 14, 3 \times 7 = 21, 4 \times 7 = 28, 5 \times 7 = 35$, ... Dividing 0, 7, 14, 21, 28, and 35 by 7 results in the whole numbers 0, 1, 2, 3, 4, and 5, respectively, showing that 7 is a factor of these numbers.

The least common multiple (**LCM**) of two (or more) whole numbers is the smallest number that is a multiple of both (or all) of them. For example, the multiples of 3 are 3, 6, 9, 12, <u>15</u>, ...; the multiples of 5 are 5, 10, <u>15</u>, 20, ... The smallest number that appears in both lists is 15, so the least common multiple of 3 and 5 is 15.

Review Video: Multiples
Visit mometrix.com/academy and enter code: 626738

Review Video: Greatest Common Factor and Least Common Multiple
Visit mometrix.com/academy and enter code: 838699

Fractions

A **fraction** is a number that is expressed as one integer written above another integer, with a dividing line between them $\left(\frac{x}{y}\right)$. It represents the **quotient** of the two numbers "x divided by y." It can also be thought of as x out of y equal parts.

The top number of a fraction is called the **numerator**, and it represents the number of parts under consideration. The 1 in $\frac{1}{4}$ means that 1 part out of the whole is being considered in the calculation.

The bottom number of a fraction is called the **denominator**, and it represents the total number of equal parts. The 4 in $\frac{1}{4}$ means that the whole consists of 4 equal parts. A fraction cannot have a denominator of zero; this is referred to as "*undefined.*"

Fractions can be manipulated, without changing the value of the fraction, by multiplying or dividing (but not adding or subtracting) both the numerator and denominator by the same number. If you divide both numbers by a common factor, you are **reducing** or simplifying the fraction. Two fractions that have the same value but are expressed differently are known as **equivalent fractions**. For example, $\frac{2}{10}, \frac{3}{15}, \frac{4}{20}$, and $\frac{5}{25}$ are all equivalent fractions. They can also all be reduced or simplified to $\frac{1}{5}$.

When two fractions are manipulated so that they have the same denominator, this is known as finding a **common denominator**. The number chosen to be that common denominator should be the least common multiple of the two original denominators. Example: $\frac{3}{4}$ and $\frac{5}{6}$; the least common multiple of 4 and 6 is 12. Manipulating to achieve the common denominator: $\frac{3}{4} = \frac{9}{12}; \frac{5}{6} = \frac{10}{12}$.

Review Video: Overview of Fractions
Visit mometrix.com/academy and enter code: 262335

Proper Fractions and Mixed Numbers

A fraction whose denominator is greater than its numerator is known as a **proper fraction**, while a fraction whose numerator is greater than its denominator is known as an **improper fraction**. Proper fractions have values *less than one* and improper fractions have values *greater than one.*

A **mixed number** is a number that contains both an integer and a fraction. Any improper fraction can be rewritten as a mixed number. Example: $\frac{8}{3} = \frac{6}{3} + \frac{2}{3} = 2 + \frac{2}{3} = 2\frac{2}{3}$. Similarly, any mixed number can be rewritten as an improper fraction. Example: $1\frac{3}{5} = 1 + \frac{3}{5} = \frac{5}{5} + \frac{3}{5} = \frac{8}{5}$.

Review Video: Proper and Improper Fractions and Mixed Numbers
Visit mometrix.com/academy and enter code: 211077

Adding and Subtracting Fractions

If two fractions have a common denominator, they can be added or subtracted simply by adding or subtracting the two numerators and retaining the same denominator. If the two fractions do not already have the same denominator, one or both of them must be manipulated to achieve a common denominator before they can be added or subtracted. Example: $\frac{1}{2} + \frac{1}{4} = \frac{2}{4} + \frac{1}{4} = \frac{3}{4}$.

Review Video: Adding and Subtracting Fractions
Visit mometrix.com/academy and enter code: 378080

MULTIPLYING FRACTIONS

Two fractions can be multiplied by multiplying the two numerators to find the new numerator and the two denominators to find the new denominator. Example: $\frac{1}{3} \times \frac{2}{3} = \frac{1 \times 2}{3 \times 3} = \frac{2}{9}$.

DIVIDING FRACTIONS

Two fractions can be divided by flipping the numerator and denominator of the second fraction and then proceeding as though it were a multiplication problem. Example: $\frac{2}{3} \div \frac{3}{4} = \frac{2}{3} \times \frac{4}{3} = \frac{8}{9}$.

> **Review Video: Multiplying and Dividing Fractions**
> Visit mometrix.com/academy and enter code: 473632

MULTIPLYING A MIXED NUMBER BY A WHOLE NUMBER OR A DECIMAL

When multiplying a mixed number by something, it is usually best to convert it to an improper fraction first. Additionally, if the multiplicand is a decimal, it is most often simplest to convert it to a fraction. For instance, to multiply $4\frac{3}{8}$ by 3.5, begin by rewriting each quantity as a whole number plus a proper fraction. Remember, a mixed number is a fraction added to a whole number and a decimal is a representation of the sum of fractions, specifically tenths, hundredths, thousandths, and so on:

$$4\frac{3}{8} \times 3.5 = \left(4 + \frac{3}{8}\right) \times \left(3 + \frac{1}{2}\right)$$

Next, the quantities being added need to be expressed with the same denominator. This is achieved by multiplying and dividing the whole number by the denominator of the fraction. Recall that a whole number is equivalent to that number divided by 1:

$$= \left(\frac{4}{1} \times \frac{8}{8} + \frac{3}{8}\right) \times \left(\frac{3}{1} \times \frac{2}{2} + \frac{1}{2}\right)$$

When multiplying fractions, remember to multiply the numerators and denominators separately:

$$= \left(\frac{4 \times 8}{1 \times 8} + \frac{3}{8}\right) \times \left(\frac{3 \times 2}{1 \times 2} + \frac{1}{2}\right)$$
$$= \left(\frac{32}{8} + \frac{3}{8}\right) \times \left(\frac{6}{2} + \frac{1}{2}\right)$$

Now that the fractions have the same denominators, they can be added:

$$= \frac{35}{8} \times \frac{7}{2}$$

Finally, perform the last multiplication and then simplify:

$$= \frac{35 \times 7}{8 \times 2} = \frac{245}{16} = \frac{240}{16} + \frac{5}{16} = 15\frac{5}{16}$$

COMPARING FRACTIONS

It is important to master the ability to compare and order fractions. This skill is relevant to many real-world scenarios. For example, carpenters often compare fractional construction nail lengths when preparing for a project, and bakers often compare fractional measurements to have the correct ratio of ingredients. There are three commonly used strategies when comparing fractions. These strategies are referred to as the common denominator approach, the decimal approach, and the cross-multiplication approach.

USING A COMMON DENOMINATOR TO COMPARE FRACTIONS

The fractions $\frac{2}{3}$ and $\frac{4}{7}$ have different denominators. $\frac{2}{3}$ has a denominator of 3, and $\frac{4}{7}$ has a denominator of 7. In order to precisely compare these two fractions, it is necessary to use a common denominator. A common denominator is a common multiple that is shared by both denominators. In this case, the denominators 3 and 7 share a multiple of 21. In general, it is most efficient to select the least common multiple for the two denominators.

Rewrite each fraction with the common denominator of 21. Then, calculate the new numerators as illustrated below.

$$\frac{2}{3} \xrightarrow{\times 7} \frac{\mathbf{14}}{21} \qquad \frac{4}{7} \xrightarrow{\times 3} \frac{\mathbf{12}}{21}$$

$$\frac{2}{3} = \frac{14}{21} \qquad \frac{4}{7} = \frac{12}{21}$$

For $\frac{2}{3}$, multiply the numerator and denominator by 7. The result is $\frac{14}{21}$.

For $\frac{4}{7}$, multiply the numerator and denominator by 3. The result is $\frac{12}{21}$.

Now that both fractions have a denominator of 21, the fractions can accurately be compared by comparing the numerators. Since 14 is greater than 12, the fraction $\frac{14}{21}$ is greater than $\frac{12}{21}$. This means that $\frac{2}{3}$ is greater than $\frac{4}{7}$.

USING DECIMALS TO COMPARE FRACTIONS

Sometimes decimal values are easier to compare than fraction values. For example, $\frac{5}{8}$ is equivalent to 0.625 and $\frac{3}{5}$ is equivalent to 0.6. This means that the comparison of $\frac{5}{8}$ and $\frac{3}{5}$ can be determined by comparing the decimals 0.625 and 0.6. When both decimal values are extended to the thousandths place, they become 0.625 and 0.600, respectively. It becomes clear that 0.625 is greater than 0.600 because 625 thousandths is greater than 600 thousandths. In other words, $\frac{5}{8}$ is greater than $\frac{3}{5}$ because 0.625 is greater than 0.6.

USING CROSS-MULTIPLICATION TO COMPARE FRACTIONS

Cross-multiplication is an efficient strategy for comparing fractions. This is a shortcut for the common denominator strategy. Start by writing each fraction next to one another. Multiply the numerator of the fraction on the left by the denominator of the fraction on the right. Write down the result next to the fraction on the left. Now multiply the numerator of the fraction on the right by the denominator of the fraction on the left. Write down the result next to the fraction on the right. Compare both products. The fraction with the larger result is the larger fraction.

Consider the fractions $\frac{4}{7}$ and $\frac{5}{9}$.

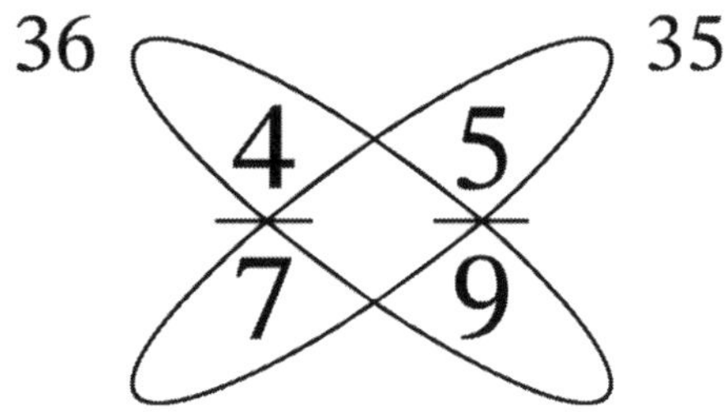

36 is greater than 35. Therefore, $\frac{4}{7}$ is greater than $\frac{5}{9}$.

Decimals

Decimals are one way to represent parts of a whole. Using the place value system, each digit to the right of a decimal point denotes the number of units of a corresponding *negative* power of ten. For example, consider the decimal 0.24. We can use a model to represent the decimal. Since a dime is worth one-tenth of a dollar and a penny is worth one-hundredth of a dollar, one possible model to represent this fraction is to have 2 dimes representing the 2 in the tenths place and 4 pennies representing the 4 in the hundredths place:

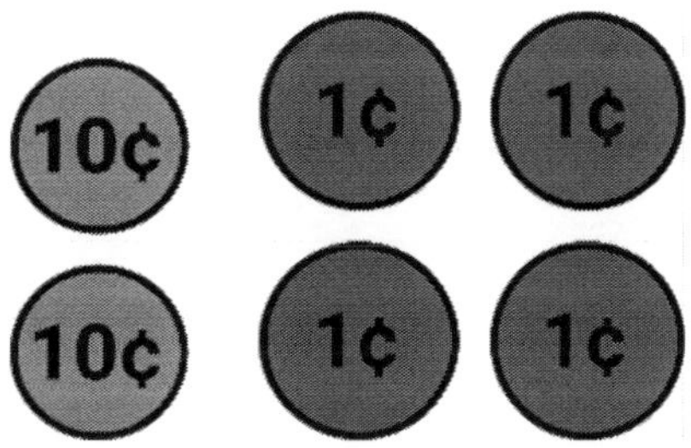

To write the decimal as a fraction, put the decimal in the numerator with 1 in the denominator. Multiply the numerator and denominator by tens until there are no more decimal places. Then simplify the fraction to lowest terms. For example, converting 0.24 to a fraction:

$$0.24 = \frac{0.24}{1} = \frac{0.24 \times 100}{1 \times 100} = \frac{24}{100} = \frac{6}{25}$$

Review Video: Decimals
Visit mometrix.com/academy and enter code: 837268

Operations with Decimals

Adding and Subtracting Decimals

When adding and subtracting decimals, the decimal points must always be aligned. Adding decimals is just like adding regular whole numbers. Example: $4.5 + 2.0 = 6.5$.

If the problem-solver does not properly align the decimal points, an incorrect answer of 4.7 may result. An easy way to add decimals is to align all of the decimal points in a vertical column visually. This will allow you to see exactly where the decimal should be placed in the final answer. Begin adding from right to left. Add each column in turn, making sure to carry the number to the left if a column adds up to more than 9. The same rules apply to the subtraction of decimals.

Review Video: Adding and Subtracting Decimals
Visit mometrix.com/academy and enter code: 381101

Multiplying Decimals

A simple multiplication problem has two components: a **multiplicand** and a **multiplier**. When multiplying decimals, work as though the numbers were whole rather than decimals. Once the final product is calculated, count the number of places to the right of the decimal in both the multiplicand and the multiplier. Then, count that number of places from the right of the product and place the decimal in that position.

For example, 12.3×2.56 has a total of three places to the right of the respective decimals. Multiply 123×256 to get 31,488. Now, beginning on the right, count three places to the left and insert the decimal. The final product will be 31.488.

Review Video: How to Multiply Decimals
Visit mometrix.com/academy and enter code: 731574

Dividing Decimals

Every division problem has a **divisor** and a **dividend**. The dividend is the number that is being divided. In the problem $14 \div 7$, 14 is the dividend and 7 is the divisor. In a division problem with decimals, the divisor must be converted into a whole number. Begin by moving the decimal in the divisor to the right until a whole number is created. Next, move the decimal in the dividend the same number of spaces to the right. For example, 4.9 into 24.5 would become 49 into 245. The decimal was moved one space to the right to create a whole number in the divisor, and then the same was done for the dividend. Once the whole numbers are created, the problem is carried out normally: $245 \div 49 = 5$.

Review Video: Dividing Decimals
Visit mometrix.com/academy and enter code: 560690

Review Video: Dividing Decimals by Whole Numbers
Visit mometrix.com/academy and enter code: 535669

Percentages

Percentages can be thought of as fractions that are based on a whole of 100; that is, one whole is equal to 100%. The word **percent** means "per hundred." Percentage problems are often presented in three main ways:

- Find what percentage of some number another number is.
  - Example: What percentage of 40 is 8?
- Find what number is some percentage of a given number.
  - Example: What number is 20% of 40?
- Find what number another number is a given percentage of.
  - Example: What number is 8 20% of?

There are three components in each of these cases: a **whole** (W), a **part** (P), and a **percentage** (%). These are related by the equation: $P = W \times \%$. This can easily be rearranged into other forms that may suit different questions better: $\% = \frac{P}{W}$ and $W = \frac{P}{\%}$. Percentage problems are often also word problems. As such, a large part of solving them is figuring out which quantities are what. For example, consider the following word problem:

In a school cafeteria, 7 students choose pizza, 9 choose hamburgers, and 4 choose tacos. What percentage of students choose tacos?

To find the whole, you must first add all of the parts: $7 + 9 + 4 = 20$. The percentage can then be found by dividing the part by the whole $\left(\% = \frac{P}{W}\right)$: $\frac{4}{20} = \frac{20}{100} = 20\%$.

Review Video: Computation with Percentages
Visit mometrix.com/academy and enter code: 693099

Calculating Percent Change

Suppose a quantity has a particular value (the *old value*) and then we add something (the *change*) to it to get another value (the *new value*). We can describe this process by the simple equation (old value) + change = (new value). If we know the old and new values, we can rearrange this equation to find the change, getting change = (new value) − (old value). For instance, if a store's price for a box of computer paper goes from $20 last week to $25 this week, this is a change of (new value) − (old value) = $25 − $20 = $5. Or, if the size of the freshman class at a college goes from 500 students one year to 440 students the next year, this is a change of (new value) − (old value) = 440 − 500 = −60 students. So, we see that change can be positive or negative.

Instead of the word *change*, we sometimes use the words *increase* or *decrease* to specify whether the value goes up or down, respectively. In the examples above, the price of computer paper increases by $5 and the freshman class decreases by 60 students. Note that the decrease is 60 students and not -60 because the word *decrease* already means that the value goes down. So, *increase* is the same as positive change and *decrease* is the opposite or negative change.

If the changing quantity represents an amount (how much of something there is), we can also calculate the **percent change**. This is the change expressed as a percentage of the old amount. To calculate this, we divide the change by the old amount and express the quotient as a percent. That is, we use the formula percent change $= \frac{\text{change}}{\text{old value}}$, converting the resulting decimal answer to a percent. In the examples above, the price of a box of computer paper has a percent change of $\frac{\text{change in price}}{\text{old price}} = \frac{\$5}{\$20} = 0.25 = 25\%$, and the size of the freshman class at the college has a percent change of $\frac{\text{change in enrollment}}{\text{old enrollment}} = \frac{-60}{500} = -0.12 = -12\%$. We can also use the terms *percent increase* and *percent decrease*, saying that the price of computer paper increases by 25% and the size of the freshman class decreases by 12%. Note that the denominator is always the old amount, never the new amount.

Example: Your landlord raises your rent from \$1,500 to \$1,700 per month. To find the percent change in your rent (rounded to the nearest tenth of a percent), you calculate as follows.

$$\text{percent change in rent} = \frac{\text{change in rent}}{\text{old rent}} = \frac{(\text{new rent}) - (\text{old rent})}{\text{old rent}}$$
$$= \frac{\$1{,}700 - \$1{,}500}{\$1{,}500} = \frac{\$200}{\$1{,}500} = 0.1333\ldots \approx 13.3\%$$

Therefore, the percent change in your rent is approximately 13.3%.

Review Video: Percent Change
Visit mometrix.com/academy and enter code: 907890

Converting Between Percentages, Fractions, and Decimals

Converting decimals to percentages and percentages to decimals is as simple as moving the decimal point. To *convert from a decimal to a percentage*, move the decimal point **two places to the right**. To *convert from a percentage to a decimal*, move it **two places to the left**. It may be helpful to remember that the percentage number will always be larger than the equivalent decimal number. Example:

$$0.23 = 23\% \qquad 5.34 = 534\% \qquad 0.007 = 0.7\%$$
$$700\% = 7.00 \qquad 86\% = 0.86 \qquad 0.15\% = 0.0015$$

To convert a fraction to a decimal, simply divide the numerator by the denominator in the fraction. To convert a decimal to a fraction, put the decimal in the numerator with 1 in the denominator. Multiply the numerator and denominator by tens until there are no more decimal places. Then simplify the fraction to lowest terms. For example, converting 0.24 to a fraction:

$$0.24 = \frac{0.24}{1} = \frac{0.24 \times 100}{1 \times 100} = \frac{24}{100} = \frac{6}{25}$$

Fractions can be converted to a percentage by finding equivalent fractions with a denominator of 100. Example:

$$\frac{7}{10} = \frac{70}{100} = 70\% \quad \frac{1}{4} = \frac{25}{100} = 25\%$$

To convert a percentage to a fraction, divide the percentage number by 100 and reduce the fraction to its simplest possible terms. Example:

$$60\% = \frac{60}{100} = \frac{3}{5} \quad 96\% = \frac{96}{100} = \frac{24}{25}$$

Review Video: Converting Fractions to Percentages and Decimals
Visit mometrix.com/academy and enter code: 306233

Review Video: Converting Percentages to Decimals and Fractions
Visit mometrix.com/academy and enter code: 287297

Review Video: Converting Decimals to Fractions and Percentages
Visit mometrix.com/academy and enter code: 986765

Review Video: Converting Decimals, Improper Fractions, and Mixed Numbers
Visit mometrix.com/academy and enter code: 696924

Rational and Irrational Numbers

The term **rational** means that the number can be expressed as a ratio or fraction. That is, a number, r, is rational if and only if it can be represented by a fraction $\frac{a}{b}$ where a and b are integers and b does not equal 0. The set of rational numbers includes integers and decimals. If there is no finite way to represent a value with a fraction of integers, then the number is **irrational**. Common irrational numbers are π and the square roots of whole numbers that are not perfect squares (e.g., $\sqrt{5}$ or $\sqrt{21}$). The sum or product of an integer and an irrational number is always irrational (e.g., 3π or $7 + \sqrt{6}$).

Review Video: Rational and Irrational Numbers
Visit mometrix.com/academy and enter code: 280645

Review Video: Ordering Rational Numbers
Visit mometrix.com/academy and enter code: 419578

Review Video: Irrational Numbers on a Number Line
Visit mometrix.com/academy and enter code: 433866

Chapter Quiz

Ready to see how well you retained what you just read? Scan the QR code to go directly to the chapter quiz interface for this study guide. If you're using a computer, simply visit the online resources page at **mometrix.com/resources719/texesmath4-8** and click the Chapter Quizzes link.

Patterns and Algebra

Proportionality

Proportions and Ratios

Proportions

There is a **proportion** between two variable quantities if there is a constant relationship between their products or quotients, a relationship that does not change as the quantities themselves change.

Given variable quantities x and y, we say that they are **directly proportional** (or that y **varies directly with** x) if their quotient or *ratio* is constant—that is, if there is a constant k such that $\frac{y}{x} = k$ is always true. Another way of saying this is that y is a constant multiple of x, so that $y = kx$ is always true. We call the number k the **constant of proportionality**. For example, if you drive at a constant 50 miles per hour, then the distance, y, that you travel in miles is 50 times the number of hours, x, that you drive. In symbols, $y = 50x$ miles (or $\frac{y}{x} = 50$ mph). So, the distance you travel, y, is directly proportional to (or varies directly with) the time you travel, x, with constant of proportionality $k = 50$ mph.

The quantities x and y are **inversely proportional** (or y varies inversely with x) if their product is constant—that is, if there is a constant k such that $xy = k$ is always true. Another way of saying this is to say that y is a constant multiple of the reciprocal of x so that $y = \frac{k}{x}$ is always true. For instance, suppose you drive at speed (rate) y mph for x hours, going a total of 120 miles. Since rate × time = distance, we get $xy = 120$ miles (or $y = \frac{120}{x}$ miles per hour). Thus, your driving speed, y, is inversely proportional to (or varies inversely with) your drive time, x, with constant of proportionality $k = 120$ miles.

Review Video: Proportions
Visit mometrix.com/academy and enter code: 505355

Ratios

A **ratio** expresses the sizes of two quantities relative to each other. For instance, suppose we have 3 copies of sheet music to share among 6 singers. We can divide the singers into groups of 2 and give each group 1 copy of the music. Thus, there is 1 copy of the music for every 2 singers, and we say that the **ratio** of sheet music to singers is 1 to 2, which we write either as a fraction $\frac{1}{2}$ or using a colon $1 : 2$. Of course, it is also true there are 3 copies for every 6 singers so that the ratio of sheet music to singers is also 3 to 6, which we write as $\frac{3}{6}$ or $3 : 6$. So, the ratios $\frac{1}{2}$ and $\frac{3}{6}$ express the same relative quantities of music and singers. We say that these ratios are equal or **equivalent**, and we note that ratios are equal precisely when their fractions are equal (so, in this case, $\frac{1}{2} = \frac{3}{6}$ as fractions). We can also express the quantities in the other order and say that the ratio of singers to music is $\frac{2}{1}$ or $2 : 1$ (or $\frac{6}{3}$ or $6 : 3$).

Review Video: Ratios
Visit mometrix.com/academy and enter code: 996914

Constant of Proportionality

If variable quantities x and y are proportional and we know a pair of corresponding values for them, then we can find their constant of proportionality. If they are directly proportional, we use the formula $\frac{y}{x} = k$. If they are inversely proportional, we use the formula $xy = k$.

Example: The cost in dollars, y, of buying fence posts is directly proportional to the number, x, that you buy. If it costs $51 to buy 17 fence posts, what is the constant of proportionality? Because of direct proportionality, we know that $\frac{y}{x} = k$. Since this works for every pair of corresponding x- and y-values, it also works for $x = 17$ and $y = 51$. This gives us $\frac{51}{17} = k$, which simplifies to $k = 3$. Note also that this is the unit price, namely $3 per fence post.

Work/Unit Rate

Unit rate expresses a quantity of one thing in terms of one unit of another. For example, if you travel 30 miles every two hours, a unit rate expresses this comparison in terms of one hour: in one hour you travel 15 miles, so your unit rate is 15 miles per hour. Other examples are how much one ounce of food costs (price per ounce) or figuring out how much one egg costs out of the dozen (price per 1 egg, instead of price per 12 eggs). The denominator of a unit rate is always 1. Unit rates are used to compare different situations to solve problems. For example, to make sure you get the best deal when deciding which kind of soda to buy, you can find the unit rate of each. If soda #1 costs $1.50 for a 1-liter bottle, and soda #2 costs $2.75 for a 2-liter bottle, it would be a better deal to buy soda #2, because its unit rate is only $1.375 per liter, which is cheaper than soda #1. Unit rates can also help determine the length of time a given event will take. For example, if you can paint 2 rooms in 4.5 hours, you can determine how long it will take you to paint 5 rooms by solving for the unit rate per room and then multiplying that by 5.

Review Video: Rates and Unit Rates
Visit mometrix.com/academy and enter code: 185363

Cross Multiplication

Finding an Unknown in Equivalent Expressions

It is often necessary to apply information given about a rate or proportion to a new scenario. For example, if you know that Jedha can run a marathon (26.2 miles) in 3 hours, how long would it take her to run 10 miles at the same pace? Start by setting up equivalent expressions:

$$\frac{26.2 \text{ mi}}{3 \text{ hr}} = \frac{10 \text{ mi}}{x \text{ hr}}$$

Now, cross multiply and solve for x:

$$26.2x = 30$$
$$x = \frac{30}{26.2} = \frac{15}{13.1}$$
$$x \approx 1.15 \text{ hrs } or \text{ 1 hr 9 min}$$

So, at this pace, Jedha could run 10 miles in about 1.15 hours or about 1 hour and 9 minutes.

Review Video: Cross Multiplying Fractions
Visit mometrix.com/academy and enter code: 893904

Linear Expressions

LINEAR EXPRESSIONS

TERMS AND COEFFICIENTS

Mathematical expressions consist of a combination of one or more values arranged in terms that are added together. As such, an expression could be just a single number, including zero. A **variable term** is the product of a real number, also called a **coefficient**, and one or more variables, each of which may be raised to an exponent. Expressions may also include numbers without a variable, called **constants** or **constant terms**. The expression $6s^2$, for example, is a single term where the coefficient is the real number 6 and the variable term is s^2. Note that if a term is written as simply a variable to some exponent, like t^2, then the coefficient is 1, because $t^2 = 1t^2$.

LINEAR EXPRESSIONS

A **single variable linear expression** is the sum of a single variable term, where the variable has no exponent, and a constant, which may be zero. For instance, the expression $2w + 7$ has $2w$ as the variable term and 7 as the constant term. It is important to realize that terms are separated by addition or subtraction. Since an expression is a sum of terms, expressions such as $5x - 3$ can be written as $5x + (-3)$ to emphasize that the constant term is negative. A real-world example of a single variable linear expression is the perimeter of a square, four times the side length, often expressed: $4s$.

In general, a **linear expression** is the sum of any number of variable terms so long as none of the variables have an exponent and none of the terms have two variables multiplied together. For example, $3m + 8n - \frac{1}{4}p + 5.5q - 1$ is a linear expression, but $3y^3$ and $5xy$ are not. In the same way, the expression for the perimeter of a general triangle $(a + b + c)$ is linear, but the expression for the area of a square (s^2) is not.

SLOPE

FINDING SLOPE GIVEN GRAPH OR TABLE

On a graph with two points, (x_1, y_1) and (x_2, y_2), the **slope** is found with the formula $m = \frac{y_2 - y_1}{x_2 - x_1}$; where $x_1 \neq x_2$ and m stands for slope. If the value of the slope is **positive**, the line has an *upward direction* from left to right. If the value of the slope is **negative**, the line has a *downward direction* from left to right. Consider the following example:

A new book goes on sale in bookstores and online stores. In the first month, 5,000 copies of the book are sold. Over time, the book continues to grow in popularity. The data for the number of copies sold is in the table below.

# of Months on Sale	1	2	3	4	5
# of Copies Sold (In Thousands)	5	10	15	20	25

So, the number of copies that are sold and the time that the book is on sale is a proportional relationship. In this example, an equation can be used to show the data: $y = 5x$, where x is the number of months that the book is on sale. Also, y is the number of copies sold. So, the slope of the corresponding line is $\frac{\text{rise}}{\text{run}} = \frac{5}{1} = 5$.

FINDING SLOPE GIVEN AN EQUATION

When given an equation of a line, it is necessary to solve for y to determine the slope of the line. Given the equation $6x + 2y = 8$, find the slope. First, subtract $6x$ from both sides of the equation, resulting in $2y = -6x + 8$. Then divide both sides of the equation by 2, resulting in $y = -3x + 4$. This then allows us to conclude that the slope of the line is $m = -3$, the coefficient of x. Once an equation is in the form $y = mx + b$, the slope and y-intercept can easily be determined. For this reason, we refer to the equation $y = mx + b$ as "slope-intercept form" of the equation of a line.

Review Video: Finding the Slope of a Line
Visit mometrix.com/academy and enter code: 766664

LINEAR EQUATIONS

Equations like $5x = 100$ and $8x - 120 = 200$ and $6x + 4y = 240$ are **linear equations**. Linear equations are named based off the number of distinct variables they include. For example, the equation $3x + 30 = 8x$ is a **one-variable linear equation** because it involves only the single variable x. It does not matter that x appears more than once. Any equations that can be written as $ax + b = 0$, where $a \neq 0$, falls into this category. Furthermore, the equation $3x - 5y = 14 + 9y$ is a **two-variable linear equation** because it involves the two variables x and y. The equation $7x + 8y - 12z + 14w = 56$ is a linear equation in four variables.

SATISFYING THE EQUATION

When given a one-variable linear equation, the goal is typically to solve it. This means that we want to find the number that makes the equation true if we substitute it for the variable. That number is the **solution,** or root, of the equation. For instance, the equation $5x = 10$ has the solution $x = 2$. This is true because when 2 is substituted for x, the result is $5 \cdot 2 = 10$, which is true. On the other hand, $x = 6$ can not be a solution because $5 \cdot 6 \neq 10$, so it is false. Two equations with the same solution are **equivalent equations**. For example, the equations $5x = 10$ and $5x + 3 = 13$ are equivalent because both have the same solution of $x = 2$.

DETERMINING A SOLUTION SET

The **solution set** is the set of all solutions of an equation. In the previous example, the solution set would be 2. Solutions to a linear equation in two variables consist of pairs of numbers. For instance, the equation $6x + 4y = 240$ has the solution $x = 20$ and $y = 30$ since $6 \cdot 20 + 4 \cdot 30 = 240$ is true. We can write this solution as the ordered pair (20,30) and plot it as a point on the coordinate plane. Such equations usually have infinitely many solutions; and if we plot the points for all these solutions we get a line, which is a picture of all the solutions. We call this **graphing the equation**. When an equation has no true solutions, it is referred to as an **empty set**.

LINEAR EQUATION FORMS

Linear equations can be written many ways. Below is a list of some forms linear equations can take:

- **Standard Form**: $Ax + By = C$; the slope is $\frac{-A}{B}$ and the y-intercept is $\frac{C}{B}$
- **Slope Intercept Form**: $y = mx + b$, where m is the slope and b is the y-intercept
- **Point-Slope Form**: $y - y_1 = m(x - x_1)$, where m is the slope and (x_1, y_1) is a point on the line

Patterns and Algebra

- **Two-Point Form**: $\frac{y-y_1}{x-x_1} = \frac{y_2-y_1}{x_2-x_1}$, where (x_1, y_1) and (x_2, y_2) are two points on the given line
- **Intercept Form**: $\frac{x}{x_1} + \frac{y}{y_1} = 1$, where $(x_1, 0)$ is the point at which a line intersects the x-axis, and $(0, y_1)$ is the point at which the same line intersects the y-axis

> **Review Video: Slope-Intercept and Point-Slope Forms**
> Visit mometrix.com/academy and enter code: 113216
>
> **Review Video: Converting Between Standard and Slope-Intercept Forms**
> Visit mometrix.com/academy and enter code: 982828
>
> **Review Video: Linear Equations Basics**
> Visit mometrix.com/academy and enter code: 793005

SOLVING EQUATIONS

MANIPULATING EQUATIONS

LIKE TERMS

Like terms are terms in an equation that have the same variable, regardless of whether they also have the same coefficient. This includes terms that *lack* a variable; all constants (i.e., numbers without variables) are considered like terms. If the equation involves terms with a variable raised to different powers, the like terms are those that have the variable raised to the same power.

For example, consider the equation $x^2 + 3x + 2 = 2x^2 + x - 7 + 2x$. In this equation, 2 and –7 are like terms; they are both constants. The terms $3x$, x, and $2x$ are like terms, they all include the variable x raised to the first power. The terms x^2 and $2x^2$ are like terms, they both include the variable x, raised to the second power. The terms $2x$ and $2x^2$ are not like terms; although they both involve the variable x, the variable is not raised to the same power in both terms. The fact that they have the same coefficient, 2, is not relevant.

> **Review Video: Rules for Manipulating Equations**
> Visit mometrix.com/academy and enter code: 838871

CARRYING OUT THE SAME OPERATION ON BOTH SIDES OF AN EQUATION

When solving an equation, the general procedure is to carry out a series of operations on both sides of an equation, choosing operations that simplify the equation when doing so. The reason why the same operation must be carried out on both sides of the equation is because that leaves the meaning of the equation unchanged, and yields a result that is equivalent to the original equation. This would not be the case if we carried out an operation on one side of an equation and not the other. Consider what an equation means: it is a statement that two values or expressions are equal. If we carry out the same operation on both sides of the equation—add 3 to both sides, for example—then the two sides of the equation are changed in the same way, and so remain equal. If we do that to only one side of the equation—add 3 to one side but not the other—then that wouldn't be true; if we change one side of the equation but not the other then the two sides are no longer equal.

COMBINING LIKE TERMS

Combining like terms refers to adding or subtracting like terms—terms with the same variable—and therefore reducing sets of like terms to a single term. The main advantage of doing this is that it simplifies the equation. Often, combining like terms can be done as the first step in solving an equation, though it can also be done later, such as after distributing terms in a product.

For example, consider the equation $2(x + 3) + 3(2 + x + 3) = -4$. The 2 and the 3 in the second set of parentheses are like terms, and we can combine them, yielding $2(x + 3) + 3(x + 5) = -4$. Now we can carry out the multiplications implied by the parentheses, distributing the outer 2 and 3 accordingly: $2x + 6 + 3x + 15 = -4$. The $2x$ and the $3x$ are like terms, and we can add them together: $5x + 6 + 15 = -4$. Now, the constants 6, 15, and –4 are also like terms, and we can combine them as well: subtracting 6 and 15 from both sides of the equation, we get $5x = -4 - 6 - 15$, or $5x = -25$, which simplifies further to $x = -5$.

Review Video: Solving Equations by Combining Like Terms
Visit mometrix.com/academy and enter code: 668506

Canceling Terms on Opposite Sides of an Equation

Two terms on opposite sides of an equation can be canceled if and only if they *exactly* match each other. They must have the same variable raised to the same power and the same coefficient. For example, in the equation $3x + 2x^2 + 6 = 2x^2 - 6$, $2x^2$ appears on both sides of the equation and can be canceled, leaving $3x + 6 = -6$. The 6 on each side of the equation *cannot* be canceled, because it is added on one side of the equation and subtracted on the other. While they cannot be canceled, however, the 6 and –6 are like terms and can be combined, yielding $3x = -12$, which simplifies further to $x = -4$.

It's also important to note that the terms to be canceled must be independent terms and cannot be part of a larger term. For example, consider the equation $2(x + 6) = 3(x + 4) + 1$. We cannot cancel the x's, because even though they match each other they are part of the larger terms $2(x + 6)$ and $3(x + 4)$. We must first distribute the 2 and 3, yielding $2x + 12 = 3x + 12 + 1$. Now we see that the terms with the x's do not match, but the 12s do, and can be canceled, leaving $2x = 3x + 1$, which simplifies to $x = -1$.

Isolating Variables

To isolate a variable means to manipulate the equation so that the variable appears by itself on one side of the equation, and does not appear at all on the other side. Generally, an equation or inequality is considered to be solved once the variable is isolated and the other side of the equation or inequality is simplified as much as possible. In the case of a two-variable equation or inequality, only one variable needs to be isolated; it will not usually be possible to simultaneously isolate both variables.

For a linear equation—an equation in which the variable only appears raised to the first power—isolating a variable can be done by first moving all the terms with the variable to one side of the equation and all other terms to the other side. (*Moving* a term really means adding the inverse of the term to both sides; when a term is *moved* to the other side of the equation its sign is flipped.) Then combine like terms on each side. Finally, divide both sides by the coefficient of the variable, if applicable. The steps need not necessarily be done in this order, but this order will always work.

Review Video: Solving Equations for Specific Variables
Visit mometrix.com/academy and enter code: 130695

Review Video: Solving Equations Involving Algebraic Fractions
Visit mometrix.com/academy and enter code: 237770

Review Video: Solving One-Step Equations
Visit mometrix.com/academy and enter code: 777004

Solving One-Variable Linear Equations

Equations with One Solution (the Usual Case)

To solve a one-variable linear equation, we use the techniques above to isolate the variable.

1. If any coefficients or constants are fractions, it is often helpful first to multiply both sides of the equation by the least common denominator (of all fractions) to clear the fractions.
2. Simplify both sides of the equation by combining any like terms.
3. Put all terms with the variable on one side of the equation and all constant terms on the other side, by adding or subtracting the same terms on both sides of the equation.
4. Divide both sides by the coefficient of the variable (or multiply both sides by its reciprocal).
5. When we have a value for the variable, we can check it by substituting the value into the original equation to make sure it produces a true result.

Consider the following example for solving the equation $\frac{2}{3}x + 8 = 14$:

$3 \cdot \left(\frac{2}{3}x + 8\right) = 3 \cdot 14$	Clear fractions by multiplying both sides by 3.
$2x + 24 = 42$	Simplify, remembering to apply the distributive property.
$2x + 24 - 24 = 42 - 24$	Subtract 24 from both sides to isolate $2x$.
$2x = 18$	Simplify by combining like terms.
$\frac{2x}{2} = \frac{18}{2}$	Divide both sides by 2 to isolate x.
$x = 9$	Simplify

Finally, we check this answer by substituting $x = 9$ into the original equation to make sure we get a true result.

$$\frac{2}{3}x + 8 = \frac{2}{3}(9) + 8 = 6 + 8 = 14$$

This is correct, so the value of x is 9.

Review Video: Solving Equations Using the Distributive Property
Visit mometrix.com/academy and enter code: 765499

Equations with More Than One Solution

Some types of non-linear equations, such as equations involving squares of variables, may have more than one solution. For example, the equation $x^2 = 4$ has two solutions: 2 and –2. Equations with absolute values can also have multiple solutions: $|x| = 1$ has the solutions $x = 1$ and $x = -1$.

It is possible for a linear equation to have more than one solution but only if the equation is true regardless of the value of the variable. We call such an equation an **identity**. In this case, the equation has infinitely many solutions, because every possible value of the variable is a solution. We discover that a linear equation is an identity when our attempts to isolate the variable cause the variable to disappear, leaving a *true* equation involving only constants. For example, consider the equation $2(3x + 5) = x + 5(x + 2)$. Distributing, we get $6x + 10 = x + 5x + 10$; combining like terms gives $6x + 10 = 6x + 10$, and the $6x$-terms cancel to leave $10 = 10$. This is clearly true, so the original equation is an identity. We could also cancel the 10's leaving $0 = 0$, which is also is clearly true—in general if both sides of the equation can be reduced to match one another exactly, the original equation is an identity.

EQUATIONS WITH NO SOLUTION

Some types of non-linear equations, such as equations involving squares of variables, may have no solution. For example, the equation $x^2 = -2$ has no solutions in the real numbers because the square of a real number must be positive. Similarly, $|x| = -1$ has no solution because the absolute value of a number is always positive.

It is also possible for a linear equation to have no solution. We call such an equation a **contradiction**. We discover that a linear equation is a contradiction when our attempts to isolate the variable cause the variable to disappear, leaving a *false* equation involving only constants. For example, the equation $2(x + 3) + x = 3x$ has no solution. We can see this by trying to solve it: first we distribute, leaving $2x + 6 + x = 3x$. Combining like terms gives us $3x + 6 = 3x$, and cancelling the term $3x$ on both sides leaves us with $6 = 0$. This is clearly false, so the original equation is a contradiction, having no solutions.

FEATURES OF EQUATIONS THAT REQUIRE SPECIAL TREATMENT

A linear equation is an equation in which variables only appear by themselves: not multiplied together, not with exponents other than one, and not inside absolute value signs or any other functions. For example, the equation $x + 1 - 3x = 5 - x$ is a linear equation; while x appears multiple times, it never appears with an exponent other than one, or inside any function. The two-variable equation $2x - 3y = 5 + 2x$ is also a linear equation. In contrast, the equation $x^2 - 5 = 3x$ is *not* a linear equation, because it involves the term x^2. The equation $\sqrt{x} = 5$ is not linear, because it involves a square root. The equation $(x - 1)^2 = 4$ is not linear because even though there's no exponent on the x directly, it appears as part of an expression that is squared. The two-variable equation $x + xy - y = 5$ is not linear because it includes the term xy, where two variables are multiplied together.

As we see above, linear equations can always be solved (or shown to have no solution) by combining like terms and performing simple operations on both sides of the equation. Some non-linear equations can be solved by similar methods, but others may require more advanced methods of solution, if they can be solved analytically at all.

SOLVING EQUATIONS INVOLVING ROOTS

In an equation involving roots, the first step is to isolate the term with the root, if possible, and then raise both sides of the equation to the appropriate power to eliminate it. Consider an example equation, $2\sqrt{x + 1} - 1 = 3$. In this case, begin by adding 1 to both sides, yielding $2\sqrt{x + 1} = 4$, and then dividing both sides by 2, yielding $\sqrt{x + 1} = 2$. Now square both sides, yielding $x + 1 = 4$. Finally, subtracting 1 from both sides yields $x = 3$.

Squaring both sides of an equation (or raising both sides to any *even* power) may, however, yield a spurious solution—a solution to the squared equation that is *not* a solution of the original equation. It's therefore necessary to plug the solution back into the original equation to make sure it works. In this case, it does: $2\sqrt{3 + 1} - 1 = 2\sqrt{4} - 1 = 2(2) - 1 = 4 - 1 = 3$.

The same procedure applies for other roots as well. For example, given the equation $3 + \sqrt[3]{2x} = 5$, we can first subtract 3 from both sides, yielding $\sqrt[3]{2x} = 2$ and isolating the root. Raising both sides to the third power yields $2x = 2^3$; i.e., $2x = 8$. We can now divide both sides by 2 to get $x = 4$.

Review Video: Solving Equations Involving Roots
Visit mometrix.com/academy and enter code: 297670

Solving Equations with Exponents

In solving an equation with powers of a variable, sometimes it is possible to eliminate all but one term involving the variable. In that case, we can isolate the power of the variable and then take the appropriate root of both sides to eliminate the exponent. For instance, for the equation $2x^3 + 17 = 5x^3 - 7$, we can subtract $5x^3$ from both sides to get $-3x^3 + 17 = -7$, and then subtract 17 from both sides to get $-3x^3 = -24$. Finally, we can divide both sides by -3 to get $x^3 = 8$. Since this isolates the cube of the variable, we can take the cube root of both sides to get $x = \sqrt[3]{8} = 2$.

One important but often overlooked point is that equations with an exponent greater than 1 may have more than one answer. The solution to $x^2 = 9$ isn't simply $x = 3$; it's $x = \pm 3$ (that is, $x = 3$ or $x = -3$). For a slightly more complicated example, consider the equation $(x - 1)^2 - 1 = 3$. Adding 1 to both sides yields $(x - 1)^2 = 4$; taking the square root of both sides yields $x - 1 = 2$. We can then add 1 to both sides to get $x = 3$. However, there's a second solution. We also have the possibility that $x - 1 = -2$, in which case $x = -1$. Both $x = 3$ and $x = -1$ are valid solutions, as can be verified by substituting them both into the original equation.

Review Video: Solving Equations with Exponents
Visit mometrix.com/academy and enter code: 514557

Review Video: Adding and Subtracting with Exponents
Visit mometrix.com/academy and enter code: 875756

Solving Equations with Absolute Values

When solving an equation with an absolute value, the first step is to isolate the absolute value term. We then consider two possibilities: when the expression inside the absolute value is positive or when it is negative. In the former case, the expression in the absolute value equals the expression on the other side of the equation; in the latter, it equals the additive inverse of that expression—the expression times negative one. We consider each case separately and finally check for spurious solutions.

For instance, consider solving $|2x - 1| + x = 5$ for x. We can first isolate the absolute value by moving the x to the other side: $|2x - 1| = -x + 5$. Now, we have two possibilities. First, that $2x - 1$ is positive, and hence $2x - 1 = -x + 5$. Rearranging and combining like terms yields $3x = 6$, and hence $x = 2$. The other possibility is that $2x - 1$ is negative, and hence $2x - 1 = -(-x + 5) = x - 5$. In this case, rearranging and combining like terms yields $x = -4$. Substituting $x = 2$ and $x = -4$ back into the original equation, we see that they are both valid solutions.

Note that the absolute value of a sum or difference applies to the sum or difference as a whole, not to the individual terms; in general, $|2x - 1|$ is not equal to $|2x + 1|$ or to $|2x| - 1$.

Review Video: Solving Absolute Value Equations
Visit mometrix.com/academy and enter code: 501208

EXTRANEOUS SOLUTIONS

An **extraneous solution** may arise when we square both sides of an equation (or raise both sides to an even power) as a step in solving it or under certain other operations on the equation. It is a solution to the squared or otherwise modified equation that is *not* a solution of the original equation. To identify an extraneous solution, it's useful when you solve an equation involving roots or absolute values to plug the solution back into the original equation to make sure it's valid.

TWO-VARIABLE EQUATIONS

Similar to methods for a one-variable equation, solving a two-variable equation involves isolating a variable: manipulating the equation so that a variable appears by itself on one side of the equation, and not at all on the other side. However, in a two-variable equation, you will usually only be able to isolate one of the variables; the other variable may appear on the other side along with constant terms, or with exponents or other functions. If an equation has multiple variables, the problem should tell you which variable to isolate.

Review Video: Solving Equations with Variables on Both Sides
Visit mometrix.com/academy and enter code: 402497

GRAPHING EQUATIONS

GRAPHICAL SOLUTIONS TO EQUATIONS

When equations are shown graphically, they are usually shown on a **Cartesian coordinate plane**. The Cartesian coordinate plane consists of two number lines placed perpendicular to each other and intersecting at the zero point, also known as the origin. The horizontal number line is known as the x-axis, with positive values to the right of the origin, and negative values to the left of the origin. The vertical number line is known as the y-axis, with positive values above the origin, and negative values below the origin. Any point on the plane can be identified by an ordered pair in the form (x, y), called coordinates. The x-value of the coordinate is called the abscissa, and the y-value of the coordinate is called the ordinate. The two number lines divide the plane into **four quadrants**: I, II, III, and IV.

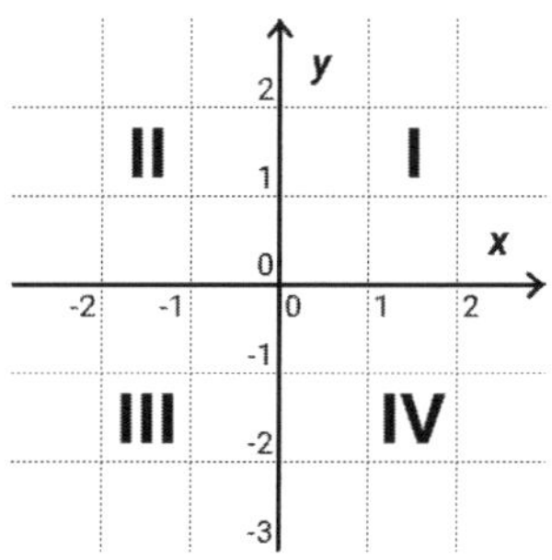

Note that in quadrant I $x > 0$ and $y > 0$, in quadrant II $x < 0$ and $y > 0$, in quadrant III $x < 0$ and $y < 0$, and in quadrant IV $x > 0$ and $y < 0$.

Recall that if the value of the slope of a line is positive, the line slopes upward from left to right. If the value of the slope is negative, the line slopes downward from left to right. If the y-coordinates are the same for two points on a line, the slope is 0 and the line is a **horizontal line**. If the x-coordinates are the same for two points on a line, there is no slope and the line is a **vertical line**.

Patterns and Algebra

Two or more lines that have equivalent slopes are **parallel lines**. **Perpendicular lines** have slopes that are negative reciprocals of each other, such as $\frac{a}{b}$ and $\frac{-b}{a}$.

Review Video: Cartesian Coordinate Plane and Graphing
Visit mometrix.com/academy and enter code: 115173

GRAPHING EQUATIONS IN TWO VARIABLES

One way of graphing an equation in two variables is to plot enough points to get an idea for its shape and then draw the appropriate curve through those points. A point can be plotted by substituting in a value for one variable and solving for the other. If the equation is linear, we only need two points and can then draw a straight line between them.

For example, consider the equation $y = 2x - 1$. This is a linear equation—both variables only appear raised to the first power—so we only need two points. When $x = 0$, $y = 2(0) - 1 = -1$. When $x = 2$, $y = 2(2) - 1 = 3$. We can therefore choose the points $(0, -1)$ and $(2, 3)$, and draw a line between them:

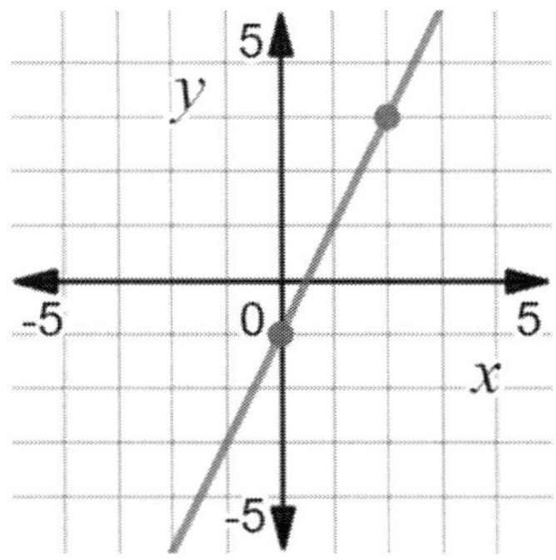

Inequalities

INEQUALITIES

Commonly in algebra and other upper-level fields of math you find yourself working with mathematical expressions that do not equal each other. The statement comparing such expressions with symbols such as $<$ (less than) or $>$ (greater than) is called an *inequality*. An example of an inequality is $7x > 5$. To solve for x, simply divide both sides by 7 and the solution is shown to be $x > \frac{5}{7}$. Graphs of the solution set of inequalities are represented on a number line. Open circles are used to show that an expression approaches a number but is never quite equal to that number.

Review Video: Solving One-Step Inequalities
Visit mometrix.com/academy and enter code: 229684

Review Video: Solving Multi-Step Inequalities
Visit mometrix.com/academy and enter code: 347842

Review Video: Solving Inequalities Using All 4 Basic Operations
Visit mometrix.com/academy and enter code: 401111

Types of Inequalities

Conditional inequalities are those with certain values for the variable that will make the condition true and other values for the variable where the condition will be false. **Absolute inequalities** can have any real number as the value for the variable to make the condition true, while there is no real number value for the variable that will make the condition false. Solving inequalities is done by following the same rules for solving equations with the exception that when multiplying or dividing by a negative number the direction of the inequality sign must be flipped or reversed. **Double inequalities** are situations where two inequality statements apply to the same variable expression. Example: $-c < ax + b < c$.

> **Review Video: Conditional and Absolute Inequalities**
> Visit mometrix.com/academy and enter code: 980164

Solving Inequalities

Determining Solutions to Inequalities

To determine whether a coordinate is a solution of an inequality, you can substitute the values of the coordinate into the inequality, simplify, and check whether the resulting statement holds true. For instance, to determine whether $(-2,4)$ is a solution of the inequality $y \geq -2x + 3$, substitute the values into the inequality, $4 \geq -2(-2) + 3$. Simplify the right side of the inequality and the result is $4 \geq 7$, which is a false statement. Therefore, the coordinate is not a solution of the inequality. You can also use this method to determine which part of the graph of an inequality is shaded. The graph of $y \geq -2x + 3$ includes the solid line $y = -2x + 3$ and, since it excludes the point $(-2,4)$ to the left of the line, it is shaded to the right of the line.

> **Review Video: Graphing Linear Inequalities**
> Visit mometrix.com/academy and enter code: 439421
>
> **Review Video: Graphing Solutions to Inequalities**
> Visit mometrix.com/academy and enter code: 391281

Flipping Inequality Signs

When given an inequality, we can always turn the entire inequality around, swapping the two sides of the inequality and changing the inequality sign. For instance, $x + 2 > 2x - 3$ is equivalent to $2x - 3 < x + 2$. Aside from that, normally the inequality does not change if we carry out the same operation on both sides of the inequality. There is, however, one principal exception: if we *multiply* or *divide* both sides of the inequality by a *negative number*, the inequality is flipped. For example, if we take the inequality $-2x < 6$ and divide both sides by -2, the inequality flips and we are left with $x > -3$. This *only* applies to multiplication and division, and only with negative numbers. Multiplying or dividing both sides by a positive number, or adding or subtracting any number regardless of sign, does not flip the inequality. Another special case that flips the inequality sign is when reciprocals are used. For instance, $3 > 2$ but the relation of the reciprocals is $\frac{1}{3} < \frac{1}{2}$.

Compound Inequalities

A **compound inequality** is an equality that consists of two inequalities combined with *and* or *or*. The two components of a proper compound inequality must be of opposite type: that is, one must be greater than (or greater than or equal to), the other less than (or less than or equal to). For instance, "$x + 1 < 2$ or $x + 1 > 3$" is a compound inequality, as is "$2x \geq 4$ and $2x \leq 6$." An *and* inequality can be written more compactly by having one inequality on each side of the common part: "$2x \geq 1$ and $2x \leq 6$," can also be written as $1 \leq 2x \leq 6$.

In order for the compound inequality to be meaningful, the two parts of an *and* inequality must overlap; otherwise, no numbers satisfy the inequality. On the other hand, if the two parts of an *or* inequality overlap, then *all* numbers satisfy the inequality and as such the inequality is usually not meaningful.

Solving a compound inequality requires solving each part separately. For example, given the compound inequality "$x + 1 < 2$ or $x + 1 > 3$," the first inequality, $x + 1 < 2$, reduces to $x < 1$, and the second part, $x + 1 > 3$, reduces to $x > 2$, so the whole compound inequality can be written as "$x < 1$ or $x > 2$." Similarly, $1 \leq 2x \leq 6$ can be solved by dividing each term by 2, yielding $\frac{1}{2} \leq x \leq 3$.

Review Video: Compound Inequalities
Visit mometrix.com/academy and enter code: 786318

Solving Inequalities Involving Absolute Values

To solve an inequality involving an absolute value, first isolate the term with the absolute value. Then proceed to treat the two cases separately as with an absolute value equation, but flipping the inequality in the case where the expression in the absolute value is negative (since that essentially involves multiplying both sides by –1.) The two cases are then combined into a compound inequality; if the absolute value is on the greater side of the inequality, then it is an *or* compound inequality, if on the lesser side, then it's an *and*.

Consider the inequality $2 + |x - 1| \geq 3$. We can isolate the absolute value term by subtracting 2 from both sides: $|x - 1| \geq 1$. Now, we're left with the two cases $x - 1 \geq 1$ or $x - 1 \leq -1$: note that in the latter, negative case, the inequality is flipped. $x - 1 \geq 1$ reduces to $x \geq 2$, and $x - 1 \leq -1$ reduces to $x \leq 0$. Since in the inequality $|x - 1| \geq 1$ the absolute value is on the greater side, the two cases combine into an *or* compound inequality, so the final, solved inequality is "$x \leq 0$ or $x \geq 2$."

Review Video: Solving Absolute Value Inequalities
Visit mometrix.com/academy and enter code: 997008

Solving Inequalities Involving Square Roots

Solving an inequality with a square root involves two parts. First, we solve the inequality as if it were an equation, isolating the square root and then squaring both sides of the equation. Second, we restrict the solution to the set of values of x for which the value inside the square root sign is non-negative.

For example, in the inequality, $\sqrt{x - 2} + 1 < 5$, we can isolate the square root by subtracting 1 from both sides, yielding $\sqrt{x - 2} < 4$. Squaring both sides of the inequality yields $x - 2 < 16$, so $x < 18$. Since we can't take the square root of a negative number, we also require the part inside the square root to be non-negative. In this case, that means $x - 2 \geq 0$. Adding 2 to both sides of the inequality yields $x \geq 2$. Our final answer is a compound inequality combining the two simple inequalities: $x \geq 2$ and $x < 18$, or $2 \leq x < 18$.

Note that we only get a compound inequality if the two simple inequalities are in opposite directions; otherwise, we take the one that is more restrictive.

The same technique can be used for other even roots, such as fourth roots. It is *not*, however, used for cube roots or other odd roots—negative numbers *do* have cube roots, so the condition that the quantity inside the root sign cannot be negative does not apply.

Review Video: Solving Inequalities Involving Square Roots
Visit mometrix.com/academy and enter code: 800288

SPECIAL CIRCUMSTANCES

Sometimes an inequality involving an absolute value or an even exponent is true for all values of x, and we don't need to do any further work to solve it. This is true if the inequality, once the absolute value or exponent term is isolated, says that term is greater than a negative number (or greater than or equal to zero). Since an absolute value or a number raised to an even exponent is *always* non-negative, this inequality is always true.

GRAPHING INEQUALITIES

GRAPHING SIMPLE INEQUALITIES

To graph a simple inequality, we first mark on the number line the value that signifies the end point of the inequality. If the inequality is strict (involves a less than or greater than), we use a hollow circle; if it is not strict (less than or equal to or greater than or equal to), we use a solid circle. We then fill in the part of the number line that satisfies the inequality: to the left of the marked point for less than (or less than or equal to), to the right for greater than (or greater than or equal to).

For example, we would graph the inequality $x < 5$ by putting a hollow circle at 5 and filling in the part of the line to the left:

GRAPHING COMPOUND INEQUALITIES

To graph a compound inequality, we fill in both parts of the inequality for an *or* inequality, or the overlap between them for an *and* inequality. More specifically, we start by plotting the endpoints of each inequality on the number line. For an *or* inequality, we then fill in the appropriate side of the line for each inequality. Typically, the two component inequalities do not overlap, which means the shaded part is *outside* the two points. For an *and* inequality, we instead fill in the part of the line that meets both inequalities.

For the inequality "$x \leq -3$ or $x > 4$," we first put a solid circle at –3 and a hollow circle at 4. We then fill the parts of the line *outside* these circles:

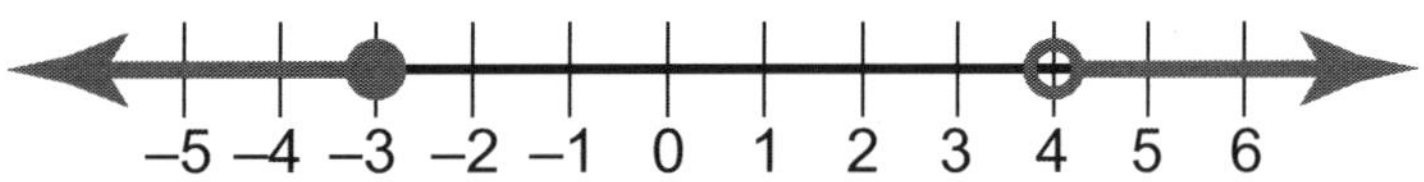

GRAPHING INEQUALITIES INCLUDING ABSOLUTE VALUES

An inequality with an absolute value can be converted to a compound inequality. To graph the inequality, first convert it to a compound inequality, and then graph that normally. If the absolute value is on the greater side of the inequality, we end up with an *or* inequality; we plot the endpoints of the inequality on the number line and fill in the part of the line *outside* those points. If the absolute value is on the smaller side of the inequality, we end up with an *and* inequality; we plot the endpoints of the inequality on the number line and fill in the part of the line *between* those points.

For example, the inequality $|x+1| \geq 4$ can be rewritten as $x \geq 3$ or $x \leq -5$. We place solid circles at the points 3 and -5 and fill in the part of the line *outside* them:

Graphing Inequalities in Two Variables

To graph an inequality in two variables, we first graph the border of the inequality. This means graphing the equation that we get if we replace the inequality sign with an equals sign. If the inequality is strict ($>$ or $<$), we graph the border with a dashed or dotted line; if it is not strict ($\geq$ or $\leq$), we use a solid line. We can then test any point not on the border to see if it satisfies the inequality. If it does, we shade in that side of the border; if not, we shade in the other side. As an example, consider $y > 2x + 2$. To graph this inequality, we first graph the border, $y = 2x + 2$. Since it is a strict inequality, we use a dashed line. Then, we choose a test point. This can be any point not on the border; in this case, we will choose the origin, (0,0). (This makes the calculation easy and is generally a good choice unless the border passes through the origin.) Putting this into the original inequality, we get $0 > 2(0) + 2$, i.e., $0 > 2$. This is *not* true, so we shade in the side of the border that does *not* include the point (0,0):

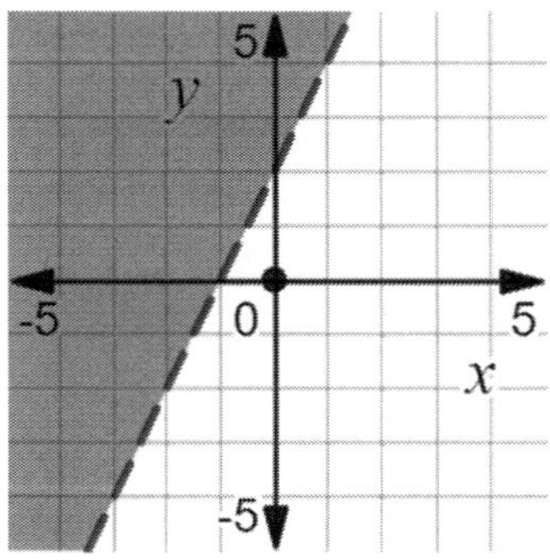

Graphing Compound Inequalities in Two Variables

One way to graph a compound inequality in two variables is to first graph each of the component inequalities. For an *and* inequality, we then shade in only the parts where the two graphs overlap; for an *or* inequality, we shade in any region that pertains to either of the individual inequalities.

Consider the graph of "$y \geq x - 1$ and $y \leq -x$":

We first shade in the individual inequalities:

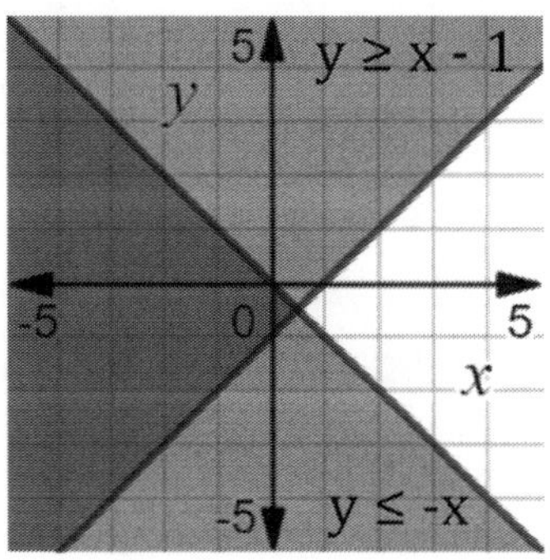

Now, since the compound inequality has an *and*, we only leave shaded the overlap—the part that pertains to *both* inequalities:

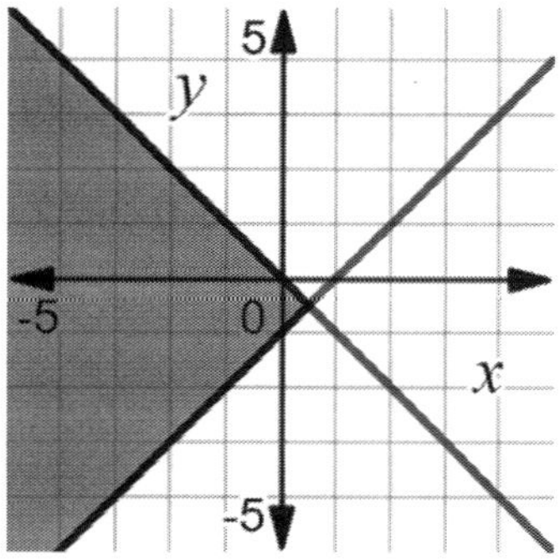

If instead the inequality had been "$y \geq x - 1$ or $y \leq -x$," our final graph would involve the *total* shaded area:

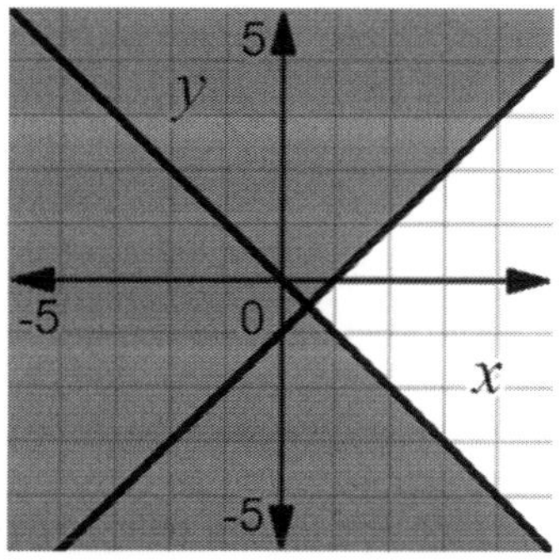

Review Video: Graphing Solutions to Inequalities
Visit mometrix.com/academy and enter code: 391281

Advanced Expressions and Equations

Systems of Equations

Solving Systems of Equations

A **system of equations** is a set of simultaneous equations that all use the same variables. A solution to a system of equations must be true for each equation in the system. **Consistent systems** are those with at least one solution. **Inconsistent systems** are systems of equations that have no solution.

Review Video: Solving Systems of Linear Equations
Visit mometrix.com/academy and enter code: 746745

Substitution

To solve a system of linear equations by **substitution**, start with the easier equation and solve for one of the variables. Express this variable in terms of the other variable. Substitute this expression in the other equation and solve for the other variable. The solution should be expressed in the form

(x, y). Substitute the values into both of the original equations to check your answer. Consider the following system of equations:

$$x + 6y = 15$$
$$3x - 12y = 18$$

Solving the first equation for x: $x = 15 - 6y$

Substitute this value in place of x in the second equation, and solve for y:

$$\begin{aligned} 3(15 - 6y) - 12y &= 18 \\ 45 - 18y - 12y &= 18 \\ 30y &= 27 \\ y &= \frac{27}{30} = \frac{9}{10} = 0.9 \end{aligned}$$

Plug this value for y back into the first equation to solve for x:

$$x = 15 - 6(0.9) = 15 - 5.4 = 9.6$$

Check both equations if you have time:

$$\begin{aligned} 9.6 + 6(0.9) &= 15 \\ 9.6 + 5.4 &= 15 \\ 15 &= 15 \end{aligned} \qquad \begin{aligned} 3(9.6) - 12(0.9) &= 18 \\ 28.8 - 10.8 &= 18 \\ 18 &= 18 \end{aligned}$$

Therefore, the solution is (9.6,0.9).

Review Video: The Substitution Method
Visit mometrix.com/academy and enter code: 565151

Review Video: Substitution and Elimination
Visit mometrix.com/academy and enter code: 958611

ELIMINATION

To solve a system of equations using **elimination**, begin by rewriting both equations in standard form $Ax + By = C$. Check to see if the coefficients of one pair of like variables add to zero. If not, multiply one or both of the equations by a non-zero number to make one set of like variables add to zero. Add the two equations to solve for one of the variables. Substitute this value into one of the original equations to solve for the other variable. Check your work by substituting into the other equation. Now, let's look at solving the following system using the elimination method:

$$5x + 6y = 4$$
$$x + 2y = 4$$

If we multiply the second equation by -3, we can eliminate the y-terms:

$$5x + 6y = 4$$
$$-3x - 6y = -12$$

Add the equations together and solve for x:

$$2x = -8$$
$$x = \frac{-8}{2} = -4$$

Plug the value for x back in to either of the original equations and solve for y:

$$-4 + 2y = 4$$
$$y = \frac{4+4}{2} = 4$$

Check both equations if you have time:

$$5(-4) + 6(4) = 4 \qquad -4 + 2(4) = 4$$
$$-20 + 24 = 4 \qquad -4 + 8 = 4$$
$$4 = 4 \qquad 4 = 4$$

Therefore, the solution is $(-4,4)$.

Review Video: The Elimination Method
Visit mometrix.com/academy and enter code: 449121

GRAPHICALLY

To solve a system of linear equations **graphically**, plot both equations on the same graph. The solution of the equations is the point where both lines cross. If the lines do not cross (are parallel), then there is **no solution**.

For example, consider the following system of equations:

$$y = 2x + 7$$
$$y = -x + 1$$

Since these equations are given in slope-intercept form, they are easy to graph; the y-intercepts of the lines are $(0,7)$ and $(0,1)$. The respective slopes are 2 and –1, thus the graphs look like this:

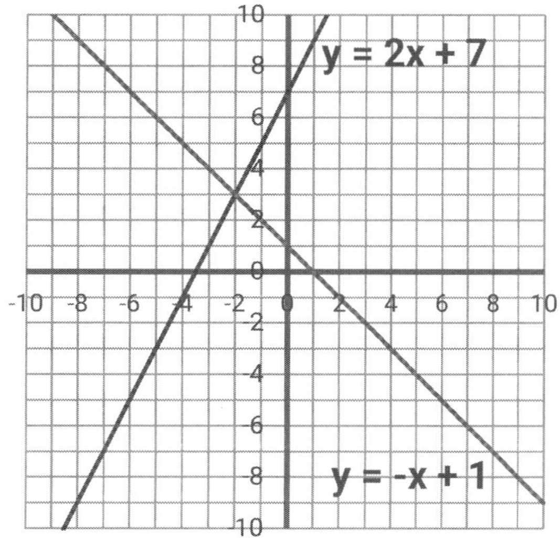

The two lines intersect at the point $(-2,3)$, thus this is the solution to the system of equations.

Solving a system graphically is generally only practical if both coordinates of the solution are integers; otherwise the intersection will lie between gridlines on the graph and the coordinates will be difficult or impossible to determine exactly. It also helps if, as in this example, the equations are in slope-intercept form or some other form that makes them easy to graph. Otherwise, another method of solution (by substitution or elimination) is likely to be more useful.

Review Video: Solving Systems by Graphing
Visit mometrix.com/academy and enter code: 634812

Solving Systems of Equations Using the Trace Feature

Using the trace feature on a calculator requires that you rewrite each equation, isolating the y-variable on one side of the equal sign. Enter both equations in the graphing calculator and plot the graphs simultaneously. Use the trace cursor to find where the two lines cross. Use the zoom feature if necessary to obtain more accurate results. Always check your answer by substituting into the original equations. The trace method is likely to be less accurate than other methods due to the resolution of graphing calculators but is a useful tool to provide an approximate answer.

Advanced Systems of Equations

Solving a System of Equations with a Linear Equation and a Quadratic Equation

Algebraically

Generally, the simplest way to solve a system of equations consisting of a linear equation and a quadratic equation algebraically is through the method of substitution. One possible strategy is to solve the linear equation for y and then substitute that expression into the quadratic equation. After expansion and combining like terms, this will result in a new quadratic equation for x, which, like all quadratic equations, may have zero, one, or two solutions. Plugging each solution for x back into one of the original equations will then produce the corresponding value of y.

For example, consider the following system of equations:

$$x + y = 1$$
$$y = (x + 3)^2 - 2$$

We can solve the linear equation for y to yield $y = -x + 1$. Substituting this expression into the quadratic equation produces $-x + 1 = (x + 3)^2 - 2$. We can simplify this equation:

$$\begin{aligned} -x + 1 &= (x + 3)^2 - 2 \\ -x + 1 &= x^2 + 6x + 9 - 2 \\ -x + 1 &= x^2 + 6x + 7 \\ 0 &= x^2 + 7x + 6 \end{aligned}$$

This quadratic equation can be factored as $(x + 1)(x + 6) = 0$. It therefore has two solutions: $x_1 = -1$ and $x_2 = -6$. Plugging each of these back into the original linear equation yields $y_1 = -x_1 + 1 = -(-1) + 1 = 2$ and $y_2 = -x_2 + 1 = -(-6) + 1 = 7$. Thus, this system of equations has two solutions, $(-1,2)$ and $(-6,7)$.

It may help to check your work by putting each x- and y-value back into the original equations and verifying that they do provide a solution.

Graphically

To solve a system of equations consisting of a linear equation and a quadratic equation graphically, plot both equations on the same graph. The linear equation will, of course, produce a straight line, while the quadratic equation will produce a parabola. These two graphs will intersect at zero, one, or two points; each point of intersection is a solution of the system.

For example, consider the following system of equations:

$$y = -2x + 2$$
$$y = -2x^2 + 4x + 2$$

The linear equation describes a line with a y-intercept of $(0,2)$ and a slope of -2.

To graph the quadratic equation, we can first find the vertex of the parabola: the x-coordinate of the vertex is $h = -\frac{b}{2a} = -\frac{4}{2(-2)} = 1$, and the y-coordinate is $k = -2(1)^2 + 4(1) + 2 = 4$. Thus, the vertex lies at $(1,4)$. To get a feel for the rest of the parabola, we can plug in a few more values of x to find more points; by putting in $x = 2$ and $x = 3$ in the quadratic equation, we find that the points $(2,2)$ and $(3,-4)$ lie on the parabola; by symmetry, so must $(0, 2)$ and $(-1,-4)$. We can now plot both equations:

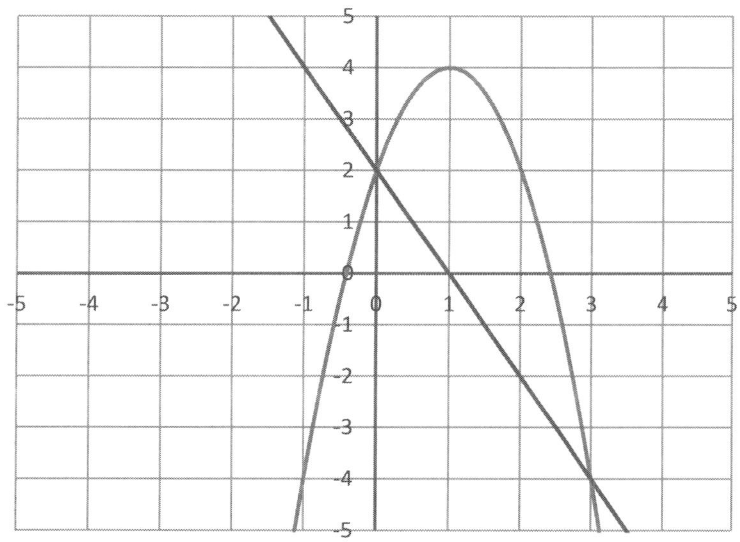

These two curves intersect at the points $(0,2)$ and $(3,-4)$, thus these are the solutions of the equation.

> **Review Video:** <u>Parabolas</u>
> Visit mometrix.com/academy and enter code: 129187
>
> **Review Video:** <u>Vertex of a Parabola</u>
> Visit mometrix.com/academy and enter code: 272300
>
> **Review Video:** <u>Solving a System of Linear and Quadratic Equations</u>
> Visit mometrix.com/academy and enter code: 194870

Patterns and Algebra

MIDPOINT AND DISTANCE FORMULAS

If you know the coordinates of the endpoints of a line segment, you can calculate the midpoint and length of the line segment. Conveniently, the length of the line segment is also the distance between the two endpoints.

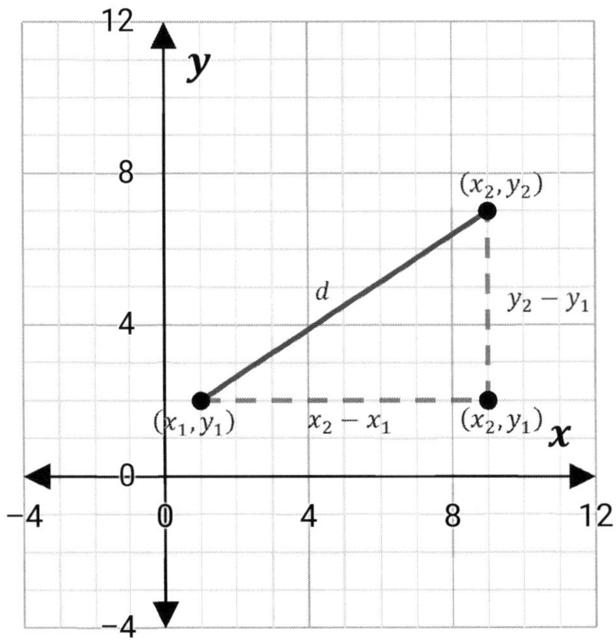

To find the **midpoint** of the line segment with endpoints (x_1, y_1) and (x_2, y_2), average the x-coordinates to get the x-coordinate of the midpoint, and average the y-coordinates to get the y-coordinate of the midpoint. Thus, the **midpoint formula** is:

$$\left(\frac{x_1 + x_2}{2}, \frac{y_1 + y_2}{2}\right)$$

The **distance** between points (x_1, y_1) and (x_2, y_2) is the same as the length of the hypotenuse of a right triangle with the two given points as endpoints, and the two sides of the right triangle parallel to the x-axis and y-axis, respectively. The length of the segment parallel to the x-axis is the difference between the x-coordinates of the two points. The length of the segment parallel to the y-axis is the difference between the y-coordinates of the two points. Use the Pythagorean theorem $a^2 + b^2 = c^2$ or $c = \sqrt{a^2 + b^2}$ to find the distance. Thus, the **distance formula** is:

$$d = \sqrt{(x_2 - x_1)^2 + (y_2 - y_1)^2}$$

Review Video: Calculations Using Points on a Graph
Visit mometrix.com/academy and enter code: 883228

Polynomials

Monomials and Polynomials

A **monomial** is a single constant, variable, or product of constants and variables, such as 7, x, $2x$, or x^3y. There will never be addition or subtraction symbols in a monomial. Like monomials have like variables, but they may have different coefficients. A **polynomial** is a monomial or the result of combining two or more monomials by sums or differences. In a polynomial we call each monomial a **term**. Two terms make a **binomial** (e.g., $2x + 3y$), three terms make a **trinomial** (e.g., $5x^2 - 4x + 9$). The **degree of a monomial** is the sum of the exponents of the variables. The **degree of a polynomial** is the highest degree of any individual term.

Review Video: Polynomials Visit mometrix.com/academy and enter code: 305005

Simplifying Polynomials

Simplifying polynomials requires combining like terms. The like terms in a polynomial expression are those that have the same variables raised to the same powers. It is often helpful to connect the like terms with arrows or lines in order to separate them from the other monomials. Once you have determined the like terms, you can rearrange the polynomial by placing them together. Remember to include the sign that is in front of each term. Once the like terms are placed together, you can apply each operation and simplify. When adding and subtracting polynomials, only add and subtract the **coefficients**, or the number part; the variable and exponent stay the same.

Adding Polynomials

To add polynomials, you need to add like terms. These terms have the same variable part. For example, the terms $4x^2$ and $3x^2$ both include x^2 terms. To find the sum of like terms, find the sum of the coefficients. Then, keep the same variable part. You can use the distributive property to distribute the plus sign to each term of the polynomial. For example:

$$(4x^2 - 5x + 7) + (3x^2 + 2x + 1) =$$
$$(4x^2 - 5x + 7) + 3x^2 + 2x + 1 =$$
$$(4x^2 + 3x^2) + (-5x + 2x) + (7 + 1) =$$
$$7x^2 - 3x + 8$$

Subtracting Polynomials

To subtract polynomials, you need to subtract like terms. To find the difference of like terms, find the difference of the coefficients. Then, keep the same variable part. You can use the distributive property to distribute the minus sign to each term of the polynomial. For example:

$$(-2x^2 - x + 5) - (3x^2 - 4x + 1) =$$
$$(-2x^2 - x + 5) - 3x^2 + 4x - 1 =$$
$$(-2x^2 - 3x^2) + (-x + 4x) + (5 - 1) =$$
$$-5x^2 + 3x + 4$$

Review Video: Adding and Subtracting Polynomials Visit mometrix.com/academy and enter code: 124088

Multiplying Polynomials

In general, multiplying polynomials is done by multiplying each term in one polynomial by each term in the other and adding the results. In the specific case for multiplying binomials, there is a useful acronym, FOIL, that can help you make sure to cover each combination of terms. The **FOIL method** for $(Ax + By)(Cx + Dy)$ would be:

F	Multiply the *first* terms of each binomial	$(\overset{first}{\widehat{Ax}} + By)(\overset{first}{\widehat{Cx}} + Dy)$	ACx^2
O	Multiply the *outer* terms	$(\overset{outer}{\widehat{Ax}} + By)(Cx + \overset{outer}{\widehat{Dy}})$	$ADxy$
I	Multiply the *inner* terms	$(Ax + \overset{inner}{\widehat{By}})(\overset{inner}{\widehat{Cx}} + Dy)$	$BCxy$
L	Multiply the *last* terms of each binomial	$(Ax + \overset{last}{\widehat{By}})(Cx + \overset{last}{\widehat{Dy}})$	BDy^2

Then, add up the result of each and combine like terms: $ACx^2 + (AD + BC)xy + BDy^2$.

For example, using the FOIL method on binomials $(x + 2)$ and $(x - 3)$:

$$\begin{array}{llll} \text{First:} & (\boxed{x} + 2)(\boxed{x} + (-3)) & \rightarrow \quad (x)(x) & = x^2 \\ \text{Outer:} & (\boxed{x} + 2)(x + \boxed{(-3)}) & \rightarrow \quad (x)(-3) & = -3x \\ \text{Inner:} & (x + \boxed{2})(\boxed{x} + (-3)) & \rightarrow \quad (2)(x) & = 2x \\ \text{Last:} & (x + \boxed{2})(x + \boxed{(-3)}) & \rightarrow \quad (2)(-3) & = -6 \end{array}$$

This results in: $(x^2) + (-3x) + (2x) + (-6)$

Combine like terms: $x^2 + (-3 + 2)x + (-6) = x^2 - x - 6$

> **Review Video: Multiplying Polynomials**
> Visit mometrix.com/academy and enter code: 598293
>
> **Review Video: Multiplying Terms Using the FOIL Method**
> Visit mometrix.com/academy and enter code: 854792

DIVIDING POLYNOMIALS

Use long division to divide a polynomial by either a monomial or another polynomial of equal or lesser degree.

When **dividing by a monomial**, divide each term of the polynomial by the monomial.

> **Review Video: Dividing Monomials**
> Visit mometrix.com/academy and enter code: 584409

When **dividing by a polynomial**, begin by arranging the terms of each polynomial in order of one variable. You may arrange in ascending or descending order, but be consistent with both polynomials. To get the first term of the quotient, divide the first term of the dividend by the first term of the divisor. Multiply the first term of the quotient by the entire divisor and subtract that product from the dividend. Repeat for the second and successive terms until you either get a remainder of zero or a remainder whose degree is less than the degree of the divisor. If the quotient has a remainder, write the answer as a mixed expression in the form:

$$\text{quotient} + \frac{\text{remainder}}{\text{divisor}}$$

For example, we can evaluate the following expression in the same way as long division:

$$\frac{x^3 - 3x^2 - 2x + 5}{x - 5}$$

$$
\begin{array}{r l}
 & \quad x^2 \quad + 2x \quad + 8 \\
x - 5 \,) & \; x^3 - 3x^2 \; - 2x \; + 5 \\
 & \underline{-(x^3 - 5x^2)} \\
 & \qquad\quad 2x^2 - 2x \\
 & \qquad\; \underline{-(2x^2 - 10x)} \\
 & \qquad\qquad\qquad 8x + 5 \\
 & \qquad\qquad\quad \underline{-(8x - 40)} \\
 & \qquad\qquad\qquad\quad 45
\end{array}
$$

$$\frac{x^3 - 3x^2 - 2x + 5}{x - 5} = x^2 + 2x + 8 + \frac{45}{x - 5}$$

Review Video: Dividing Polynomials by Monomials
Visit mometrix.com/academy and enter code: 253551

Review Video: Dividing Trinomials by Binomials
Visit mometrix.com/academy and enter code: 651465

When **factoring** a polynomial, first see whether you can factor out a nontrivial greatest common factor (GCF). For example, the trinomial $3x^5 - 18x^4 + 15x^3$ has a GCF of $3x^3$ since the GCF of 3, 18, and 15 is 3 and the GCF of x^5, x^4, and x^3 is x^3. Factoring out the GCF simplifies the expression to $3x^3(x^2 - 6x + 5)$.

To factor a quadratic trinomial (this comes up frequently), first check whether it is a perfect square trinomial (see bulleted list below). If not, see if you can factor it by trial and error by making clever choices of values for a and b (or a, b, c, and d) in the formulas below (this amounts to trying to use the FOIL mnemonic backwards):

$$x^2 + (a + b)x + ab = (x + a)(x + b)$$
$$(ac)x^2 + (ad + bc)x + bd = (ax + b)(cx + d)$$

For instance, you would try to factor the trinomial $x^2 - 6x + 5$ using the equation $x^2 + (a + b)x + ab = (x + a)(x + b)$. This means that you need to find integers a and b such that $a + b = -6$ and $ab = 5$. Starting with $ab = 5$, you can see that the only ways to write 5 as a product of integers are $(1)(5) = 5$ and $(-1)(-5) = 5$. So, it is easy to see that you want $a = -1$ and $b = -5$ since $a + b = -1 + (-5) = -6$ and $ab = (-1)(-5) = 5$. This tells you that $x^2 - 6x + 5 = (x - 1)(x - 5)$.

For polynomials with four terms (usually a cubic polynomial), sometimes factoring by grouping works: You group the two higher-power terms and the two lower-power terms, factor the GCF out of each group, and then factor out the resulting common binomial factor, if there is one. For example, $x^3 + 5x^2 + 3x + 15 = (x^3 + 5x^2) + (3x + 15) = x^2(x + 5) + 3(x + 5) = (x^2 + 3)(x + 5)$.

Once you have found the factors, write the original polynomial as the product of all the factors. Make sure all of the factors are either monomials, or else linear or irreducible quadratic polynomials (*irreducible* means they have no real zeros, which is easy to check with the quadratic formula). Check your work by multiplying the factors to make sure you get the original polynomial.

Review Video: Factoring Out Common Monomial Factors
Visit mometrix.com/academy and enter code: 398578

Review Video: Factoring Trinomials of the Form x^2+bx+c
Visit mometrix.com/academy and enter code: 270556

Below are patterns of some special products to remember to help make factoring easier:

- Perfect square trinomials: $x^2 + 2xy + y^2 = (x + y)^2$ or $x^2 - 2xy + y^2 = (x - y)^2$. For example, $x^2 + 10x + 25 = (x + 5)^2$.
- Difference between two squares: $x^2 - y^2 = (x + y)(x - y)$. For example, $x^2 - 9 = (x + 3)(x - 3)$.
- Sum of two cubes: $x^3 + y^3 = (x + y)(x^2 - xy + y^2)$. For example, $x^3 + 27 = (x + 3)(x^2 - 3x + 9)$.
    - Note: the second factor is *not* the same as a perfect square trinomial, so do not try to factor it further.
- Difference between two cubes: $x^3 - y^3 = (x - y)(x^2 + xy + y^2)$. For example, $x^3 - 1000 = (x - 10)(x^2 + 10x + 100)$.
    - Again, the second factor is *not* the same as a perfect square trinomial.
- Perfect cubes: $x^3 + 3x^2y + 3xy^2 + y^3 = (x + y)^3$ and $x^3 - 3x^2y + 3xy^2 - y^3 = (x - y)^3$

Review Video: Factoring the Difference of Two Squares
Visit mometrix.com/academy and enter code: 128954

Rational and Irrational Expressions

Rational Expressions

Rational expressions are fractions with polynomials in both the numerator and the denominator; the value of the polynomial in the denominator cannot be equal to zero. Be sure to keep track of values that make the denominator of the original expression zero as the final result inherits the same restrictions. For example, a denominator of $x - 3$ indicates that the expression is not defined when $x = 3$ and, as such, regardless of any operations done to the expression, it remains undefined there.

To **add or subtract** rational expressions, first find the common denominator, then rewrite each fraction as an equivalent fraction with the common denominator. Finally, add or subtract the numerators to get the numerator of the answer, and keep the common denominator as the denominator of the answer.

When **multiplying** rational expressions, factor each polynomial and cancel like factors (a factor which appears in both the numerator and the denominator). Then, multiply all remaining factors in the numerator to get the numerator of the product, and multiply the remaining factors in the denominator to get the denominator of the product. Remember: cancel entire factors, not individual terms.

To **divide** rational expressions, take the reciprocal of the divisor (the rational expression you are dividing by) and multiply by the dividend.

Review Video: Rational Expressions
Visit mometrix.com/academy and enter code: 415183

Simplifying Rational Expressions

To simplify a rational expression, factor the numerator and denominator completely. Factors that are the same and appear in the numerator and denominator have a ratio of 1. For example, look at the following expression:

$$\frac{x-1}{1-x^2}$$

The denominator, $(1-x^2)$, is a difference of squares. It can be factored as $(1-x)(1+x)$. The factor $1-x$ and the numerator $x-1$ are opposites and have a ratio of –1. Rewrite the numerator as $-1(1-x)$. So, the rational expression can be simplified as follows:

$$\frac{x-1}{1-x^2} = \frac{-1(1-x)}{(1-x)(1+x)} = \frac{-1}{1+x}$$

Note that since the original expression is only defined for $x \neq \{-1, 1\}$, the simplified expression has the same restrictions.

Review Video: Reducing Rational Expressions
Visit mometrix.com/academy and enter code: 788868

Review Video: Simplifying Algebraic Expressions with Parentheses
Visit mometrix.com/academy and enter code: 850843

Irrational Expressions

Irrational expressions are mathematical expressions that contain an irrational number and cannot be simplified into a rational form. Usually, this includes expressions that contain radicals or constants such as π. Most commonly, you will encounter these in the forms of expressions containing roots of non-perfect squares.

Basic Operations on Radical Expressions

To add or subtract radical numbers, the numbers within the radicals must match, similar to finding a common denominator in fractions:

$$a\sqrt{x} + b\sqrt{x} = (a+b)\sqrt{x}$$

$$a\sqrt{x} - b\sqrt{x} = (a-b)\sqrt{x}$$

To multiply radicals, the numbers outside the radical are multiplied together and the numbers inside the radical are multiplied together:

$$a\sqrt{x} \times b\sqrt{y} = ab\sqrt{xy}$$

To divide radicals, the radical must be eliminated from the denominator by multiplying both numerator and denominator by a value that will make the denominator a rational number:

$$\frac{a\sqrt{x}}{b\sqrt{y}} = \frac{a\sqrt{x}\sqrt{y}}{b\sqrt{y}\sqrt{y}} = \frac{a\sqrt{xy}}{by}$$

Review Video: Adding and Subtracting Radical Expressions
Visit mometrix.com/academy and enter code: 752176

Example

To solve $\frac{(3\sqrt{6})(2\sqrt{3})}{4\sqrt{5}}$, we first multiply the numerator, inside the radical and out: $3 \times 2\sqrt{6 \times 3} = 6\sqrt{18} = 18\sqrt{2}$. To divide, we multiply both numerator and denominator by a value that will eliminate the radical:

$$\frac{18\sqrt{2} \times \sqrt{5}}{4\sqrt{5} \times \sqrt{5}} = \frac{18\sqrt{10}}{4 \times 5} = \frac{18\sqrt{10}}{20} = \frac{9\sqrt{10}}{10}$$

Algebraic Theorems

According to the **fundamental theorem of algebra**, every non-constant, single-variable polynomial has exactly as many roots as the polynomial's highest exponent. For example, if x^4 is the largest exponent of a term, the polynomial will have exactly 4 roots. However, some of these roots may have multiplicity or be complex numbers. For instance, in the polynomial function $f(x) = x^4 - 4x + 3$, the only real root is 1, though it has multiplicity of 2 – that is, it occurs twice. The other two roots, $(-1 - i\sqrt{2})$ and $(-1 + i\sqrt{2})$, are complex, consisting of both real and non-real components.

The **remainder theorem** is useful for determining the remainder when a polynomial is divided by a binomial. The remainder theorem states that if a polynomial function $f(x)$ is divided by a binomial $x - a$, where a is a real number, the remainder of the division will be the value of $f(a)$. If $f(a) = 0$, then a is a root of the polynomial.

The **factor theorem** is related to the remainder theorem and states that if $f(a) = 0$ then $(x - a)$ is a factor of the function.

According to the **rational root theorem,** any rational root of a polynomial function $f(x) = a_n x^n + a_{n-1}x^{n-1} + \cdots + a_1 x + a_0$ with integer coefficients will, when reduced to its lowest terms, be a positive or negative fraction such that the numerator is a factor of a_0 and the denominator is a factor of a_n. For instance, if the polynomial function $f(x) = x^3 + 3x^2 - 4$ has any rational roots, the numerators of those roots can only be factors of 4 (1, 2, 4), and the denominators can only be factors of 1 (1). The function in this example has roots of 1 (or $\frac{1}{1}$) and -2 (or $\frac{-2}{1}$).

Quadratics

Solving Quadratic Equations

A quadratic equation is an equation that can be written (possibly after simplification) in the form $ax^2 + bx + c = 0$. Thus, the **solutions** of this equation are precisely the **zeros** of the quadratic polynomial $P(x) = ax^2 + bx + c$. On the graph of this polynomial the zeros, if any, appear as

x-intercepts. There are several ways to find these solutions including the quadratic formula, factoring, completing the square, and graphing the function.

> **Review Video: Quadratic Equations Overview**
> Visit mometrix.com/academy and enter code: 476276
>
> **Review Video: Solutions of a Quadratic Equation on a Graph**
> Visit mometrix.com/academy and enter code: 328231

QUADRATIC FORMULA

The **quadratic formula** gives the zeros of a quadratic polynomial. It always works, but it is sometimes a little harder to use than other methods. To use it to solve a quadratic equation, rewrite the equation in the form $ax^2 + bx + c = 0$, where a, b, and c are coefficients. Now, as explained above, the solutions of the equation are the zeros of the quadratic polynomial $P(x) = ax^2 + bx + c$. To find them, substitute the values of a, b, and c into the Quadratic Formula:

$$x = \frac{-b \pm \sqrt{b^2 - 4ac}}{2a}$$

After simplification this formula produces two, one, or zero real solutions, depending on whether the **discriminant** (the number $b^2 - 4ac$ under the radical) is positive, zero, or negative. It is a good practice to check each solution by substituting it into the original equation. Incidentally, if the discriminant is negative, then the equation does have two complex solutions, but you often ignore these as meaningless in real-world settings.

> **Review Video: Using the Quadratic Formula**
> Visit mometrix.com/academy and enter code: 163102

FACTORING

To solve a quadratic equation by factoring, begin by rewriting the equation in the standard form, $ax^2 + bx + c = 0$. In the important special case that $a = 1$, the goal of factoring is to find numbers f and g such that $x^2 + bx + c = (x + f)(x + g) = x^2 + (f + g)x + fg$. In other words, you want to choose f and g to make $fg = c$ and $f + g = b$. To do this, find pairs of numbers (factors) whose product is c and look for a pair whose sum is b.

For example, suppose you want to find the solutions of the equation $x^2 + 6x - 16 = 0$ by factoring. Here $b = 6$ and $c = -16$. First, you find the pairs of numbers whose product is -16. These are -4 and 4, -8 and 2, -2 and 8, -1 and 16, and 1 and -16. The pair -2 and 8 has a sum of 6. This means $f = -2$ and $g = 8$. So, the factorization is $x^2 + 6x - 16 = (x + f)(x + g) = (x - 2)(x + 8)$, allowing you to rewrite the original equation as $(x - 2)(x + 8) = 0$. The only way for a product to equal zero is for one of the factors to equal zero; so, either $x - 2 = 0$ (in which case $x = 2$) or $x + 8 = 0$ (in which case $x = -8$). Thus, the equation has the solution $x = 2$ or $x = -8$.

In the case that $a \neq 1$, you can attempt to factor the quadratic polynomial $ax^2 + bx + c$ in the form $(mx + f)(nx + g)$ by a similar trial-and-error procedure, but the work tends to be much harder.

> **Review Video: Factoring Quadratic Equations**
> Visit mometrix.com/academy and enter code: 336566

COMPLETING THE SQUARE

The technique of completing the square comes from a simple observation: Suppose you have the expression $x^2 + bx$. If you take half the linear coefficient, b, square it, and add the result to the expression, the result is always a perfect square trinomial:

$$x^2 + bx + \left(\frac{b}{2}\right)^2 = \left(x + \frac{b}{2}\right)^2$$

For example, if you begin with $x^2 + 6x$ and add the square of half of 6 (half of 6 is 3, and $3^2 = 9$), then you get a perfect square trinomial:

$$x^2 + 6x + 9 = (x + 3)^2$$

This also works if b is negative. For instance, if you begin with the expression $x^2 - 10x$ and complete the square by adding 25 (half of -10 is -5, and $(-5)^2 = 25$), then you get another perfect square trinomial:

$$x^2 - 10x + 25 = (x - 5)^2$$

Now, suppose you want to solve the equation $x^2 + bx + c = 0$. Subtract c from both sides, to get the equation $x^2 + bx = -c$. Complete the square on the left side by adding $(b/2)^2$, but also add this same term to the right side so that the new equation is equivalent to the old one:

$$x^2 + bx + \left(\frac{b}{2}\right)^2 = -c + \left(\frac{b}{2}\right)^2$$
$$\left(x + \frac{b}{2}\right)^2 = -c + \left(\frac{b}{2}\right)^2$$

Take square roots of both sides:

$$x + \frac{b}{2} = \pm\sqrt{-c + \left(\frac{b}{2}\right)^2}$$

Remember to include $\pm$ since every positive number has both a positive and a negative square root. Subtract $b/2$ from both sides to isolate the variable x to finish the problem:

$$x = -\frac{b}{2} \pm \sqrt{-c + \left(\frac{b}{2}\right)^2}$$

This may sound complicated, but in practice it is not hard. For example, suppose you want to solve the equation $x^2 + 6x - 16 = 0$ by completing the square. First, add 16 to both sides:

$$x^2 + 6x = 16$$

Half of 6 is 3 and $3^2 = 9$, so complete the square by adding 9 to both sides of the equation:

$$x^2 + 6x + 9 = 16 + 9$$
$$(x + 3)^2 = 25$$

Now take square root of both sides, remembering to include the $\pm$:

$$\sqrt{(x+3)^2} = \pm\sqrt{25}$$
$$x + 3 = \pm 5$$
$$x = -3 \pm 5$$

So we see that the two solutions to the equation are $x = 2$ and $x = -8$.

> **Review Video: Completing the Square**
> Visit mometrix.com/academy and enter code: 982479

Using Given Solutions to Find a Quadratic Equation

To find a quadratic equation with given numbers as solutions, simply find a quadratic polynomial that has those numbers as zeros and set that polynomial equal to zero. This is easy because a polynomial has the number p as a zero precisely when it has the binomial $x - p$ as a factor. Thus, for instance, to find a quadratic polynomial with zeros at $x = 3$ and $x = -5$, construct the polynomial $P(x) = (x-3)(x-(-5)) = (x-3)(x+5) = x^2 + 2x - 15$. Setting this equal to zero produces an equation, $x^2 + 2x - 15 = 0$, whose solutions are $x = 3$ and $x = -5$.

Of course, any constant multiple $P(x) = a(x-3)(x+5)$ will also have the same zeros. For instance, if you choose $a = 4$, then you get the polynomial $P(x) = 4(x-3)(x+5) = 4x^2 + 8x - 60$, which also has zeros at $x = 3$ and $x = -5$. From this you can get another equation, $4x^2 + 8x - 60 = 0$, with solutions $x = 3$ and $x = -5$.

Functions

Basics of Functions

Definition of a Function

A function is a rule that assigns to every number in a given set (called the **domain**) exactly one corresponding value. For example, if our domain is the set $\{-2,1,2,3\}$, we can define a function by assigning to each number its square. This function assigns to -2 the value 4, to 1 the value 1, to 2 the value 4, and to 3 the value 9 (since $(-2)^2 = 4$, $1^2 = 1$, $2^2 = 4$, and $3^2 = 9$). The set of all the values assigned by a function is the **range** of the function. The range of the function in our example is the set $\{1, 4, 9\}$. We may think of a function as a kind of machine: we give it a number as an input, and it uses its rule to produce a number as an output. In the squaring function above, the input 3 produces the output 9.

> **Review Video: What is a Function?**
> Visit mometrix.com/academy and enter code: 784611

Function Notation

We usually name a function by a letter, often the letter f (for *function*—if we need to talk about more than one function, we name the second one g, the third one h, etc.). To specify the value (the output) corresponding to a particular number in the domain (the input), we write the function letter followed by the input number in parentheses. For instance, in the example above the notation $f(3)$ means the value that the function assigns to the number 3, namely 9—that is, $f(3) = 9$. We read the symbols $f(3)$ as, "f of 3," and we call 3 the **argument** of the function and 9 the **value** of the function (so *argument* means *input* and *value* means *output*).

Using function notation we can define the squaring function above by listing the values the function assigns to each argument in the domain: $f(-2) = 4$. $f(1) = 1, f(2) = 4$, and $f(3) = 9$. More efficiently, we can define the function by the single equation $f(x) = x^2$, which says that if x is a number from the domain, then we calculate the value assigned to it by substituting the number x in the formula x^2. For instance, we calculate $f(5) = 5^2 = 25$. Similarly, if we define a function g by the equation $g(x) = x^2 - 4x + 7$, then we calculate the value $g(3)$ by substituting 3 for each x in the formula: $g(3) = 3^2 - 4 \cdot 3 + 7 = 9 - 12 + 7 = 4$.

OTHER WAYS TO DEFINE FUNCTIONS

Instead of denoting the value of the function by $f(x)$, sometimes we simply use another letter, usually y. For instance, instead of defining the squaring function by the equation $f(x) = x^2$, we might use the equation $y = x^2$. In this case, we refer to x (the input) as the **independent variable** and y (the output) as the **dependent variable** because the value, y, depends on the number we choose for x.

A formula (with y or $f(x)$) is the most common way to define a function; but sometimes, if the domain is small enough, we prefer to list explicitly the possible inputs and their corresponding outputs. Some ways of doing this appear above, but a more common approach is to put the input-output pairs in a table. For instance, we can define the squaring function above by the table

x	-2	1	2	3
y	4	1	4	9

We see that the domain of this function is the set of all numbers in the x-row and the range is the set of all numbers in the y-row. We note that numbers cannot repeat in the x-row (because a function assigns exactly one value to each argument in the domain) but they can repeat in the y-row (because the function can assign the same value to multiple arguments—for instance, the number 4 appears twice in the y-row).

We can also define a function by writing the inputs and corresponding outputs as ordered pairs of x- and y-values. For instance, we can write the squaring function above as the set of ordered pairs $\{(-2,4), (1,1), (2,4), (3,9)\}$. Further, by treating these ordered pairs as coordinates and plotting the corresponding points on the coordinate plane, we get the **graph** of the function:

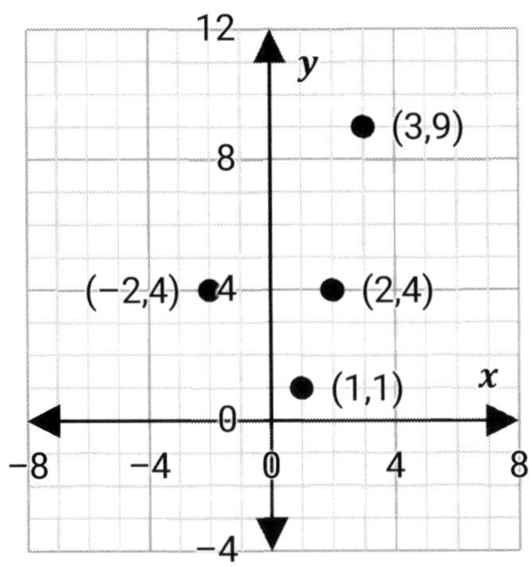

Turning this around, we can potentially use a graph to define a function, namely the function consisting of the coordinate pairs of all the points in the graph. This always works unless the graph

has two points with the same x-coordinate (because then the function would assign two different y-values to the same x). It is easy to detect such points: because they have the same x-coordinate, a vertical line passes through both of them. Thus, a graph always defines a function unless it is possible to draw a vertical line that intersects the graph in two or more points. We call this condition the **vertical line test**. For example, if our graph is a circle, then by the Vertical Line Test the graph does not define a function because there are vertical lines that will intersect the circle in two different points.

MORE ON DOMAINS AND RANGES

When we define a function by a formula and do not specify the domain, then by default the domain consists of all real numbers for which the formula produces an answer. For instance, suppose we define a function f by the formula $f(x) = 1/x$. If $x = 0$, then $1/x = 1/0$, which is undefined. But if x is any other real number, then we can calculate the value of $1/x$. So, the default domain of this function is all real numbers except zero. Because of this domain convention, the graph of a function defined by a formula usually consists of infinitely many points that "connect to" each other in a way that produces a line or curve (see examples below) rather than the isolated points we see in the squaring function above.

If we have the graph of a function, its domain consists of all numbers on the x-axis with corresponding points on the graph and its range consists of all numbers on the y-axis with corresponding points on the graph. For example, consider the function $f(x) = x^2 + 3$:

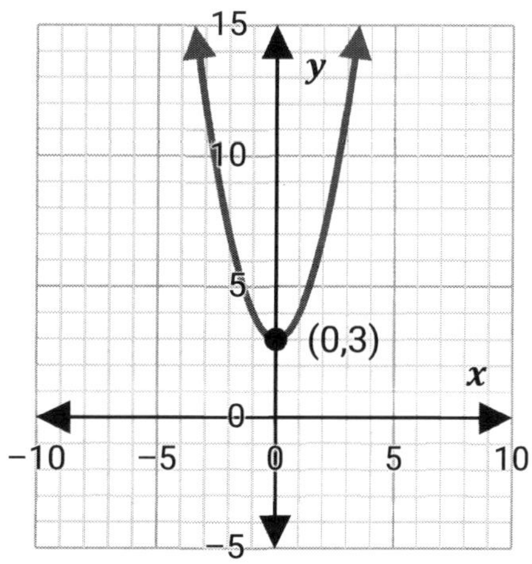

Since the graph continues infinitely to the left and right beyond what we can see, every point on the x-axis has a corresponding point on the graph; so, the domain of this function is all real numbers. On the other hand, the lowest point on this graph has a y-value of 3, and the graph passes through all higher y-values. So, the range of this function is all real numbers greater than or equal to 3, which we can denote algebraically by $y \geq 3$ or, using interval notation, by $[3, \infty)$.

Review Video: How to Find Domain and Range
Visit mometrix.com/academy and enter code: 778133

Review Video: Domain and Range of Quadratic Functions
Visit mometrix.com/academy and enter code: 331768

MONOTONIC AND EVEN/ODD FUNCTIONS

A function, f, is **increasing** if it always assigns larger values to larger arguments. It is **decreasing** if it always assigns smaller values to larger arguments. That is, f is increasing if $a < b$ always guarantees $f(a) < f(b)$, and it is decreasing if $a < b$ always guarantees $f(a) > f(b)$. The graph of an increasing function consistently rises from left to right, and the graph of a decreasing function consistently falls from left to right. For example, the function $f(x) = 2x$ is an increasing function because doubling a larger number always gives us a larger result than doubling a smaller number. The graph of $f(x) = 2x$ is a line with slope $m = 2$, which, as we expect, rises from left to right. We call a function **monotonic** if it is either increasing or decreasing.

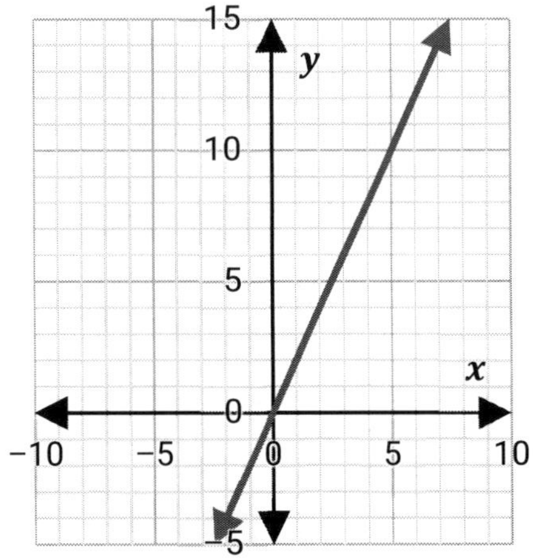

A function, f, is **even** if changing the sign of its argument produces the same value. It is **odd** if changing the sign of its argument produces the same value except with the opposite sign. That is, f is even if $f(-x) = f(x)$ and odd if $f(-x) = -f(x)$ for every argument x. The function $f(x) = x^2 + 3$ is even because substituting opposite arguments always produces the same value. For instance, $f(5) = 28$ and $f(-5) = 28$ because $5^2 + 3 = 25 + 3 = 28$ and $(-5)^2 + 3 = 25 + 3 = 28$. The function $f(x) = 2x$ is odd because substituting opposite arguments always produces opposite values. For instance, $f(10) = 20$ and $f(-10) = -20$ because $2(10) = 20$ and $2(-10) = -20$. The graph of an even function is always symmetric with respect to the y-axis, making the left and right halves of the graph mirror images of each other, as in the graph of the even function $f(x) = x^2 + 3$ above. The graph of an odd function is always symmetric with respect to the origin. This means that if we rotate the graph 180° around the origin (think of sticking a pin through the origin on a sheet of graph paper and rotating the paper halfway around) the graph looks the same, as in the graph of the odd function $f(x) = 2x$ above.

It is worth noting that most functions are neither increasing nor decreasing (that is, they are not monotonic) and most functions are neither even nor odd. For example, the function $f(x) = x^2 -$

x is neither increasing nor decreasing and neither even nor odd: its graph neither rises nor falls consistently, and it is symmetric with respect to neither the y-axis nor the origin.

Review Video: Even and Odd Functions
Visit mometrix.com/academy and enter code: 278985

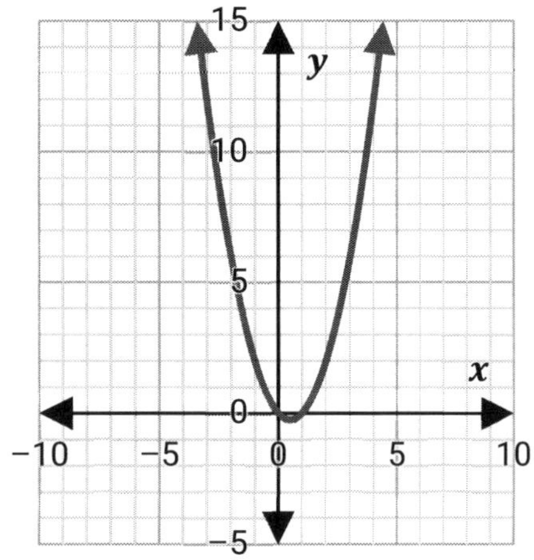

Invertible (One-to-One) Functions

A function, f, is one-to-one if it never assigns the same value to different arguments—that is, if $f(a)$ and $f(b)$ are different whenever a and b are different. The graph of a one-to-one function never has two points that lie on the same horizontal line because such points would have different x-values but the same y-value. Thus, a function is one-to-one if it is impossible to draw a horizontal line that intersects its graph in more than one point. We call this condition the **horizonal line test**. For example, the graph of the function $f(x) = 2x$ above is a line that rises from left to right. Every horizontal line intersects this line in exactly one point, so the function $f(x) = 2x$ is one-to-one. This is also clear without the graph because it is impossible to double two different numbers and get the same answer.

When a function, f, is one-to-one, it is possible to define its inverse function, f^{-1}, that "undoes" what f does, assigning to each output from f the input that produced it. That is, for each x in the domain of f, if $y = f(x)$, then $f^{-1}(y) = x$. For example, the inverse of the function $f(x) = 2x$ above is $f^{-1}(y) = y/2$. So, for instance, $f(5) = 2 \cdot 5 = 10$, and $f^{-1}(10) = 10/2 = 5$ (and similarly for every other value of x). Thus, the domain of f^{-1} is the range of f and vice versa. If a function, f, has an inverse, we say that f is **invertible**. Since a function has an inverse precisely when it is one-to-one, the terms *invertible* and *one-to-one* are synonyms.

If f is an invertible function defined by a formula, then to find its inverse we simply write the equation $y = f(x)$ and solve it for x (that is, we isolate the x). The result will be the equation $f^{-1}(y) = x$. For instance, starting with the function $f(x) = 2x$, we write $y = 2x$ and isolate the x by dividing both sides of the equation by 2. This gives us $y/2 = x$, so we know that $f^{-1}(y) = y/2$. Although this procedure is theoretically simple, in practice the algebra can be difficult.

Common Functions

Certain functions and certain kinds of functions are particularly useful, coming up frequently in mathematics and its applications. Once we know some basic function terminology and concepts, it is useful to begin developing a mental library of the most common and useful functions.

Review Video: Common Functions
Visit mometrix.com/academy and enter code: 629798

Constant Functions

A function of the form $f(x) = a$, where a is a real number, is a **constant function**. This function assigns the same value, a, to every real argument x. For instance, given the constant function $f(x) = 5$, we have $f(2) = 5$, $f(100) = 5$, and $f(-7.1) = 5$.

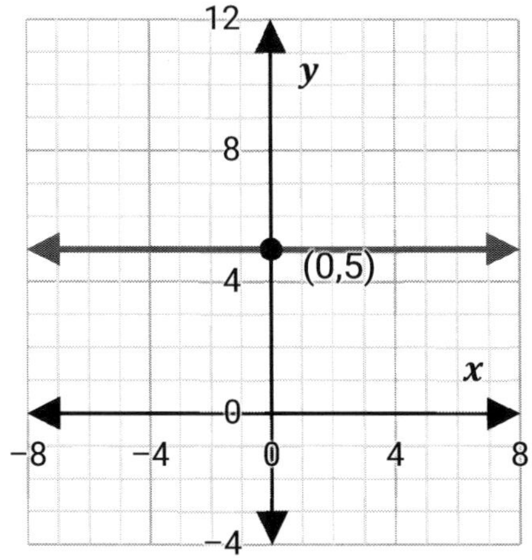

The domain of a constant function is the set of all real numbers, and the range is the set containing the single number a. Its graph is a horizontal line passing through the number $y = a$ on the y-axis (we call the number at which a function's graph intersects the y-axis the ***y*-intercept** of the function).

THE IDENTITY FUNCTION

The function $f(x) = x$ is the **identity function**. Its value always equals its argument. Thus, for instance, $f(2) = 2$, $f(100) = 100$, and $f(-7.1) = -7.1$.

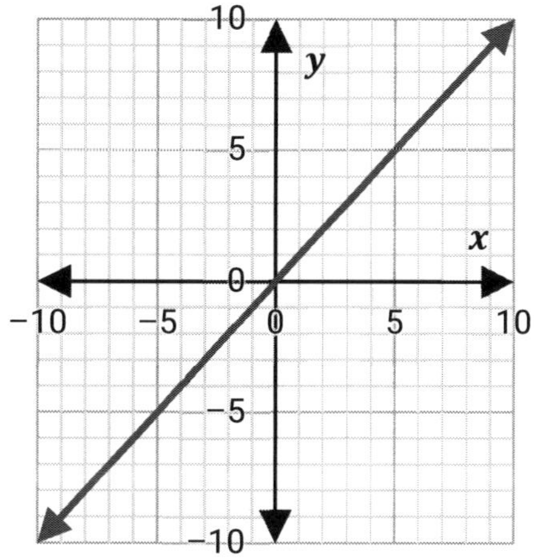

Its domain and range are the set of all real numbers. It is both an increasing function and an odd function. Its graph is a line that passes through the origin and rises from left to right at a 45° angle to the horizontal. Since it passes through the origin, its y intercept is $y = 0$ and it also has an **x-intercept** (a number at which the function's graph intersects the x-axis) of $x = 0$.

LINEAR FUNCTIONS

A function of the form $f(x) = ax + b$, where a and b are real numbers (with $a \neq 0$), is a **linear function** (the identity function is a linear function with $a = 1$ and $b = 0$). Its domain and range are the set of all real numbers. Its graph is a line (the word *linear* contains the root word *line*) with one x-intercept (at $x = -b/a$), with a y-intercept at $y = b$, and with a direction and steepness that depend on the coefficient a, which we call the **slope**. Specifically, the slope a is the amount the y-value increases for each increase of 1 in the x-value. Thus, for $a > 0$, the line rises from left to right (making f an increasing function), and larger values of a produce steeper ascents. Similarly, for $a < 0$, the line falls from left to right (making f a decreasing function), and smaller (more negative) values of a produce steeper descents. For instance, the graph of the linear function

$f(x) = (1/2)x + 3$ is a line that passes through the point $y = 3$ on the y-axis and that rises by $1/2$ unit for every unit that x increases.

Review Video: Linear Functions
Visit mometrix.com/academy and enter code: 200735

Review Video: Graphing Linear Functions
Visit mometrix.com/academy and enter code: 699478

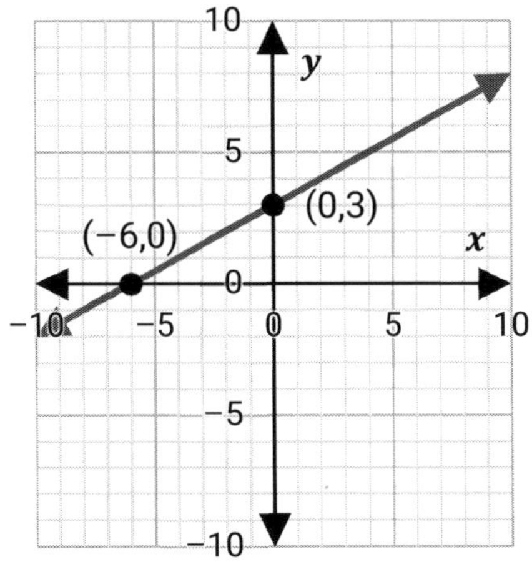

In many contexts it is standard to use the letter m for slope and thus to write the general form of a linear function as $f(x) = mx + b$, known as **slope-intercept form**.

The Squaring Function

The function $f(x) = x^2$ is the **squaring function**.

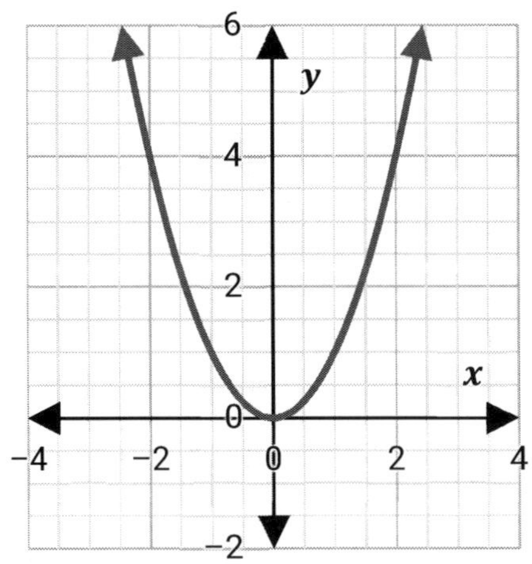

Its graph is U-shaped, opening upward as shown, a shape known as a **parabola**. It has a lowest point, its **vertex**, at the origin, which is also the location of its single x-intercept and single y-intercept. Thus, its **minimum** is $y = 0$, its domain is the set of all real numbers, and its range is the set of nonnegative real numbers (that is, $y \geq 0$). It is an even function and thus symmetric with respect to the y-axis (which we call the **axis of symmetry**), meaning that the left half of the graph is the mirror image of the right half, with the mirror standing on the y-axis.

QUADRATIC FUNCTIONS

A function of the form $f(x) = ax^2 + bx + c$, where a, b, and c are real numbers (with $a \neq 0$), is a **quadratic function** (the squaring function is a quadratic function with $a = 1$, $b = 0$, and $c = 0$). Its domain is the set of all real numbers, and its graph is a parabola. It is symmetric with respect to its axis of symmetry, the vertical line $x = -b/(2a)$. If $a > 0$, the parabola opens upward, so that its vertex is at its lowest point (its minimum) and its range consists of all real numbers greater than or equal to this minimum y-value. If $a < 0$, the parabola opens downward, so that its vertex is at its highest point (its maximum) and its range consists of all real numbers less than or equal to this maximum y-value. Its y-intercept is $y = c$ since $f(0) = c$, and it may have zero, one, or two x-intercepts. For example, the function $f(x) = x^2 - 6x + 5$ has $a = 1$, $b = -6$, and $c = 5$.

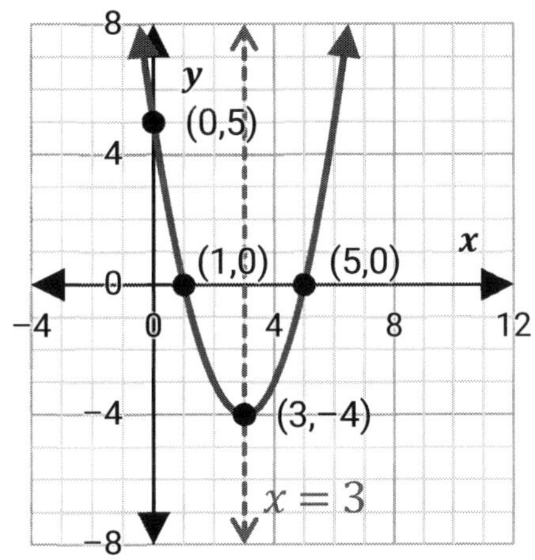

Its graph opens upward (because $a > 0$) and its axis of symmetry is the vertical line $x = 3$ (since $-b/(2a) = -(-6)/(2 \cdot 1) = 3$). Its y-intercept is at $y = 5$. It turns out to have its vertex at the point $(3, -4)$, making its minimum value $y = -4$. So, its domain is the set of all real numbers, and its range is $y \geq -4$. It also turns out to have two x-intercepts, at $x = 1$ and at $x = 5$ (since $f(1) = 0$ and $f(5) = 0$).

POLYNOMIAL FUNCTIONS

A function of the form $f(x) = a^n x^n + a^{n-1} x^{n-1} + \cdots + a_2 x^2 + a_1 x + a_0$, where n is a whole number and $a_0, a_1, a_2, \ldots a_{n-1}, a_n$ are real numbers, is a **polynomial function of degree *n***. Its domain is the set of all real numbers (it is complicated to describe its range in general), and its y-intercept is $y = a_0$ (since $f(0) = a_0$). Constant functions, linear functions, and quadratic functions are polynomial functions of degrees 0, 1, and 2, respectively. In general, a polynomial function of degree n has up to n zeros (x-intercepts) and up to $n - 1$ "bends." For example, the fourth degree polynomial function $f(x) = x^4 - 11x^3 + 41x^2 - 61x + 30$, whose graph appears here, has four x-intercepts (at $x = 1, x = 2, x = 3$, and $x = 5$) and three "bends," and its y-intercept (not visible on the graph) is at $y = 30$.

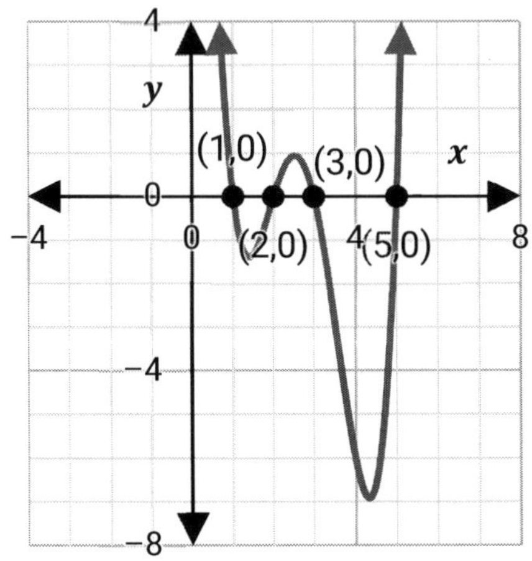

RATIONAL FUNCTIONS

A function of the form $f(x) = P(x)/Q(x)$, where P and Q are polynomials, is a rational function (we note that the word *rational* includes the root word *ratio*, indicating that a rational function is a ratio of polynomial functions). The domain of a rational function is all real numbers except the zeros of $Q(x)$ since division by zero is undefined (the range can be difficult to describe in general). Its y-intercept is $f(0)$, if this is defined; and its x-intercepts are the zeros of $P(x)$ that are in the domain of f, if there are any. A rational function may also have vertical asymptotes (vertical lines that the graph approaches without crossing) and a horizontal asymptote (a horizontal line that the curve approaches as x becomes very small or very large (toward the left and right edges of the graph). For example, the rational function $f(x) = (2x^2 + x - 1)/(x^2 + x - 2)$ has as its domain the set of all real numbers except $x = -2$ and $x = 1$ (since those numbers make the denominator zero).

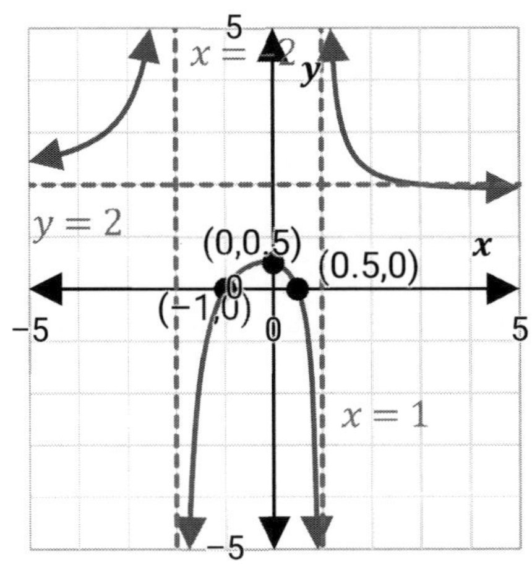

It has a y-intercept of $y = 1/2$ since $f(0) = (-1)/(-2) = 1/2$, and it has x-intercepts at $x = -1$ and at $x = 1/2$ since those numbers make the numerator zero. It has vertical asymptotes at $x = -2$ and $x = 1$ (not coincidentally, these are the numbers omitted from the domain) and a horizontal asymptote at $y = 2$. It is important to note that vertical asymptotes cannot be crossed in rational functions, but horizontal asymptotes can be crossed if the function tends near the asymptote at infinity and does not go past all possible turning points.

Review Video: Simplifying Rational Polynomial Functions
Visit mometrix.com/academy and enter code: 351038

Review Video: Horizontal Asymptotes
Visit mometrix.com/academy and enter code: 747796

The Square Root Function

The function $f(x) = \sqrt{x}$ is the square root function.

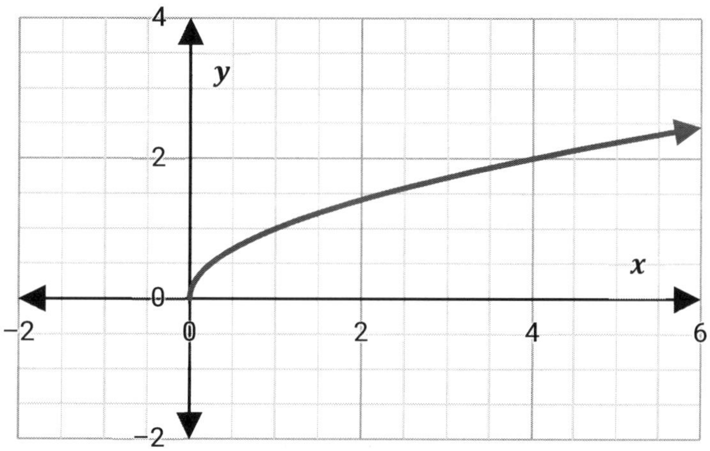

It is an increasing function, and its domain and range are both the set of all nonnegative real numbers. It has one x-intercept and one y-intercept, both appearing at the origin. Its graph is the upper half of a parabola opening to the right. The square root function is the inverse of the squaring function with domain restricted to the nonnegative real numbers (that is, $f(x) = x^2$ for $x \geq 0$).

Piecewise-Defined Functions

As the name suggests, a **piecewise-defined function** (or, simply, a **piecewise function**) is a function defined by different rules on different pieces of the domain. We define such a function using the following form:

Function Name	Rule to Apply	Piece of the Domain on Which the Rule Applies
$f(x) =$	Rule 1,	First Piece of the Domain
	Rule 2,	Second Piece of the Domain
	Rule 3,	Third Piece of the Domain
	etc.,	etc.

The pieces of the domain should not overlap, and together they should cover the whole domain. For example, we might craft a piecewise-defined function by

$$f(x) = \begin{cases} x^2, & \text{if } x < 2 \\ 3x - 5, & \text{if } x \geq 2 \end{cases}$$

The two pieces of the domain—namely, $x < 2$ and $x \geq 2$—do not overlap, and together they include all real numbers. To evaluate the function for a particular argument x, we determine which piece of the domain includes x and then apply the corresponding rule. For instance, to find $f(4)$, we note that $4 \geq 2$; so, we apply the rule $3x - 5$ to get the value $f(4) = 3 \cdot 4 - 5 = 7$. Similarly, to find $f(-6)$, we note that $-6 < 2$; so, we apply the rule x^2 to get the value $f(-6) = (-6)^2 = 36$.

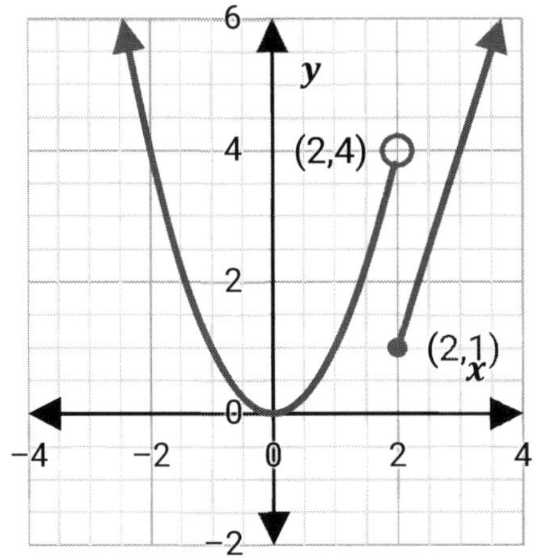

To graph this function, we sketch the graph of the parabola $y = x^2$ on the part of the plane where $x < 2$ and we sketch the line $y = 3x - 5$ on the part of the plane where $x \geq 2$. This produces a graph with a jump at $x = 2$ (a discontinuity—piecewise-defined functions are useful for producing graphs with discontinuities). We plot an open circle at the point (2,4), the end of the left part of the graph, to show that this point is not part of the graph. And we plot a solid dot at the point (2,1), the start of the right part of the graph, to show that this point *is* part of the graph.

Review Video: Piecewise Functions
Visit mometrix.com/academy and enter code: 707921

The Absolute Value Function

A particularly useful piecewise-defined function is the absolute value function. It is so important that instead of naming it $f(x)$ or $g(x)$, we denote it using the special notation $|x|$. Its definition is

$$|x| = \begin{cases} -x, & \text{if } x < 0 \\ x, & \text{if } x \geq 0 \end{cases}$$

For instance, $|8| = 8$ (since $8 \geq 0$) and $|-5| = -(-5) = 5$, since $-5 < 0$. So, the absolute value function acts like the identity function for nonnegative numbers (it leaves them unchanged), and it gives the opposite of negative numbers (it effectively strips off the minus sign). Thus, we can think of the absolute value of a real number as its distance from zero on the number line, without taking into consideration whether the number is larger than or smaller than zero. For instance, $|-3| = 3$ and $|3| = 3$, showing that both -3 and 3 are three units away from zero. The absolute value function is an even function with a V-shaped graph that looks like the line $y = x$ (the identity function) on the right "half" of the plane (for $x \geq 0$) and the line $y = -x$ on the left "half" of the plane (for $x < 0$).

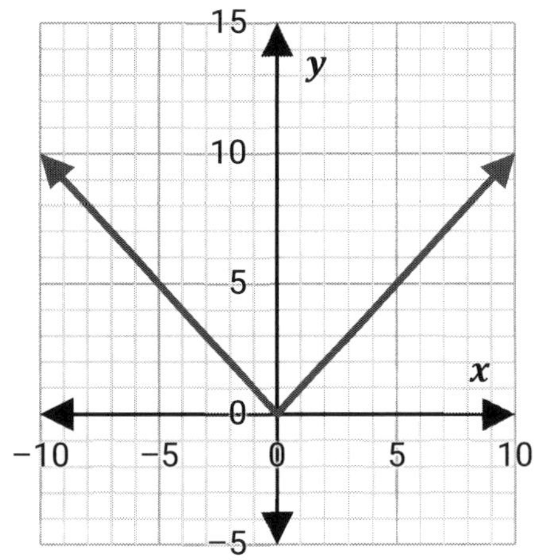

WORKING WITH FUNCTIONS

MANIPULATION OF FUNCTIONS

Translation occurs when values are added to or subtracted from the x- or y-values. If a constant is added to the y-portion of each point, the graph shifts up. If a constant is subtracted from the y-portion of each point, the graph shifts down. This is represented by the expression $f(x) \pm k$, where k is a constant. If a constant is added to the x-portion of each point, the graph shifts left. If a constant is subtracted from the x-portion of each point, the graph shifts right. This is represented by the expression $f(x \pm k)$, where k is a constant.

Stretching, compression, and reflection occur when different parts of a function are multiplied by different groups of constants. If the function as a whole is multiplied by a real number constant greater than 1, $(k \times f(x))$, the graph is stretched vertically. If k in the previous equation is greater than zero but less than 1, the graph is compressed vertically. If k is less than zero, the graph is reflected about the x-axis, in addition to being either stretched or compressed vertically if k is less than or greater than –1, respectively. If instead, just the x-term is multiplied by a constant greater than 1 $(f(k \times x))$, the graph is compressed horizontally. If k in the previous equation is greater than zero but less than 1, the graph is stretched horizontally. If k is less than zero, the graph is reflected about the y-axis, in addition to being either stretched or compressed horizontally if k is greater than or less than –1, respectively.

Review Video: Manipulation of Functions
Visit mometrix.com/academy and enter code: 669117

APPLYING THE BASIC OPERATIONS TO FUNCTIONS

For each of the basic operations, we will use these functions as examples: $f(x) = x^2$ and $g(x) = x$.

To find the sum of two functions f and g, assuming the domains are compatible, simply add the two functions together: $(f + g)(x) = f(x) + g(x) = x^2 + x$.

To find the difference of two functions f and g, assuming the domains are compatible, simply subtract the second function from the first: $(f - g)(x) = f(x) - g(x) = x^2 - x$.

To find the product of two functions f and g, assuming the domains are compatible, multiply the two functions together: $(f \times g)(x) = f(x) \times g(x) = x^2 \times x = x^3$.

To find the quotient of two functions f and g, assuming the domains are compatible, divide the first function by the second: $\left(\frac{f}{g}\right)(x) = \frac{f(x)}{g(x)} = \frac{x^2}{x} = x\,; x \neq 0$.

The example given in each case is fairly simple, but on a given problem, if you are looking only for the value of the sum, difference, product, or quotient of two functions at a particular x-value, it may be simpler to solve the functions individually and then perform the given operation using those values.

The composite of two functions f and g, written as $(f \circ g)(x)$ simply means that the output of the second function is used as the input of the first. This can also be written as $f\big(g(x)\big)$. In general, this can be solved by substituting $g(x)$ for all instances of x in $f(x)$ and simplifying. Using the example functions $f(x) = x^2 - x + 2$ and $g(x) = x + 1$, we can find that $(f \circ g)(x)$ or $f\big(g(x)\big)$ is equal to $f(x+1) = (x+1)^2 - (x+1) + 2$, which simplifies to $x^2 + x + 2$.

It is important to note that $(f \circ g)(x)$ is not necessarily the same as $(g \circ f)(x)$. The process is not always commutative like addition or multiplication expressions. It *can* be commutative, but most often this is not the case.

Evaluating Linear Functions

A **function** can be expressed as an equation that relates an input to an output where each input corresponds to exactly one output. The input of a function is defined by the x-variable, and the output is defined by the y-variable. For example, consider the function $y = 2x + 6$. The value of y, the output, is determined by the value of the x, the input. If the value of x is 3, the value of y is $y = 2(3) + 6 = 6 + 6 = 12$. This means that when $x = 3$, $y = 12$. This can be expressed as the ordered pair (3,12).

It is common for function equations to use the form $f(x) =$ instead of $y =$. However, $f(x)$ and y represent the same thing. We read $f(x)$ as "f of x." The expression "f of x" implies that the value of f depends on the value of x. The function used in the example above could be expressed as $y = 2x + 6$ or $f(x) = 2x + 6$. Both functions represent the same line when graphed.

Functions that are expressed in the form $f(x) =$ are evaluated in the same way the equations are evaluated in the form $y =$. For example, when evaluating the function $f(x) = 3x - 2$ for $f(6)$, substitute 6 in for x, and simplify. In this case, $f(x) = 3x - 2$ becomes $f(6) = 3(6) - 2 = 18 - 2 = 16$. When x is 6, $f(x)$ is 16.

Example: To find the value of $f(8)$, calculate as follows:

$$f(x) = 3x - 2$$
$$f(8) = 3(8) - 2$$
$$f(8) = 22$$

Review Video: Evaluating Functions
Visit mometrix.com/academy and enter code: 588515

ADVANCED FUNCTIONS

STEP FUNCTIONS

The double brackets indicate a step function. For a step function, the value inside the double brackets is rounded down to the nearest integer. The graph of the function $f_0(x) = [\![x]\!]$ appears on the left graph. In comparison $f(x) = 2\left[\!\left[\frac{1}{3}(x-1)\right]\!\right]$ is on the right graph. The coefficient of 2 shows that it's stretched vertically by a factor of 2 (so there's a vertical distance of 2 units between successive "steps"). The coefficient of $\frac{1}{3}$ in front of the x shows that it's stretched horizontally by a factor of 3 (so each "step" is three units long), and the $x - 1$ shows that it's displaced one unit to the right.

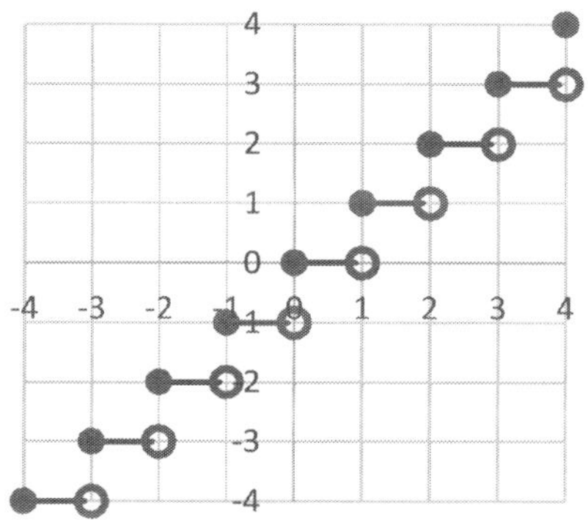

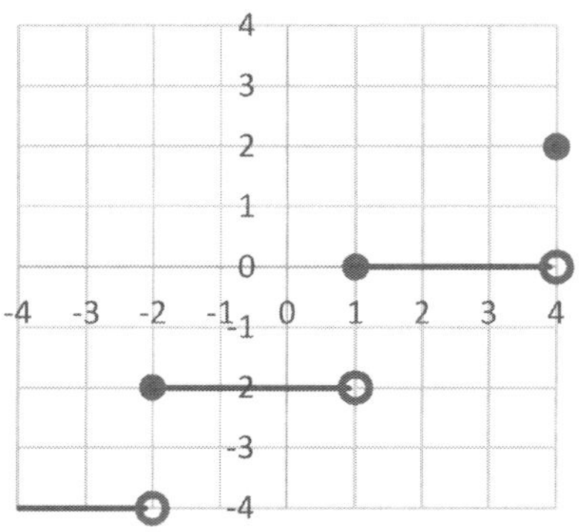

TRANSCENDENTAL FUNCTIONS

Roughly speaking, algebraic functions are functions defined by formulas involving numbers and variables combined by addition, subtraction, multiplication, division, powers (but not variable powers), and roots. **Transcendental functions** are functions that are not algebraic. A function that includes logarithms, trigonometric functions, or variables as exponents, is transcendental, not algebraic, even if the function also includes polynomials or roots.

EXPONENTIAL FUNCTIONS

Exponential functions are functions that have the form $y = b^x$, where base $b > 0$ and $b \neq 1$. The exponential function can also be written $f(x) = b^x$. The following properties apply to exponential expressions:

Property	Description
$a^x a^y = a^{x+y}$	The product of exponentials with the same base equals the base raised to the sum of the powers
$a^x / a^y = a^{x-y}$	The quotient of exponentials with the same base equals the base raised to the difference of the powers
$(a^x)^y = a^{xy}$	An exponential raised to a power equals the base raised to the product of the powers
$(ab)^x = a^x b^x$	Exponentiation distributes over multiplication
$(a/b)^x = a^x / b^x$	Exponentiation distributes over division

Patterns and Algebra

The graph of an example exponential function, $f(x) = 2^x$, is below:

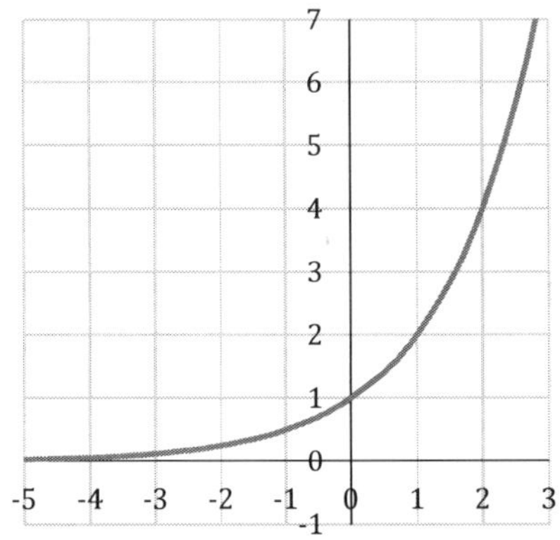

Note in the graph that the y-value approaches zero to the left and infinity to the right. One of the key features of an exponential function is that there will be one end that goes off to infinity and another that asymptotically approaches a lower bound. Common forms of exponential functions include the following:

Geometric sequences: The terms of a geometric sequence have the form $a_n = a_1 \times r^{n-1}$, where a_n is the value of the nth term, a_1 is the initial term, and r is the common ratio between succesive terms. Note that $a_1 \times r^{1-1} = a_1 \times r^0 = a_1 \times 1 = a_1$

Review Video: Geometric Sequences
Visit mometrix.com/academy and enter code: 140779

General exponential growth or decay: The general exponential growth or decay function is $f(t) = a(1 + r)^t$, where the value of $f(t)$ is the amount (of whatever quantity we are measuring) at time t, the constant a is the initial amount (the amount at time $t = 0$), and the constant r is the fixed rate of increase (if $r > 0$) or decrease (if $r < 0$) per unit time. For example, if we invest \$1000 at an interest rate of 6% interest compounded annually and we measure time in years, then our investment will grow according to an exponential model with $a = \$1000$ and $r = 6\% = 0.06$. Thus, after t years the value of our investment will be $f(t) = \$1000(1 + 0.06)^t$. After 5 years, for instance, the investment will grow to $f(5) = \$1000(1 + 0.06)^5 \approx \$1338.23$.

Compound interest: We can modify the general exponential growth function above slightly to get a formula for interest compounded n times per year. Replacing the constant a with P (for principal, the initial amount we invest), the total value of our investment after t years is $f(t) = P\left(1 + \frac{r}{n}\right)^{nt}$, where r is the nominal annual interest rate. Thus, if we change our \$1000 investment above by having the interest rate be 6% compounded *semiannually* (two times per year—so $n = 2$), the value of our investment after t years is $f(t) = \$1000\left(1 + \frac{0.06}{2}\right)^{2t} = \$1000(1 + 0.03)^{2t}$. After 5 years, for instance, the investment will grow to $f(5) = \$1000(1 + 0.03)^{10} \approx \$1343.92$. This is slightly higher than the previous investment because the interest compounds twice as often.

Review Video: Compound Interest Formula
Visit mometrix.com/academy and enter code: 100366

Review Video: Interest Functions
Visit mometrix.com/academy and enter code: 559176

Population growth and continuously compounded interest: When a quantity grows (or decays) continuously at a rate that stays constant relative to the size the quantity has already attained, then we can model its size at time t with the function $f(t) = ae^{rt}$, where a is the initial amount, r is the relative growth rate (which we often call simply the **growth rate**), and e is the irrational constant known as Euler's number (approximately 2.718; scientific calculators have a button for finding e^x, which is known as the **natural exponential function**). For instance, under some circumstances, if an initial population (of people, plants, or animals, for example) of size a grows at constant relative rate r, then the size of the population at time t is $f(t) = ae^{rt}$. Similarly, if we invest principal P (instead of a) for t years at nominal annual interest rate r compounded *continuously*, then after t years the value of the investment is $f(t) = Pe^{rt}$.

For example, suppose the initial population of a town is $a = 1{,}200$ people and the relative annual growth rate is $r = 5\% = 0.05$. Then the population of the town after t years is $f(t) = ae^{rt} = 1200e^{0.05t}$. After 10 years, for instance, the town population is $f(10) = 1200e^{0.05\cdot 10} = 1200e^{0.5} \approx 1978$ people.

> **Review Video: Population Growth**
> Visit mometrix.com/academy and enter code: 109278

LOGARITHMIC FUNCTIONS

The **logarithmic function base b** is the function $y = \log_b x$ or $f(x) = \log_b x$, where the base b may be any positive number except one. The most common bases for logarithms are base 10 (the **common logarithm**) and base e (the **natural logarithm**). We usually write the common logarithm as $y = \log x$ (that is, $\log x$, with no base listed, means $\log_{10} x$) and the natural logarithm as $y = \ln x$ (that is, $\ln x$ means $\log_e x$).

Exponential functions and logarithmic functions with the same base are inverse functions. That is, if $f(x) = b^x$, then $f^{-1}(x) = \log_b x$. This means that the two equations $y = b^x$ (exponential form) and $x = \log_b y$ (logarithmic form) express the same relationship between the quantities x and y. We often solve problems involving logarithms by rewriting them in exponential form, and vice versa. Also, because of this inverse relationship, logarithms and exponentials cancel each other. That is, $\log_b b^x = x$ and $b^{\log_b x} = x$.

The following properties apply to logarithmic expressions:

Property	Description
$\log_b 1 = 0$	The log of 1 is equal to 0 for any base
$\log_b b = 1$	The log of the base is equal to 1
$\log_b b^p = p$	The log of the base raised to a power is equal to that power
$\log_b MN = \log_b M + \log_b N$	The log of a product is the sum of the log of each factor
$\log_b \frac{M}{N} = \log_b M - \log_b N$	The log of a quotient is equal to the log of the dividend minus the log of the divisor
$\log_b M^p = p \log_b M$	The log of a value raised to a power is equal to the power times the log of the value

Logarithms are helpful in solving equations in which the variable appears in an exponent. For instance, consider the example above in which we model the population of a town by the function $f(t) = 1200e^{0.05t}$. Suppose we want to know how long it will take the population of the town to double to 2400 people from its original value of 1200. We find this by solving the equation $1200e^{0.05t} = 2400$. First, we divide both sides of the equation by 1200 to get $e^{0.05t} = 2$. Then we take natural logarithms of both sides to get $\ln e^{0.05t} = \ln 2$, which simplifies (because natural logarithms and natural exponentials are inverse functions) to $0.05t = \ln 2$. Finally, we divide both sides by 0.05 to get $t = (\ln 2)/0.05$, which we evaluate with a calculator to get $t \approx 13.9$ years.

The graph of an example logarithmic function, $f(x) = \log_2(x + 2)$, is below:

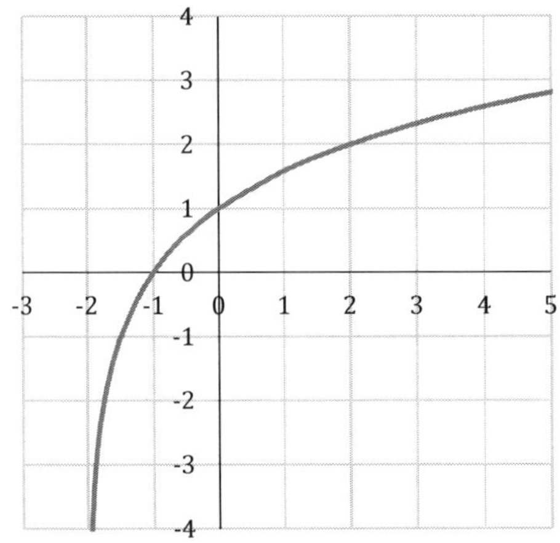

Review Video: Logarithmic Function
Visit mometrix.com/academy and enter code: 658985

Sequences and Series

Sequences

A **sequence** is an ordered set of numbers that continues in a defined pattern. The function that defines a sequence has a domain composed of the set of positive integers. Each member of the sequence is an element, or individual term. Each element is identified by the notation a_n, where a is the term of the sequence, and n is the integer identifying which term in the sequence a is.

There are two different ways to represent a sequence that contains the element a_n. The first is the simple notation $\{a_n\}$. The second is the expanded notation of a sequence: $a_1, a_2, a_3, \dots a_n, \dots$. Notice that the expanded form does not end with the nth term. There is no indication that the nth term is the last term in the sequence, only that the nth term is an element of the sequence.

Arithmetic Sequences

An **arithmetic sequence**, or arithmetic progression, is a special kind of sequence in which a specific quantity, called the common difference, is added to each term to make the next term. The common difference may be positive or negative. The general form of an arithmetic sequence containing n terms is $a_1, a_1 + d, a_1 + 2d, \dots, a_1 + (n-1)d$, where d is the common difference. The general formula for any term of an arithmetic sequence is $a_n = a_1 + (n-1)d$, where a_n is the term you are looking for and d is the common difference. To find the sum of the first n terms of an arithmetic sequence, use the formula $s_n = \frac{n}{2}(a_1 + a_n)$.

Review Video: Arithmetic Sequence
Visit mometrix.com/academy and enter code: 676885

MONOTONIC SEQUENCES

A **monotonic sequence** is a sequence that is either nonincreasing or nondecreasing. A **nonincreasing** sequence is one whose terms either get progressively smaller in value or remain the same. Such a sequence is always bounded above, that is, all elements of the sequence must be less than some real number. A **nondecreasing** sequence is one whose terms either get progressively larger in value or remain the same. Such a sequence is always bounded below, that is, all elements of the sequence must be greater than some real number.

RECURSIVE SEQUENCES

When one element of a sequence is defined in terms of a previous element or elements of the sequence, the sequence is a **recursive sequence**. For example, given the recursive definition $a_1 = 1; a_2 = 1; a_n = a_{n-1} + a_{n-2}$ for all $n > 2$, you get the sequence 1,1,2,3,5,8, … . This is known as the Fibonacci sequence: a continuing sequence of numbers in which each number (after a_2) is the sum of the two previous numbers. The Fibonacci sequence can be defined as starting with either 1,1 or 0,1. Both definitions are considered correct in mathematics. Make sure you know which definition you are working with when dealing with Fibonacci numbers.

Sometimes in a recursive sequence, the terms can be found using a general formula that does not involve the previous terms of the sequence. Such a formula is called a **closed-form** expression for a recursive definition—an alternate formula that will generate the same sequence of numbers. However, not all sequences based on recursive definitions will have a closed-form expression. Some sequences will require the use of the recursive definition.

THE GOLDEN RATIO AND THE FIBONACCI SEQUENCE

The golden ratio is approximately 1.6180339887 and is often represented by the Greek letter phi, Φ. The exact value of Φ is $\frac{(1+\sqrt{5})}{2}$ and it is one of the solutions to $x - \frac{1}{x} = 1$. The golden ratio can be found using the Fibonacci sequence, since the ratio of a term to the previous term approaches Φ as the sequence approaches infinity:

n	a_n	a_{n-1}	$\frac{a_n}{a_{n-1}}$
3	2	1	2
4	3	2	1.5
5	5	3	$1.\overline{6}$
6	8	5	1.6
7	13	8	1.625
8	21	13	$1.\overline{615384}$
9	34	21	$1.\overline{619047}$
⋮	⋮	⋮	⋮
20	6,765	4,181	1.618033963 …

GEOMETRIC SEQUENCES

A geometric sequence is a sequence in which each term is multiplied by a constant number (called the common ratio) to get the next term. Essentially, it's the same concept as an arithmetic sequence, but with multiplication instead of addition.

Consider the following example of a geometric sequence: Andy opens a savings account with $10. During each subsequent week, he plans to double the amount from the previous week.

Sequence: $10, 20, 40, 80, 160, \ldots$

Function: $a_n = 10 \times 2^{n-1}$

This is a geometric sequence with a common ratio of 2. All geometric sequences represent exponential functions. The nth term in any geometric sequence is $a_n = a_1 \times r^{n-1}$, where a_n represents the value of the nth term, a_1 is the initial term, r is the common ratio, and n is the number of terms. Thus, substituting the initial value of 10 and common ratio of 2 gives the function $a_n = 10 \times 2^{n-1}$.

Review Video: Geometric Sequences
Visit mometrix.com/academy and enter code: 140779

Advanced Sequences and Series

Limit of a Sequence

Some sequences will have a **limit**—a value the sequence approaches, or sometimes even reaches, but never passes. A sequence with a limit is called a **convergent** sequence because all the values of the sequence seemingly converge at that point. Sequences that do not converge at a particular limit are **divergent** sequences. The easiest way to determine whether a sequence converges or diverges is to find the limit of the sequence. If the limit is a real number, the sequence is convergent. If the limit is infinity, the sequence is divergent.

Remember the following rules for finding limits:

- $\lim\limits_{n\to\infty} k = k$, for all real numbers k
- $\lim\limits_{n\to\infty} \frac{1}{n} = 0$
- $\lim\limits_{n\to\infty} n = \infty$
- $\lim\limits_{n\to\infty} \frac{k}{n^p} = 0$, for all real numbers k and positive rational numbers p
- The limit of the sum of two sequences is equal to the sum of the limits of the two sequences: $\lim\limits_{n\to\infty} (a_n + b_n) = \lim\limits_{n\to\infty} a_n + \lim\limits_{n\to\infty} b_n$
- The limit of the difference between two sequences is equal to the difference between the limits of the two sequences: $\lim\limits_{n\to\infty} (a_n - b_n) = \lim\limits_{n\to\infty} a_n - \lim\limits_{n\to\infty} b_n$
- The limit of the product of two sequences is equal to the product of the limits of the two sequences: $\lim\limits_{n\to\infty} (a_n \times b_n) = \lim\limits_{n\to\infty} a_n \times \lim\limits_{n\to\infty} b_n$
- The limit of the quotient of two sequences is equal to the quotient of the limits of the two sequences, with some exceptions: $\lim\limits_{n\to\infty} \left(\frac{a_n}{b_n}\right) = \frac{\lim_{n\to\infty} a_n}{\lim_{n\to\infty} b_n}$. In the quotient formula, it is important that $b_n \neq 0$ and that $\lim\limits_{n\to\infty} b_n \neq 0$.
- The limit of a sequence multiplied by a scalar is equal to the scalar multiplied by the limit of the sequence: $\lim\limits_{n\to\infty} ka_n = k \lim\limits_{n\to\infty} a_n$, where k is any real number

Review Video: Limit of a Sequence
Visit mometrix.com/academy and enter code: 847732

Infinite Series

Both arithmetic and geometric sequences have formulas to find the sum of the first n terms in the sequence, assuming you know what the first term is. The sum of all the terms in a sequence is called a series. An **infinite series** is an infinite sum. In other words, it is what you get by adding up all the terms in an infinite sequence: $\sum_{n=1}^{\infty} a_n = a_1 + a_2 + a_3 + \cdots + a_n + \cdots$. This notation can be shortened to $\sum_{n=1}^{\infty} a_n$ or $\sum a_n$.

While we can't add up an infinite list of numbers one at a time, we can still determine the infinite sum. As we add the terms in a series, we can imagine an infinite sequence of partial sums, where the first partial sum is the first element of the series, the second partial sum is the sum of the first two elements of the series, and the nth partial sum is the sum of the first n elements of the series.

Every infinite sequence of partial sums (infinite series) either converges or diverges. As with the test for convergence in a sequence, finding the limit of the sequence of partial sums will indicate whether it is a converging series or a diverging series. If there exists a real number S such that $\lim_{n\to\infty} S_n = S$, where S_n is the sequence of partial sums, then the series converges. If the limit equals infinity, then the series diverges. If $\lim_{n\to\infty} S_n = S$ and S is a real number, then S is also the convergence value of the series.

To find the sum as n approaches infinity for the sum of two convergent series, find the sum as n approaches infinity for each individual series and add the results.

$$\sum_{n=1}^{\infty}(a_n + b_n) = \sum_{n=1}^{\infty} a_n + \sum_{n=1}^{\infty} b_n$$

The same idea works for subtraction.

$$\sum_{n=1}^{\infty}(a_n - b_n) = \sum_{n=1}^{\infty} a_n - \sum_{n=1}^{\infty} b_n$$

To find the sum as n approaches infinity for the product of a constant (also called a scalar) and a convergent series, find the sum as n approaches infinity for the series and multiply the result by the scalar.

$$\sum_{n=1}^{\infty} ka_n = k\sum_{n=1}^{\infty} a_n$$

Review Video: Infinite Series
Visit mometrix.com/academy and enter code: 271404

The nth **term test for divergence** means taking the limit of a sequence a_n as n goes to infinity $\left(\lim_{n\to\infty} a_n\right)$ and checking whether the limit is zero. If the limit is not zero, then the series $\sum a_n$ is a diverging series. This test only works to prove divergence, however. If the limit is zero, the test is inconclusive, meaning the series could be either convergent or divergent.

Review Video: Nth Term Test for Divergence
Visit mometrix.com/academy and enter code: 346400

Matrices

Matrix Basics

A **matrix** (plural: matrices) is a rectangular array of numbers or variables, often called **elements**, which are arranged in columns and rows. A matrix is generally represented by a capital letter, with its elements represented by the corresponding lowercase letter with two subscripts indicating the row and column of the element. For example, n_{ab} represents the element in row a column b of matrix N.

$$N = \begin{bmatrix} n_{11} & n_{12} & n_{13} \\ n_{21} & n_{22} & n_{23} \end{bmatrix}$$

A matrix can be described in terms of the number of rows and columns it contains in the format $a \times b$, where a is the number of rows and b is the number of columns. The matrix shown above is a 2×3 matrix. Any $a \times b$ matrix where $a = b$ is a square matrix. A **vector** is a matrix that has exactly one column (**column vector**) or exactly one row (**row vector**).

The **main diagonal** of a matrix is the set of elements on the diagonal from the top left to the bottom right of a matrix. Because of the way it is defined, only square matrices will have a main diagonal. For the matrix shown below, the main diagonal consists of the elements $n_{11}, n_{22}, n_{33}, n_{44}$.

$$\begin{bmatrix} n_{11} & n_{12} & n_{13} & n_{14} \\ n_{21} & n_{22} & n_{23} & n_{24} \\ n_{31} & n_{32} & n_{33} & n_{34} \\ n_{41} & n_{42} & n_{43} & n_{44} \end{bmatrix}$$

A 3×4 matrix such as the one shown below would not have a main diagonal because there is no straight line of elements between the top left corner and the bottom right corner that joins the elements.

$$\begin{bmatrix} n_{11} & n_{12} & n_{13} & n_{14} \\ n_{21} & n_{22} & n_{23} & n_{24} \\ n_{31} & n_{32} & n_{33} & n_{34} \end{bmatrix}$$

A **diagonal matrix** is a square matrix that has a zero for every element in the matrix except the elements on the main diagonal. All the elements on the main diagonal must be nonzero numbers.

$$\begin{bmatrix} n_{11} & 0 & 0 & 0 \\ 0 & n_{22} & 0 & 0 \\ 0 & 0 & n_{33} & 0 \\ 0 & 0 & 0 & n_{44} \end{bmatrix}$$

If every element on the main diagonal of a diagonal matrix is equal to one, the matrix is called an **identity matrix**. The identity matrix is often represented by the letter I.

$$I = \begin{bmatrix} 1 & 0 & 0 & 0 \\ 0 & 1 & 0 & 0 \\ 0 & 0 & 1 & 0 \\ 0 & 0 & 0 & 1 \end{bmatrix}$$

A **zero matrix** is a matrix that has zero as the value for every element in the matrix.

$$\begin{bmatrix} 0 & 0 & 0 & 0 \\ 0 & 0 & 0 & 0 \\ 0 & 0 & 0 & 0 \\ 0 & 0 & 0 & 0 \end{bmatrix}$$

The zero matrix is the *identity for matrix addition*. Do not confuse the zero matrix with the identity matrix.

The **negative of a matrix** is also known as the additive inverse of a matrix. If matrix N is the given matrix, then matrix $-N$ is its negative. This means that every element n_{ab} is equal to $-n_{ab}$ in the negative. To find the negative of a given matrix, change the sign of every element in the matrix and keep all elements in their original corresponding positions in the matrix.

If two matrices have the same order and all corresponding elements in the two matrices are the same, then the two matrices are **equal matrices**.

A matrix N may be **transposed** to matrix N^T by changing all rows into columns and changing all columns into rows. The easiest way to accomplish this is to swap the positions of the row and column notations for each element. For example, suppose the element in the second row of the third column of matrix N is $n_{23} = 6$. In the transposed matrix N^T, the transposed element would be $n_{32} = 6$, and it would be placed in the third row of the second column.

$$N = \begin{bmatrix} 1 & 2 & 3 \\ 4 & 5 & 6 \end{bmatrix}; \; N^T = \begin{bmatrix} 1 & 4 \\ 2 & 5 \\ 3 & 6 \end{bmatrix}$$

To quickly transpose a matrix by hand, begin with the first column and rewrite a new matrix with those same elements in the same order in the first row. Write the elements from the second column of the original matrix in the second row of the transposed matrix. Continue this process until all columns have been completed. If the original matrix is identical to the transposed matrix, the matrices are symmetric.

Basic Operations with Matrices

There are two categories of basic operations with regard to matrices: operations between a matrix and a scalar, and operations between two matrices.

Scalar Operations

A scalar being added to a matrix is treated as though it were being added to each element of the matrix. The same is true for subtraction, multiplication and division:

$$M + \text{k} = \begin{bmatrix} m_{11} + k & m_{12} + k \\ m_{21} + k & m_{22} + k \end{bmatrix}$$
$$M - k = \begin{bmatrix} m_{11} - k & m_{12} - k \\ m_{21} - k & m_{22} - k \end{bmatrix}$$
$$M \times k = \begin{bmatrix} m_{11} \times k & m_{12} \times k \\ m_{21} \times k & m_{22} \times k \end{bmatrix}$$
$$M \div k = \begin{bmatrix} m_{11} \div k & m_{12} \div k \\ m_{21} \div k & m_{22} \div k \end{bmatrix}$$

Matrix Addition and Subtraction

All four of the basic operations can be used with operations between matrices (although division is usually discarded in favor of multiplication by the inverse), but there are restrictions on the situations in which they can be used. Matrices that meet all the qualifications for a given operation are called **conformable matrices**. However, conformability is specific to the operation; two matrices that are conformable for addition are not necessarily conformable for multiplication.

For two matrices to be conformable for addition or subtraction, they must be of the same dimension; otherwise, the operation is not defined. If matrix M is a 3×2 matrix and matrix N is a 2×3 matrix, the operations $M + N$ and $M - N$ are meaningless. If matrices M and N are the same size, the operation is as simple as adding or subtracting all of the corresponding elements:

$$\begin{bmatrix} m_{11} & m_{12} \\ m_{21} & m_{22} \end{bmatrix} + \begin{bmatrix} n_{11} & n_{12} \\ n_{21} & n_{22} \end{bmatrix} = \begin{bmatrix} m_{11} + n_{11} & m_{12} + n_{12} \\ m_{21} + n_{21} & m_{22} + n_{22} \end{bmatrix}$$

$$\begin{bmatrix} m_{11} & m_{12} \\ m_{21} & m_{22} \end{bmatrix} - \begin{bmatrix} n_{11} & n_{12} \\ n_{21} & n_{22} \end{bmatrix} = \begin{bmatrix} m_{11} - n_{11} & m_{12} - n_{12} \\ m_{21} - n_{21} & m_{22} - n_{22} \end{bmatrix}$$

The result of addition or subtraction is a matrix of the same dimension as the two original matrices involved in the operation.

Matrix Multiplication

The first thing it is necessary to understand about matrix multiplication is that it is not commutative. In scalar multiplication, the operation is commutative, meaning that $a \times b = b \times a$. For matrix multiplication, this is not the case: $A \times B \neq B \times A$. The terminology must be specific when describing matrix multiplication. The operation $A \times B$ can be described as A multiplied (or **post-multiplied**) by B, or B **pre-multiplied** by A.

For two matrices to be conformable for multiplication, they need not be of the same dimension, but specific dimensions must correspond. Taking the example of two matrices M and N to be multiplied $M \times N$, matrix M must have the same number of columns as matrix N has rows. Put another way, if matrix M has the dimensions $a \times b$ and matrix N has the dimensions $c \times d$, b must equal c if the two matrices are to be conformable for this multiplication. The matrix that results from the multiplication will have the dimensions $a \times d$. If a and d are both equal to 1, the product is simply a scalar. Square matrices of the same dimensions are always conformable for multiplication, and their product is always a matrix of the same size.

The simplest type of matrix multiplication is a 1×2 matrix (a row vector) times a 2×1 matrix (a column vector). These will multiply in the following way:

$$[m_{11} \quad m_{12}] \times \begin{bmatrix} n_{11} \\ n_{21} \end{bmatrix} = m_{11}n_{11} + m_{12}n_{21}$$

The two matrices are conformable for multiplication because matrix M has the same number of columns as matrix N has rows. Because the other dimensions are both 1, the result is a scalar. Expanding our matrices to 1×3 and 3×1, the process is the same:

$$[m_{11} \quad m_{12} \quad m_{13}] \times \begin{bmatrix} n_{11} \\ n_{21} \\ n_{31} \end{bmatrix} = m_{11}n_{11} + m_{12}n_{21} + m_{13}n_{31}$$

Once again, the result is a scalar. This type of basic matrix multiplication is the building block for the multiplication of larger matrices.

To multiply larger matrices, treat each **row from the first matrix** and each **column from the second matrix** as individual vectors and follow the pattern for multiplying vectors. The scalar value found from multiplying the first-row vector by the first column vector is placed in the first row, first column of the new matrix. The scalar value found from multiplying the second-row vector by the first column vector is placed in the second row, first column of the new matrix. Continue this pattern until each row of the first matrix has been multiplied by each column of the second matrix.

Below is an example of the multiplication of a 3×2 matrix and a 2×3 matrix.

$$\begin{bmatrix} m_{11} & m_{12} \\ m_{21} & m_{22} \\ m_{31} & m_{32} \end{bmatrix} \times \begin{bmatrix} n_{11} & n_{12} & n_{13} \\ n_{21} & n_{22} & n_{23} \end{bmatrix} = \begin{bmatrix} m_{11}n_{11} + m_{12}n_{21} & m_{11}n_{12} + m_{12}n_{22} & m_{11}n_{13} + m_{12}n_{23} \\ m_{21}n_{11} + m_{22}n_{21} & m_{21}n_{12} + m_{22}n_{22} & m_{21}n_{13} + m_{22}n_{23} \\ m_{31}n_{11} + m_{32}n_{21} & m_{31}n_{12} + m_{32}n_{22} & m_{31}n_{13} + m_{32}n_{23} \end{bmatrix}$$

This process starts by taking the first column of the second matrix and running it through each row of the first matrix. Removing all but the first M row and first N column, we would see only the following:

$$[m_{11} \; m_{12}] \times \begin{bmatrix} n_{11} \\ n_{21} \end{bmatrix} = m_{11}n_{11} + m_{12}n_{21}$$

The first product would then be $m_{11}n_{11} + m_{12}n_{21}$. This process will be continued for each column of the N matrix to find the first full row of the product matrix, as shown below.

$$[m_{11}n_{11} + m_{12}n_{21} \quad m_{11}n_{12} + m_{12}n_{22} \quad m_{11}n_{13} + m_{12}n_{23}]$$

After completing the first row, the next step would be to simply move to the second row of the M matrix and repeat the process until all of the rows have been finished. The result is a 3×3 matrix.

$$\begin{bmatrix} m_{11} & m_{12} \\ m_{21} & m_{22} \\ m_{31} & m_{32} \end{bmatrix} \times \begin{bmatrix} n_{11} & n_{12} & n_{13} \\ n_{21} & n_{22} & n_{23} \end{bmatrix} = \begin{bmatrix} m_{11}n_{11} + m_{12}n_{21} & m_{11}n_{12} + m_{12}n_{22} & m_{11}n_{13} + m_{12}n_{23} \\ m_{21}n_{11} + m_{22}n_{21} & m_{21}n_{12} + m_{22}n_{22} & m_{21}n_{13} + m_{22}n_{23} \\ m_{31}n_{11} + m_{32}n_{21} & m_{31}n_{12} + m_{32}n_{22} & m_{31}n_{13} + m_{32}n_{23} \end{bmatrix}$$

If the operation were done in reverse $(N \times M)$, the result would be a 2×2 matrix.

$$\begin{bmatrix} n_{11} & n_{12} & n_{13} \\ n_{21} & n_{22} & n_{23} \end{bmatrix} \times \begin{bmatrix} m_{11} & m_{12} \\ m_{21} & m_{22} \\ m_{31} & m_{32} \end{bmatrix} = \begin{bmatrix} m_{11}n_{11} + m_{21}n_{12} + m_{31}n_{13} & m_{12}n_{11} + m_{22}n_{12} + m_{32}n_{13} \\ m_{11}n_{21} + m_{21}n_{22} + m_{31}n_{23} & m_{12}n_{21} + m_{22}n_{22} + m_{32}n_{23} \end{bmatrix}$$

Review Video: Matrices: The Basics
Visit mometrix.com/academy and enter code: 516658

Advanced Matrices

Elementary Row Operations

Elementary row operations include multiplying a row by a non-zero scalar, adding scalar multiples of two rows, and switching rows. These operations can be done using matrix multiplication with specialized transformation matrices. Elementary row operations are left multiplied, $A' = MA$.To do the same type of operations on the columns, then the transformation matrix is right multiplied, $A' = AM$. **Row switching** is achieved by swapping the corresponding rows in the identity matrix. For example, consider switching row 2 and row 3 in a 3×3 matrix:

$$M_{R_2 \leftrightarrow R_3} = \begin{bmatrix} 1 & 0 & 0 \\ 0 & 0 & 1 \\ 0 & 1 & 0 \end{bmatrix}$$

The transformation matrix for **row multiplication** is also based on the identity matrix with the scalar multiplication factor in place of the 1 in the corresponding row. Multiplying row 1 by –4 in a 3×3 matrix:

$$M_{-4R_1 \to R_1} = \begin{bmatrix} -4 & 0 & 0 \\ 0 & 1 & 0 \\ 0 & 0 & 1 \end{bmatrix}$$

The transformation matrix for **row addition** consists of the identity matrix with a 1 in the element corresponding to the two rows being added in the column where you want the result to go. Adding row 2 to row 1 in a 3×3 matrix:

$$M_{R_1 + R_2 \to R_1} = \begin{bmatrix} 1 & 1 & 0 \\ 0 & 1 & 0 \\ 0 & 0 & 1 \end{bmatrix}$$

Review Video: Matrices: Elementary Row Operations
Visit mometrix.com/academy and enter code: 493170

Determinants and Inverses of Matrices

The **determinant** of a matrix is a scalar value that is calculated by taking into account all the elements of a square matrix. A determinant only exists for square matrices. Finding the determinant of a 2×2 matrix is as simple as remembering a simple equation. For a 2×2 matrix

$M = \begin{bmatrix} m_{11} & m_{12} \\ m_{21} & m_{22} \end{bmatrix}$, the determinant is obtained by the equation $|M| = m_{11}m_{22} - m_{12}m_{21}$. Anything larger than 2×2 requires multiple steps. Take matrix $N = \begin{bmatrix} a & b & c \\ d & e & f \\ g & h & j \end{bmatrix}$. The determinant of N is calculated as $|N| = a\begin{vmatrix} e & f \\ h & j \end{vmatrix} - b\begin{vmatrix} d & f \\ g & j \end{vmatrix} + c\begin{vmatrix} d & e \\ g & h \end{vmatrix}$ or $|N| = a(ej - fh) - b(dj - fg) + c(dh - eg)$.

There is a shortcut for 3×3 matrices: add the products of each unique set of elements diagonally left-to-right and subtract the products of each unique set of elements diagonally right-to-left. In matrix N, the left-to-right diagonal elements are (a, e, j), (b, f, g), and (c, d, h). The right-to-left diagonal elements are (a, f, h), (b, d, j), and (c, e, g). $\det(N) = aej + bfg + cdh - afh - bdj - ceg$.

Calculating the determinants of matrices larger than 3×3 is rarely, if ever, done by hand.

The **inverse** of a matrix M is the matrix that, when multiplied by matrix M, yields a product that is the identity matrix. Multiplication of matrices will be explained in greater detail shortly. Not all matrices have inverses. Only a square matrix whose determinant is not zero has an inverse. If a matrix has an inverse, that inverse is unique to that matrix. For any matrix M that has an inverse, the inverse is represented by the symbol M^{-1}. To calculate the inverse of a 2×2 square matrix, use the following pattern:

$$M = \begin{bmatrix} m_{11} & m_{12} \\ m_{21} & m_{22} \end{bmatrix};\ M^{-1} = \begin{bmatrix} \frac{m_{22}}{|M|} & \frac{-m_{12}}{|M|} \\ \frac{-m_{21}}{|M|} & \frac{m_{11}}{|M|} \end{bmatrix}$$

Another way to find the inverse of a matrix by hand is use an augmented matrix and elementary row operations. An **augmented matrix** is formed by appending the entries from one matrix onto the end of another. For example, given a 2×2 invertible matrix $N = \begin{bmatrix} a & b \\ c & d \end{bmatrix}$, you can find the inverse N^{-1} by creating an augmented matrix by appending a 2×2 identity matrix: $\left[\begin{array}{cc|cc} a & b & 1 & 0 \\ c & d & 0 & 1 \end{array}\right]$. To find the inverse of the original 2×2 matrix, perform elementary row operations to convert the original matrix on the left to an identity matrix: $\left[\begin{array}{cc|cc} 1 & 0 & e & f \\ 0 & 1 & g & h \end{array}\right]$. For instance, the first step might be to multiply the second row by $\frac{b}{d}$ and then subtract it from the first row to make its second column a zero. The end result is that the 2×2 section on the right will become the inverse of the original matrix: $N^{-1} = \begin{bmatrix} e & f \\ g & h \end{bmatrix}$.

Review Video: Transposition, Determinants, and Augmentation of Matrices
Visit mometrix.com/academy and enter code: 521365

Reduced Row-Echelon Forms

When a system of equations has a solution, finding the transformation of the augmented matrix will result in one of three reduced row-echelon forms. Only one of these forms will give a unique solution to the system of equations, however. The following examples show the solutions indicated by particular results:

$\begin{bmatrix} 1 & 0 & 0 & x_0 \\ 0 & 1 & 0 & y_0 \\ 0 & 0 & 1 & z_0 \end{bmatrix}$ gives the unique solution $x = x_0;\ y = y_0; z = z_0$

$\begin{bmatrix} 1 & 0 & k_1 & x_0 \\ 0 & 1 & k_2 & y_0 \\ 0 & 0 & 0 & 0 \end{bmatrix}$ gives a non-unique solution $x = x_0 - k_1 z; y = y_0 - k_2 z$

$\begin{bmatrix} 1 & j_1 & k_1 & x_0 \\ 0 & 0 & 0 & 0 \\ 0 & 0 & 0 & 0 \end{bmatrix}$ gives a non-unique solution $x = x_0 - j_1 y - k_1 z$

Geometric Transformations

The four *geometric transformations* are **translations, reflections, rotations,** and **dilations**. When geometric transformations are expressed as matrices, the process of performing the transformations is simplified. For calculations of the geometric transformations of a planar figure, make a $2 \times n$ matrix, where n is the number of vertices in the planar figure. Each column represents the rectangular coordinates of one vertex of the figure, with the top row containing the values of the x-coordinates and the bottom row containing the values of the y-coordinates. For example, given a planar triangular figure with coordinates (x_1, y_1), (x_2, y_2), and (x_3, y_3), the corresponding matrix is $\begin{bmatrix} x_1 & x_2 & x_3 \\ y_1 & y_2 & y_3 \end{bmatrix}$. You can then perform the necessary transformations on this matrix to determine the coordinates of the resulting figure.

Review Video: Matrices: Geometric Transformations
Visit mometrix.com/academy and enter code: 612781

Translation

A **translation** moves a figure along the x-axis, the y-axis, or both axes without changing the size or shape of the figure. To calculate the new coordinates of a planar figure following a translation, set up a matrix of the coordinates and a matrix of the translation values and add the two matrices.

$$\begin{bmatrix} h & h & h \\ v & v & v \end{bmatrix} + \begin{bmatrix} x_1 & x_2 & x_3 \\ y_1 & y_2 & y_3 \end{bmatrix} = \begin{bmatrix} h + x_1 & h + x_2 & h + x_3 \\ v + y_1 & v + y_2 & v + y_3 \end{bmatrix}$$

where h is the number of units the figure is moved along the x-axis (horizontally) and v is the number of units the figure is moved along the y-axis (vertically).

Reflection

To find the **reflection** of a planar figure over the x-axis, set up a matrix of the coordinates of the vertices and pre-multiply the matrix by the 2×2 matrix $\begin{bmatrix} 1 & 0 \\ 0 & -1 \end{bmatrix}$ so that $\begin{bmatrix} 1 & 0 \\ 0 & -1 \end{bmatrix} \begin{bmatrix} x_1 & x_2 & x_3 \\ y_1 & y_2 & y_3 \end{bmatrix} = \begin{bmatrix} x_1 & x_2 & x_3 \\ -y_1 & -y_2 & -y_3 \end{bmatrix}$. To find the reflection of a planar figure over the y-axis, set up a matrix of the coordinates of the vertices and pre-multiply the matrix by the 2×2 matrix $\begin{bmatrix} -1 & 0 \\ 0 & 1 \end{bmatrix}$ so that $\begin{bmatrix} -1 & 0 \\ 0 & 1 \end{bmatrix} \begin{bmatrix} x_1 & x_2 & x_3 \\ y_1 & y_2 & y_3 \end{bmatrix} = \begin{bmatrix} -x_1 & -x_2 & -x_3 \\ y_1 & y_2 & y_3 \end{bmatrix}$. To find the reflection of a planar figure over the line $y = x$, set up a matrix of the coordinates of the vertices and pre-multiply the matrix by the 2×2

matrix $\begin{bmatrix} 0 & 1 \\ 1 & 0 \end{bmatrix}$ so that $\begin{bmatrix} 0 & 1 \\ 1 & 0 \end{bmatrix}\begin{bmatrix} x_1 & x_2 & x_3 \\ y_1 & y_2 & y_3 \end{bmatrix} = \begin{bmatrix} y_1 & y_2 & y_3 \\ x_1 & x_2 & x_3 \end{bmatrix}$. Remember that the order of multiplication is important when multiplying matrices. The commutative property does not apply.

ROTATION

To find the coordinates of the figure formed by rotating a planar figure about the origin θ degrees in a counterclockwise direction, set up a matrix of the coordinates of the vertices and pre-multiply the matrix by the 2×2 matrix $\begin{bmatrix} \cos\theta & -\sin\theta \\ \sin\theta & \cos\theta \end{bmatrix}$. For example, if you want to rotate a figure 90° clockwise around the origin, you would have to convert the degree measure to 270° counterclockwise and solve the 2×2 matrix you have set as the pre-multiplier: $\begin{bmatrix} \cos 270° & \sin 270° \\ -\sin 270° & \cos 270° \end{bmatrix} = \begin{bmatrix} 0 & -1 \\ 1 & 0 \end{bmatrix}$. Use this as the pre-multiplier for the matrix $\begin{bmatrix} x_1 & x_2 & x_3 \\ y_1 & y_2 & y_3 \end{bmatrix}$ and solve to find the new coordinates.

DILATION

To find the **dilation** of a planar figure by a scale factor of k, set up a matrix of the coordinates of the vertices of the planar figure and pre-multiply the matrix by the 2×2 matrix $\begin{bmatrix} k & 0 \\ 0 & k \end{bmatrix}$ so that $\begin{bmatrix} k & 0 \\ 0 & k \end{bmatrix}\begin{bmatrix} x_1 & x_2 & x_3 \\ y_1 & y_2 & y_3 \end{bmatrix} = \begin{bmatrix} kx_1 & kx_2 & kx_3 \\ ky_1 & ky_2 & ky_3 \end{bmatrix}$. This is effectively the same as multiplying the matrix by the scalar k, but the matrix equation would still be necessary if the figure were being dilated by different factors in vertical and horizontal directions. The scale factor k will be greater than 1 if the figure is being enlarged, and between 0 and 1 if the figure is being shrunk. Again, remember that when multiplying matrices, the order of the matrices is important. The commutative property does not apply, and the matrix with the coordinates of the figure must be the second matrix.

MATRIX SYSTEMS

SOLVING SYSTEMS OF EQUATIONS

Matrices can be used to represent the coefficients of a system of linear equations and can be very useful in solving those systems. Take for instance three equations with three variables where all a, b, c, and d are known constants:

$$a_1x + b_1y + c_1z = d_1$$
$$a_2x + b_2y + c_2z = d_2$$
$$a_3x + b_3y + c_3z = d_3$$

To solve this system, define three matrices:

$$A = \begin{bmatrix} a_1 & b_1 & c_1 \\ a_2 & b_2 & c_2 \\ a_3 & b_3 & c_3 \end{bmatrix};\ D = \begin{bmatrix} d_1 \\ d_2 \\ d_3 \end{bmatrix};\ X = \begin{bmatrix} x \\ y \\ z \end{bmatrix}$$

The three equations in our system can be fully represented by a single matrix equation:

$$AX = D$$

Patterns and Algebra

We know that the identity matrix times X is equal to X, and we know that any matrix multiplied by its inverse is equal to the identity matrix.

$$A^{-1}AX = IX = X; \text{thus } X = A^{-1}D$$

Our goal then is to find the inverse of A, or A^{-1}. Once we have that, we can pre-multiply matrix D by A^{-1} (post-multiplying here is an undefined operation) to find matrix X.

Systems of equations can also be solved using the transformation of an augmented matrix in a process similar to that for finding a matrix inverse. Begin by arranging each equation of the system in the following format:

$$\begin{gathered} a_1x + b_1y + c_1z = d_1 \\ a_2x + b_2y + c_2z = d_2 \\ a_3x + b_3y + c_3z = d_3 \end{gathered}$$

Define matrices A and D and combine them into augmented matrix A_a:

$$A = \begin{bmatrix} a_1 & b_1 & c_1 \\ a_2 & b_2 & c_2 \\ a_3 & b_3 & c_3 \end{bmatrix}; D = \begin{bmatrix} d_1 \\ d_2 \\ d_3 \end{bmatrix}; A_a = \begin{bmatrix} a_1 & b_1 & c_1 & d_1 \\ a_2 & b_2 & c_2 & d_2 \\ a_3 & b_3 & c_3 & d_3 \end{bmatrix}$$

To solve the augmented matrix and the system of equations, use elementary row operations to form an identity matrix in the first 3×3 section. When this is complete, the values in the last column are the solutions to the system of equations:

$$\begin{bmatrix} 1 & 0 & 0 & x \\ 0 & 1 & 0 & y \\ 0 & 0 & 1 & z \end{bmatrix}$$

If an identity matrix is not possible, the system of equations has no unique solution. Sometimes only a partial solution will be possible. The following are partial solutions you may find:

$\begin{bmatrix} 1 & 0 & k_1 & x_0 \\ 0 & 1 & k_2 & y_0 \\ 0 & 0 & 0 & 0 \end{bmatrix}$ gives the non-unique solution $x = x_0 - k_1z;\ y = y_0 - k_2z$

$\begin{bmatrix} 1 & j_1 & k_1 & x_0 \\ 0 & 0 & 0 & 0 \\ 0 & 0 & 0 & 0 \end{bmatrix}$ gives the non-unique solution $x = x_0 - j_1y - k_1z$

This process can be used to solve systems of equations with any number of variables, but three is the upper limit for practical purposes. Anything more ought to be done with a graphing calculator.

Review Video: Matrices: Data Systems
Visit mometrix.com/academy and enter code: 579763

Permutations and Combinations

Permutations and Combinations

Factorials

The **factorial** is a function that can be performed on any **non-negative integer**. It is represented by the ! sign written after the integer on which it is being performed. The factorial of an integer is the product of all positive integers less than or equal to the number. For example, 4! (read "4 factorial") is calculated as $4 \times 3 \times 2 \times 1 = 24$.

Since 0 is not itself a positive integer, nor does it have any positive integers less than it, 0! cannot be calculated using this method. Instead, 0! is defined by convention to equal 1. This makes sense if you consider the pattern of descending factorials:

$$\begin{aligned} 5! &= 120 \\ 4! &= \frac{5!}{5} = \frac{120}{5} = 24 \\ 3! &= \frac{4!}{4} = \frac{24}{4} = 6 \\ 2! &= \frac{3!}{3} = \frac{6}{3} = 2 \\ 1! &= \frac{2!}{2} = \frac{2}{2} = 1 \\ 0! &= \frac{1!}{1} = \frac{1}{1} = 1 \end{aligned}$$

Permutations

For any given set of data, the individual elements in the set may be arranged in different groups containing different numbers of elements arranged in different orders. For example, given the set of integers from one to three, inclusive, the elements of the set are 1, 2, and 3: written as $\{1, 2, 3\}$. They may be arranged as follows: 1, 2, 3, 12, 21, 13, 31, 23, 32, 123, 132, 213, 231, 312, and 321. These ordered sequences of elements from the given set of data are called **permutations**. It is important to note that in permutations, the order of the elements in the sequence is important. The sequence 123 is not the same as the sequence 213. Also, no element in the given set may be used more times as an element in a permutation than it appears as an element in the original set. For example, 223 is not a permutation in the above example because the number 2 only appears one time in the given set.

To find the number of permutations of r items from a set of n items, use the formula ${}_nP_r = \frac{n!}{(n-r)!}$. When using this formula, each element of r must be unique. Also, this assumes that different arrangements of the same set of elements yields different outcomes. For example, 123 is not the same as 321; order is important.

A special case arises while finding the number of possible permutations of n items from a set of n items. Because $n = r$, the equation for the number of permutations becomes simply $P = n!$ The same result is true for $r = n - 1$. Both of these cases are a result of the fact that 0! and 1! are both equal to 1.

If a set contains one or more groups of **indistinguishable or interchangeable elements** (e.g., the set $\{1, 2, 3, 3\}$, which has a group of two indistinguishable 3's), there is a different formula for finding distinct permutations of all n elements. Use the formula $P = \frac{n!}{m_1!m_2!...m_k!}$, where P is the number of permutations, n is the total number of elements in the set, and m_1 through m_k are the number of identical elements in each group (e.g., for the set $\{1,1,2,2,2,3,3\}$, $m_1 = 2$, $m_2 = 3$, and $m_3 = 2$). It is important to note that each repeated number is counted as its own element for the purpose of defining n (e.g., for the set $\{1,1,2,2,2,3,3\}$, $n = 7$, not 3).

To find the number of possible permutations of **any number of elements** in a set of unique elements, you must apply the permutation formulas multiple times. For example, to find the total number of possible permutations of the set $\{1,2,3\}$ first apply the permutation formula for situations where $n = r$ as follows: $P = n! = 3! = 6$. This gives the number of permutations of the three elements when all three elements are used. To find the number of permutations when only two of the three elements are used, use the formula ${}_nP_r = \frac{n!}{(n-r)!}$, where n is 3 and r is 2.

$${}_nP_r = \frac{n!}{(n-r)!} \Rightarrow {}_3P_2 = \frac{3!}{(3-2)!} = \frac{6}{1} = 6$$

To find the number of permutations when one element is used, use the formula ${}_nP_r = \frac{n!}{(n-r)!}$, where n is 3 and r is 1.

$${}_nP_r = \frac{n!}{(n-r)!} \Rightarrow {}_3P_1 = \frac{3!}{(3-1)!} = \frac{3!}{2!} = \frac{6}{2} = 3$$

Find the sum of the three formulas: $6 + 6 + 3 = 15$ total possible permutations.

Alternatively, the general formula for total possible permutations can be written as follows:

$$P_T = \sum_{i=1}^{n} \frac{n!}{(i-1)!}$$

Combinations

Combinations are essentially defined as permutations where the order in which the elements appear does not matter. Going back to the earlier example of the set $\{1,2,3\}$, the possible combinations that can be made from that set are 1, 2, 3, 12, 13, 23, and 123.

In a set containing n elements, the number of combinations of r items from the set can be found using the formula ${}_nC_r = \frac{n!}{r!(n-r)!}$. Notice the similarity to the formula for permutations. In effect, you are dividing the number of permutations by $r!$ to get the number of combinations, and the formula may be written ${}_nC_r = \frac{{}_nP_r}{r!}$. When finding the number of combinations, it is important to remember that the elements in the set must be unique (i.e., there must not be any duplicate items), and that no item may be used more than once in any given sequence.

Chapter Quiz

Ready to see how well you retained what you just read? Scan the QR code to go directly to the chapter quiz interface for this study guide. If you're using a computer, simply visit the online resources page at **mometrix.com/resources719/texesmath4-8** and click the Chapter Quizzes link.

Geometry and Measurement

Measurement

Rounding and Estimation

Rounding is reducing the digits in a number while still trying to keep the value similar. The result will be less accurate but in a simpler form and easier to use. Whole numbers can be rounded to the nearest ten, hundred, or thousand, for instance.

To round a number, we make it a little smaller (rounding down) or a little larger (rounding up) to get a number that ends in zeros. We specify the number of zeros by naming the last place that we will not "zero out." For example, to round 8,327 to the nearest hundred, we round down to 8,300, zeroing out every digit to the right of the hundreds place. To round 4,728 to the nearest thousand, we round up to 5,000, increasing the thousands digit by one (to make the number larger) and zeroing out every digit to the right of the thousands place.

We decide whether to round down or up by looking at the first digit we are going to zero out. If it is less than 5 (namely, 0, 1, 2, 3, or 4) we round down. If it is greater than or equal to 5 (namely, 5, 6, 7, 8, or 9) we round up by adding 1 to the place we are rounding to. So, rounding 8,327 to the nearest hundred, we round down to 8,300 because the tens digit, 2, is less than 5. And rounding 4,728 to the nearest thousand, we round up to 5,000, increasing the thousands digit by 1, because the hundreds digit, 7, is greater than or equal to 5.

This even works with decimals. For example, rounding 39.7426 to the nearest tenth, we round down to 39.7000 (or simply 39.7) because the hundredths digit, 4, is less than 5. And rounding 0.019823 to the nearest thousandth, we round up to 0.020000 (or simply 0.02) by increasing the thousandths digit by 1, because the ten-thousandths digit, 8, is greater than or equal to 5.

When you are asked to estimate the solution to a problem, you will need to provide only an approximate figure or **estimation** for your answer. In this situation, you will need to round each number in the calculation to the level indicated (nearest hundred, nearest thousand, etc.) or to a level that makes sense for the numbers involved. When estimating a sum **all numbers must be rounded to the same level**. You cannot round one number to the nearest thousand while rounding another to the nearest hundred.

For instance, suppose you are considering buying four pieces of equipment for your home office. Their prices are \$485, \$1,217, \$750, and \$643. To estimate their total cost, you might round each price to the nearest hundred and add the rounded figures, getting an estimate of $\$500 + \$1,200 + \$800 + \$600 = \$3,100$. By estimating instead of making an exact calculation, you give up a little accuracy to get a simpler calculation.

Review Video: Rounding and Estimation
Visit mometrix.com/academy and enter code: 126243

Scientific Notation

Scientific notation is a way of writing large numbers in a shorter form. The form $a \times 10^n$ is used in scientific notation, where a is greater than or equal to 1 but less than 10, and n is the number of places the decimal must move to get from the original number to a. Example: The number 230,400,000 is cumbersome to write. To write the value in scientific notation, place a decimal point between the first and second numbers, and include all digits through the last non-zero digit ($a = 2.304$). To find the appropriate power of 10, count the number of places the decimal point had to move ($n = 8$). The number is positive if the decimal moved to the left, and negative if it moved to the right. We can then write 230,400,000 as 2.304×10^8. If we look instead at the number 0.00002304, we have the same value for a, but this time the decimal moved 5 places to the right ($n = -5$). Thus, 0.00002304 can be written as 2.304×10^{-5}. Using this notation makes it simple to compare very large or very small numbers. By comparing exponents, it is easy to see that 3.28×10^4 is smaller than 1.51×10^5, because 4 is less than 5.

Review Video: Scientific Notation
Visit mometrix.com/academy and enter code: 976454

Metric and Customary Measurements

Metric Measurement Prefixes

Giga-	One billion	1 *giga*watt is one billion watts
Mega-	One million	1 *mega*hertz is one million hertz
Kilo-	One thousand	1 *kilo*gram is one thousand grams
Deci-	One-tenth	1 *deci*meter is one-tenth of a meter
Centi-	One-hundredth	1 *centi*meter is one-hundredth of a meter
Milli-	One-thousandth	1 *milli*liter is one-thousandth of a liter
Micro-	One-millionth	1 *micro*gram is one-millionth of a gram

Review Video: How the Metric System Works
Visit mometrix.com/academy and enter code: 163709

Measurement Conversion

When converting between units, the goal is to maintain the same meaning but change the way it is displayed. In order to go from a larger unit to a smaller unit, multiply the number of the known amount by the equivalent amount. When going from a smaller unit to a larger unit, divide the number of the known amount by the equivalent amount.

For complicated conversions, it may be helpful to set up conversion fractions. In these fractions, one fraction is the **conversion factor**. The other fraction has the unknown amount in the numerator. So, the known value is placed in the denominator. Sometimes, the second fraction has the known value from the problem in the numerator and the unknown in the denominator. Multiply the two fractions to get the converted measurement. Note that since the numerator and the denominator of the factor are equivalent, the value of the fraction is 1. That is why we can say that the result in the new units is equal to the result in the old units even though they have different numbers.

It can often be necessary to chain known conversion factors together. As an example, consider converting 512 square inches to square meters. We know that there are 2.54 centimeters in an inch and 100 centimeters in a meter, and we know we will need to square each of these factors to achieve the conversion we are looking for.

$$\frac{512\text{ in}^2}{1} \times \left(\frac{2.54\text{ cm}}{1\text{ in}}\right)^2 \times \left(\frac{1\text{ m}}{100\text{ cm}}\right)^2 = \frac{512\text{ }\cancel{\text{in}^2}}{1} \times \left(\frac{6.4516\text{ }\cancel{\text{cm}^2}}{1\text{ }\cancel{\text{in}^2}}\right) \times \left(\frac{1\text{ m}^2}{10{,}000\text{ }\cancel{\text{cm}^2}}\right) = 0.330\text{ m}^2$$

Review Video: Measurement Conversions
Visit mometrix.com/academy and enter code: 316703

Review Video: Converting Kilograms to Pounds
Visit mometrix.com/academy and enter code: 241463

Common Units and Equivalents

Metric Equivalents

1000 μg (microgram)	1 mg
1000 mg (milligram)	1 g
1000 g (gram)	1 kg
1000 kg (kilogram)	1 metric ton
1000 mL (milliliter)	1 L
1000 μm (micrometer)	1 mm
1000 mm (millimeter)	1 m
100 cm (centimeter)	1 m
1000 m (meter)	1 km

Distance and Area Measurement

Unit	Abbreviation	US equivalent	Metric equivalent
Inch	in	1 inch	2.54 centimeters
Foot	ft	12 inches	0.305 meters
Yard	yd	3 feet	0.914 meters
Mile	mi	5280 feet	1.609 kilometers
Acre	ac	4840 square yards	0.405 hectares
Square Mile	sq. mi. or mi.^{2}	640 acres	2.590 square kilometers

Capacity Measurements

Unit	Abbreviation	US equivalent	Metric equivalent
Fluid Ounce	fl oz	8 fluid drams	29.573 milliliters
Cup	c	8 fluid ounces	0.237 liter
Pint	pt.	16 fluid ounces	0.473 liter
Quart	qt.	2 pints	0.946 liter
Gallon	gal.	4 quarts	3.785 liters
Teaspoon	t or tsp.	1 fluid dram	5 milliliters
Tablespoon	T or tbsp.	4 fluid drams	15 or 16 milliliters
Cubic Centimeter	cc or cm^3	0.271 drams	1 milliliter

Weight Measurements

Unit	Abbreviation	US equivalent	Metric equivalent
Ounce	oz	16 drams	28.35 grams
Pound	lb	16 ounces	453.6 grams
Ton	tn.	2,000 pounds	907.2 kilograms

Volume and Weight Measurement Clarifications

Always be careful when using ounces and fluid ounces. They are not equivalent.

1 pint = 16 fluid ounces	1 fluid ounce ≠ 1 ounce
1 pound = 16 ounces	1 pint ≠ 1 pound

Having one pint of something does not mean you have one pound of it. In the same way, just because something weighs one pound does not mean that its volume is one pint.

In the United States, the word "ton" by itself refers to a short ton or a net ton. Do not confuse this with a long ton (also called a gross ton) or a metric ton (also spelled *tonne*), which have different measurement equivalents.

$$1 \text{ US ton} = 2000 \text{ pounds} \quad \neq \quad 1 \text{ metric ton} = 1000 \text{ kilograms}$$

Precision, Accuracy, and Error

Measurements of physical quantities (e.g., length, area, volume, weight, mass, and time) in the real world are never perfect. Measurements miss the true value, and repeated measurements produce different values. For this reason, fields that depend on good measurement have technical terms, precision and accuracy, that describe how particular ways of measuring a quantity produce good or bad results. Note that these terms apply not to single measurements but to repeated measurements of the same quantity using the same procedure.

Precision describes the consistency of measurements. Measurements that cluster closely together, with little variation from one measurement to the next, have high precision. Measurements that vary a great deal from one measurement to the next have low precision.

Accuracy describes the closeness of measurements to the true value of the quantity being measured or, more technically, the tendency of measurements to cluster around the true value (though we do not usually know the true value; otherwise, we would not bother to measure it).

An analogy from archery may help. An outstanding archer aiming at the center of the target (the true value) produces a tight cluster of arrows around the center (high accuracy, high precision). Under the same circumstances a modestly good archer produces a loose cluster around the center (high accuracy, low precision). If, however, there is a strong crosswind and the archers do nothing to compensate for it, the outstanding archer's shots will cluster tightly around a point away from the center (low accuracy, high precision); and the modestly good archer's shots will cluster loosely around a point away from the center (low accuracy, low precision).

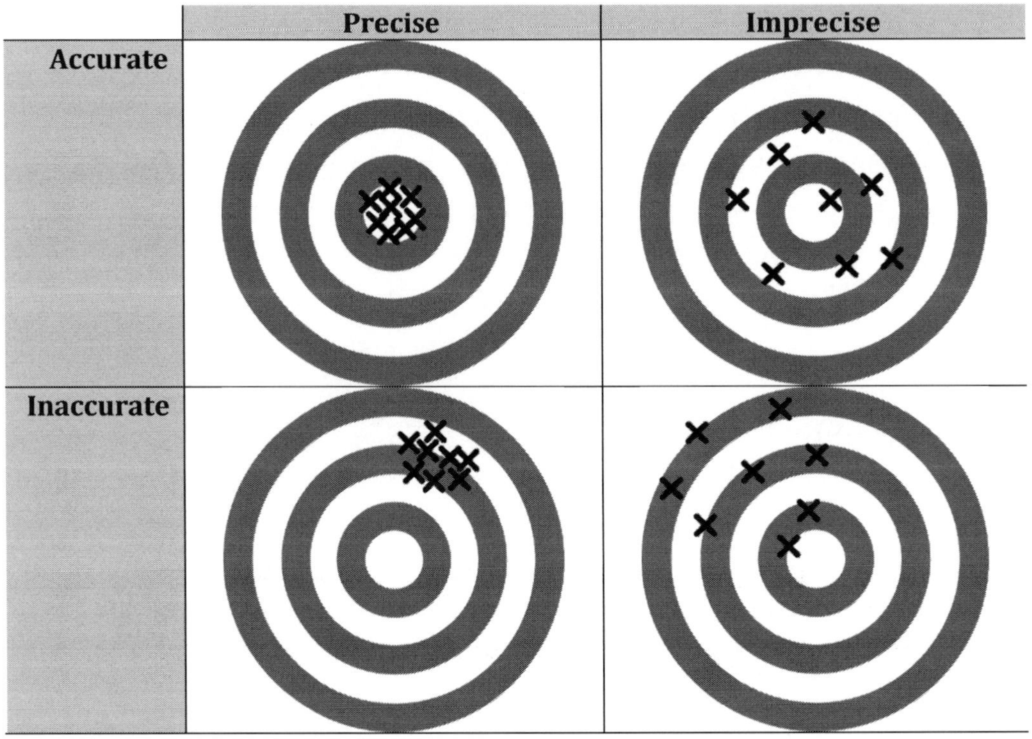

Error in measurement is not a mistake but simply the difference between the true value and the measured value. Since we seldom know the true value, we seldom know the exact error; but sometimes we know a limit on how big the error can be (an error bound), in which case we can use the plus-or-minus sign, $\pm$, to indicate how far the true value might lie from the measured value. For instance, if we measure the length of a metal bar as 25.6 cm and we know the error in our measurement is no more than 0.03 cm (some sources call this **approximate error**), then we might report the length of the bar as 25.6 ± 0.03 cm, which means it lies between 25.57 cm and 25.63 cm.

A particularly important application of this comes from the necessity of rounding whenever we make a measurement. For instance, if we measure the length of a pencil using a ruler marked off in whole inches (no fractions), then we must round our measurement to the nearest inch. Thus, if we report the length as 8 inches, it means that the actual value lies somewhere between 7.5 inches and 8.5 inches, which is to say 8 ± 0.5 inches. This built-in error bound due to rounding is called the **maximum possible error**, and it is always half the magnitude of the smallest unit used in the measurement. Determining the smallest unit can be somewhat subtle, involving the rules for significant figures commonly used in physics, chemistry, and other fields.

Review Video: Precision, Accuracy, and Error
Visit mometrix.com/academy and enter code: 520377

Points, Lines, and Planes

POINTS, LINES, AND PLANES

POINTS AND LINES

A **point** is a fixed location in space, has no size or dimensions, and is commonly represented by a dot. A **line** is a set of points that extends infinitely in two opposite directions. It has length, but no width or depth. A line can be defined by any two distinct points that it contains. A **line segment** is a portion of a line that has definite endpoints. A **ray** is a portion of a line that extends from a single point on that line in one direction along the line. It has a definite beginning, but no ending.

Points are **collinear** if there is a single line that passes through all of them. Otherwise, they are noncollinear. Two points are always collinear since two points define a line. Three points may be noncollinear. For example, the three vertices of a triangle are noncollinear since there is no line that goes through all three of them.

INTERACTIONS BETWEEN LINES

Intersecting lines are lines that have exactly one point in common. **Concurrent lines** are multiple lines that intersect at a single point. **Perpendicular lines** are lines that intersect at right angles. They are represented by the symbol ⊥. The shortest distance from a line to a point not on the line is a perpendicular segment from the point to the line. **Parallel lines** are lines in the same plane that have no points in common and never meet. Two distinct lines in a given plane are always either intersecting or parallel. **Skew lines** are two distinct lines in a three dimensional space that do not intersect and may also not be parallel because there is no single plane that contains them both.

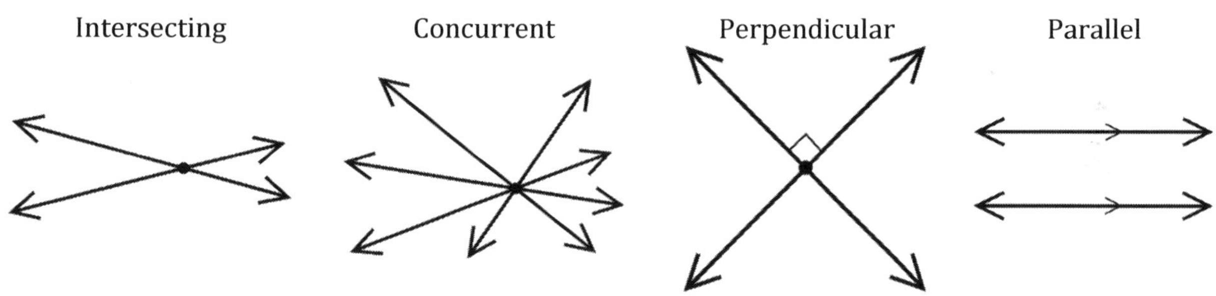

Review Video: Parallel and Perpendicular Lines
Visit mometrix.com/academy and enter code: 815923

A **transversal** is a line that intersects at least two other lines, which may or may not be parallel to one another. A transversal that intersects parallel lines is a common occurrence in geometry. A **bisector** is a line or line segment that divides another line segment into two equal lengths. A

perpendicular bisector of a line segment is composed of points that are equidistant from the endpoints of the segment it is dividing.

Transversal　　Bisector　　Perpendicular bisector

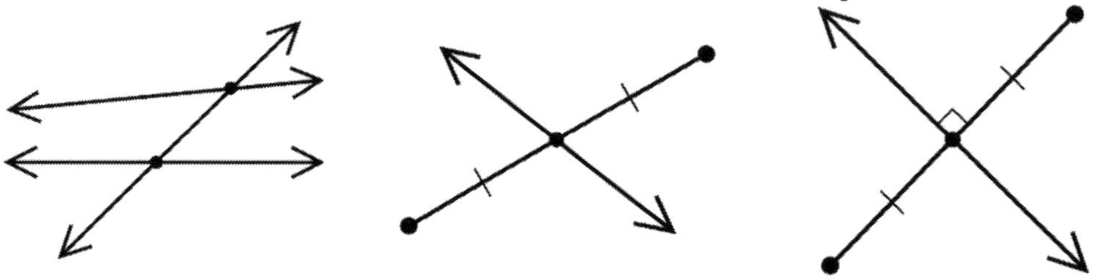

The **projection of a point on a line** is the point at which a perpendicular line drawn from the given point to the given line intersects the line. This is also the shortest distance from the given point to the line. The **projection of a segment on a line** is a segment whose endpoints are the points formed when perpendicular lines are drawn from the endpoints of the given segment to the given line. This is similar to the length a diagonal line appears to be when viewed from above.

Projection of a point on a line　　Projection of a segment on a line

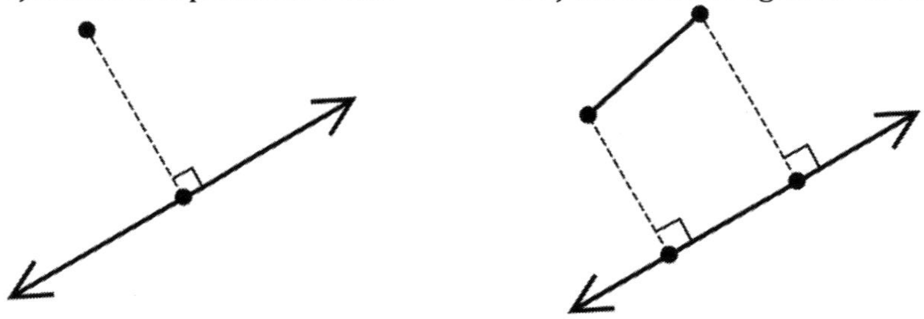

PLANES

A **plane** is a two-dimensional flat surface defined by three non-collinear points. A plane extends an infinite distance in all directions in those two dimensions. It contains an infinite number of points, parallel lines and segments, intersecting lines and segments, as well as parallel or intersecting rays. A plane will never contain a three-dimensional figure or skew lines. Two given planes are either parallel or they intersect at a line. A plane may intersect a circular conic surface to form **conic sections**, such as a parabola, hyperbola, circle or ellipse.

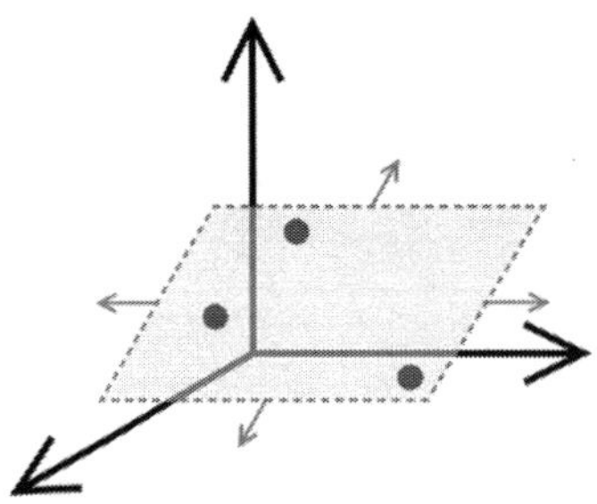

Review Video: Lines and Planes
Visit mometrix.com/academy and enter code: 554267

Angles

ANGLES

ANGLES AND VERTICES

An **angle** is formed when two lines or line segments meet at a common point. It may be a common starting point for a pair of segments or rays, or it may be the intersection of lines. Angles are represented by the symbol ∠.

The **vertex** is the point at which two segments or rays meet to form an angle. If the angle is formed by intersecting rays, lines, and/or line segments, the vertex is the point at which four angles are formed. The pairs of angles opposite one another are called vertical angles, and their measures are equal.

- An **acute** angle is an angle with a degree measure less than 90°.
- A **right** angle is an angle with a degree measure of exactly 90°.
- An **obtuse** angle is an angle with a degree measure greater than 90° but less than 180°.
- A **straight angle** is an angle with a degree measure of exactly 180°.
- A **reflex angle** is an angle with a degree measure greater than 180° but less than 360°.
- A **full angle** is an angle with a degree measure of exactly 360°.

Review Video: Angles
Visit mometrix.com/academy and enter code: 264624

RELATIONSHIPS BETWEEN ANGLES

Two angles whose sum is exactly 90° are said to be **complementary**. The two angles may or may not be adjacent. In a right triangle, the two acute angles are complementary.

Two angles whose sum is exactly 180° are said to be **supplementary**. The two angles may or may not be adjacent. Two intersecting lines always form two pairs of supplementary angles. Adjacent supplementary angles will always form a straight line.

Two angles that have the same vertex and share a side are said to be **adjacent**. Vertical angles are not adjacent because they share a vertex but no common side.

Review Video: Adjacent Angles
Visit mometrix.com/academy and enter code: 100375

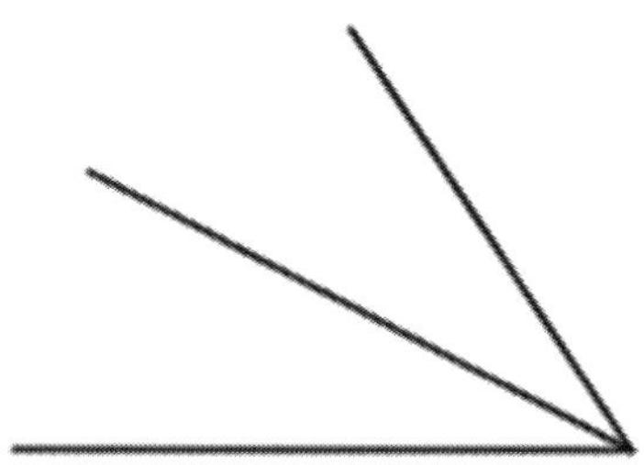

Adjacent
Share vertex and side

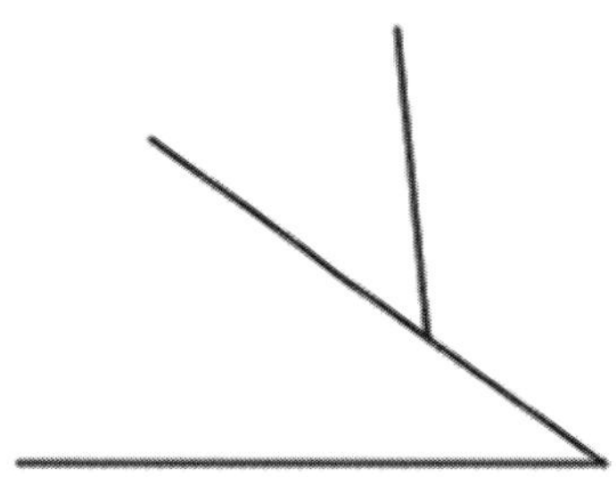

Not adjacent
Share part of a side, but not vertex

Geometry and Measurement

When two lines are cut by a transversal, the angles that are between the two lines are **interior angles**. In the diagram below, angles 3, 4, 5, and 6 are interior angles.

When two lines are cut by a transversal, the angles that are outside the lines are **exterior angles**. In the diagram below, angles 1, 2, 7, and 8 are exterior angles.

When two lines are cut by a transversal, the angles that are in the same position relative to the transversal and the cut lines are **corresponding angles**. The diagram below has four pairs of corresponding angles: angles 1 and 5, angles 2 and 6, angles 3 and 7, and angles 4 and 8. Corresponding angles formed by parallel lines are congruent.

When two lines are cut by a transversal, the two interior angles that are on opposite sides of the transversal are called **alternate interior angles**. In the diagram below, there are two pairs of alternate interior angles: angles 3 and 6, and angles 4 and 5. Alternate interior angles formed by parallel lines are congruent. Similarly, the two interior angles on the same side of the transversal (angles 3 and 5, and angles 4 and 6) are supplementary when the transversed lines are parallel. Some books call these angles **same side interior angles**.

When two lines are cut by a transversal, the two exterior angles that are on opposite sides of the transversal are called **alternate exterior angles**. In the diagram below, there are two pairs of alternate exterior angles: angles 1 and 8, and angles 2 and 7. Alternate exterior angles formed by parallel lines are congruent. Similarly, the two exterior angles on the same side of the transversal (angles 1 and 7, and angles 2 and 8) are supplementary when the transversed lines are parallel. Some books call these angles **same side exterior angles**.

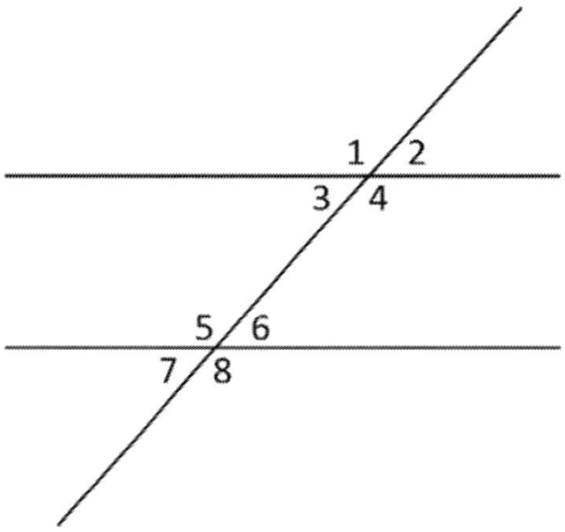

When two lines intersect, four angles are formed. The non-adjacent angles at this vertex are called vertical angles. Vertical angles are congruent. In the diagram, $\angle ABD \cong \angle CBE$ and $\angle ABC \cong \angle DBE$. The other pairs of angles, $(\angle ABC, \angle CBE)$ and $(\angle ABD, \angle DBE)$, are supplementary, meaning the pairs sum to 180°.

Review Video: Congruent Angles
Visit mometrix.com/academy and enter code: 642874

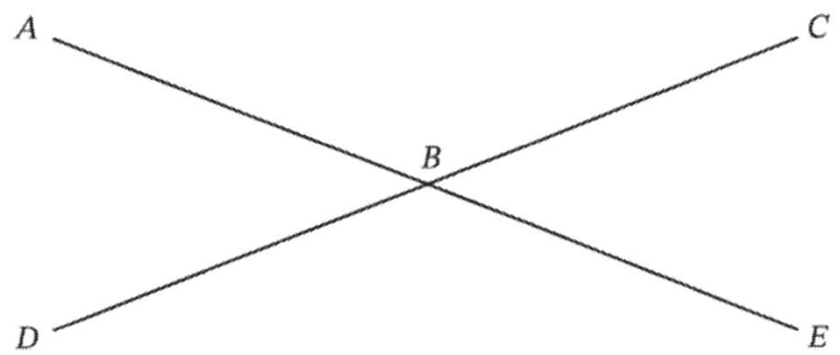

Polygons

POLYGONS

A **polygon** is a closed, two-dimensional figure with three or more straight line segments called **sides**. The point at which two sides of a polygon intersect is called the **vertex**. In a polygon, the number of sides is always equal to the number of vertices. A polygon with all sides congruent and all angles equal is called a **regular polygon**. Common polygons are:

Triangle = 3 sides
Quadrilateral = 4 sides
Pentagon = 5 sides
Hexagon = 6 sides
Heptagon = 7 sides
Octagon = 8 sides
Nonagon = 9 sides
Decagon = 10 sides
Dodecagon = 12 sides

More generally, an n-gon is a polygon that has n angles and n sides.

Review Video: Intro to Polygons
Visit mometrix.com/academy and enter code: 271869

The sum of the interior angles of an n-sided polygon is $(n - 2) \times 180°$. For example, in a triangle $n = 3$. So the sum of the interior angles is $(3 - 2) \times 180° = 180°$. In a quadrilateral, $n = 4$, and the sum of the angles is $(4 - 2) \times 180° = 360°$.

Review Video: Sum of Interior Angles
Visit mometrix.com/academy and enter code: 984991

CONVEX AND CONCAVE POLYGONS

A **convex polygon** is a polygon whose diagonals all lie within the interior of the polygon. A **concave polygon** is a polygon with at least one diagonal that is outside the polygon. In the diagram below, quadrilateral $ABCD$ is concave because diagonal $\overline{AC}$ lies outside the polygon and quadrilateral $EFGH$ is convex because both diagonals lie inside the polygon.

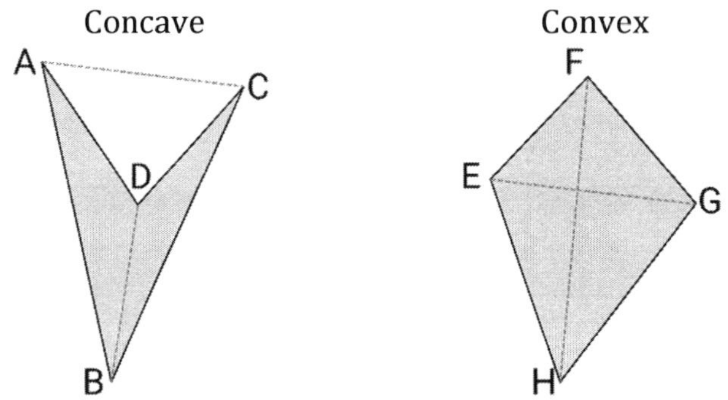

Apothem and Radius

A line segment from the center of a regular polygon that is perpendicular to a side of the polygon is called the **apothem**. A line segment from the center of a regular polygon to a vertex of the polygon is called a **radius**. In a regular polygon, the apothem can be used to find the area of the polygon using the formula $A = \frac{1}{2}ap$, where a is the apothem, and p is the perimeter.

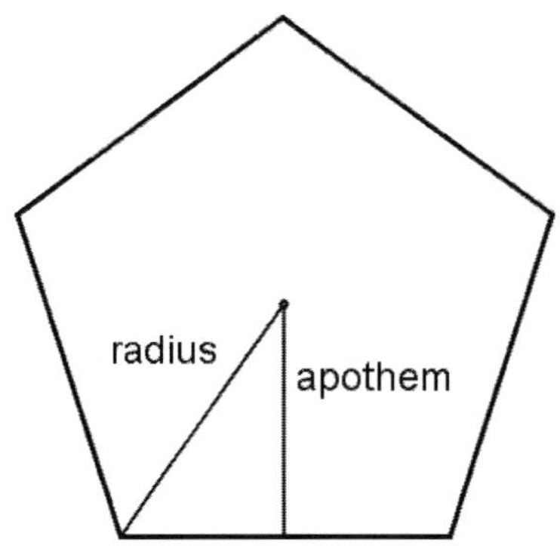

A **diagonal** is a line segment that joins two non-adjacent vertices of a polygon. The number of diagonals a polygon has can be found by using the formula:

$$\text{number of diagonals} = \frac{n(n-3)}{2}$$

Note that n is the number of sides in the polygon. This formula works for all polygons, not just regular polygons.

Congruence and Similarity

Congruent figures are geometric figures that have the same size and shape. For congruent polygons all corresponding angle measures are equal, and all corresponding side lengths are equal. Congruence is indicated by the symbol $\cong$. For instance, the expression $ABC \cong DEF$ indicates that the triangles below are congruent. The order of the letters is important, indicating which parts of the polygons correspond to each other. For example, since the letters A and D both come first, $\angle A$ and $\angle D$ have the same measure.

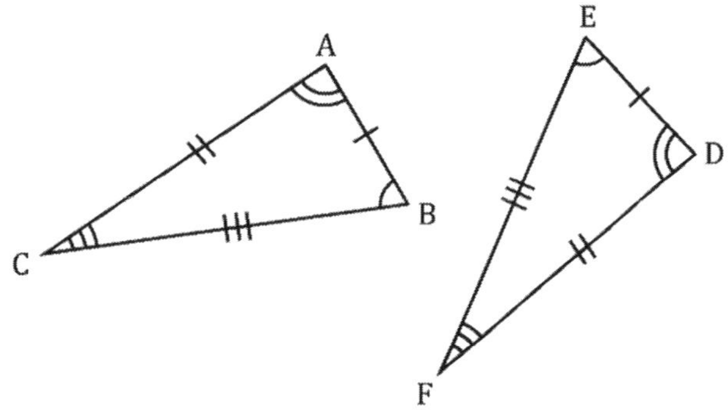

Similar figures are geometric figures that have the same shape, but do not necessarily have the same size. For similar polygons all corresponding angle measures are equal, and all corresponding side lengths are proportional, but they do not have to be equal. It is indicated by the symbol ~. For instance, the expression $ABC \sim DEF$ indicates that the triangles below are similar. Again, the order of the letters indicates which parts of the polygons correspond to each other.

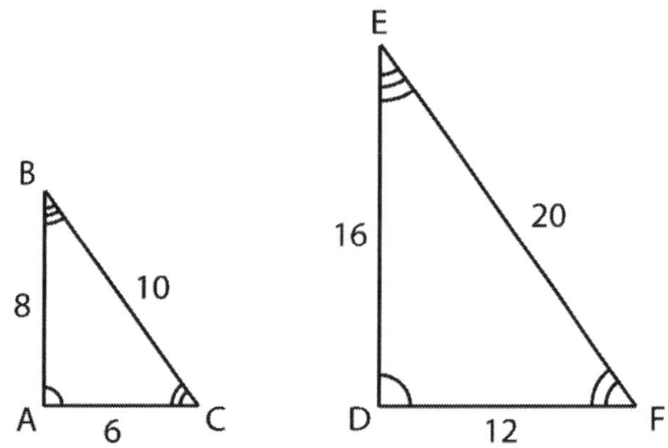

Note that all congruent figures are also similar, but not all similar figures are congruent.

Review Video: Congruent Shapes
Visit mometrix.com/academy and enter code: 492281

Line of Symmetry

A line that divides a figure or object into congruent parts that are mirror images of each other across the line is called a **line of symmetry**. An object may have no lines of symmetry, one line of symmetry, or multiple (i.e., more than one) lines of symmetry.

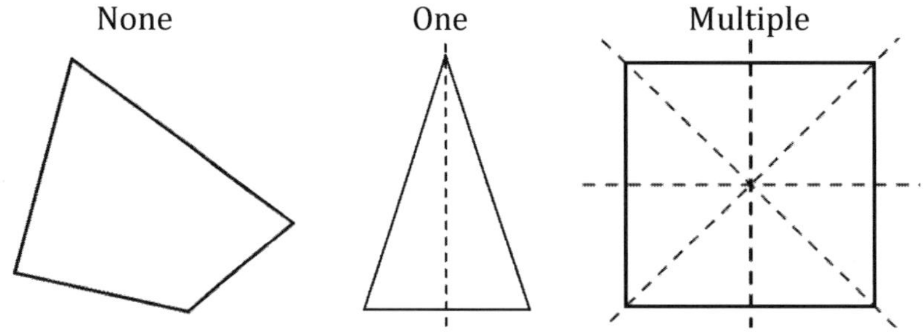

Review Video: Symmetry
Visit mometrix.com/academy and enter code: 528106

Triangles

A triangle is a three-sided figure with the sum of its interior angles being 180°. The **perimeter of any triangle** is found by summing the three side lengths; $P = a + b + c$. For an equilateral triangle, this is the same as $P = 3a$, where a is any side length, since all three sides are the same length.

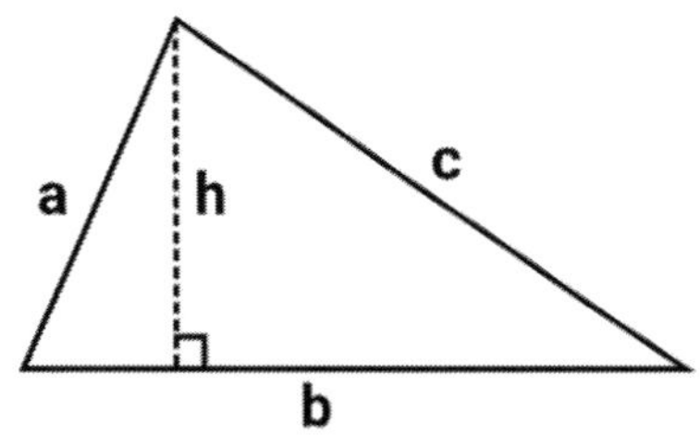

Review Video: Proof that a Triangle is 180 Degrees
Visit mometrix.com/academy and enter code: 687591

Review Video: Area and Perimeter of a Triangle
Visit mometrix.com/academy and enter code: 853779

The **area of any triangle** can be found by taking half the product of one side length referred to as the base, often given the variable b and the perpendicular distance from that side to the opposite vertex called the altitude or height and given the variable h. In equation form that is $A = \frac{1}{2}bh$. Another formula that works for any triangle is $A = \sqrt{s(s-a)(s-b)(s-c)}$, where s is the semiperimeter: $\frac{a+b+c}{2}$, and a, b, and c are the lengths of the three sides. Special cases include isosceles triangles, $A = \frac{1}{2}b\sqrt{a^2 - \frac{b^2}{4}}$, where b is the unique side and a is the length of one of the two congruent sides, and equilateral triangles, $A = \frac{\sqrt{3}}{4}a^2$, where a is the length of a side.

Review Video: Area of Any Triangle
Visit mometrix.com/academy and enter code: 138510

PARTS OF A TRIANGLE

An **altitude** of a triangle is a line segment drawn from one vertex perpendicular to the opposite side. In the diagram that follows, $\overline{BE}$, $\overline{AD}$, and $\overline{CF}$ are altitudes. The length of an altitude is also called the height of the triangle. The three altitudes in a triangle are always concurrent. The point of concurrency of the altitudes of a triangle, O, is called the **orthocenter**. Note that in an obtuse triangle, the orthocenter will be outside the triangle, and in a right triangle, the orthocenter is the vertex of the right angle.

A **median** of a triangle is a line segment drawn from one vertex to the midpoint of the opposite side. In the diagram that follows, $\overline{BH}$, $\overline{AG}$, and $\overline{CI}$ are medians. This is not the same as the altitude, except the altitude to the base of an isosceles triangle and all three altitudes of an equilateral triangle. The point of concurrency of the medians of a triangle, T, is called the **centroid**. This is the same point as the orthocenter only in an equilateral triangle. Unlike the orthocenter, the centroid is always inside the triangle. The centroid can also be considered the exact center of the triangle. Any shape triangle can be perfectly balanced on a tip placed at the centroid. The centroid is also the point that is two-thirds the distance from the vertex to the opposite side.

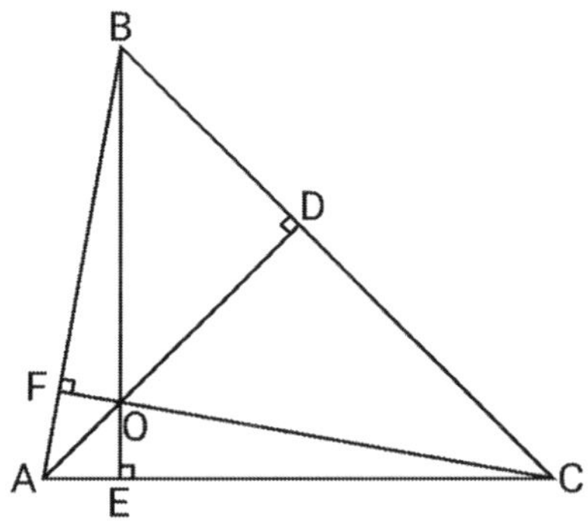

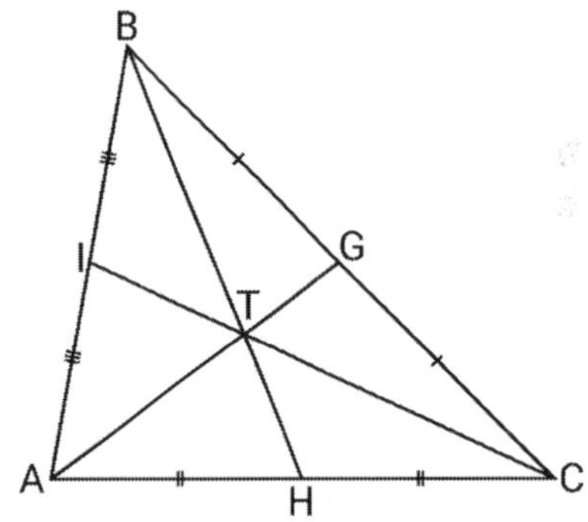

Review Video: Centroid, Incenter, Circumcenter, and Orthocenter
Visit mometrix.com/academy and enter code: 598260

TRIANGLE PROPERTIES

CLASSIFICATIONS OF TRIANGLES

A **scalene triangle** is a triangle with no congruent sides. A scalene triangle will also have three angles of different measures. The angle with the largest measure is opposite the longest side, and the angle with the smallest measure is opposite the shortest side. An **acute triangle** is a triangle whose three angles are all less than 90°. If two of the angles are equal, the acute triangle is also an **isosceles triangle**. An isosceles triangle will also have two congruent angles opposite the two congruent sides. If the three angles are all equal, the acute triangle is also an **equilateral triangle**. An equilateral triangle will also have three congruent angles, each 60°. All equilateral triangles are also acute triangles. An **obtuse triangle** is a triangle with exactly one angle greater than 90°. The other two angles may or may not be equal. If the two remaining angles are equal, the obtuse triangle is also an isosceles triangle. A **right triangle** is a triangle with exactly one angle equal to 90°. All right triangles follow the Pythagorean theorem. A right triangle can never be acute or obtuse.

The table below illustrates how each descriptor places a different restriction on the triangle:

Angles / Sides	**Acute:** All angles < 90°	**Obtuse:** One angle > 90°	**Right:** One angle = 90°
Scalene: No equal side lengths	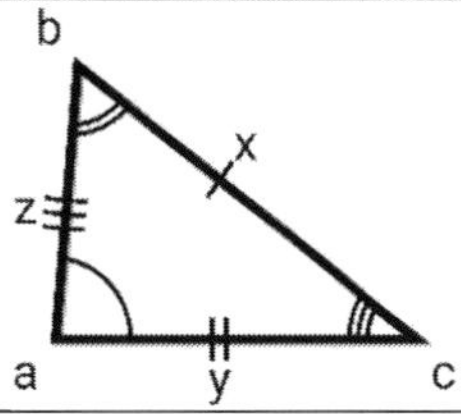 $90° > \angle a > \angle b > \angle c$ $x > y > z$	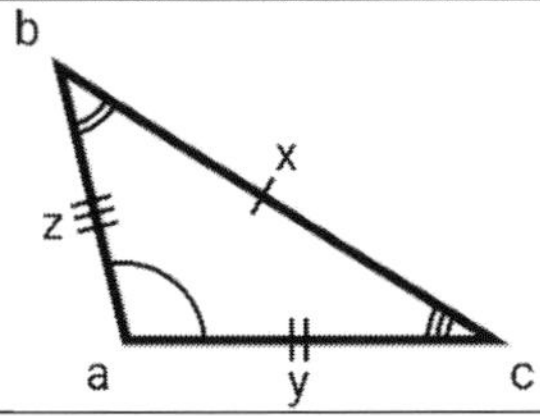 $\angle a > 90° > \angle b > \angle c$ $x > y > z$	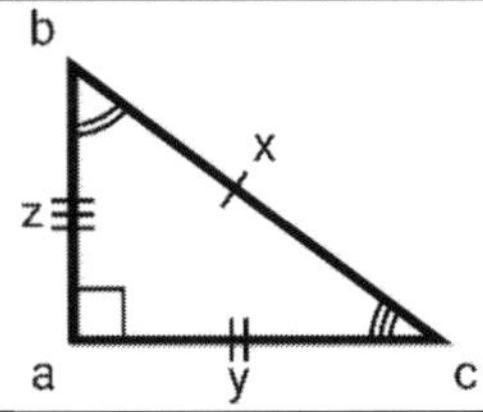 $90° = \angle a > \angle b > \angle c$ $x > y > z$
Isosceles: Two equal side lengths	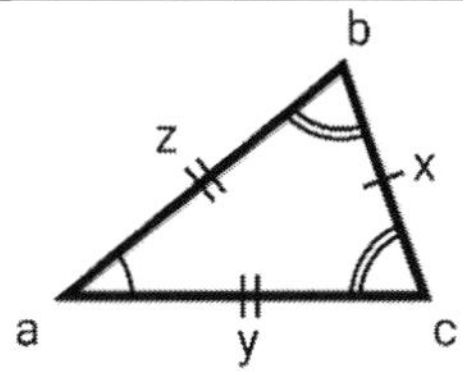 $90° > \angle a, \angle b, or\ \angle c$ $\angle b = \angle c, \quad y = z$	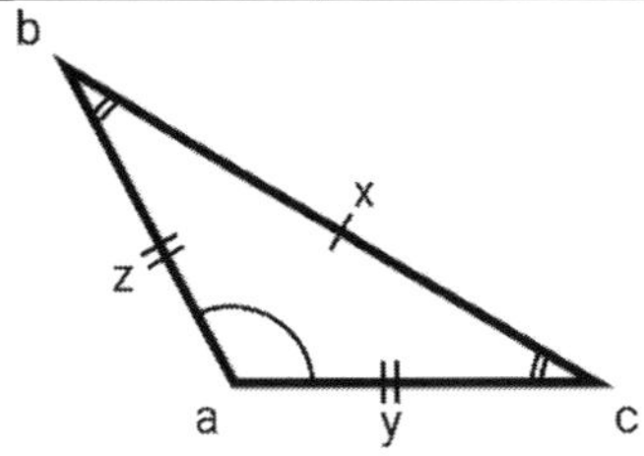 $\angle a > 90° > \angle b = \angle c$ $x > y = z$	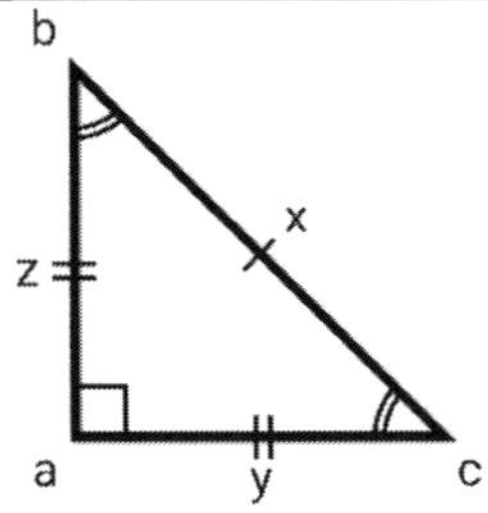 $\angle a = 90°$ $\angle b = \angle c = 45°$ $x > y = z$
Equilateral: Three equal side lengths	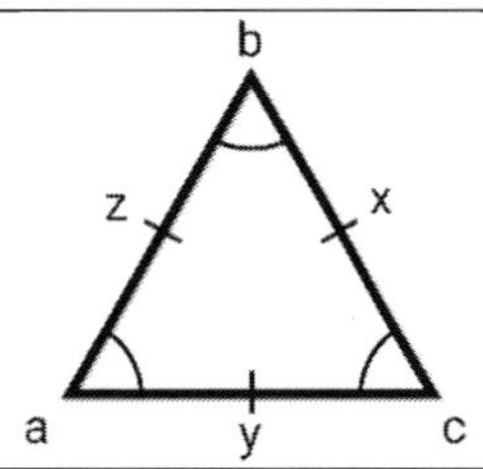 $60° = \angle a = \angle b = \angle c$ $x = y = z$		

Review Video: Introduction to Types of Triangles
Visit mometrix.com/academy and enter code: 511711

General Rules for Triangles

The **triangle inequality theorem** states that the sum of the measures of any two sides of a triangle is always greater than the measure of the third side. If the sum of the measures of two sides were equal to the third side, a triangle would be impossible because the two sides would lie flat across the third side and there would be no vertex. If the sum of the measures of two of the sides was less than the third side, a closed figure would be impossible because the two shortest sides would never meet. In other words, for a triangle with sides lengths *A*, *B*, and *C*: $A + B > C$, $B + C > A$, and $A + C > B$.

The sum of the measures of the interior angles of a triangle is always 180°. Therefore, a triangle can never have more than one angle greater than or equal to 90°.

In any triangle, the angles opposite congruent sides are congruent, and the sides opposite congruent angles are congruent. The largest angle is always opposite the longest side, and the smallest angle is always opposite the shortest side.

The line segment that joins the midpoints of any two sides of a triangle is always parallel to the third side and exactly half the length of the third side.

Review Video: General Rules (Triangle Inequality Theorem)
Visit mometrix.com/academy and enter code: 166488

Similarity and Congruence Rules

Similar triangles are triangles whose corresponding angles are equal and whose corresponding sides are proportional. Represented by AAA. Similar triangles whose corresponding sides are congruent are also congruent triangles.

Triangles can be shown to be **congruent** in 5 ways:

- **SSS**: Three sides of one triangle are congruent to the three corresponding sides of the second triangle.
- **SAS**: Two sides and the included angle (the angle formed by those two sides) of one triangle are congruent to the corresponding two sides and included angle of the second triangle.
- **ASA**: Two angles and the included side (the side that joins the two angles) of one triangle are congruent to the corresponding two angles and included side of the second triangle.
- **AAS**: Two angles and a non-included side of one triangle are congruent to the corresponding two angles and non-included side of the second triangle.
- **HL**: The hypotenuse and leg of one right triangle are congruent to the corresponding hypotenuse and leg of the second right triangle.

Review Video: Similar Triangles
Visit mometrix.com/academy and enter code: 398538

Quadrilaterals

A **quadrilateral** is a closed two-dimensional geometric figure that has four straight sides. The sum of the interior angles of any quadrilateral is 360°.

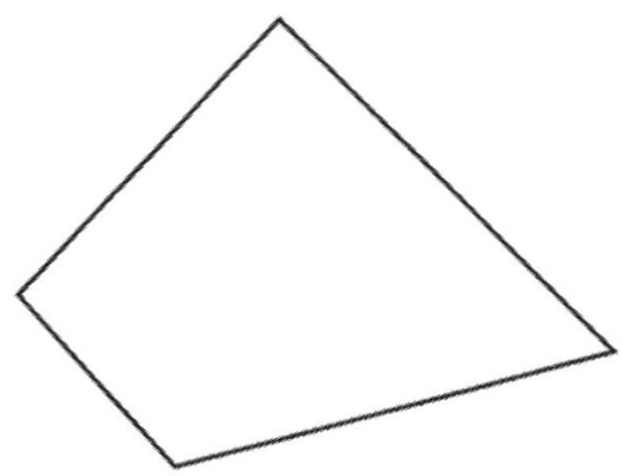

Review Video: Diagonals of Parallelograms, Rectangles, and Rhombi
Visit mometrix.com/academy and enter code: 320040

KITE

A **kite** is a quadrilateral with two pairs of adjacent sides that are congruent. A result of this is perpendicular diagonals. A kite can be concave or convex and has one line of symmetry.

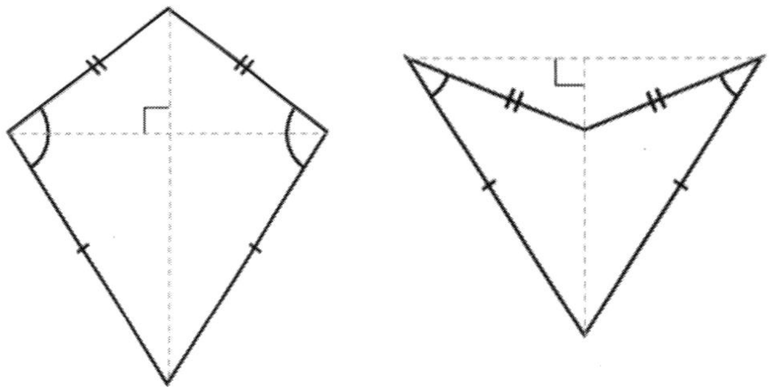

TRAPEZOID

Trapezoid: A trapezoid is defined as a quadrilateral that has at least one pair of parallel sides. There are no rules for the second pair of sides. So, there are no rules for the diagonals and no lines of symmetry for a trapezoid.

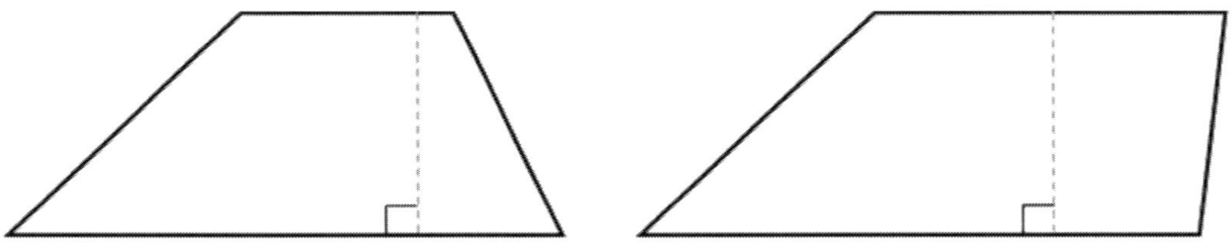

The **area of a trapezoid** is found by the formula $A = \frac{1}{2}h(b_1 + b_2)$, where h is the height (segment joining and perpendicular to the parallel bases), and b_1 and b_2 are the two parallel sides (bases). Do not use one of the other two sides as the height unless that side is also perpendicular to the parallel bases.

The **perimeter of a trapezoid** is found by the formula $P = a + b_1 + c + b_2$, where a, b_1, c, and b_2 are the four sides of the trapezoid.

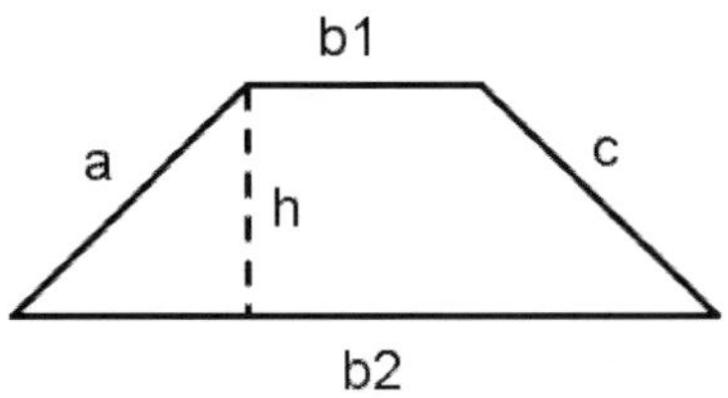

Review Video: Area and Perimeter of a Trapezoid
Visit mometrix.com/academy and enter code: 587523

Isosceles trapezoid: A trapezoid with equal base angles. This gives rise to other properties including: the two nonparallel sides have the same length, the two non-base angles are also equal, and there is one line of symmetry through the midpoints of the parallel sides.

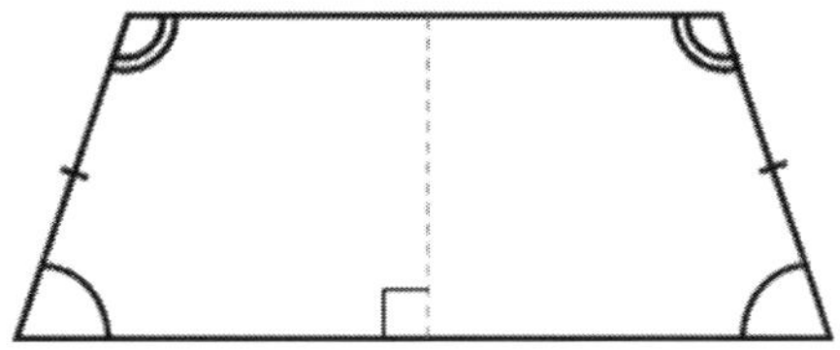

PARALLELOGRAM

A **parallelogram** is a quadrilateral that has two pairs of opposite parallel sides. As such it is a special type of trapezoid. The sides that are parallel are also congruent. The opposite interior angles are always congruent, and the consecutive interior angles are supplementary. The diagonals of a parallelogram divide each other. Each diagonal divides the parallelogram into two congruent triangles. A parallelogram has no line of symmetry, but does have 180-degree rotational symmetry about the midpoint.

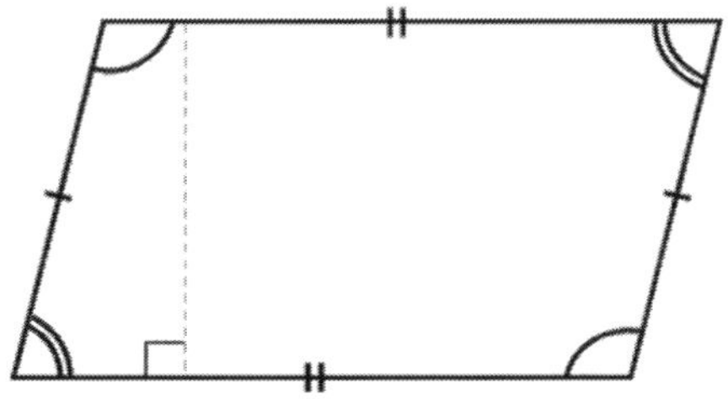

The **area of a parallelogram** is found by the formula $A = bh$, where b is the length of the base, and h is the height. Note that the base and height correspond to the length and width in a rectangle, so this formula would apply to rectangles as well. Do not confuse the height of a parallelogram with the length of the second side. The two are only the same measure in the case of a rectangle.

The **perimeter of a parallelogram** is found by the formula $P = 2a + 2b$ or $P = 2(a + b)$, where a and b are the lengths of the two sides.

Review Video: Area and Perimeter of a Parallelogram
Visit mometrix.com/academy and enter code: 718313

RECTANGLE

A **rectangle** is a quadrilateral with four right angles. All rectangles are parallelograms and trapezoids, but not all parallelograms or trapezoids are rectangles. The diagonals of a rectangle are congruent. Rectangles have two lines of symmetry (through each pair of opposing midpoints) and 180-degree rotational symmetry about the midpoint.

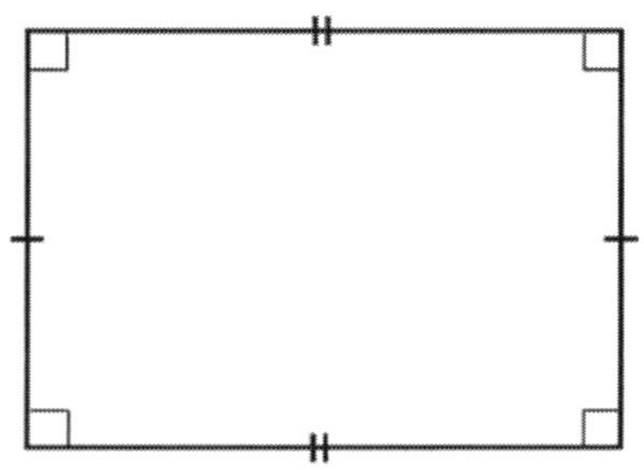

The **area of a rectangle** is found by the formula $A = lw$, where A is the area of the rectangle, l is the length (usually considered to be the longer side) and w is the width (usually considered to be the shorter side). The numbers for l and w are interchangeable.

The **perimeter of a rectangle** is found by the formula $P = 2l + 2w$ or $P = 2(l + w)$, where l is the length, and w is the width. It may be easier to add the length and width first and then double the result, as in the second formula.

Rhombus

A **rhombus** is a quadrilateral with four congruent sides. All rhombuses are parallelograms and kites; thus, they inherit all the properties of both types of quadrilaterals. The diagonals of a rhombus are perpendicular to each other. Rhombi have two lines of symmetry (along each of the diagonals) and 180° rotational symmetry. The **area of a rhombus** is half the product of the diagonals: $A = \frac{d_1 d_2}{2}$ and the perimeter of a rhombus is: $P = 2\sqrt{(d_1)^2 + (d_2)^2}$.

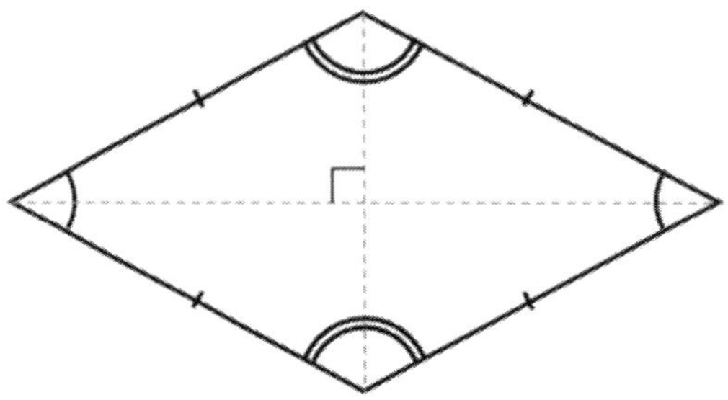

Square

A **square** is a quadrilateral with four right angles and four congruent sides. Squares satisfy the criteria of all other types of quadrilaterals. The diagonals of a square are congruent and perpendicular to each other. Squares have four lines of symmetry (through each pair of opposing midpoints and along each of the diagonals) as well as 90° rotational symmetry about the midpoint.

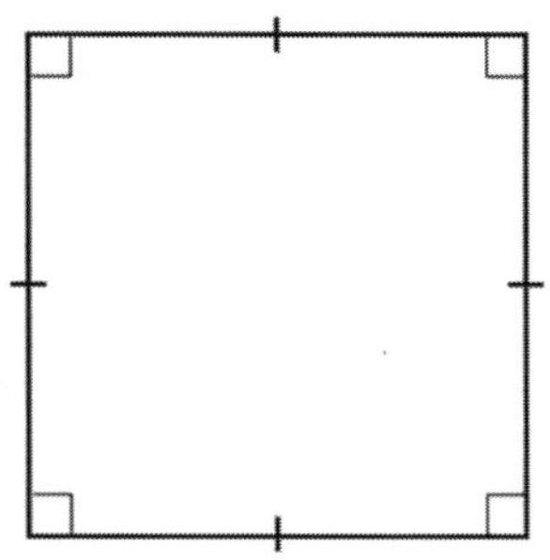

The **area of a square** is found by using the formula $A = s^2$, where s is the length of one side. The **perimeter of a square** is found by using the formula $P = 4s$, where s is the length of one side. Because all four sides are equal in a square, it is faster to multiply the length of one side by 4 than to add the same number four times. You could use the formulas for rectangles and get the same answer.

Review Video: Area and Perimeter of Rectangles and Squares
Visit mometrix.com/academy and enter code: 428109

HIERARCHY OF QUADRILATERALS

The hierarchy of quadrilaterals is as follows:

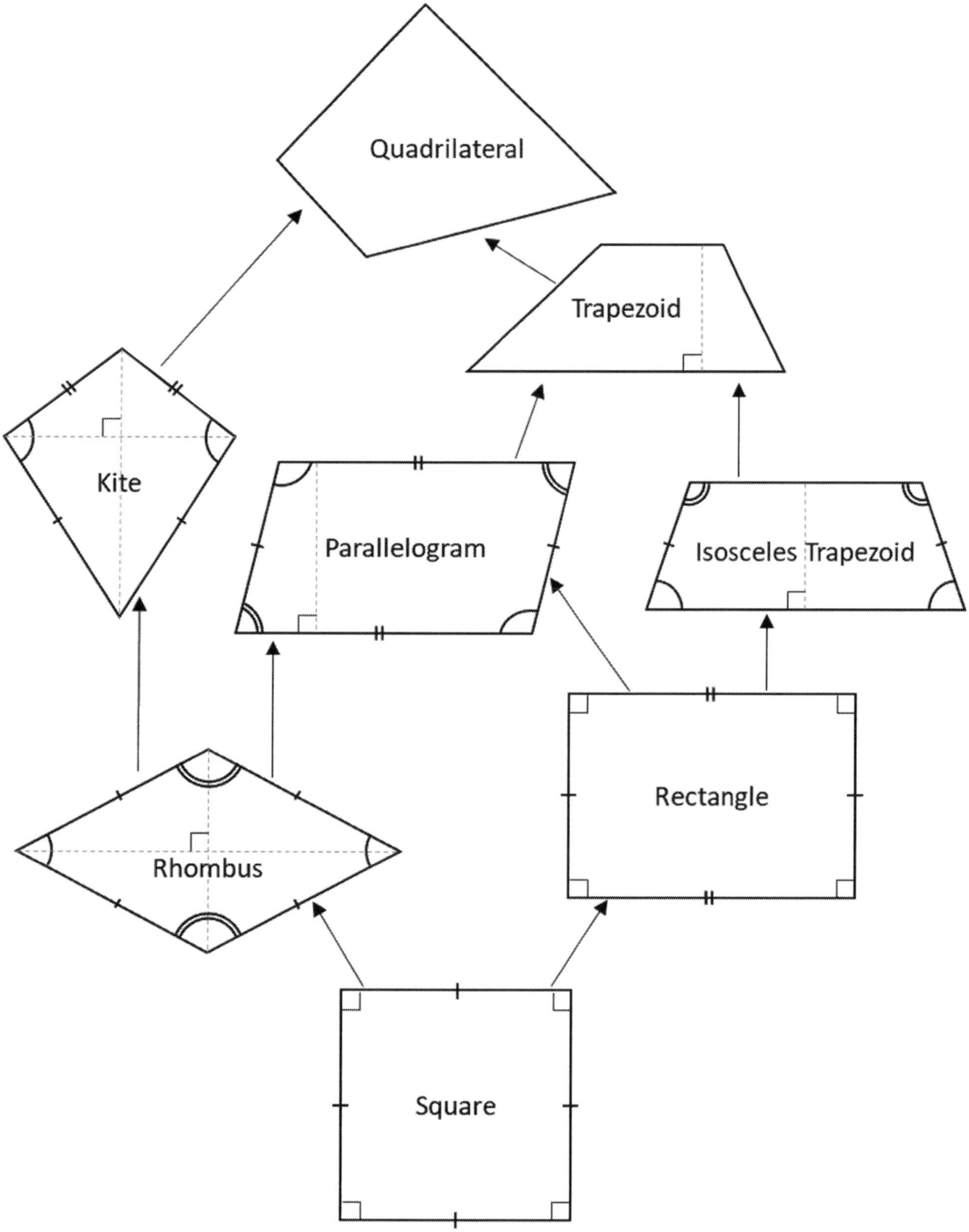

Circles

Circles

The **center** of a circle is the single point from which every point on the circle is **equidistant**. The **radius** is a line segment that joins the center of the circle and any one point on the circle. All radii of a circle are equal. Circles that have the same center but not the same length of radii are **concentric**. The **diameter** is a line segment that passes through the center of the circle and has both endpoints on the circle. The length of the diameter is exactly twice the length of the radius. Point O in the diagram below is the center of the circle, segments $\overline{OX}$, $\overline{OY}$, and $\overline{OZ}$ are radii; and segment $\overline{XZ}$ is a diameter.

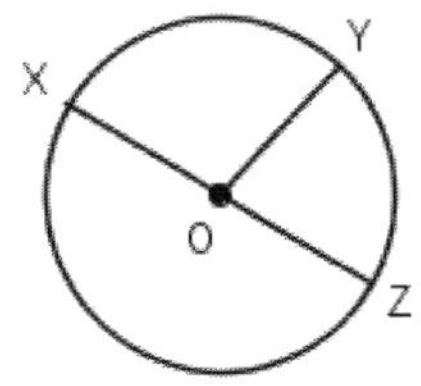

Review Video: Points of a Circle
Visit mometrix.com/academy and enter code: 420746

Review Video: Diameter, Radius, and Circumference
Visit mometrix.com/academy and enter code: 448988

The **area of a circle** is found by the formula $A = \pi r^2$, where r is the length of the radius. If the diameter of the circle is given, remember to divide it in half to get the length of the radius before proceeding.

The **circumference** of a circle is found by the formula $C = 2\pi r$, where r is the radius. Again, remember to convert the diameter if you are given that measure rather than the radius.

Review Video: Area and Circumference of a Circle
Visit mometrix.com/academy and enter code: 243015

Inscribed and Circumscribed Figures

These terms can both be used to describe a given arrangement of figures, depending on perspective. If each of the vertices of figure A lie on figure B, then it can be said that figure A is **inscribed** in figure B, but it can also be said that figure B is **circumscribed** about figure A. The following table and examples help to illustrate the concept. Note that the figures cannot both be circles, as they would be completely overlapping and neither would be inscribed or circumscribed.

Given	Description	Equivalent Description	Figures
Each of the sides of a pentagon is tangent to a circle	The circle is inscribed in the pentagon	The pentagon is circumscribed about the circle	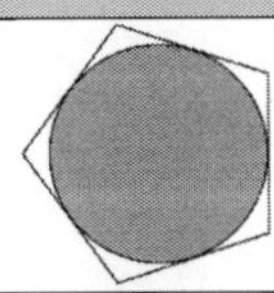
Each of the vertices of a pentagon lie on a circle	The pentagon is inscribed in the circle	The circle is circumscribed about the pentagon	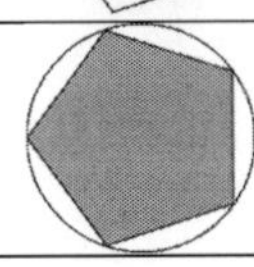

Circle Properties

Arcs

An **arc** is a portion of a circle. Specifically, an arc is the set of points between and including two points on a circle. An arc does not contain any points inside the circle. When a segment is drawn from the endpoints of an arc to the center of the circle, a sector is formed. A **minor arc** is an arc that has a measure less than 180°. A **major arc** is an arc that has a measure of at least 180°. Every minor arc has a corresponding major arc that can be found by subtracting the measure of the minor arc from 360°. A **semicircle** is an arc whose endpoints are the endpoints of the diameter of a circle. A semicircle is exactly half of a circle.

Arc length is the length of that portion of the circumference between two points on the circle. The formula for arc length is $s = \frac{\pi r \theta}{180°}$, where s is the arc length, r is the length of the radius, and θ is the angular measure of the arc in degrees, or $s = r\theta$, where θ is the angular measure of the arc in radians (2π radians $= 360$ degrees).

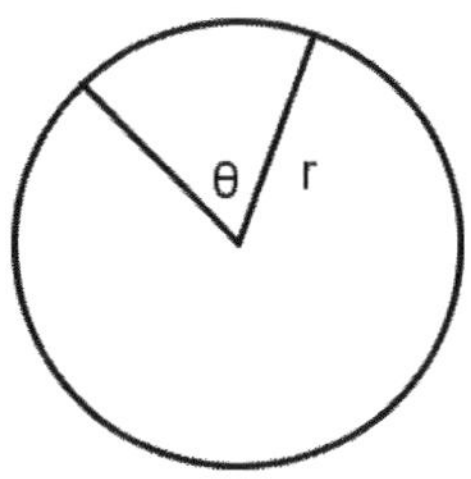

Angles of Circles

A **central angle** is an angle whose vertex is the center of a circle and whose legs intercept an arc of the circle. The measure of a central angle is equal to the measure of the minor arc it intercepts.

An **inscribed angle** is an angle whose vertex lies on a circle and whose legs contain chords of that circle. The portion of the circle intercepted by the legs of the angle is called the intercepted arc. The measure of the intercepted arc is exactly twice the measure of the inscribed angle. In the following diagram, angle ABC is an inscribed angle. $\widehat{AC} = 2(\text{m}\angle ABC)$.

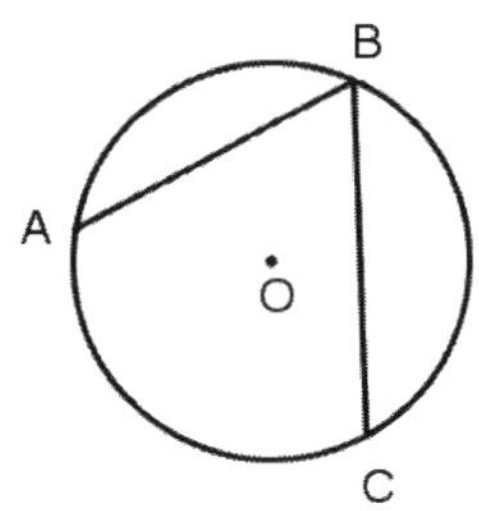

Any angle inscribed in a semicircle is a right angle. The intercepted arc is 180°, making the inscribed angle half that, or 90°. In the diagram below, angle ABC is inscribed in semicircle ABC, making angle ABC equal to 90°.

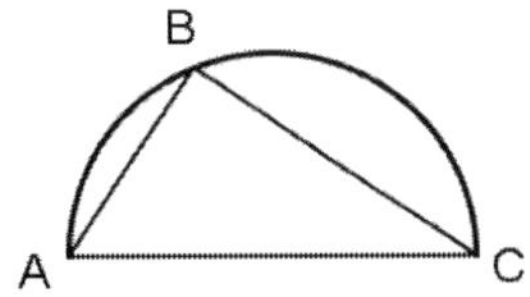

Review Video: Arcs and Angles of Circles
Visit mometrix.com/academy and enter code: 652838

Secants, Chords, and Tangents

A **secant** is a line that intersects a circle in two points. The segment of a secant line that is contained within the circle is called a **chord**. Two secants may intersect inside the circle, on the circle, or outside the circle. When the two secants intersect on the circle, an inscribed angle is formed. When two secants intersect inside a circle, the measure of each of two vertical angles is equal to half the sum of the two intercepted arcs. Consider the following diagram where $m\angle AEB = \frac{1}{2}(\widehat{AB} + \widehat{CD})$ and $m\angle BEC = \frac{1}{2}(\widehat{BC} + \widehat{AD})$.

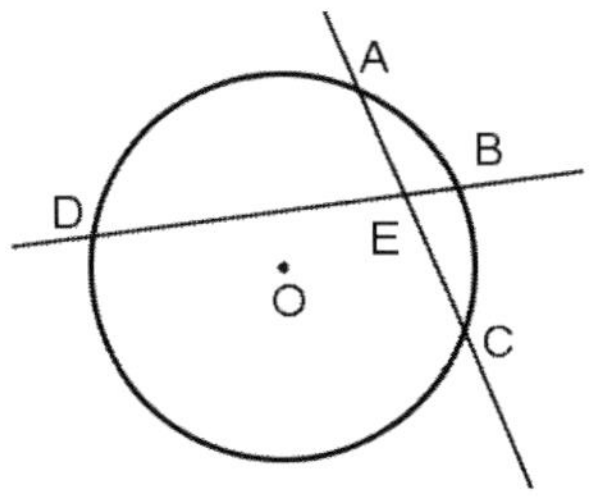

When two secants intersect outside a circle, the measure of the angle formed is equal to half the difference of the two arcs that lie between the two secants. In the diagram below, $m\angle AEB = \frac{1}{2}(\widehat{AB} - \widehat{CD})$.

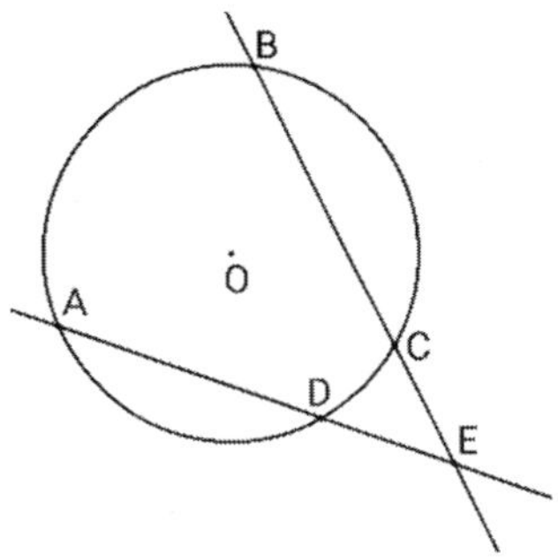

A **tangent** is a line in the same plane as a circle that touches the circle in exactly one point. The point at which a tangent touches a circle is called the **point of tangency**. While a line segment can be tangent to a circle as part of a line that is tangent, it is improper to say a tangent can be simply a line segment that touches the circle in exactly one point.

In the diagram below, $\overleftrightarrow{EB}$ is a secant and contains chord $\overline{EB}$, and $\overleftrightarrow{CD}$ is tangent to circle A. Notice that $\overline{FB}$ is not tangent to the circle. $\overline{FB}$ is a line segment that touches the circle in exactly one point, but if the segment were extended, it would touch the circle in a second point. In the diagram below, point B is the point of tangency.

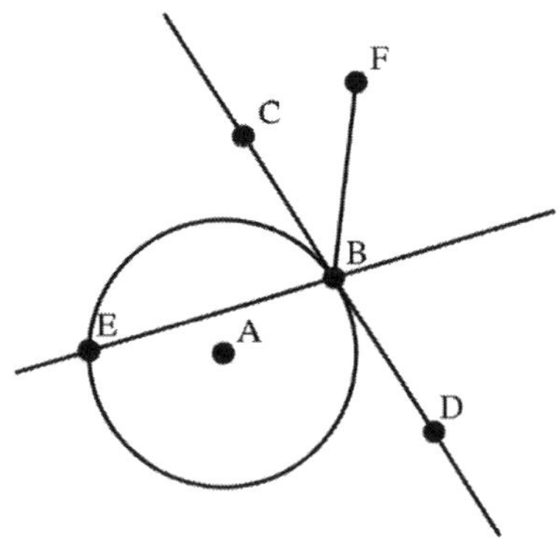

Review Video: Secants, Chords, and Tangents
Visit mometrix.com/academy and enter code: 258360

Review Video: Tangent Lines of a Circle
Visit mometrix.com/academy and enter code: 780167

Sectors

A **sector** is the portion of a circle formed by two radii and their intercepted arc. While the arc length is exclusively the points that are also on the circumference of the circle, the sector is the entire area bounded by the arc and the two radii.

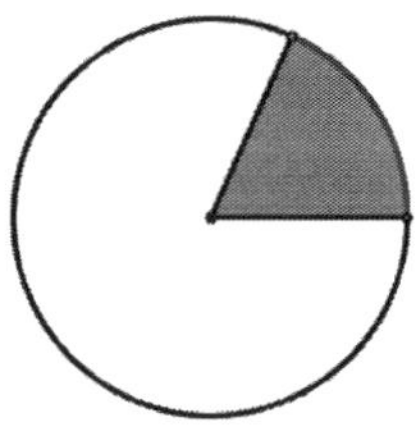

The **area of a sector** of a circle is found by the formula, $A = \frac{\theta r^2}{2}$, where A is the area, θ is the measure of the central angle in radians, and r is the radius. To find the area with the central angle in degrees, use the formula, $A = \frac{\theta \pi r^2}{360}$, where θ is the measure of the central angle and r is the radius.

Transformations

Transformations

Rotation

A **rotation** is a transformation that turns a figure around a point called the **center of rotation**, which can lie anywhere in the plane. If a line is drawn from a point on a figure to the center of rotation, and another line is drawn from the center to the rotated image of that point, the angle between the two lines is the **angle of rotation**. The vertex of the angle of rotation is the center of rotation.

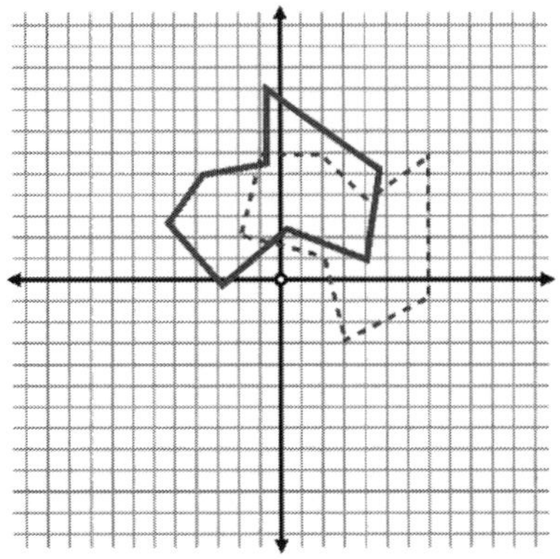

Review Video: Rotation
Visit mometrix.com/academy and enter code: 602600

Translation and Dilation

A **translation** is a transformation which slides a figure from one position in the plane to another position in the plane. The original figure and the translated figure have the same size, shape, and orientation. A **dilation** is a transformation which proportionally stretches or shrinks a figure by a **scale factor**. The dilated image is the same shape and orientation as the original image but a different size. A polygon and its dilated image are similar.

Translation

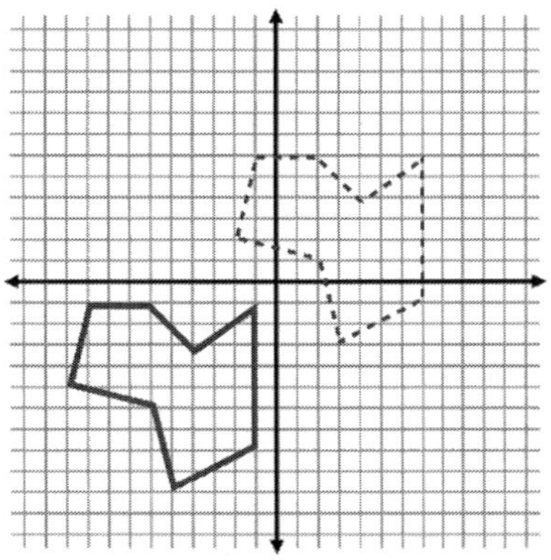

Dilation

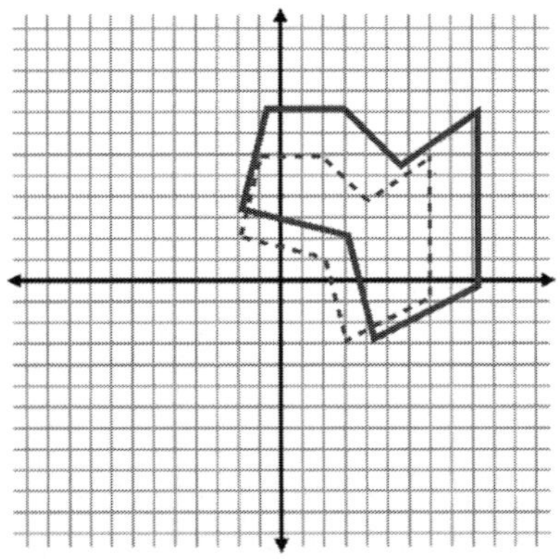

Review Video: Translation
Visit mometrix.com/academy and enter code: 718628

Review Video: Dilation
Visit mometrix.com/academy and enter code: 471630

A **reflection of a figure over a line** (a "flip") creates a congruent image that is the same distance from the line as the original figure but on the opposite side. The **line of reflection** is the perpendicular bisector of any line segment drawn from a point on the original figure to its reflected image (unless the point and its reflected image happen to be the same point, which happens when a figure is reflected over one of its own sides). A **reflection of a figure over a point** (an inversion) in two dimensions is the same as the rotation of the figure 180° about that point. The image of the figure is congruent to the original figure. The **point of reflection** is the midpoint of a line segment which connects a point in the figure to its image (unless the point and its reflected image happen to be the same point, which happens when a figure is reflected in one of its own points).

Reflection of a figure over a line

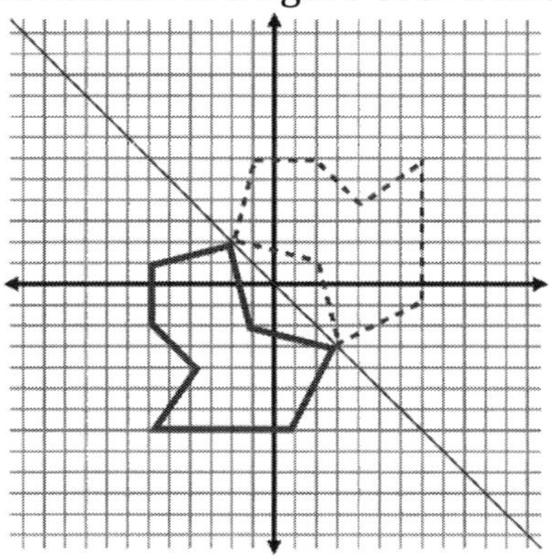

Reflection of a figure over a point

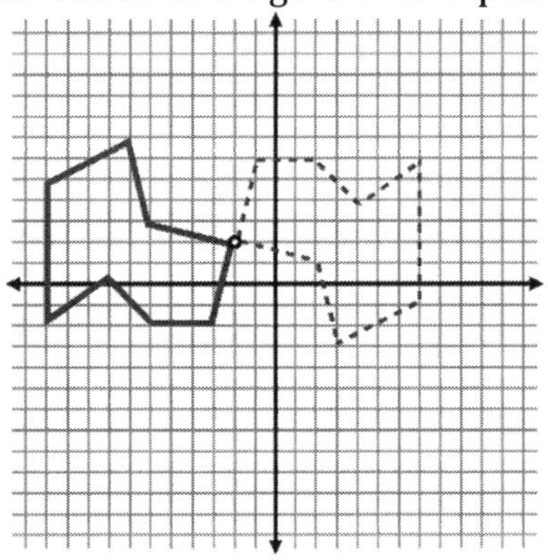

Review Video: Reflection
Visit mometrix.com/academy and enter code: 955068

3D Shapes

3D SHAPES

SOLIDS

The **surface area of a solid object** is the area of all sides or exterior surfaces. For objects such as prisms and pyramids, a further distinction is made between base surface area (B) and lateral surface area (LA). For a prism, the total surface area (SA) is $SA = LA + 2B$. For a pyramid or cone, the total surface area is $SA = LA + B$.

The **surface area of a sphere** can be found by the formula $A = 4\pi r^2$, where r is the radius. The volume is given by the formula $V = \frac{4}{3}\pi r^3$, where r is the radius. Both quantities are generally given in terms of π.

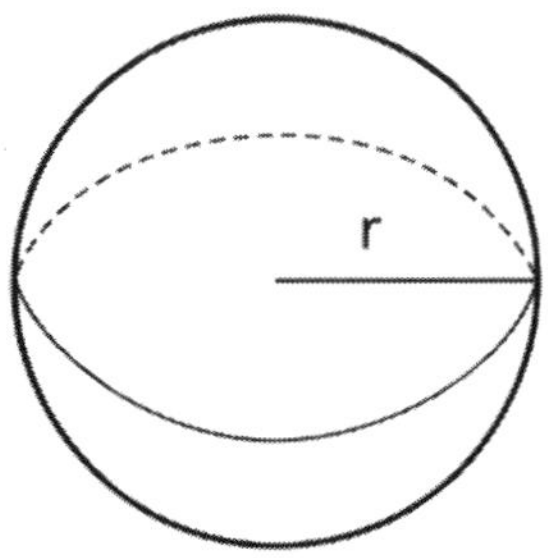

Review Video: Volume and Surface Area of a Sphere
Visit mometrix.com/academy and enter code: 786928

Review Video: How to Calculate the Volume of 3D Objects
Visit mometrix.com/academy and enter code: 163343

Geometry and Measurement

The **volume of any prism** is found by the formula $V = Bh$, where B is the area of the base, and h is the height (perpendicular distance between the bases). The surface area of any prism is the sum of the areas of both bases and all sides. It can be calculated as $SA = 2B + Ph$, where P is the perimeter of the base.

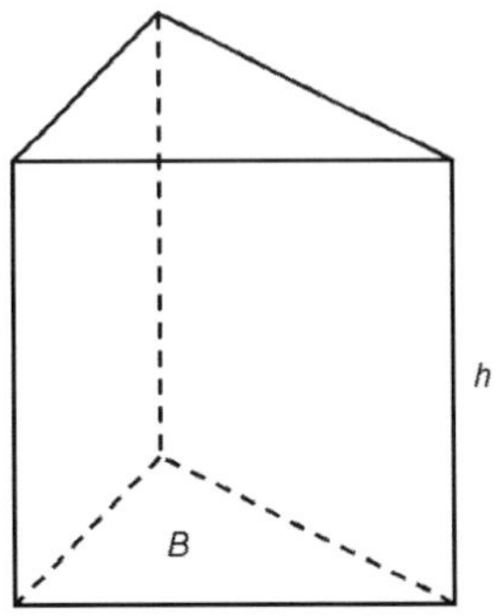

Review Video: Volume and Surface Area of a Prism
Visit mometrix.com/academy and enter code: 420158

For a **rectangular prism**, the volume can be found by the formula $V = lwh$, where V is the volume, l is the length, w is the width, and h is the height. The surface area can be calculated as $SA = 2lw + 2hl + 2wh$ or $SA = 2(lw + hl + wh)$.

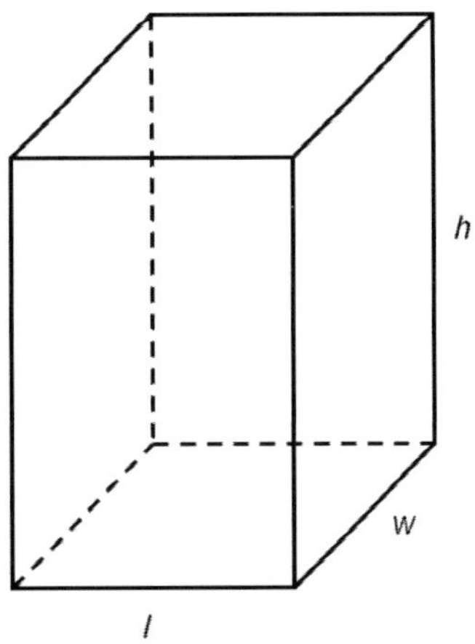

Review Video: Volume and Surface Area of a Rectangular Prism
Visit mometrix.com/academy and enter code: 282814

The **volume of a cube** can be found by the formula $V = s^3$, where s is the length of a side. The surface area of a cube is calculated as $SA = 6s^2$, where SA is the total surface area and s is the length of a side. These formulas are the same as the ones used for the volume and surface area of a rectangular prism, but simplified since all three quantities (length, width, and height) are the same.

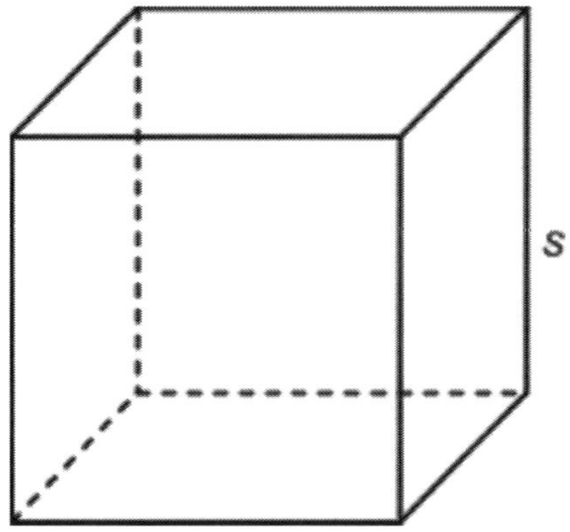

Review Video: Volume and Surface Area of a Cube
Visit mometrix.com/academy and enter code: 664455

The **volume of a cylinder** can be calculated by the formula $V = \pi r^2 h$, where r is the radius, and h is the height. The surface area of a cylinder can be found by the formula $SA = 2\pi r^2 + 2\pi rh$. The first term is the base area multiplied by two, and the second term is the perimeter of the base multiplied by the height.

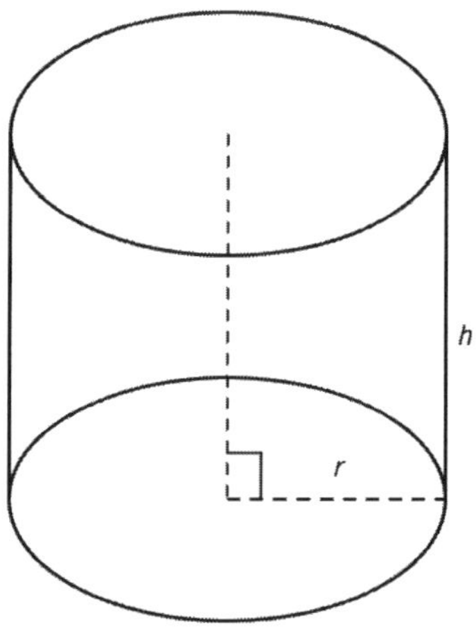

Review Video: Volume and Surface Area of a Right Circular Cylinder
Visit mometrix.com/academy and enter code: 226463

The **volume of a pyramid** is found by the formula $V = \frac{1}{3}Bh$, where B is the area of the base, and h is the height (perpendicular distance from the vertex to the base). Notice this formula is the same as $\frac{1}{3}$ times the volume of a prism. Like a prism, the base of a pyramid can be any shape.

Finding the **surface area of a pyramid** is not as simple as the other shapes we've looked at thus far. If the pyramid is a right pyramid, meaning the base is a regular polygon and the vertex is directly over the center of that polygon, the surface area can be calculated as $SA = B + \frac{1}{2}Ph_s$, where P is the perimeter of the base, and h_s is the slant height (distance from the vertex to the midpoint of one side of the base). If the pyramid is irregular, the area of each triangle side must be calculated individually and then summed, along with the base.

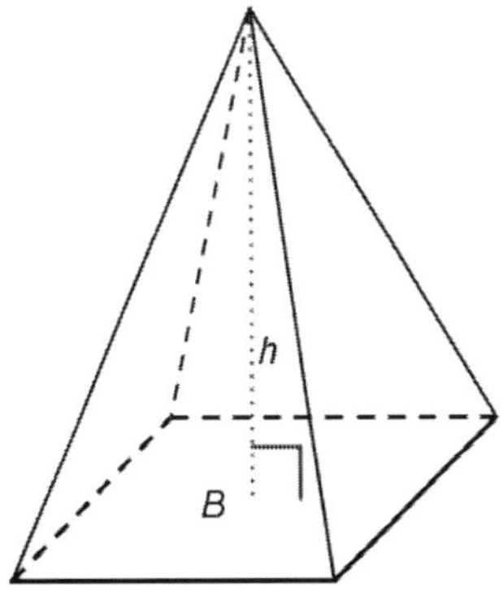

Review Video: Volume and Surface Area of a Pyramid
Visit mometrix.com/academy and enter code: 621932

The **volume of a cone** is found by the formula $V = \frac{1}{3}\pi r^2 h$, where r is the radius, and h is the height. Notice this is the same as $\frac{1}{3}$ times the volume of a cylinder. The surface area can be calculated as $SA = \pi r^2 + \pi rs$, where s is the slant height. The slant height can be calculated using the Pythagorean theorem to be $\sqrt{r^2 + h^2}$, so the surface area formula can also be written as $SA = \pi r^2 + \pi r\sqrt{r^2 + h^2}$.

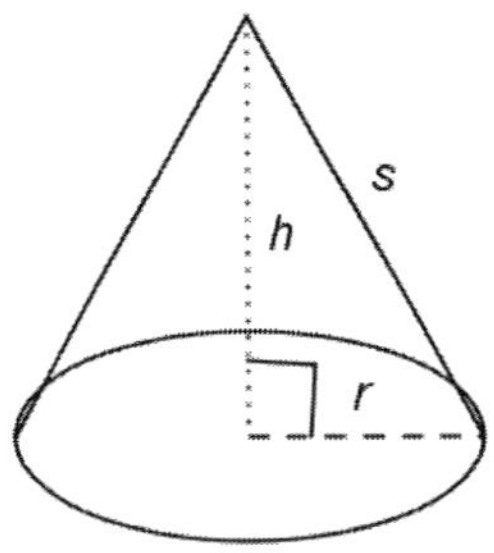

Review Video: Volume and Surface Area of a Right Circular Cone
Visit mometrix.com/academy and enter code: 573574

Conic Sections

Conic sections are a family of shapes that can be thought of as cross sections of a pair of infinite right cones stacked vertex to vertex. This is easiest to see with a visual representation:

A three-dimensional look at representative conic sections. (Note that a hyperbola intersects both cones.)

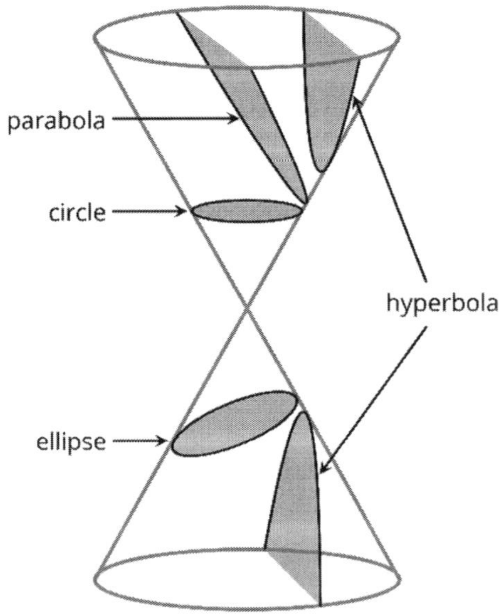

A side-on look at representative conic sections. (Note that the parabola is parallel to the slant of the cones.)

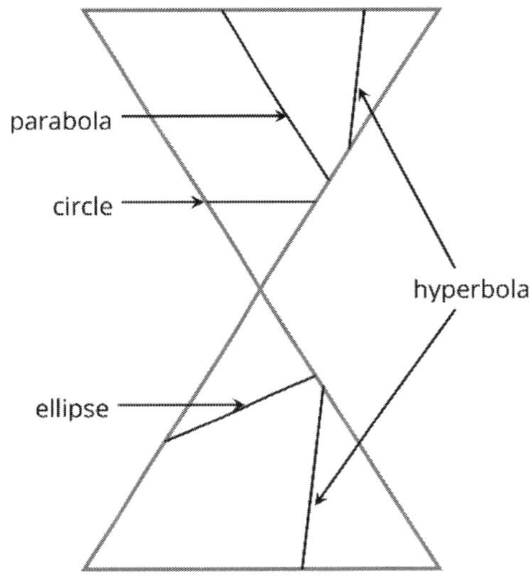

In short, a circle is a horizontal cross section, a parabola is a cross section parallel to the slant of the cone, an ellipse is a cross section at an angle *less than* the slant of the cone, and a hyperbola is a cross section at an angle *greater than* the slant of the cone.

Trigonometric Formulas

Pythagorean Theorem

The side of a triangle opposite the right angle is called the **hypotenuse**. The other two sides are called the legs. The Pythagorean theorem states a relationship among the legs and hypotenuse of a right triangle: $(a^2 + b^2 = c^2)$, where a and b are the lengths of the legs of a right triangle, and c is the length of the hypotenuse. Note that this formula will only work with right triangles.

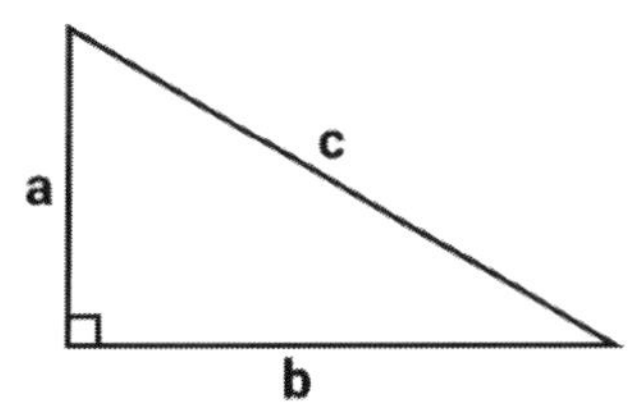

Review Video: Pythagorean Theorem
Visit mometrix.com/academy and enter code: 906576

Trigonometric Formulas

In the diagram below, angle C is the right angle, and side c is the hypotenuse. Side a is the side opposite to angle A and side b is the side opposite to angle B. Using ratios of side lengths as a means to calculate the sine, cosine, and tangent of an acute angle only works for right triangles.

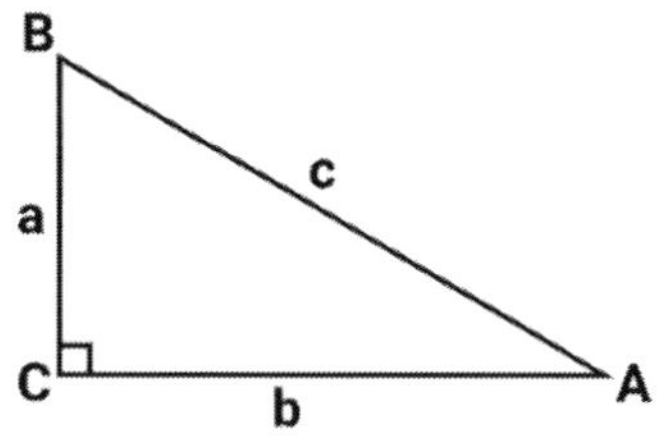

$$\sin A = \frac{\text{opposite side}}{\text{hypotenuse}} = \frac{a}{c} \qquad \csc A = \frac{1}{\sin A} = \frac{\text{hypotenuse}}{\text{opposite side}} = \frac{c}{a}$$
$$\cos A = \frac{\text{adjacent side}}{\text{hypotenuse}} = \frac{b}{c} \qquad \sec A = \frac{1}{\cos A} = \frac{\text{hypotenuse}}{\text{adjacent side}} = \frac{c}{b}$$
$$\tan A = \frac{\text{opposite side}}{\text{adjacent side}} = \frac{a}{b} \qquad \cot A = \frac{1}{\tan A} = \frac{\text{adjacent side}}{\text{opposite side}} = \frac{b}{a}$$

Laws of Sines and Cosines

The **law of sines** states that $\frac{\sin A}{a} = \frac{\sin B}{b} = \frac{\sin C}{c}$, where A, B, and C are the angles of a triangle, and a, b, and c are the sides opposite their respective angles. This formula will work with all triangles, not just right triangles.

The **law of cosines** is given by the formula $c^2 = a^2 + b^2 - 2ab(\cos C)$, where a, b, and c are the sides of a triangle, and C is the angle opposite side c. This is a generalized form of the Pythagorean theorem that can be used on any triangle.

Review Video: Law of Sines
Visit mometrix.com/academy and enter code: 206844

Review Video: Law of Cosines
Visit mometrix.com/academy and enter code: 158911

Basic Trigonometry

Trigonometric Functions

The basic trigonometric functions are sine (abbreviated 'sin'), cosine (abbreviated 'cos'), and tangent (abbreviated 'tan'). The simplest way to think of them is as describing the ratio of the side lengths of a right triangle in relation to the angles of the triangle.

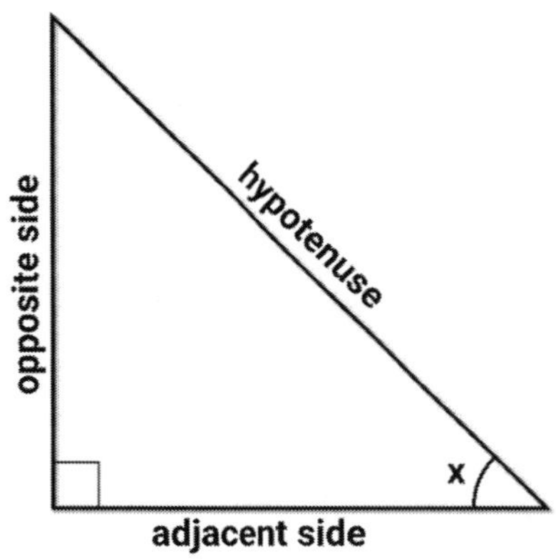

$$\sin x = \frac{\text{opposite side}}{\text{hypotenuse}}$$
$$\cos x = \frac{\text{adjacent side}}{\text{hypotenuse}}$$
$$\tan x = \frac{\text{opposite side}}{\text{adjacent side}}$$

APPLYING TRIGONOMETRIC FUNCTIONS

Suppose we have a point (x, y) at distance r from the origin such that the line segment between this point and the origin forms an angle of measure θ with the positive x-axis (We allow θ to be any real number, with the angle measured counterclockwise from the x-axis if $\theta > 0$ and clockwise if $\theta < 0$). Then we can define the trigonometric functions sine, cosine, and tangent by the formulas $\sin\theta = y/r$, $\cos\theta = x/r$, and $\tan\theta = y/x$ (and their reciprocal functions cosecant, secant, and cotangent accordingly). These functions are periodic because increasing the angle θ by 2π radians (that is, 360°) turns the line segment all the way around the origin so that it ends at the same point (x, y) again.

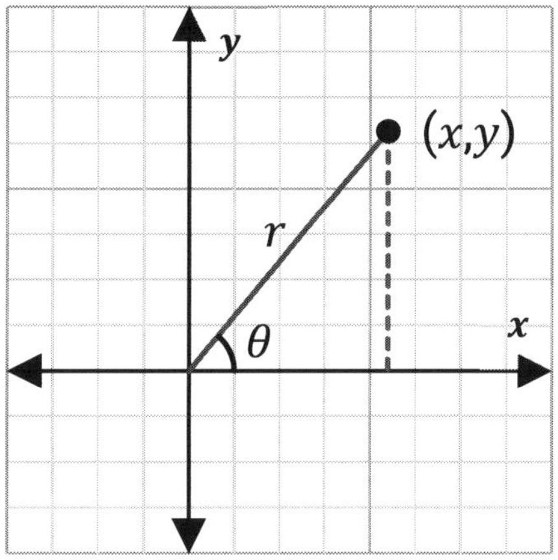

If the angle in the above diagram is acute, we can think of the line segment as the hypotenuse of a right triangle so that we get the familiar formulas $\sin\theta = (\text{opposite leg})/\text{hypotenuse}$, $\cos\theta = (\text{adjacent leg})/\text{hypotenuse}$, and $\tan\theta = (\text{opposite leg})/(\text{adjacent leg})$. In this form, the trigonometric functions are useful for finding missing sides of triangles. For example, suppose that standing 30 feet from the base of a tree, we have to look up at a 58° angle to see the top of the tree (see diagram). If we let x be the height of the tree, then we get the equation $\tan 58° = x/(30\text{ feet})$. Multiplying both sides of the equation by 30 gives us the height of the tree, namely, $x = 30\tan 58° \approx 48$ feet.

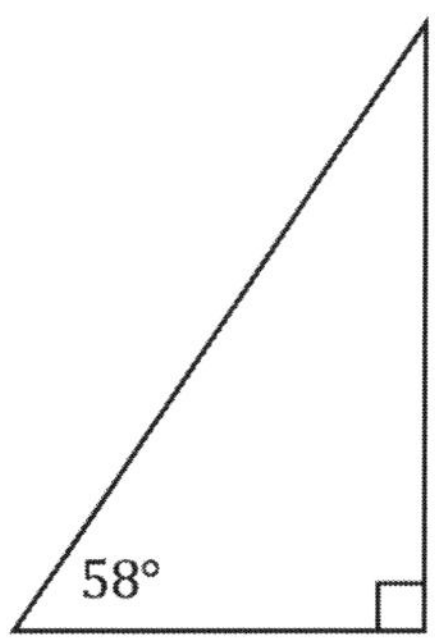

GRAPHING TRIGONOMETRIC FUNCTIONS

SINE

To graph the sine function, we let x (rather than θ) be the angle measure (usually in radians) and y be the value of the sine. That is, we graph the equation $y = \sin x$. From the definition of sine above we can show that $\sin 0 = 0$, $\sin(\pi/2) = 1$, $\sin\pi = 0$, $\sin(3\pi/2) = -1$, and $\sin 2\pi = 0$. Thus, the graph of the sine function begins at the origin, peaks at the point $(\pi/2, 1)$, crosses the x-axis at $(\pi, 0)$, has its lowest point at $(3\pi/2, -1)$, and returns to the x-axis at $(2\pi, 0)$. Because the sine function is periodic with period 2π radians (or 360°), this curve represents one complete cycle of the graph. The remainder of the graph of $y = \sin x$ consists of infinitely many repetitions of this cycle, producing the familiar "sine wave."

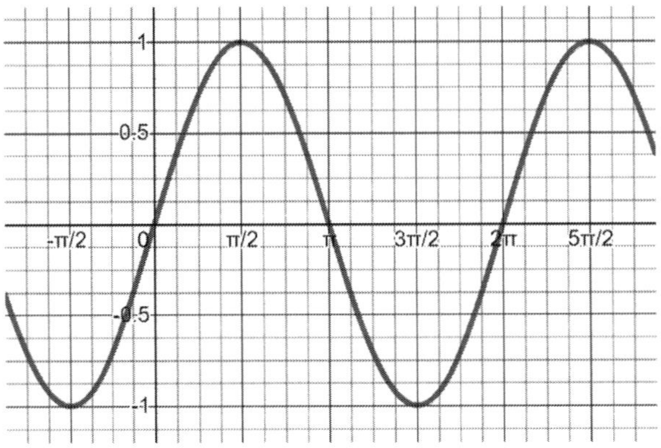

Review Video: Sine
Visit mometrix.com/academy and enter code: 193339

By suitable choice of the parameters A, B, C, and D, we can construct a "custom" sine function $y = A\sin(Bx + C) + D$ with any desired amplitude (the vertical distance the curve extends above and below its midline), period (distance between successive peaks), phase shift (horizontal shift), and midline (the horizontal line halfway between the peaks and troughs).

COSINE

Similarly, the graph of the cosine function is the graph of the equation $y = \cos x$. Proceeding as above, we get a graph with the same shape as that of the sine function but shifted by $\pi/2$ to the left.

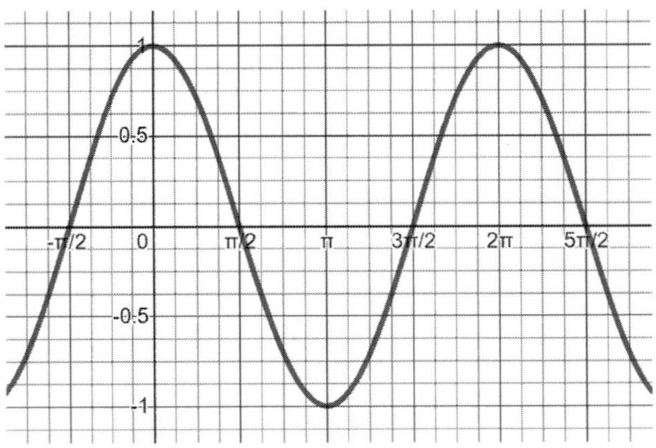

Review Video: Cosine
Visit mometrix.com/academy and enter code: 361120

As for the sine function, we can construct custom cosine graphs with desired amplitude, period, phase shift, and midline by choosing suitable values of the parameters in the equation $y = A\cos(Bx + C) + D$.

TANGENT

The graph of the tangent function (that is, the graph of the equation $y = \tan x$) turns out to be periodic with period π radians (or 180°). It consists of an infinite sequence of smooth curves crossing the x-axis at every multiple of π radians (180°) and having as asymptotes the vertical lines $x = \frac{k\pi}{2}$ radians ($x = k \times 90°$), for every odd integer k (which also means that the domain of the tangent function excludes these x-values).

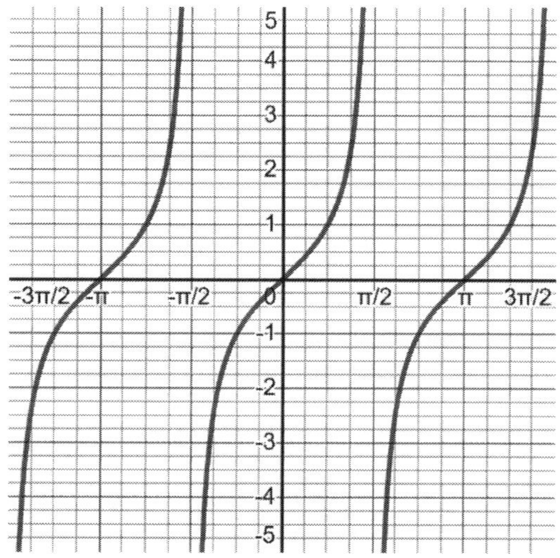

Review Video: Tangent
Visit mometrix.com/academy and enter code: 947639

COMPLEX NUMBERS

Complex numbers consist of a real component and an imaginary component. Complex numbers are expressed in the form $a + bi$ with real component a and imaginary component bi. The imaginary unit i is equal to $\sqrt{-1}$. That means $i^2 = -1$. The imaginary unit provides a way to find the square root of a negative number. For example, $\sqrt{-25}$ is $5i$. You should expect questions asking you to add, subtract, multiply, divide, and simplify complex numbers. You may see a question that says, "Add $3 + 2i$ and $5 - 7i$" or "Subtract $4 + i\sqrt{5}$ from $2 + i\sqrt{5}$." Or you may see a question that says, "Multiply $6 + 2i$ by $8 - 4i$" or "Divide $1 - 3i$ by $9 - 7i$."

OPERATIONS ON COMPLEX NUMBERS

Operations with complex numbers resemble operations with variables in algebra. When adding or subtracting complex numbers, you can only combine like terms—real terms with real terms and imaginary terms with imaginary terms. For example, if you are asked to simplify the expression $-2 + 4i - (-3 + 7i) - 5i$, you should first remove the parentheses to yield $-2 + 4i + 3 - 7i - 5i$. Combining like terms yields $1 - 8i$. One interesting aspect of imaginary numbers is that if i has an exponent greater than 1, it can be simplified. Example: $i^2 = -1$, $i^3 = -i$, and $i^4 = 1$. When multiplying complex numbers, remember to simplify each i with an exponent greater than 1. For example, you might see a question that says, "Simplify $(2 - i)(3 + 2i)$." You need to distribute and multiply to get $6 + 4i - 3i - 2i^2$. This is further simplified to $6 + i - 2(-1)$, or $8 + i$.

SIMPLIFYING EXPRESSIONS WITH COMPLEX DENOMINATORS

If an expression contains an i in the denominator, it must be simplified. Remember, roots cannot be left in the denominator of a fraction. Since i is equivalent to $\sqrt{-1}$, i cannot be left in the denominator of a fraction. You must rationalize the denominator of a fraction that contains a complex denominator by multiplying the numerator and denominator by the conjugate of the denominator. The conjugate of the complex number $a + bi$ is $a - bi$. You can simplify $\frac{2}{5i}$ by simply multiplying $\frac{2}{5i} \times \frac{i}{i}$, which yields $-\frac{2}{5}i$. And you can simplify $\frac{5+3i}{2-4i}$ by multiplying $\frac{5+3i}{2-4i} \times \frac{2+4i}{2+4i}$. This yields $\frac{10+20i+6i-12}{4-8i+8i+16}$ which simplifies to $\frac{-2+26i}{20}$ or $\frac{-1+13i}{10}$, which can also be written as $-\frac{1}{10} + \frac{13}{10}i$.

The Unit Circle

Degrees, Radians, and the Unit Circle

It is important to understand the deep connection between trigonometry and circles. Specifically, the two main units, **degrees** (°) and **radians** (rad), that are used to measure angles are related this way: 360° in one full circle and 2π radians in one full circle: $(360° = 2\pi \text{ rad})$. The conversion factor relating the two is often stated as $\frac{180°}{\pi}$. For example, to convert $\frac{3\pi}{2}$ radians to degrees, multiply by the conversion factor: $\frac{3\pi}{2} \times \frac{180°}{\pi} = 270°$. As another example, to convert 60° to radians, divide by the conversion factor or multiply by the reciprocal: $60° \times \frac{\pi}{180°} = \frac{\pi}{3}$ radians.

Recall that the standard equation for a circle is $(x - h)^2 + (y - k)^2 = r^2$. A **unit circle** is a circle with a radius of 1 $(r = 1)$ that has its center at the origin $(h = 0, k = 0)$. Thus, the equation for the unit circle simplifies from the standard equation down to $x^2 + y^2 = 1$.

Standard position is the position of an angle of measure θ whose vertex is at the origin, the initial side crosses the unit circle at the point $(1, 0)$, and the terminal side crosses the unit circle at some other point (a, b). In the standard position, $\sin\theta = b$, $\cos\theta = a$, and $\tan\theta = \frac{b}{a}$.

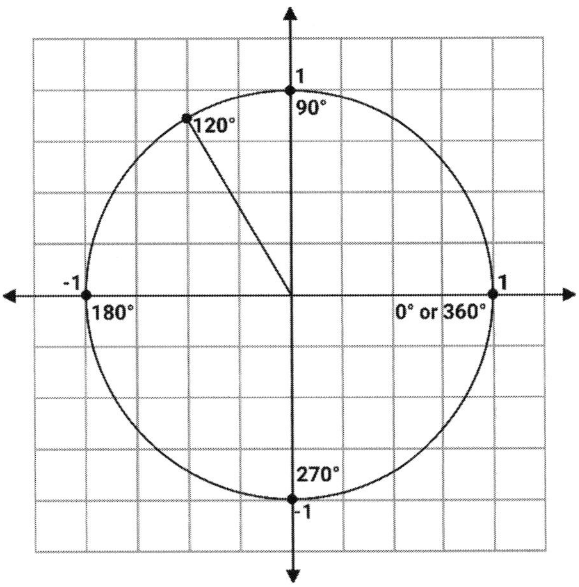

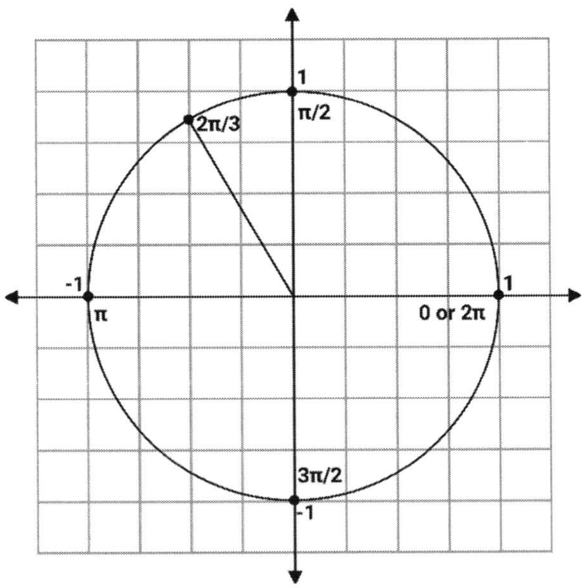

Review Video: Unit Circle
Visit mometrix.com/academy and enter code: 333922

Table of Commonly Encountered Angles

$0° = 0$ radians, $30° = \frac{\pi}{6}$ radians, $45° = \frac{\pi}{4}$ radians, $60° = \frac{\pi}{3}$ radians, and $90° = \frac{\pi}{2}$ radians

$\sin 0° = 0$	$\cos 0° = 1$	$\tan 0° = 0$
$\sin 30° = \frac{1}{2}$	$\cos 30° = \frac{\sqrt{3}}{2}$	$\tan 30° = \frac{\sqrt{3}}{3}$
$\sin 45° = \frac{\sqrt{2}}{2}$	$\cos 45° = \frac{\sqrt{2}}{2}$	$\tan 45° = 1$
$\sin 60° = \frac{\sqrt{3}}{2}$	$\cos 60° = \frac{1}{2}$	$\tan 60° = \sqrt{3}$
$\sin 90° = 1$	$\cos 90° = 0$	$\tan 90° = \text{undefined}$
$\csc 0° = \text{undefined}$	$\sec 0° = 1$	$\cot 0° = \text{undefined}$
$\csc 30° = 2$	$\sec 30° = \frac{2\sqrt{3}}{3}$	$\cot 30° = \sqrt{3}$
$\csc 45° = \sqrt{2}$	$\sec 45° = \sqrt{2}$	$\cot 45° = 1$
$\csc 60° = \frac{2\sqrt{3}}{3}$	$\sec 60° = 2$	$\cot 60° = \frac{\sqrt{3}}{3}$
$\csc 90° = 1$	$\sec 90° = \text{undefined}$	$\cot 90° = 0$

The values in the upper half of this table are values you should have memorized or be able to find quickly and those in the lower half can easily be determined as the reciprocal of the corresponding function.

Defined and Reciprocal Functions

The tangent function is defined as the ratio of the sine to the cosine: $\tan x = \frac{\sin x}{\cos x}$.

To take the reciprocal of a number means to place that number as the denominator of a fraction with a numerator of 1. The reciprocal functions are thus defined quite simply.

Cosecant	$\csc x$	$\frac{1}{\sin x}$
Secant	$\sec x$	$\frac{1}{\cos x}$
Cotangent	$\cot x$	$\frac{1}{\tan x}$

It is important to know these reciprocal functions, but they are not as commonly used as the three basic functions.

Review Video: Defined and Reciprocal Functions
Visit mometrix.com/academy and enter code: 996431

Geometry and Measurement

Inverse Trigonometric Functions

Inverse Functions

Each of the trigonometric functions accepts an angular measure, either degrees or radians, and gives a numerical value as the output. The inverse functions do the opposite; they accept a numerical value and give an angular measure as the output.

The inverse of sine, or arcsine, commonly written as either $\sin^{-1} x$ or $\arcsin x$, gives the angle whose sine is x. Similarly:

The inverse of $\cos x$ is written as $\cos^{-1} x$ or $\arccos x$ and means the angle whose cosine is x.
The inverse of $\tan x$ is written as $\tan^{-1} x$ or $\arctan x$ and means the angle whose tangent is x.
The inverse of $\csc x$ is written as $\csc^{-1} x$ or $\text{arccsc}\, x$ and means the angle whose cosecant is x.
The inverse of $\sec x$ is written as $\sec^{-1} x$ or $\text{arcsec}\, x$ and means the angle whose secant is x.
The inverse of $\cot x$ is written as $\cot^{-1} x$ or $\text{arccot}\, x$ and means the angle whose cotangent is x.

Review Video: Inverse Trig Functions
Visit mometrix.com/academy and enter code: 156054

Important Note About Solving Trigonometric Equations

When solving for an angle with a known trigonometric value, you must consider the sign and include all angles with that value. Your calculator will probably only give one value as an answer, typically in the following ranges:

- For $\sin^{-1} x$, $\left[-\frac{\pi}{2}, \frac{\pi}{2}\right]$ or $[-90°, 90°]$
- For $\cos^{-1} x$, $[0, \pi]$ or $[0°, 180°]$
- For $\tan^{-1} x$, $\left[-\frac{\pi}{2}, \frac{\pi}{2}\right]$ or $[-90°, 90°]$

It is important to determine if there is another angle in a different quadrant that also satisfies the problem. To do this, find the other quadrant(s) with the same sign for that trigonometric function and find the angle that has the same reference angle. Then check whether this angle is also a solution.

- In the first quadrant, all six trigonometric functions are positive.
- In the second quadrant, sin and csc are positive.
- In the third quadrant, tan and cot are positive.
- In the fourth quadrant, cos and sec are positive.

If you remember the phrase, "ALL Students Take Classes," you will be able to remember the sign of each trigonometric function in each quadrant. ALL represents all the signs in the first quadrant. The "S" in "Students" represents the sine function and its reciprocal in the second quadrant. The "T" in "Take" represents the tangent function and its reciprocal in the third quadrant. The "C" in "Classes" represents the cosine function and its reciprocal.

Trigonometric Identities

Sum and Difference

To find the sine, cosine, or tangent of the sum or difference of two angles, use one of the following formulas where α and β are two angles with known sine, cosine, or tangent values as needed:

$$\sin(\alpha \pm \beta) = \sin\alpha\cos\beta \pm \cos\alpha\sin\beta$$
$$\cos(\alpha \pm \beta) = \cos\alpha\cos\beta \mp \sin\alpha\sin\beta$$
$$\tan(\alpha \pm \beta) = \frac{\tan\alpha \pm \tan\beta}{1 \mp \tan\alpha\tan\beta}$$

Half Angle

To find the sine or cosine of half of a known angle, use the following formulas where θ is an angle with a known exact cosine value:

$$\sin\left(\frac{\theta}{2}\right) = \pm\sqrt{\frac{(1 - cos\theta)}{2}}$$

$$\cos\left(\frac{\theta}{2}\right) = \pm\sqrt{\frac{(1 + \cos\theta)}{2}}$$

To determine the sign of the answer, you must recognize which quadrant the given angle is in and apply the correct sign for the trigonometric function you are using. If you need to find an expression for the exact sine or cosine of an angle that you do not know, such as sine 22.5°, you can rewrite the given angle as a half angle, such as $\sin\left(\frac{45°}{2}\right)$, and use the formula above:

$$\sin\left(\frac{45°}{2}\right) = \pm\sqrt{\frac{(1 - \cos(45°))}{2}} = \pm\sqrt{\frac{\left(1 - \frac{\sqrt{2}}{2}\right)}{2}} = \pm\sqrt{\frac{(2 - \sqrt{2})}{4}} = \pm\frac{1}{2}\sqrt{(2 - \sqrt{2})}$$

To find the tangent or cotangent of half of a known angle, use the following formulas where θ is an angle with known exact sine and cosine values:

$$\tan\frac{\theta}{2} = \frac{sin\theta}{1 + \cos\theta}$$
$$\cot\frac{\theta}{2} = \frac{\sin\theta}{1 - \cos\theta}$$

These formulas will work for finding the tangent or cotangent of half of any angle unless the cosine of θ happens to make the denominator of the identity equal to 0.

The Pythagorean theorem states that $a^2 + b^2 = c^2$ for all right triangles. The trigonometric identity that derives from this principle is stated in this way: $\sin^2\theta + \cos^2\theta = 1$.

Geometry and Measurement

Dividing each term by either $\sin^2\theta$ or $\cos^2\theta$ yields two other identities, respectively:

$$1+\cot^2\theta=\csc^2\theta$$
$$\tan^2\theta+1=\sec^2\theta$$

Review Video: Sum and Difference Trigonometric Identities
Visit mometrix.com/academy and enter code: 468838

Double Angles

In each case, use one of the double angle formulas. To find the sine or cosine of twice a known angle, use one of the following formulas:

$$\sin(2\theta)=2\sin\theta\cos\theta$$

$$\begin{aligned}\cos(2\theta)&=\cos^2\theta-\sin^2\theta\\&=2\cos^2\theta-1\\&=1-2\sin^2\theta\end{aligned}$$

To find the tangent or cotangent of twice a known angle, use the formulas where θ is an angle with known exact sine, cosine, tangent, and cotangent values:

$$\tan(2\theta)=\frac{2\tan\theta}{1-\tan^2\theta}$$
$$\cot(2\theta)=\frac{\cot\theta-\tan\theta}{2}$$

Products

To find the product of the sines and cosines of two different angles, use one of the following formulas where α and β are two unique angles:

$$\sin\alpha\sin\beta=\frac{1}{2}[\cos(\alpha-\beta)-\cos(\alpha+\beta)]$$
$$\cos\alpha\cos\beta=\frac{1}{2}[\cos(\alpha+\beta)+\cos(\alpha-\beta)]$$
$$\sin\alpha\cos\beta=\frac{1}{2}[\sin(\alpha+\beta)+\sin(\alpha-\beta)]$$
$$\cos\alpha\sin\beta=\frac{1}{2}[\sin(\alpha+\beta)-\sin(\alpha-\beta)]$$

Review Video: Half-Angle, Double Angle, and Product Trig Identities
Visit mometrix.com/academy and enter code: 274252

Complementary

The trigonometric cofunction identities use the trigonometric relationships of complementary angles (angles whose sum is 90°). These are:

$$\cos x=\sin(90°-x)$$
$$\csc x=\sec(90°-x)$$
$$\cot x=\tan(90°-x)$$

Domain, Range, and Asymptotes in Trigonometry

The domain is the set of all possible real number values of x on the graph of a trigonometric function. Some graphs will impose limits on the values of x.

The range is the set of all possible real number values of y on the graph of a trigonometric function. Some graphs will impose limits on the values of y.

Asymptotes are lines that the graph of a trigonometric function approaches but never reaches. Asymptotes exist for values of x in the graphs of the tangent, cotangent, secant, and cosecant. The sine and cosine graphs do not have any asymptotes.

Domain, Range, and Asymptotes of the Six Trigonometric Functions

The domain, range, and asymptotes for each of the trigonometric functions are as follows:

- In the **sine** function, the domain is all real numbers, the range is $-1 \leq y \leq 1$, and there are no asymptotes.
- In the **cosine** function, the domain is all real numbers, the range is $-1 \leq y \leq 1$, and there are no asymptotes.
- In the **tangent** function, the domain is $x \in \mathbb{R}; x \neq \frac{\pi}{2} + k\pi$, the range is all real numbers, and the asymptotes are the lines $x = \frac{\pi}{2} + k\pi$.
- In the **cosecant** function, the domain is $x \in \mathbb{R}; x \neq k\pi$, the range is $(-\infty, -1]$ and $[1, \infty)$, and the asymptotes are the lines $x = k\pi$.
- In the **secant** function, the domain is $x \in \mathbb{R}; x \neq \frac{\pi}{2} + k\pi$, the range is $(-\infty, 1]$ and $[1, \infty)$, and the asymptotes are the lines $x = \frac{\pi}{2} + k\pi$.
- In the **cotangent** function, the domain is $x \in \mathbb{R}; x \neq k\pi$, the range is all real numbers, and the asymptotes are the lines $x = k\pi$.

In each of the above cases, k represents any integer.

Rectangular and Polar Coordinates

Rectangular coordinates are those that lie on the square grids of the Cartesian plane. They should be quite familiar to you. The polar coordinate system is based on a circular graph, rather than the square grid of the Cartesian system. Points in the polar coordinate system are in the format (r, θ), where r is the distance from the origin (think radius of the circle) and θ is the smallest positive angle (moving counterclockwise around the circle) made with the positive horizontal axis.

To convert a point from rectangular (x, y) format to polar (r, θ) format, use the formula (x, y) to $(r, \theta) \Rightarrow r = \sqrt{x^2 + y^2}; \theta = \arctan\frac{y}{x}$ when $x \neq 0$.

If x is positive, use the positive square root value for r. If x is negative, use the negative square root value for r. If $x = 0$, use the following rules:

- If $y = 0$, then $\theta = 0$.
- If $y > 0$, then $\theta = \frac{\pi}{2}$.
- If $y < 0$, then $\theta = \frac{3\pi}{2}$.

Geometry and Measurement

To convert a point from polar (r, θ) format to rectangular (x, y) format, use the formula (r, θ) to $(x, y) \Rightarrow x = r\cos\theta\,;\, y = r\sin\theta$.

De Moivre's Theorem

De Moivre's theorem is used to find the powers of complex numbers (numbers that contain the imaginary number i) written in polar form. Given a trigonometric expression that contains i, such as $z = r\cos x + ir\sin x$, where r is a real number and x is an angle measurement in polar form, use the formula $z^n = r^n(\cos nx + i\sin nx)$, where r and n are real numbers, x is the angle measure in polar form, and i is the imaginary number $i = \sqrt{-1}$. The expression $\cos x + i\sin x$ can be written $\text{cis}\, x$, making the formula appear in the format $z^n = r^n \text{ cis } nx$.

Note that De Moivre's theorem is only for angles in polar form. If you are given an angle in degrees, you must convert to polar form before using the formula.

Parabolas, Ellipses, and Hyperbolas

Parabolas

A **parabola** is the set of all points in a plane that are equidistant from a fixed line, called the **directrix**, and a fixed point not on the line, called the **focus**. The **axis** is the line perpendicular to the directrix that passes through the focus.

For parabolas that open up or down, the standard equation is $(x - h)^2 = 4c(y - k)$, where h, c, and k are coefficients. If c is positive, the parabola opens up. If c is negative, the parabola opens down. The vertex is the point (h, k). The directrix is the line having the equation $y = -c + k$, and the focus is the point $(h, c + k)$.

For parabolas that open left or right, the standard equation is $(y - k)^2 = 4c(x - h)$, where k, c, and h are coefficients. If c is positive, the parabola opens to the right. If c is negative, the parabola opens to the left. The vertex is the point (h, k). The directrix is the line having the equation $x = -c + h$, and the focus is the point $(c + h, k)$.

Review Video: Parabolas
Visit mometrix.com/academy and enter code: 129187

Review Video: Vertex of a Parabola
Visit mometrix.com/academy and enter code: 272300

Review Video: How to Convert Between Standard Form and Vertex Form
Visit mometrix.com/academy and enter code: 916601

Ellipses and Hyperbolas

Ellipse

An **ellipse** is the set of all points in a plane whose total distance from two fixed points called the **foci** (singular: focus) is constant, and whose center is the midpoint between the foci.

The standard equation of an ellipse that is wider than it is tall is $\frac{(x-h)^2}{a^2} + \frac{(y-k)^2}{b^2} = 1$, where a and b are coefficients. The center is the point (h, k) and the foci are the points $(h + c, k)$ and $(h - c, k)$, where $c^2 = a^2 - b^2$ and $a^2 > b^2$.

The major axis has length $2a$, and the minor axis has length $2b$.

Eccentricity (e) is a measure of how elongated an ellipse is, and is the ratio of the distance between the foci to the length of the major axis. Eccentricity will have a value between 0 and 1. The closer to 0 the eccentricity is, the closer the ellipse is to being a circle. The formula for eccentricity is $e = \frac{c}{a}$.

Review Video: Ellipse
Visit mometrix.com/academy and enter code: 703899

HYPERBOLA

A **hyperbola** is the set of all points in a plane, whose distance from two fixed points, called foci, has a constant difference.

The standard equation of a horizontal hyperbola is $\frac{(x-h)^2}{a^2} - \frac{(y-k)^2}{b^2} = 1$, where a, b, h, and k are real numbers. The center is the point (h,k), the vertices are the points $(h+a,k)$ and $(h-a,k)$, and the foci are the points that every point on one of the parabolic curves is equidistant from. The foci are found using the formulas $(h+c,k)$ and $(h-c,k)$, where $c^2 = a^2 + b^2$. The asymptotes are two lines the graph of the hyperbola approaches but never reaches, and are given by the equations $y = \left(\frac{b}{a}\right)(x-h) + k$ and $y = -\left(\frac{b}{a}\right)(x-h) + k$.

The standard equation of a vertical hyperbola is $\frac{(y-k)^2}{a^2} - \frac{(x-h)^2}{b^2} = 1$, where a, b, k, and h are real numbers. The center is the point (h,k), the vertices are the points $(h,k+a)$ and $(h,k-a)$, and the foci are the points that every point on one of the hyperbolic curves is equidistant from and are found using the formulas $(h,k+c)$ and $(h,k-c)$, where $c^2 = a^2 + b^2$. The asymptotes are two lines the graph of the hyperbola approaches but never reaches, and are given by the equations $y = \left(\frac{a}{b}\right)(x-h) + k$ and $y = -\left(\frac{a}{b}\right)(x-h) + k$.

Review Video: Hyperbolas
Visit mometrix.com/academy and enter code: 509429

Chapter Quiz

Ready to see how well you retained what you just read? Scan the QR code to go directly to the chapter quiz interface for this study guide. If you're using a computer, simply visit the online resources page at **mometrix.com/resources719/texesmath4-8** and click the Chapter Quizzes link.

Probability and Statistics

Displaying Data

Displaying Information

Frequency Tables

Frequency tables show how frequently each unique value appears in a set. A **relative frequency table** is one that shows the proportions of each unique value compared to the entire set. Relative frequencies are given as percentages; however, the total percent for a relative frequency table will not necessarily equal 100 percent due to rounding. An example of a frequency table with relative frequencies is below.

Favorite Color	Frequency	Relative Frequency
Blue	4	13%
Red	7	22%
Green	3	9%
Purple	6	19%
Cyan	12	38%

Review Video: Data Interpretation of Graphs
Visit mometrix.com/academy and enter code: 200439

Circle Graphs

Circle graphs, also known as *pie charts*, provide a visual depiction of the relationship of each type of data compared to the whole set of data. The circle graph is divided into sections by drawing radii to create central angles whose percentage of the circle is equal to the individual data's percentage of the whole set. Each 1% of data is equal to 3.6° in the circle graph. Therefore, data represented by a 90° section of the circle graph makes up 25% of the whole. When complete, a circle graph often looks like a pie cut into uneven wedges. The pie chart below shows the data from the frequency table referenced earlier where people were asked their favorite color.

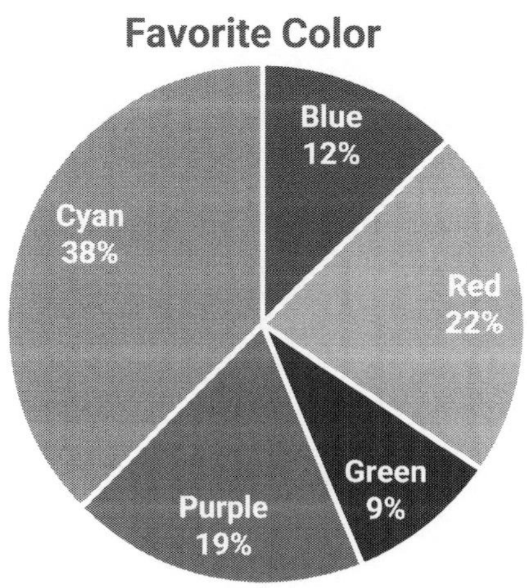

Pictographs

A **pictograph** is a graph, generally in the horizontal orientation, that uses pictures or symbols to represent the data. Each pictograph must have a key that defines the picture or symbol and gives the quantity each picture or symbol represents. Pictures or symbols on a pictograph are not always shown as whole elements. In this case, the fraction of the picture or symbol shown represents the same fraction of the quantity a whole picture or symbol stands for. For example, a row with $3\frac{1}{2}$ ears of corn, where each ear of corn represents 100 stalks of corn in a field, would equal $3\frac{1}{2} \times 100 = 350$ stalks of corn in the field.

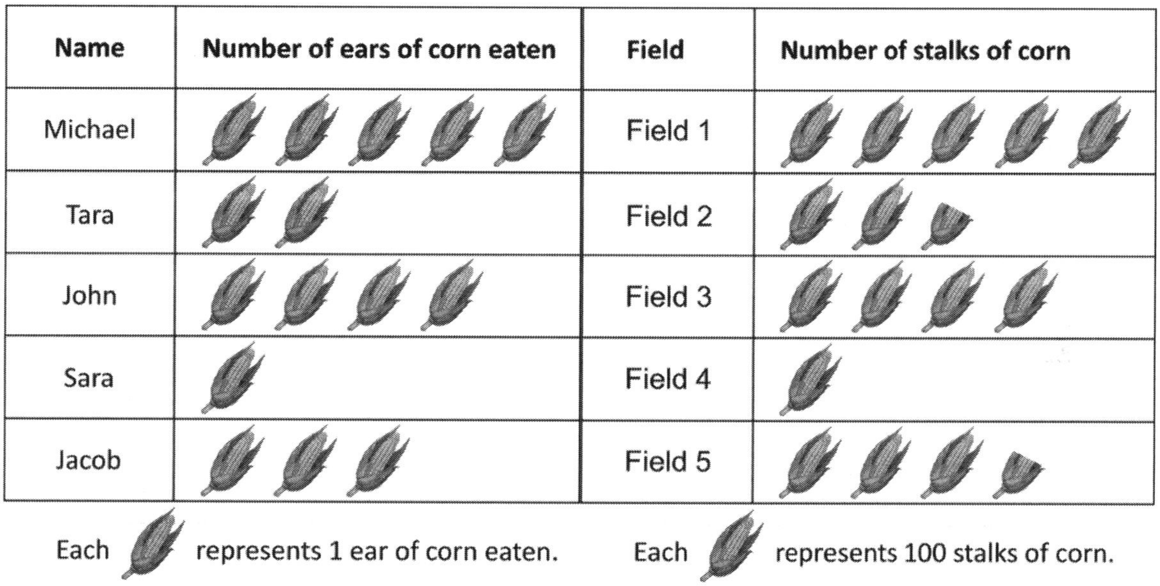

Review Video: Pictographs
Visit mometrix.com/academy and enter code: 147860

Line Graphs

Line graphs have one or more lines of varying styles (solid or broken) to show the different values for a set of data. The individual data are represented as ordered pairs, much like on a Cartesian plane. In this case, the x- and y-axes are defined in terms of their units, such as dollars or time. The individual plotted points are joined by line segments to show whether the value of the data is increasing (line sloping upward), decreasing (line sloping downward), or staying the same (horizontal line). Multiple sets of data can be graphed on the same line graph to give an easy visual comparison. An example of this would be graphing achievement test scores for different groups of students over the same time period to see which group had the greatest increase or decrease in performance from year to year (as shown below).

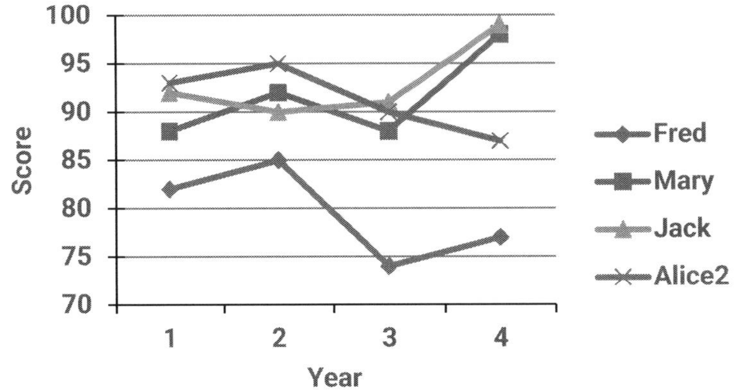

Review Video: How to Create a Line Graph
Visit mometrix.com/academy and enter code: 480147

Line Plots

A **line plot**, also known as a *dot plot*, has plotted points that are not connected by line segments. In this graph, the horizontal axis lists the different possible values for the data, and the vertical axis lists the number of times the individual value occurs. A single dot is graphed for each value to show the number of times it occurs. This graph is more closely related to a bar graph than a line graph. Do not connect the dots in a line plot or it will misrepresent the data.

Review Video: Line Plot
Visit mometrix.com/academy and enter code: 754610

Stem and Leaf Plots

A **stem and leaf plot** is useful for depicting groups of data that fall into a range of values. Each piece of data is separated into two parts: the first, or left, part is called the stem; the second, or right, part is called the leaf. Each stem is listed in a column from smallest to largest. Each leaf that has the common stem is listed in that stem's row from smallest to largest. For example, in a set of two-digit numbers, the digit in the tens place is the stem, and the digit in the ones place is the leaf. With a stem and leaf plot, you can easily see which subset of numbers (10s, 20s, 30s, etc.) is the largest. This information is also readily available by looking at a histogram, but a stem and leaf plot also allows you to look closer and see exactly which values fall in that range. Using a sample set of test scores (82, 88, 92, 93, 85, 90, 92, 95, 74, 88, 90, 91, 78, 87, 98, 99), we can assemble a stem and leaf plot like the one below.

Test Scores

7	4	8							
8	2	5	7	8	8				
9	0	0	1	2	2	3	5	8	9

Review Video: Stem and Leaf Plots
Visit mometrix.com/academy and enter code: 302339

BAR GRAPHS

A **bar graph** is one of the few graphs that can be drawn correctly in two different configurations – both horizontally and vertically. A bar graph is similar to a line plot in the way the data is organized on the graph. Both axes must have their categories defined for the graph to be useful. Rather than placing a single dot to mark the point of the data's value, a bar, or thick line, is drawn from zero to the exact value of the data, whether it is a number, percentage, or other numerical value. Longer bar lengths correspond to greater data values. To read a bar graph, read the labels for the axes to find the units being reported. Then, look where the bars end in relation to the scale given on the corresponding axis and determine the associated value.

The bar chart below represents the responses from our favorite-color survey.

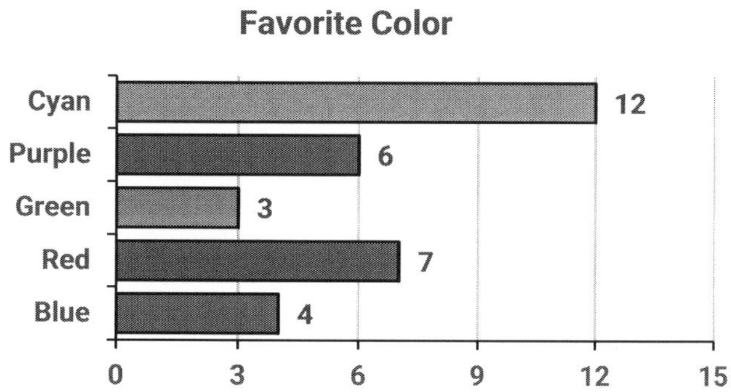

HISTOGRAMS

At first glance, a **histogram** looks like a vertical bar graph. The difference is that a bar graph has a separate bar for each piece of data and a histogram has one continuous bar for each *range* of data. For example, a histogram may have one bar for the range 0–9, one bar for 10–19, etc. While a bar graph has numerical values on one axis, a histogram has numerical values on both axes. Each range is of equal size, and they are ordered left to right from lowest to highest. The height of each column on a histogram represents the number of data values within that range. Like a stem and leaf plot, a histogram makes it easy to glance at the graph and quickly determine which range has the greatest quantity of values. A simple example of a histogram is below.

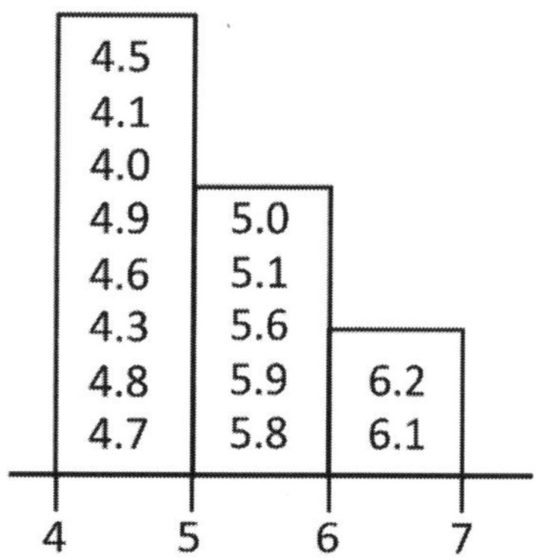

5-NUMBER SUMMARY

The **5-number summary** of a set of data gives a very informative picture of the set. The five numbers in the summary include the minimum value, maximum value, and the three quartiles. This information gives the reader the range and median of the set, as well as an indication of how the data is spread about the median.

Box and Whisker Plots

A **box-and-whiskers plot** is a graphical representation of the 5-number summary. To draw a box-and-whiskers plot, plot the points of the 5-number summary on a number line. Draw a box whose ends are through the points for the first and third quartiles. Draw a vertical line in the box through the median to divide the box in half. Draw a line segment from the first quartile point to the minimum value, and from the third quartile point to the maximum value.

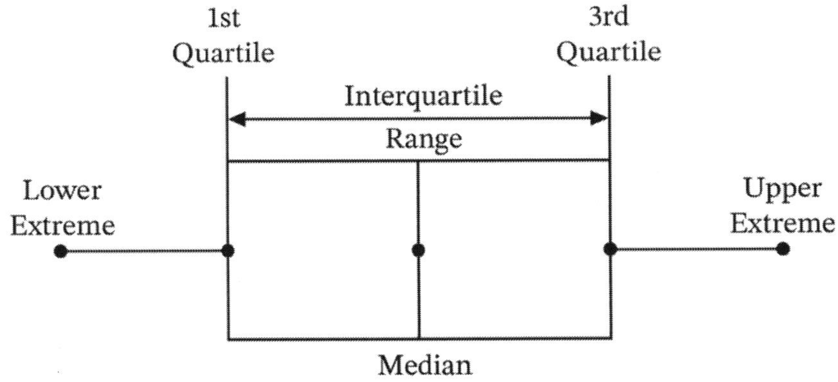

Review Video: Box and Whisker Plots
Visit mometrix.com/academy and enter code: 810817

Example

Given the following data (32, 28, 29, 26, 35, 27, 30, 31, 27, 32), we first sort it into numerical order: 26, 27, 27, 28, 29, 30, 31, 32, 32, 35. We can then find the median. Since there are ten values, we take the average of the 5th and 6th values to get 29.5. We find the lower quartile by taking the median of the data smaller than the median. Since there are five values, we take the 3rd value, which is 27. We find the upper quartile by taking the median of the data larger than the overall median, which is 32. Finally, we note our minimum and maximum, which are simply the smallest and largest values in the set: 26 and 35, respectively. Now we can create our box plot:

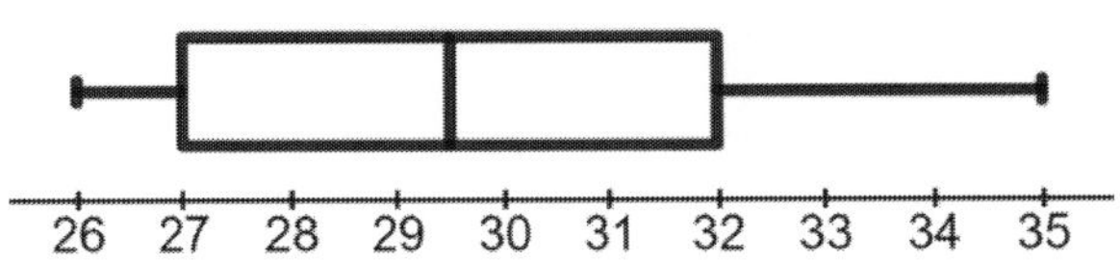

This plot is fairly "long" on the right whisker, showing one or more unusually high values (but not quite outliers). The other quartiles are similar in length, showing a fairly even distribution of data.

Interquartile Range

The **interquartile range, or IQR**, is the difference between the upper and lower quartiles. It measures how the data is dispersed: a high IQR means that the data is more spread out, while a low IQR means that the data is clustered more tightly around the median. To find the IQR, subtract the lower quartile value (Q_1) from the upper quartile value (Q_3).

EXAMPLE

To find the upper and lower quartiles, we first find the median and then take the median of all values above it and all values below it. In the following data set (16, 18, 13, 24, 16, 51, 32, 21, 27, 39), we first rearrange the values in numerical order: 13, 16, 16, 18, 21, 24, 27, 32, 39, 51. There are 10 values, so the median is the average of the 5th and 6th: $\frac{21+24}{2} = \frac{45}{2} = 22.5$. We do not actually need this value to find the upper and lower quartiles. We look at the set of numbers below the median: 13, 16, 16, 18, 21. There are five values, so the 3rd is the median (16), or the value of the lower quartile (Q_1). Then we look at the numbers above the median: 24, 27, 32, 39, 51. Again there are five values, so the 3rd is the median (32), or the value of the upper quartile (Q_3). We find the IQR by subtracting Q_1 from Q_3: $32 - 16 = 16$.

68-95-99.7 RULE

The **68–95–99.7 rule** describes how a normal distribution of data should appear when compared to the mean. This is also a description of a normal bell curve. According to this rule, 68 percent of the data values in a normally distributed set should fall within one standard deviation of the mean (34 percent above and 34 percent below the mean), 95 percent of the data values should fall within two standard deviations of the mean (47.5 percent above and 47.5 percent below the mean), and 99.7 percent of the data values should fall within three standard deviations of the mean, again, equally distributed on either side of the mean. This means that only 0.3 percent of all data values should fall more than three standard deviations from the mean. On the graph below, the normal curve is centered on the y-axis. The x-axis labels are how many standard deviations away from the center you are. Therefore, it is easy to see how the 68-95-99.7 rule can apply.

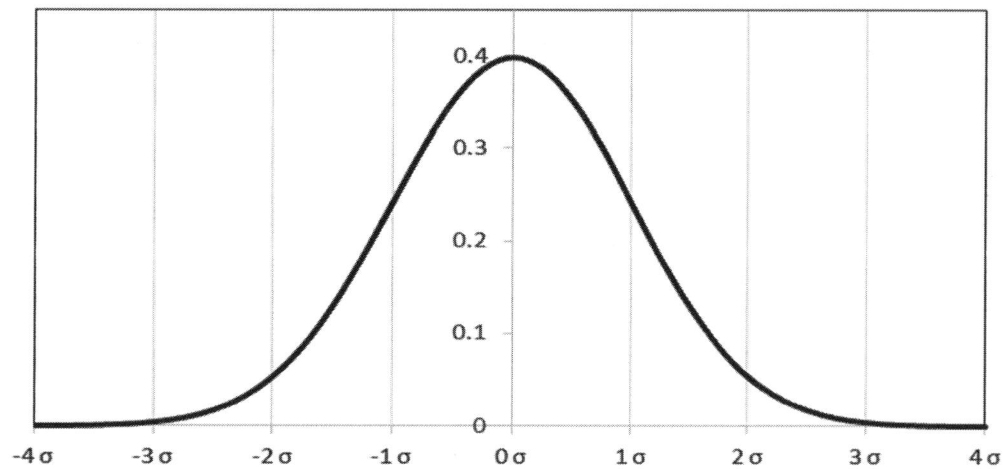

Probability and Statistics

Scatter Plots

Bivariate Data

Bivariate data is simply data from two different variables. (The prefix *bi-* means *two*.) In a *scatter plot*, each value in the set of data is plotted on a grid similar to a Cartesian plane, where each axis represents one of the two variables. By looking at the pattern formed by the points on the grid, you can often determine whether or not there is a relationship between the two variables, and what that relationship is, if it exists. The variables may be directly proportionate, inversely proportionate, or show no proportion at all. It may also be possible to determine if the data is linear, and if so, to find an equation to relate the two variables. The following scatter plot shows the relationship between preference for brand "A" and the age of the consumers surveyed.

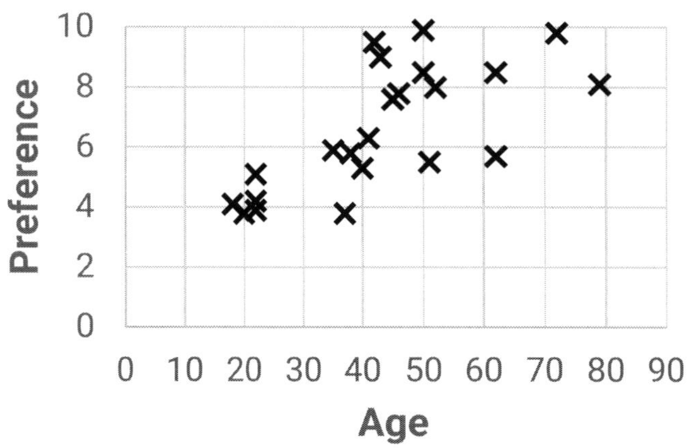

SCATTER PLOTS

Scatter plots are also useful in determining the type of function represented by the data and finding the simple regression. Linear scatter plots may be positive or negative. Nonlinear scatter plots are generally exponential or quadratic. Below are some common types of scatter plots:

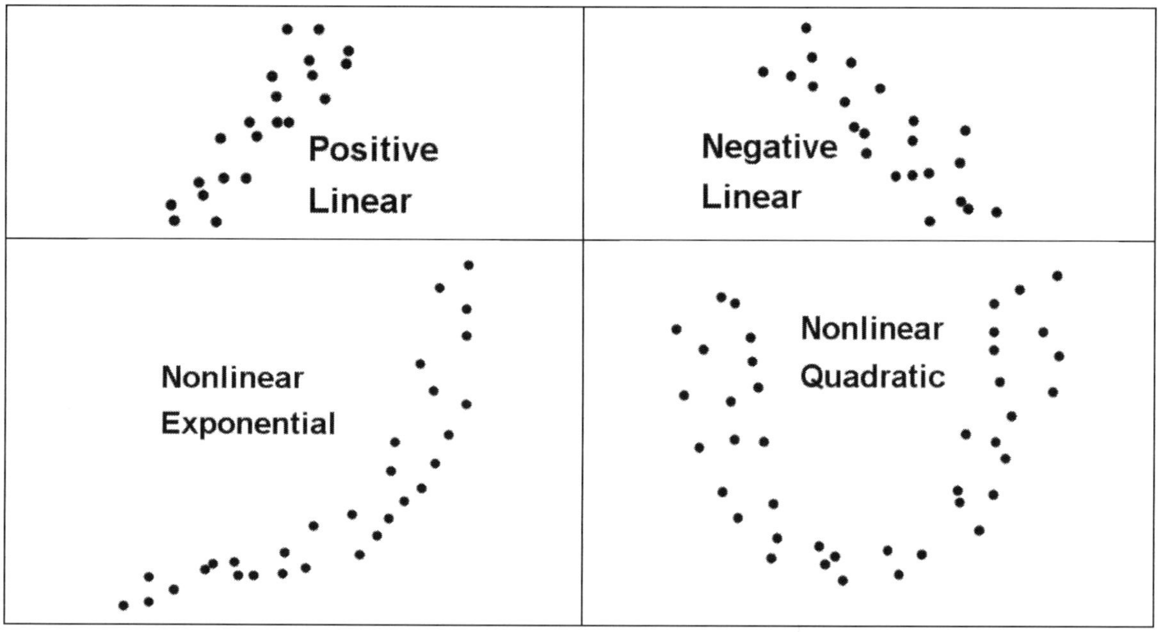

Review Video: Scatter Plot
Visit mometrix.com/academy and enter code: 596526

Statistics

INTRODUCTION TO STATISTICS

Statistics is the branch of mathematics that deals with collecting, recording, interpreting, illustrating, and analyzing large amounts of **data**. The following terms are often used in the discussion of data and **statistics**:

- **Data** – the collective name for pieces of information (singular is datum)
- **Quantitative data** – measurements (such as length, mass, and speed) that provide information about quantities in numbers
- **Qualitative data** – information (such as colors, scents, tastes, and shapes) that cannot be measured using numbers
- **Discrete data** – information that can be expressed only by a specific value, such as whole or half numbers. (e.g., since people can be counted only in whole numbers, a population count would be discrete data.)
- **Continuous data** – information (such as time and temperature) that can be expressed by any value within a given range
- **Primary data** – information that has been collected directly from a survey, investigation, or experiment, such as a questionnaire or the recording of daily temperatures. (Primary data that has not yet been organized or analyzed is called **raw data**.)
- **Secondary data** – information that has been collected, sorted, and processed by the researcher

Probability and Statistics

- **Ordinal data** – information that can be placed in numerical order, such as age or weight
- **Nominal data** – information that *cannot* be placed in numerical order, such as names or places

Data Collection

Population

In statistics, the **population** is the entire collection of people, plants, etc., that data can be collected from. For example, a study to determine how well students in local schools perform on a standardized test would have a population of all the students enrolled in those schools, although a study may include just a small sample of students from each school. A **parameter** is a numerical value that gives information about the population, such as the mean, median, mode, or standard deviation. Remember that the symbol for the mean of a population is μ and the symbol for the standard deviation of a population is σ.

Sample

A **sample** is a portion of the entire population. Whereas a parameter helped describe the population, a **statistic** is a numerical value that gives information about the sample, such as mean, median, mode, or standard deviation. Keep in mind that the symbols for mean and standard deviation are different when they are referring to a sample rather than the entire population. For a sample, the symbol for mean is $\bar{x}$ and the symbol for standard deviation is s. The mean and standard deviation of a sample may or may not be identical to that of the entire population due to a sample only being a subset of the population. However, if the sample is random and large enough, statistically significant values can be attained. Samples are generally used when the population is too large to justify including every element or when acquiring data for the entire population is impossible.

Inferential Statistics

Inferential statistics is the branch of statistics that uses samples to make predictions about an entire population. This type of statistic is often seen in political polls, where a sample of the population is questioned about a particular topic or politician to gain an understanding of the attitudes of the entire population of the country. Often, exit polls are conducted on election days using this method. Inferential statistics can have a large margin of error if you do not have a valid sample.

Sampling Distribution

Statistical values calculated from various samples of the same size make up the **sampling distribution**. For example, if several samples of identical size are randomly selected from a large population and then the mean of each sample is calculated, the distribution of values of the means would be a sampling distribution.

The **sampling distribution of the mean** is the distribution of the sample mean, $\bar{x}$, derived from random samples of a given size. It has three important characteristics. First, the mean of the sampling distribution of the mean is equal to the mean of the population that was sampled. Second, assuming the standard deviation is non-zero, the standard deviation of the sampling distribution of the mean equals the standard deviation of the sampled population divided by the square root of the sample size. This is sometimes called the standard error. Finally, as the sample size gets larger, the sampling distribution of the mean gets closer to a normal distribution via the central limit theorem.

Survey Study

A **survey study** is a method of gathering information from a small group in an attempt to gain enough information to make accurate general assumptions about the population. Once a survey study is completed, the results are then put into a summary report.

Survey studies are generally in the format of surveys, interviews, or questionnaires as part of an effort to find opinions of a particular group or to find facts about a group.

It is important to note that the findings from a survey study are only as accurate as the sample chosen from the population.

Correlational Studies

Correlational studies seek to determine how much one variable is affected by changes in a second variable. For example, correlational studies may look for a relationship between the amount of time a student spends studying for a test and the grade that student earned on the test or between student scores on college admissions tests and student grades in college.

It is important to note that correlational studies cannot show a cause and effect, but rather can show only that two variables are or are not potentially correlated.

Experimental Studies

Experimental studies take correlational studies one step farther, in that they attempt to prove or disprove a cause-and-effect relationship. These studies are performed by conducting a series of experiments to test the hypothesis. For a study to be scientifically accurate, it must have both an experimental group that receives the specified treatment and a control group that does not get the treatment. This is the type of study pharmaceutical companies do as part of drug trials for new medications. Experimental studies are only valid when the proper scientific method has been followed. In other words, the experiment must be well-planned and executed without bias in the testing process, all subjects must be selected at random, and the process of determining which subject is in which of the two groups must also be completely random.

Observational Studies

Observational studies are the opposite of experimental studies. In observational studies, the tester cannot change or in any way control all of the variables in the test. For example, a study to determine which gender does better in math classes in school is strictly observational. You cannot change a person's gender, and you cannot change the subject being studied. The big downfall of observational studies is that you have no way of proving a cause-and-effect relationship because you cannot control outside influences. Events outside of school can influence a student's performance in school, and observational studies cannot take that into consideration.

Random Samples

For most studies, a **random sample** is necessary to produce valid results. Random samples should not have any particular influence to cause sampled subjects to behave one way or another. The goal is for the random sample to be a **representative sample**, or a sample whose characteristics give an accurate picture of the characteristics of the entire population. To accomplish this, you must make sure you have a proper **sample size**, or an appropriate number of elements in the sample.

Biases

In statistical studies, biases must be avoided. **Bias** is an error that causes the study to favor one set of results over another. For example, if a survey to determine how the country views the president's job performance only speaks to registered voters in the president's party, the results will be skewed because a disproportionately large number of responders would tend to show approval, while a disproportionately large number of people in the opposite party would tend to express disapproval. **Extraneous variables** are, as the name implies, outside influences that can affect the outcome of a study. They are not always avoidable but could trigger bias in the result.

DATA ANALYSIS

DISPERSION

A **measure of dispersion** is a single value that helps to "interpret" the measure of central tendency by providing more information about how the data values in the set are distributed about the measure of central tendency. The measure of dispersion helps to eliminate or reduce the disadvantages of using the mean, median, or mode as a single measure of central tendency, and give a more accurate picture of the dataset as a whole. To have a measure of dispersion, you must know or calculate the range, standard deviation, or variance of the data set.

RANGE

The **range** of a set of data is the difference between the greatest and lowest values of the data in the set. To calculate the range, you must first make sure the units for all data values are the same, and then identify the greatest and lowest values. If there are multiple data values that are equal for the highest or lowest, just use one of the values in the formula. Write the answer with the same units as the data values you used to do the calculations.

Review Video: Statistical Range
Visit mometrix.com/academy and enter code: 778541

SAMPLE STANDARD DEVIATION

Standard deviation is a measure of dispersion that compares all the data values in the set to the mean of the set to give a more accurate picture. To find the **standard deviation of a sample**, use the formula

$$s = \sqrt{\frac{\sum_{i=1}^{n}(x_i - \bar{x})^2}{n - 1}}$$

Note that s is the standard deviation of a sample, x_i represents the individual values in the data set, $\bar{x}$ is the mean of the data values in the set, and n is the number of data values in the set. The higher the value of the standard deviation is, the greater the variance of the data values from the mean. The units associated with the standard deviation are the same as the units of the data values.

Review Video: Standard Deviation
Visit mometrix.com/academy and enter code: 419469

SAMPLE VARIANCE

The **variance of a sample** is the square of the sample standard deviation (denoted s^2). While the mean of a set of data gives the average of the set and gives information about where a specific data value lies in relation to the average, the variance of the sample gives information about the degree to which the data values are spread out and tells you how close an individual value is to the average compared to the other values. The units associated with variance are the same as the units of the data values squared.

PERCENTILE

Percentiles and quartiles are other methods of describing data within a set. **Percentiles** tell what percentage of the data in the set fall below a specific point. For example, achievement test scores are often given in percentiles. A score at the 80th percentile is one which is equal to or higher than 80 percent of the scores in the set. In other words, 80 percent of the scores were lower than that score.

Quartiles are percentile groups that make up quarter sections of the data set. The first quartile is the 25th percentile. The second quartile is the 50th percentile; this is also the median of the dataset. The third quartile is the 75th percentile.

SKEWNESS

Skewness is a way to describe the symmetry or asymmetry of the distribution of values in a dataset. If the distribution of values is symmetrical, there is no skew. In general the closer the mean of a data set is to the median of the data set, the less skew there is. Generally, if the mean is to the right of the median, the data set is *positively skewed*, or right-skewed, and if the mean is to the left of the median, the data set is *negatively skewed*, or left-skewed. However, this rule of thumb is not infallible. When the data values are graphed on a curve, a set with no skew will be a perfect bell curve.

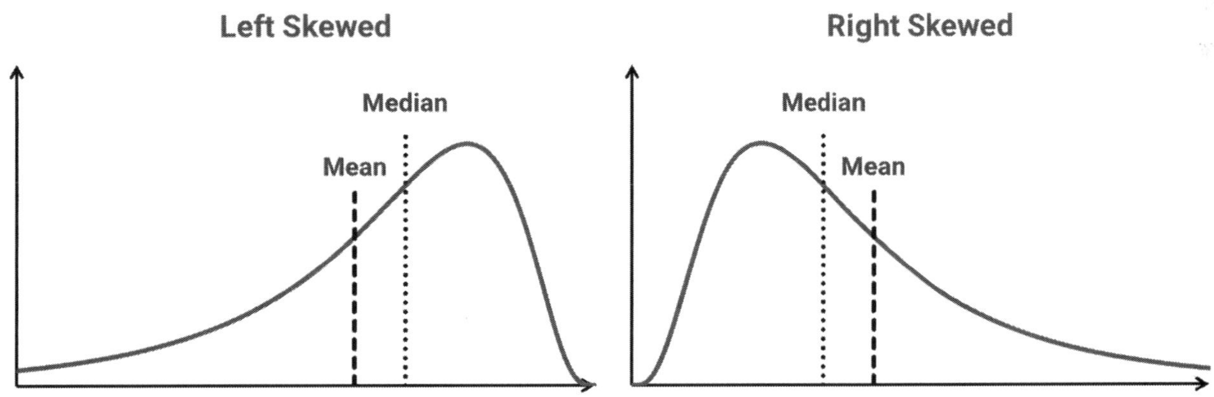

To estimate skew, use the formula:

$$\text{skew} = \frac{\sqrt{n(n-1)}}{n-2}\left(\frac{\frac{1}{n}\sum_{i=1}^{n}(x_i - \bar{x})^3}{\left(\frac{1}{n}\sum_{i=1}^{n}(x_i - \bar{x})^2\right)^{\frac{3}{2}}}\right)$$

Note that n is the datapoints in the set, x_i is the ith value in the set, and $\bar{x}$ is the mean of the set.

Review Video: Skew
Visit mometrix.com/academy and enter code: 661486

UNIMODAL VS. BIMODAL

If a distribution has a single peak, it would be considered **unimodal**. If it has two discernible peaks it would be considered **bimodal**. Bimodal distributions may be an indication that the set of data being considered is actually the combination of two sets of data with significant differences. A

uniform distribution is a distribution in which there is *no distinct peak or variation* in the data. No values or ranges are particularly more common than any other values or ranges.

OUTLIER

An outlier is an extremely high or extremely low value in the data set. It may be the result of measurement error, in which case, the outlier is not a valid member of the data set. However, it may also be a valid member of the distribution. Unless a measurement error is identified, the experimenter cannot know for certain if an outlier is or is not a member of the distribution. There are arbitrary methods that can be employed to designate an extreme value as an outlier. One method designates an outlier (or possible outlier) to be any value less than $Q_1 - 1.5(IQR)$ or any value greater than $Q_3 + 1.5(IQR)$.

DATA ANALYSIS

SIMPLE REGRESSION

In statistics, **simple regression** is using an equation to represent a relation between independent and dependent variables. The independent variable is also referred to as the explanatory variable or the predictor and is generally represented by the variable x in the equation. The dependent variable, usually represented by the variable y, is also referred to as the response variable. The equation may be any type of function – linear, quadratic, exponential, etc. The best way to handle this task is to use the regression feature of your graphing calculator. This will easily give you the curve of best fit and provide you with the coefficients and other information you need to derive an equation.

LINE OF BEST FIT

In a scatter plot, the **line of best fit** is the line that best shows the trends of the data. The line of best fit is given by the equation $\hat{y} = ax + b$, where a and b are the regression coefficients. The regression coefficient a is also the slope of the line of best fit, and b is also the y-coordinate of the point at which the line of best fit crosses the y-axis. Not every point on the scatter plot will be on the line of best fit. The differences between the y-values of the points in the scatter plot and the corresponding y-values according to the equation of the line of best fit are the residuals. The line of best fit is also called the least-squares regression line because it is also the line that has the lowest sum of the squares of the residuals.

CORRELATION COEFFICIENT

The **correlation coefficient** is the numerical value that indicates how strong the relationship is between the two variables of a linear regression equation. A correlation coefficient of −1 is a perfect negative correlation. A correlation coefficient of +1 is a perfect positive correlation. Correlation coefficients close to −1 or +1 are very strong correlations. A correlation coefficient equal to zero indicates there is no correlation between the two variables. This test is a good indicator of whether or not the equation for the line of best fit is accurate. The formula for the correlation coefficient is

$$r = \frac{\sum_{i=1}^{n}(x_i - \bar{x})(y_i - \bar{y})}{\sqrt{\sum_{i=1}^{n}(x_i - \bar{x})^2}\sqrt{\sum_{i=1}^{n}(y_i - \bar{y})^2}}$$

where r is the correlation coefficient, n is the number of data values in the set, (x_i, y_i) is a point in the set, and $\bar{x}$ and $\bar{y}$ are the means.

Z-Score

A **z-score** is an indication of how many standard deviations a given value falls from the sample mean. To calculate a z-score, use the formula:

$$\frac{x - \bar{x}}{\sigma}$$

In this formula x is the data value, $\bar{x}$ is the mean of the sample data, and σ is the standard deviation of the population. If the z-score is positive, the data value lies above the mean. If the z-score is negative, the data value falls below the mean. These scores are useful in interpreting data such as standardized test scores, where every piece of data in the set has been counted, rather than just a small random sample. In cases where standard deviations are calculated from a random sample of the set, the z-scores will not be as accurate.

Central Limit Theorem

According to the **central limit theorem**, regardless of what the original distribution of a sample is, the distribution of the means tends to get closer and closer to a normal distribution as the sample size gets larger and larger (this is necessary because the sample is becoming more all-encompassing of the elements of the population). As the sample size gets larger, the distribution of the sample mean will approach a normal distribution with a mean of the population mean and a variance of the population variance divided by the sample size.

Measures of Central Tendency

A **measure of central tendency** is a statistical value that gives a reasonable estimate for the center of a group of data. There are several different ways of describing the measure of central tendency. Each one has a unique way it is calculated, and each one gives a slightly different perspective on the data set. Whenever you give a measure of central tendency, always make sure the units are the same. If the data has different units, such as hours, minutes, and seconds, convert all the data to the same unit, and use the same unit in the measure of central tendency. If no units are given in the data, do not give units for the measure of central tendency.

Mean

The **statistical mean** of a group of data is the same as the arithmetic average of that group. To find the mean of a set of data, first convert each value to the same units, if necessary. Then find the sum of all the values, and count the total number of data values, making sure you take into consideration each individual value. If a value appears more than once, count it more than once. Divide the sum of the values by the total number of values and apply the units, if any. Note that the mean does not have to be one of the data values in the set, and may not divide evenly.

$$\text{mean} = \frac{\text{sum of the data values}}{\text{quantity of data values}}$$

For instance, the mean of the data set $\{88, 72, 61, 90, 97, 68, 88, 79, 86, 93, 97, 71, 80, 84, 89\}$ would be the sum of the fifteen numbers divided by 15:

$$\frac{88 + 72 + 61 + 90 + 97 + 68 + 88 + 79 + 86 + 93 + 97 + 71 + 80 + 84 + 89}{15} = \frac{1242}{15} = 82.8$$

While the mean is relatively easy to calculate and averages are understood by most people, the mean can be very misleading if it is used as the sole measure of central tendency. If the data set has

Probability and Statistics

outliers (data values that are unusually high or unusually low compared to the rest of the data values), the mean can be very distorted, especially if the data set has a small number of values. If unusually high values are countered with unusually low values, the mean is not affected as much. For example, if five of twenty students in a class get a 100 on a test, but the other 15 students have an average of 60 on the same test, the class average would appear as 70. Whenever the mean is skewed by outliers, it is always a good idea to include the median as an alternate measure of central tendency.

A **weighted mean**, or weighted average, is a mean that uses "weighted" values. The formula is weighted mean $= \frac{w_1x_1+w_2x_2+w_3x_3...+w_nx_n}{w_1+w_2+w_3+\cdots+w_n}$. Weighted values, such as $w_1, w_2, w_3, ... w_n$ are assigned to each member of the set $x_1, x_2, x_3, ... x_n$. When calculating the weighted mean, make sure a weight value for each member of the set is used.

Review Video: All About Averages
Visit mometrix.com/academy and enter code: 176521

MEDIAN

The **statistical median** is the value in the middle of the set of data. To find the median, list all data values in order from smallest to largest or from largest to smallest. Any value that is repeated in the set must be listed the number of times it appears. If there are an odd number of data values, the median is the value in the middle of the list. If there is an even number of data values, the median is the arithmetic mean of the two middle values.

For example, the median of the data set {88, 72, 61, 90, 97, 68, 88, 79, 86, 93, 97, 71, 80, 84, 88} is 86 since the ordered set is {61, 68, 71, 72, 79, 80, 84, **86**, 88, 88, 88, 90, 93, 97, 97}.

The big disadvantage of using the median as a measure of central tendency is that is relies solely on a value's relative size as compared to the other values in the set. When the individual values in a set of data are evenly dispersed, the median can be an accurate tool. However, if there is a group of rather large values or a group of rather small values that are not offset by a different group of values, the information that can be inferred from the median may not be accurate because the distribution of values is skewed.

MODE

The **statistical mode** is the data value that occurs the greatest number of times in the data set. It is possible to have exactly one mode, more than one mode, or no mode. To find the mode of a set of data, arrange the data like you do to find the median (all values in order, listing all multiples of data values). Count the number of times each value appears in the data set. If all values appear an equal number of times, there is no mode. If one value appears more than any other value, that value is the mode. If two or more values appear the same number of times, but there are other values that appear fewer times and no values that appear more times, all of those values are the modes.

For example, the mode of the data set {**88**, 72, 61, 90, 97, 68, **88**, 79, 86, 93, 97, 71, 80, 84, **88**} is 88.

The main disadvantage of the mode is that the values of the other data in the set have no bearing on the mode. The mode may be the largest value, the smallest value, or a value anywhere in between in the set. The mode only tells which value or values, if any, occurred the greatest number of times. It does not give any suggestions about the remaining values in the set.

Review Video: Mean, Median, and Mode
Visit mometrix.com/academy and enter code: 286207

Probability

PROBABILITY

Probability is the likelihood of a certain outcome occurring for a given event. An **event** is any situation that produces a result. It could be something as simple as flipping a coin or as complex as launching a rocket. Determining the probability of an outcome for an event can be equally simple or complex. As such, there are specific terms used in the study of probability that need to be understood:

- **Compound event**—an event that involves two or more independent events (rolling a pair of dice and taking the sum)
- **Desired outcome** (or success)—an outcome that meets a particular set of criteria (a roll of 1 or 2 if we are looking for numbers less than 3)
- **Independent events**—two or more events whose outcomes do not affect one another (two coins tossed at the same time)
- **Dependent events**—two or more events whose outcomes affect one another (two cards drawn consecutively from the same deck)
- **Certain outcome**—probability of outcome is 100% or 1
- **Impossible outcome**—probability of outcome is 0% or 0
- **Mutually exclusive outcomes**—two or more outcomes whose criteria cannot all be satisfied in a single event (a coin coming up heads and tails on the same toss)
- **Random variable**—refers to all possible outcomes of a single event which may be discrete or continuous.

Review Video: Intro to Probability
Visit mometrix.com/academy and enter code: 212374

SAMPLE SPACE

The total set of all possible results of a test or experiment is called a **sample space**, or sometimes a universal sample space. The sample space, represented by one of the variables S, Ω, or U (for universal sample space) has individual elements called outcomes. Other terms for outcome that may be used interchangeably include elementary outcome, simple event, or sample point. The number of outcomes in a given sample space could be infinite or finite, and some tests may yield multiple unique sample sets. For example, tests conducted by drawing playing cards from a standard deck would have one sample space of the card values, another sample space of the card suits, and a third sample space of suit-denomination combinations. For most tests, the sample spaces considered will be finite.

An **event**, represented by the variable E, is a portion of a sample space. It may be one outcome or a group of outcomes from the same sample space. If an event occurs, then the test or experiment will generate an outcome that satisfies the requirement of that event. For example, given a standard deck of 52 playing cards as the sample space, and defining the event as the collection of face cards, then the event will occur if the card drawn is a J, Q, or K. If any other card is drawn, the event is said to have not occurred.

For every sample space, each possible outcome has a specific likelihood, or probability, that it will occur. The probability measure, also called the **distribution**, is a function that assigns a real number probability, from zero to one, to each outcome. For a probability measure to be accurate, every outcome must have a real number probability measure that is greater than or equal to zero and less than or equal to one. Also, the probability measure of the sample space must equal one, and the probability measure of the union of multiple outcomes must equal the sum of the individual probability measures.

Probabilities of events are expressed as real numbers from zero to one. They give a numerical value to the chance that a particular event will occur. The probability of an event occurring is the sum of the probabilities of the individual elements of that event. For example, in a standard deck of 52 playing cards as the sample space and the collection of face cards as the event, the probability of drawing a specific face card is $\frac{1}{52} = 0.019$, but the probability of drawing any one of the twelve face cards is $12(0.019) = 0.228$. Note that rounding of numbers can generate different results. If you multiplied 12 by the fraction $\frac{1}{52}$ before converting to a decimal, you would get the answer $\frac{12}{52} = 0.231$.

Theoretical and Experimental Probability

Theoretical probability can usually be determined without actually performing the event. The likelihood of an outcome occurring, or the probability of an outcome occurring, is given by the formula:

$$P(A) = \frac{\text{Number of acceptable outcomes}}{\text{Number of possible outcomes}}$$

Note that $P(A)$ is the probability of an outcome A occurring, and each outcome is just as likely to occur as any other outcome. If each outcome has the same probability of occurring as every other possible outcome, the outcomes are said to be equally likely to occur. The total number of acceptable outcomes must be less than or equal to the total number of possible outcomes. If the two are equal, then the outcome is certain to occur and the probability is 1. If the number of acceptable outcomes is zero, then the outcome is impossible and the probability is 0. For example, if there are 20 marbles in a bag and 5 are red, then the theoretical probability of randomly selecting a red marble is 5 out of 20, $\left(\frac{5}{20} = \frac{1}{4}, 0.25, \text{or } 25\%\right)$.

If the theoretical probability is unknown or too complicated to calculate, it can be estimated by an experimental probability. **Experimental probability**, also called empirical probability, is an estimate of the likelihood of a certain outcome based on repeated experiments or collected data. In other words, while theoretical probability is based on what *should* happen, experimental probability is based on what *has* happened. Experimental probability is calculated in the same way as theoretical probability, except that actual outcomes are used instead of possible outcomes. The more experiments performed or datapoints gathered, the better the estimate should be.

Theoretical and experimental probability do not always line up with one another. Theoretical probability says that out of 20 coin-tosses, 10 should be heads. However, if we were actually to toss 20 coins, we might record just 5 heads. This doesn't mean that our theoretical probability is incorrect; it just means that this particular experiment had results that were different from what was predicted. A practical application of empirical probability is the insurance industry. There are no set functions that define lifespan, health, or safety. Insurance companies look at factors from hundreds of thousands of individuals to find patterns that they then use to set the formulas for insurance premiums.

Review Video: Empirical Probability
Visit mometrix.com/academy and enter code: 513468

Objective and Subjective Probability

Objective probability is based on mathematical formulas and documented evidence. Examples of objective probability include raffles or lottery drawings where there is a pre-determined number of possible outcomes and a predetermined number of outcomes that correspond to an event. Other cases of objective probability include probabilities of rolling dice, flipping coins, or drawing cards. Most gambling games are based on objective probability.

In contrast, **subjective probability** is based on personal or professional feelings and judgments. Often, there is a lot of guesswork following extensive research. Areas where subjective probability is applicable include sales trends and business expenses. Attractions set admission prices based on subjective probabilities of attendance based on varying admission rates in an effort to maximize their profit.

Complement of an Event

Sometimes it may be easier to calculate the possibility of something not happening, or the **complement of an event**. Represented by the symbol $\bar{A}$, the complement of A is the probability that event A does not happen. When you know the probability of event A occurring, you can use the formula $P(\bar{A}) = 1 - P(A)$, where $P(\bar{A})$ is the probability of event A not occurring, and $P(A)$ is the probability of event A occurring.

Addition Rule

The **addition rule** for probability is used for finding the probability of a compound event. Use the formula $P(A \cup B) = P(A) + P(B) - P(A \cap B)$, where $P(A \cap B)$ is the probability of both events occurring to find the probability of a compound event. The probability of both events occurring at the same time must be subtracted to eliminate any overlap in the first two probabilities.

Conditional Probability

Given two events A and B, the **conditional probability** $P(A|B)$ is the probability that event A will occur, given that event B has occurred. The conditional probability cannot be calculated simply from $P(A)$ and $P(B)$; these probabilities alone do not give sufficient information to determine the conditional probability. It can, however, be determined if you are also given the probability of the intersection of events A and B, $P(A \cap B)$, the probability that events A and B both occur. Specifically, $P(A|B) = \frac{P(A \cap B)}{P(B)}$. For instance, suppose you have a jar containing two red marbles and two blue marbles, and you draw two marbles at random. Consider event A being the event that the first marble drawn is red, and event B being the event that the second marble drawn is blue. If we want to find the probability that B occurs given that A occurred, $P(B|A)$, then we can compute it using the fact that $P(A)$ is $\frac{1}{2}$, and $P(A \cap B)$ is $\frac{1}{3}$. (The latter may not be obvious, but may be determined by finding the product of $\frac{1}{2}$ and $\frac{2}{3}$). Therefore $P(B|A) = \frac{P(A \cap B)}{P(A)} = \frac{1/3}{1/2} = \frac{2}{3}$.

Conditional Probability in Everyday Situations

Conditional probability often arises in everyday situations in, for example, estimating the risk or benefit of certain activities. The conditional probability of having a heart attack given that you exercise daily may be smaller than the overall probability of having a heart attack. The conditional probability of having lung cancer given that you are a smoker is larger than the overall probability of having lung cancer. Note that changing the order of the conditional probability changes the meaning: the conditional probability of having lung cancer given that you are a smoker is a very different thing from the probability of being a smoker given that you have lung cancer. In an extreme case, suppose that a certain rare disease is caused only by eating a certain food, but even then, it is unlikely. Then the conditional probability of having that disease given that you eat the dangerous food is nonzero but low, but the conditional probability of having eaten that food given that you have the disease is 100%!

Review Video: Conditional Probability
Visit mometrix.com/academy and enter code: 397924

Independence

The conditional probability $P(A|B)$ is the probability that event A will occur given that event B occurs. If the two events are independent, we do not expect that whether or not event B occurs should have any effect on whether or not event A occurs. In other words, we expect $P(A|B) = P(A)$.

This can be proven using the usual equations for conditional probability and the joint probability of independent events. The conditional probability $P(A|B) = \frac{P(A \cap B)}{P(B)}$. If A and B are independent, then $P(A \cap B) = P(A)P(B)$. So $P(A|B) = \frac{P(A)P(B)}{P(B)} = P(A)$. By similar reasoning, if A and B are independent then $P(B|A) = P(B)$.

Multiplication Rule

The **multiplication rule** can be used to find the probability of two independent events occurring using the formula $P(A \cap B) = P(A) \times P(B)$, where $P(A \cap B)$ is the probability of two independent events occurring, $P(A)$ is the probability of the first event occurring, and $P(B)$ is the probability of the second event occurring.

The multiplication rule can also be used to find the probability of two dependent events occurring using the formula $P(A \cap B) = P(A) \times P(B|A)$, where $P(A \cap B)$ is the probability of two dependent events occurring and $P(B|A)$ is the probability of the second event occurring after the first event has already occurred.

Use a **combination of the multiplication** rule and the rule of complements to find the probability that at least one outcome of the element will occur. This is given by the general formula $P(\text{at least one event occurring}) = 1 - P(\text{no outcomes occurring})$. For example, to find the probability that at least one even number will show when a pair of dice is rolled, find the probability that two odd numbers will be rolled (no even numbers) and subtract from one. You can always use a tree diagram or make a chart to list the possible outcomes when the sample space is small, such as in the dice-rolling example, but in most cases it will be much faster to use the multiplication and complement formulas.

Review Video: Multiplication Rule
Visit mometrix.com/academy and enter code: 782598

Union and Intersection of Two Sets of Outcomes

If A and B are each a set of elements or outcomes from an experiment, then the **union** (symbol ∪) of the two sets is the set of elements found in set A or set B. For example, if $A = \{2, 3, 4\}$ and $B = \{3, 4, 5\}$, $A \cup B = \{2, 3, 4, 5\}$. Note that the outcomes 3 and 4 appear only once in the union. For statistical events, the union is equivalent to "or"; $P(A \cup B)$ is the same thing as $P(A \text{ or } B)$. The **intersection** (symbol ∩) of two sets is the set of outcomes common to both sets. For the above sets

A and B, $A \cap B = \{3, 4\}$. For statistical events, the intersection is equivalent to "and"; $P(A \cap B)$ is the same thing as $P(A \text{ and } B)$. It is important to note that union and intersection operations commute. That is:

$$A \cup B = B \cup A \text{ and } A \cap B = B \cap A$$

PERMUTATIONS AND COMBINATIONS IN PROBABILITY

When trying to calculate the probability of an event using the $\frac{\text{desired outcomes}}{\text{total outcomes}}$ formula, you may frequently find that there are too many outcomes to individually count them. **Permutation** and **combination formulas** offer a shortcut to counting outcomes. A permutation is an arrangement of a specific number of a set of objects in a specific order. The number of **permutations** of r items given a set of n items can be calculated as ${}_nP_r = \frac{n!}{(n-r)!}$. Combinations are similar to permutations, except there are no restrictions regarding the order of the elements. While ABC is considered a different permutation than BCA, ABC and BCA are considered the same combination. The number of **combinations** of r items given a set of n items can be calculated as ${}_nC_r = \frac{n!}{r!(n-r)!}$ or ${}_nC_r = \frac{{}_nP_r}{r!}$.

Suppose you want to calculate how many different 5-card hands can be drawn from a deck of 52 cards. This is a combination since the order of the cards in a hand does not matter. There are 52 cards available, and 5 to be selected. Thus, the number of different hands is ${}_{52}C_5 = \frac{52!}{5! \times 47!} =$ 2,598,960.

Review Video: Probability - Permutation and Combination
Visit mometrix.com/academy and enter code: 907664

TREE DIAGRAMS

For a simple sample space, possible outcomes may be determined by using a **tree diagram** or an organized chart. In either case, you can easily draw or list out the possible outcomes. For example, to determine all the possible ways three objects can be ordered, you can draw a tree diagram:

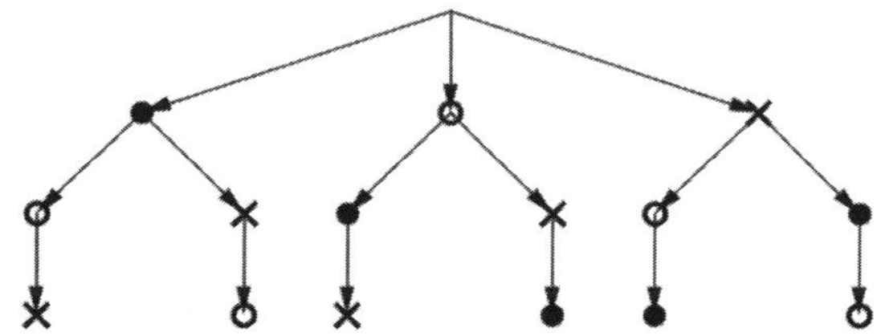

Review Video: Tree Diagrams
Visit mometrix.com/academy and enter code: 829158

You can also make a chart to list all the possibilities:

First object	Second object	Third object
●	x	o
●	o	x
o	●	x
o	x	●
x	●	o
x	o	●

Either way, you can easily see there are six possible ways the three objects can be ordered.

If two events have no outcomes in common, they are said to be **mutually exclusive**. For example, in a standard deck of 52 playing cards, the event of all card suits is mutually exclusive to the event of all card values. If two events have no bearing on each other so that one event occurring has no influence on the probability of another event occurring, the two events are said to be independent. For example, rolling a standard six-sided die multiple times does not change that probability that a particular number will be rolled from one roll to the next. If the outcome of one event does affect the probability of the second event, the two events are said to be dependent. For example, if cards are drawn from a deck, the probability of drawing an ace after an ace has been drawn is different than the probability of drawing an ace if no ace (or no other card, for that matter) has been drawn.

In probability, the **odds in favor of an event** are the number of times the event will occur compared to the number of times the event will not occur. To calculate the odds in favor of an event, use the formula $\frac{P(A)}{1-P(A)}$, where $P(A)$ is the probability that the event will occur. Many times, odds in favor is given as a ratio in the form $\frac{a}{b}$ or $a:b$, where a is the probability of the event occurring and b is the complement of the event, the probability of the event not occurring. If the odds in favor are given as 2:5, that means that you can expect the event to occur two times for every 5 times that it does not occur. In other words, the probability that the event will occur is $\frac{2}{2+5}=\frac{2}{7}$.

In probability, the **odds against an event** are the number of times the event will not occur compared to the number of times the event will occur. To calculate the odds against an event, use the formula $\frac{1-P(A)}{P(A)}$, where $P(A)$ is the probability that the event will occur. Many times, odds against is given as a ratio in the form $\frac{b}{a}$ or $b:a$, where b is the probability the event will not occur (the complement of the event) and a is the probability the event will occur. If the odds against an event are given as 3:1, that means that you can expect the event to not occur 3 times for every one time it does occur. In other words, 3 out of every 4 trials will fail.

Two-Way Frequency Tables

If we have a two-way frequency table, it is generally a straightforward matter to read off the probabilities of any two events A and B, as well as the joint probability of both events occurring, $P(A \cap B)$. We can then find the conditional probability $P(A|B)$ by calculating $P(A|B)=\frac{P(A\cap B)}{P(B)}$. We could also check whether or not events are independent by verifying whether $P(A)P(B)=P(A\cap B)$.

For example, a certain store's recent T-shirt sales:

	Small	Medium	Large	Total
Blue	25	40	35	100
White	27	25	22	74
Black	8	23	15	46
Total	60	88	72	220

Suppose we want to find the conditional probability that a customer buys a black shirt (event A), given that the shirt he buys is size small (event B). From the table, the probability $P(B)$ that a customer buys a small shirt is $\frac{60}{220} = \frac{3}{11}$. The probability $P(A \cap B)$ that he buys a small, black shirt is $\frac{8}{220} = \frac{2}{55}$. The conditional probability $P(A|B)$ that he buys a black shirt, given that he buys a small shirt, is therefore $P(A|B) = \frac{2/55}{3/11} = \frac{2}{15}$.

Similarly, if we want to check whether the event a customer buys a blue shirt, A, is independent of the event that a customer buys a medium shirt, B. From the table, $P(A) = \frac{100}{220} = \frac{5}{11}$ and $P(B) = \frac{88}{220} = \frac{4}{10}$. Also, $P(A \cap B) = \frac{40}{220} = \frac{2}{11}$. Since $\left(\frac{5}{11}\right)\left(\frac{4}{10}\right) = \frac{20}{110} = \frac{2}{11}$, $P(A)P(B) = P(A \cap B)$ and these two events are indeed independent.

Expected Value

Expected value is a method of determining the expected outcome in a random situation. It is a sum of the weighted probabilities of the possible outcomes. Multiply the probability of an event occurring by the weight assigned to that probability (such as the amount of money won or lost). A practical application of the expected value is to determine whether a game of chance is really fair. If the sum of the weighted probabilities is equal to zero, the game is generally considered fair because the player has a fair chance to at least break even. If the expected value is less than zero, then players are expected to lose more than they win. For example, a lottery drawing might allow the player to choose any three-digit number, 000–999. The probability of choosing the winning number is 1:1000. If it costs \$1 to play, and a winning number receives \$500, the expected value is $\left(-\$1 \times \frac{999}{1{,}000}\right) + \left(\$499 \times \frac{1}{1{,}000}\right) = -\$0.50$. You can expect to lose on average 50 cents for every dollar you spend.

Review Video: Expected Value
Visit mometrix.com/academy and enter code: 643554

Expected Value and Simulators

A die roll simulator will show the results of n rolls of a die. The result of each die roll may be recorded. For example, suppose a die is rolled 100 times. All results may be recorded. The numbers of 1s, 2s, 3s, 4s, 5s, and 6s, may be counted. The experimental probability of rolling each number will equal the ratio of the frequency of the rolled number to the total number of rolls. As the number of rolls increases, or approaches infinity, the experimental probability will approach the theoretical probability of $\frac{1}{6}$. Thus, the expected value for the roll of a die is shown to be $\left(1 \times \frac{1}{6}\right) + \left(2 \times \frac{1}{6}\right) + \left(3 \times \frac{1}{6}\right) + \left(4 \times \frac{1}{6}\right) + \left(5 \times \frac{1}{6}\right) + \left(6 \times \frac{1}{6}\right)$, or 3.5.

Chapter Quiz

Ready to see how well you retained what you just read? Scan the QR code to go directly to the chapter quiz interface for this study guide. If you're using a computer, simply visit the online resources page at **mometrix.com/resources719/texesmath4-8** and click the Chapter Quizzes link.

Mathematical Processes and Perspectives

Statement Logic

Premise and Argument

A premise is a statement that precedes a conclusion, in an argument. It is the proposition, or assumption, of an argument. An argument will have two or more premises.

Example:

If it is hot, then I will go swimming. (Premise)
It is hot. (Premise)
Therefore, I will go swimming. (Conclusion)

Simple and Compound Statements

A **statement** in propositional logic is any sentence or expression that has a truth value—that is, that may in principle be considered true or false. "Hello!", for example, is not a statement; there's no sense in which it could be considered true or false. On the other hand, "$2 = 3$" *is* a statement, albeit a clearly false one. A **compound statement** is a statement that contains one or more other statements, combined or modified in some way. A **simple statement**, or a **proposition**, is a statement that cannot be broken down further into smaller statements.

For example, consider the statement, "If it rains tomorrow, then the streets will be flooded and traffic will be slow." This is a compound statement, because two smaller statements are embedded within it: "it rains tomorrow" and "the streets will be flooded and traffic will be slow." the former cannot be broken down further, and is therefore a simple statement, but the latter is another compound statement, because it includes two simple statements: "the streets will be flooded" and "traffic will be slow."

Common operations used to combine and modify simple statements into compound statements include conjunction, disjunction, negation, and implication.

Logical Reasoning

Conjunction

Conjunction is an operation that combines two or more statements into a compound statement that is true if and only if all of the component statements are true. When the statements are written out, conjunction is marked by the word "and." For example, the statement "Roses are red and violets are blue" is a compound statement that is a conjunction of the two simple statements "roses are red" and "violets are blue."

Conjunction is represented by the operator $\wedge$. In the previous example, if proposition P is "roses are red" and proposition Q is "violets are blue," then the compound statement "roses are red and violets are blue" would be written as "$P \wedge Q$."

Disjunction

Disjunction is an operation that combines two or more statements into a compound statement that is true if and only if at least one of the component statements is true. When the statements are written out, disjunction is marked by the word "or." For example, the statement "I'll clean the closet today, or you'll clean it tomorrow" is a compound statement that is a disjunction of the simple statements "I'll clean the closet today" and "you'll clean the closet tomorrow."

Disjunction is represented by the operator ∨. In the previous example, if proposition P is "I'll clean the closet today" and proposition Q is "you'll clean the closet tomorrow," then the compound statement "I'll clean the closet today, or you'll clean it tomorrow" would be written as "$P \vee Q$."

Note that while in everyday language "or" implies exclusivity, as one or the other option but not both, in formal logic disjunction includes the possibility of both propositions being true. If I clean the closet today *and* you clean it tomorrow, then the sample statement "I'll clean the closet today, or you'll clean it tomorrow" is true.

Conditional and Biconditional Statements

A conditional statement, or **implication**, is a compound statement of the form "if P, then Q." for instance, the statement "if a snake has rattles, then it's venomous" is a conditional statement. It can also be written "P implies Q" ("that a snake has rattles implies that it's venomous") or "P only if Q" ("a snake has rattles only if it's venomous"). the conditional statement is true when both P and Q are true, and even when P is false, regardless of Q. In other words, the conditional statement is false only when P is true and Q is false. the conditional statement is written as "$P \to Q$." P is called the **premise** of the statement, and Q the **conclusion**.

A **biconditional statement** is a combination of two conditional statements: both "if P, then Q" and "if Q, then P." To state it more concisely, "P if and only if Q." an example is "A number is even if and only if it is divisible by 2." the biconditional statement is true when P and Q are either both true or both false; it is false if P is true and Q is false or vice versa. the biconditional statement is written "$P \leftrightarrow Q$."

Existential and Universal Quantifiers

A **quantifier** is a logical construct used in a compound statement to give information on the number of subjects for which a statement is true. The **existential quantifier** specifies that the statement is true for at least one subject. It is usually introduced as "there exists," such as "there exists a real number that is equal to its own square." The symbol ∃ is used to signify the existential quantifier. For example, the preceding statement could be written as "$\exists x \in \mathbb{R}\ x = x^2$." The **universal quantifier** specifies that the statement is true for *every* subject. It is usually said as "all" or "for all", such as "all real numbers are less than their own squares plus one." The symbol ∀ is used to signify the universal quantifier. For example, the preceding statement could be written as

$$\forall x \in \mathbb{R}\ x < x^2 + 1$$

Sometimes it is useful to specify that there exists *exactly* one subject that meets a given criterion. In other words, there exists a *unique* such subject. This can be signified by adding an exclamation mark after the existential quantifier: "$\exists!\, x \in \mathbb{R}\ |x| = 0$" means "there exists a unique real number that has an absolute value of zero."

Truth Tables

A truth table shows the truth value of one or more compound statements for each possible combination of truth values of the propositions within it. The truth table contains one column for each **proposition**, and one column for each of the **compound statements** to be analyzed. It has one row for each combination of **truth values** of the propositions. Since each proposition has two possible truth values, the number of possible combinations for N propositions is 2^N, so the truth table will have 2^N rows.

The table below is a simple truth table for some common compound statements involving two propositions.

P	Q	$P \wedge Q$	$P \vee Q$	$\neg P$	$\neg Q$	$P \to Q$	$Q \to P$	$P \leftrightarrow Q$
T	T	T	T	F	F	T	T	T
T	F	F	T	F	T	F	T	F
F	T	F	T	T	F	T	F	F
F	F	F	F	T	T	T	T	T

Truth tables are useful for comparing two compound statements to see if they are equivalent. They are also useful for analyzing whether complicated compound statements are true or false. A table can have a column for each of the increasingly complex compound statements that combine to form the total statement.

Review Video: Truth Tables
Visit mometrix.com/academy and enter code: 293095

Truth Table to Validate the Rule of Detachment

The Rule of Detachment states that given the premises, $P \to Q$ and P, the valid conclusion is Q.

In other words, for every case where $(P \to Q) \wedge P$ is true, Q will also be true. The truth table below illustrates this fact:

P	Q	$P \to Q$	$(P \to Q) \wedge P$
T	T	T	T
T	F	F	F
F	T	T	F
F	F	T	F

Notice the first cell under $(P \to Q) \wedge P$ is true, while the first cell under Q is also true. Thus, for every case where $(P \to Q) \wedge P$ was true, Q was also true.

TRUTH TABLE TO VALIDATE THE CHAIN RULE

The Chain Rule states that given the premises, $P \rightarrow Q$ and $Q \rightarrow R$, the valid conclusion is $P \rightarrow R$.

In other words, for every case where $(P \rightarrow Q) \wedge (Q \rightarrow R)$ is true, $P \rightarrow R$ will also be true. The truth table below illustrates this fact:

P	Q	R	$P \rightarrow Q$	$Q \rightarrow R$	$(P \rightarrow Q) \wedge (Q \rightarrow R)$	$P \rightarrow R$
T	T	T	T	T	T	T
T	T	F	T	F	F	F
T	F	T	F	T	F	T
T	F	F	F	T	F	F
F	T	T	T	T	T	T
F	T	F	T	F	F	T
F	F	T	T	T	T	T
F	F	F	T	T	T	T

Notice that for every case where $(P \rightarrow Q) \wedge (Q \rightarrow R)$ was true, $P \rightarrow R$ was also true.

For example, consider the premises below:

If I hike a mountain, I will not eat a sandwich.
If I do not eat a sandwich, I will drink some water.
I will not drink some water.

Write a valid conclusive statement. Explain how you arrived at your answer. Be specific in your explanation.

Valid conclusive statement: I will not hike a mountain.

Application of the chain rule and rule of contraposition give the valid conclusion of $\neg P$. According to the chain rule, given $P \rightarrow \neg Q$ and $\neg Q \rightarrow R$, then $P \rightarrow R$. According to the rule of contraposition, $P \rightarrow R$ and $\neg R$ yields $\neg P$. On a truth table, for every place where $(P \rightarrow R) \wedge \neg R$ is true, $\neg P$ is also true. Thus, this is a valid conclusive statement.

Converse, Inverse, and Contrapositive Statements

The converse of a conditional statement is a conditional statement with the premise and conclusion interchanged. the converse of $P \rightarrow Q$ is $Q \rightarrow P$. The **inverse** has the premise and conclusion both negated. The inverse of $P \rightarrow Q$ is $\neg P \rightarrow \neg Q$. The **contrapositive** has the premise and conclusion both negated *and* interchanged. The contrapositive of $P \rightarrow Q$ is $\neg Q \rightarrow \neg P$.

For example, given the **conditional statement**, "If there is a key in the lock, then someone is home," the **converse** is "if someone is home, then there is a key in the lock," the **inverse** is "if there is not a key in the lock, then no one is home," and the **contrapositive** is "if no one is home, then there is not a key in the lock."

Note that the converse and inverse of a statement are *not* logically equivalent to the original statement. For instance, the statement "if $x = 4$, then $x > 2$" is true, but its converse "if $x > 2$, then $x = 4$" is not, because there are many numbers greater than 2, not just 4. A statement *is*, however, logically equivalent to its contrapositive—and the converse and inverse, while not equivalent to the original statement, are equivalent to each other. The following truth table summarizes the relationships:

P	Q	$\neg P$	$\neg Q$	$P \to Q$ (statement)	$Q \to P$ (converse)	$\neg P \to \neg Q$ (inverse)	$\neg Q \to \neg P$ (contrapositive)
T	T	F	F	T	T	T	T
T	F	F	T	F	T	T	F
F	T	T	F	T	F	F	T
F	F	T	T	T	T	T	T

Review Video: Converse, Inverse, and Contrapositive
Visit mometrix.com/academy and enter code: 822844

Negation

In propositional logic, negation refers to the inversion of the truth value of a statement. The **negation** of a statement is true if the original statement is false, and false if the original statement is true. Negation can be signified by the word "not." For instance, the negation of the statement "Bob's cat is black" is "Bob's cat is not black." the symbol for negation is $\neg$. So, if the proposition P is "Bob's cat is black," then $\neg P$ would be "Bob's cat is not black." Two negations cancel each other out: $\neg\neg P = P$, or "not not P equals P."

It's important to be careful when combining negation with **quantifiers**. The negation of "there exists a cow that has a blue horn" is not "there exists a cow that does not have a blue horn." Rather, the negation is "there does not exist a cow that has a blue horn." the statements $\neg\exists x\ P(x)$ and $\exists x\ \neg P(x)$ are not equivalent. The same is true for the universal quantifier: $\neg\forall x\ P(x)$ and $\forall x\ \neg P(x)$ do not mean the same thing. There is, however, a connection between the negated quantifiers: $\neg\exists x\ P(x)$ is equivalent to $\forall x\ \neg P(x)$, and $\exists x\ \neg P(x)$ is equivalent to $\neg\forall x\ P(x)$.

Review Video: Negation
Visit mometrix.com/academy and enter code: 429150

De Morgan's Laws

De Morgan's Laws are a set of useful relations connecting negation, conjunction, and disjunction. They can be stated briefly as "the negation of a conjunction is the disjunction of the negations" and "the negation of a disjunction is the conjunction of the negations." This can be written as:

$$\neg(P \wedge Q) \leftrightarrow (\neg P) \vee (\neg Q) \text{ and } \neg(P \vee Q) \leftrightarrow (\neg P) \wedge (\neg Q)$$

For instance, if proposition P is "$x > 3$" and proposition Q is "$y > 3$", then De Morgan's Laws state that "it is not true that both x and y are greater than 3" is equivalent to "either x is not greater than 3, or y is not greater than 3."

The validity of **De Morgan's Laws** can be shown with truth tables. Note that the columns highlighted in the same color match:

P	Q	$\neg P$	$\neg Q$	$(\neg P) \wedge (\neg Q)$	$(\neg P) \vee (\neg Q)$	$P \wedge Q$	$P \vee Q$	$\neg(P \wedge Q)$	$\neg(P \vee Q)$
T	T	F	F	F	F	T	T	F	F
T	F	F	T	F	T	F	T	T	F
F	T	T	F	F	T	F	T	T	F
F	F	T	T	T	T	F	F	T	T

Types of Reasoning

Inductive Reasoning

Inductive reasoning is a method used to make a conjecture, based on patterns and observations. The conclusion of an inductive argument may be true or false.

Mathematical Example:

A cube has 6 faces, 8 vertices, and 12 edges. A square pyramid has 5 faces, 5 vertices, and 8 edges. A triangular prism has 5 faces, 6 vertices, and 9 edges. Thus, the sum of the numbers of faces and vertices, minus the number of edges, will always equal 2, for any solid.

Non-Mathematical Example:

Almost all summer days in Tucson are hot. It is a summer day in Tucson. Therefore, it will probably be hot.

Deductive Reasoning

Deductive reasoning is a method that proves a hypothesis or set of premises. The conclusion of a valid deductive argument will be true, given that the premises are true. Deductive reasoning utilizes logic to determine a conclusion. For instance, consider the following application of the chain rule:

If a ding is a dong, then a ping is a pong.	$p \rightarrow q$
If a ping is a pong, then a ring is a ting.	$q \rightarrow r$
A ding is a dong.	p
Therefore, a ring is a ting.	$\therefore r$

Formal Reasoning

Formal reasoning, in mathematics, involves justification using formal steps and processes to arrive at a conclusion. Formal reasoning is utilized when writing proofs and using logic. For example, when applying logic, validity of a conclusion is determined by truth tables. A set of premises will yield a given conclusion. This type of thinking is formal reasoning. Writing a geometric proof also employs formal reasoning. Example:

If a quadrilateral has four congruent sides, it is a rhombus.
If a shape is a rhombus, then the diagonals are perpendicular.
A quadrilateral has four congruent sides.

Therefore, the diagonals are perpendicular.

Informal Reasoning

Informal reasoning, in mathematics, uses patterns and observations to make conjectures. The conjecture may be true or false. Several, or even many, examples may show a certain pattern, shedding light on a possible conclusion. However, informal reasoning does not provide a justifiable conclusion. A conjecture may certainly be deemed as likely or probable. However, informal reasoning will not reveal a certain conclusion. Consider the following example:

Mathematical Idea – Given a sequence that starts with 1 and each term decreases by a factor of $\frac{1}{2}$, the limit of the sum of the sequence will be 2.

Informal Reasoning – The sum of 1 and $\frac{1}{2}$ is $1\frac{1}{2}$. The sum of 1, $\frac{1}{2}$, and $\frac{1}{4}$ is $1\frac{3}{4}$. The sum of 1, $\frac{1}{2}$, $\frac{1}{4}$, and $\frac{1}{8}$ is $1\frac{7}{8}$. Thus, it appears that as the sequence approaches infinity, the sum of the sequence approaches 2.

Proofs

A **proof** serves to show the deductive or inductive process that relates the steps leading from a hypothesis to a conclusion. A proof may be direct $(p \to q)$, meaning that a conclusion is shown to be true, given a hypothesis. There are also proofs by contradiction $(p \wedge {\sim}q)$, whereby the hypothesis is assumed to be true, and the negation of the conclusion is assumed to be true. (In other words, the statement is assumed to be false.) Proofs by contraposition $({\sim}q \to {\sim}p)$ show that the negation of the conclusion leads to the negation of the hypothesis. (In other words, the negation of the conclusion is assumed to be true, and it must be shown that the negation of the hypothesis is also true.) A mathematical induction proof seeks to show that $P(1)$ is true and that $P(k+1)$ is true, given that $P(k)$ is true. Direct proofs, proofs by contradiction, and proofs by contraposition use deductive methods, while a mathematical induction proof uses an inductive method.

Direct proofs are those that assume a statement to be true. The purpose of such a proof is to show that the conclusion is true, given that the hypothesis is true. A sample of a direct proof is shown below:

Prove "If m divides a and m divides b, then m divides $a + b$."

Proof:

- Assume m divides a and m divides b.
- Thus, a equals the product of m and some integer factor, p, by the definition of division, and b equals the product of m and some integer factor, q, by the definition of division. According to substitution, $a + b$ may be rewritten as $(m \times p) + (m \times q)$. Factoring out the m gives $m(p + q)$. Since m divides $p + q$, and $p + q$ is an integer, according to the closure property, we have shown that m divides $a + b$, by the definition of division.

Indirect proofs (or proofs by contradiction) are those that assume a statement to be false. The purpose of such a proof is to show that a hypothesis is false, given the negation of the conclusion, indicating that the conclusion must be true. A sample of an indirect proof is shown below:

Prove "If $3x + 7$ is odd, then x is even."

Proof:

- Assume $3x + 7$ is odd and x is odd.
- According to the definition of odd, $x = 2a + 1$, where a is an element of the integers.
- Thus, by substitution, $3x + 7 = 3(2a + 1) + 7$, which simplifies as $6a + 3 + 7$, or $6a + 10$, which may be rewritten as $2(3a + 5)$. Any even integer may be written as the product of 2 and some integer, k. Thus, we have shown the hypothesis to be false, meaning that the conditional statement must be true.

A **proof by contraposition** is one written in the form, $\sim Q \to \sim P$. In other words, a proof by contraposition seeks to show that the negation of Q will yield the negation of P. A sample of a proof by contraposition is shown below:

Prove "If $5x + 7$ is even, then x is odd."

Proof:

- Assume that if x is even, then $5x + 7$ is odd.
- Assume x is even.
- Thus, by the definition of an even integer, $x = 2a$.

By substitution, $5x + 7$ may be rewritten as $5(2a) + 7$, which simplifies as $10a + 7$. This expression cannot be written as the product of 2 and some factor, k. Thus, $5x + 7$ is odd, by definition of an odd integer. So, when $5x + 7$ is even, x is odd, according to contraposition.

A **proof by contradiction** is one written in the form, $p \wedge \sim q$. In other words, a proof by contradiction seeks to show the negation of q will result in a false hypothesis, indicating that the conclusion of the statement, as written, must be true. In other words, the conditional statement of $p \to q$ is true.

Mathematical Induction Proof Utilizing Inductive Reasoning

A mathematical induction proof utilizes inductive reasoning in its assumption that if $P(k)$ is true, then $P(k + 1)$ is also true. The induction hypothesis is $P(k)$. This step utilizes inductive reasoning because an observation is used to make the conjecture that $P(k + 1)$ is also true.

Example:

For all natural numbers, n, the sum is equal to $(n + 1)\left(\frac{n}{2}\right)$.
Show that $P(1)$ is true.
$1 = (1 + 1)\left(\frac{1}{2}\right)$.
Assume $P(k)$ is true.
$1 + 2 + 3 + 4 + \cdots + k = (k + 1)\left(\frac{k}{2}\right)$.

This previous step is the inductive hypothesis. This hypothesis may be used to write the conjecture that $P(k+1)$ is also true: $(1+2+3+4+\cdots+k)+(k+1)=[(k+1)+1]\left(\frac{k+1}{2}\right)$

$$(k+1)\left(\frac{k}{2}\right)+(k+1)=[(k+1)+1]\left(\frac{k}{2}+\frac{1}{2}\right)$$
$$(k+1)\left(\frac{k}{2}\right)+(k+1)=\left(\frac{k}{2}(k+1)+\frac{k}{2}\right)+\left(\frac{1}{2}(k+1)+\frac{1}{2}(1)\right)$$
$$(k+1)\left(\frac{k}{2}\right)+(k+1)=\frac{k}{2}(k+1)+\frac{k}{2}+\frac{k+1}{2}+\frac{1}{2}$$
$$(k+1)\left(\frac{k}{2}\right)+(k+1)=\frac{k}{2}(k+1)+\frac{2k+2}{2}$$
$$(k+1)\left(\frac{k}{2}\right)+(k+1)=\frac{k}{2}(k+1)+(k+1)$$

Mathematical Learning, Instruction, and Assessment

Instruction and Assessment

INSTRUCTION

MATHEMATICAL JARGON

Mathematical language is hard for beginners. Words such as "or" and "only" have more precise meanings than in everyday speech. Also confusing to beginners are words such as "open" and "field" that have been given specific mathematical meanings. **Mathematical jargon** includes technical terms such as homeomorphism and integrable. But there is a reason for special notation and technical jargon. Mathematics requires more precision than everyday speech. Mathematicians refer to this precision of language and logic as rigor.

RIGOR

Rigor is fundamentally a matter of mathematical proof. Mathematicians want their theorems to follow from axioms by means of systematic reasoning. This is to avoid mistaken "theorems", based upon fallible intuitions, of which many instances have occurred in the history of the subject. The level of rigor expected in mathematics has varied over time; the Greeks expected detailed arguments, but at the time of Isaac Newton the methods employed were less rigorous. Problems inherent in the definitions used by Newton would lead to a resurgence of careful analysis and formal proof in the 19th century. Today, mathematicians continue to argue amongst themselves about computer-assisted proofs. Because large computations are hard to verify, such proofs may not be sufficiently rigorous. Axioms in traditional thought were "self-evident truths," but that conception is problematic. At a formal level, an axiom is just a string of symbols which has an intrinsic meaning only in the context of all derivable formulas of an axiomatic system. It was the goal of Hilbert's program to put all of mathematics on a firm axiomatic basis, but according to Gödel's incompleteness theorem every (sufficiently powerful) axiomatic system has undecidable formulas; and thus, a final axiomatization of mathematics is impossible. Nonetheless mathematics is often imagined to be (as far as its formal content) nothing but set theory in some axiomatization, in the sense that every mathematical statement or proof could be cast into formulas within set theory.

NUMERALS AND NAMING SYSTEMS

Some of the systems for representing numbers in previous and present cultures are well known. Roman numerals use a few letters of the alphabet to represent numbers up to the thousands, but are not intended for arbitrarily large numbers and can only represent positive integers. Arabic numerals are a family of systems originating in India, passing to medieval Islamic civilization and then to Europe, and now are the standard in global culture. They have undergone many curious changes with time and geography, but can represent arbitrarily large numbers and have been adapted to negative numbers, fractions, and other real numbers.

Less-well-known systems include some that are written and can be read today, such as the Hebrew and Greek method of using the letters of the alphabet, in order, for digits 1–9, tens 10–90, and hundreds 100–900.

A completely different system is that of the quipu, which the Inca used to record numbers on knotted strings.

Finger Counting

Many systems of finger counting have been, and still are, used in various parts of the world. Most are not as obvious as holding up a number of fingers. The position of fingers may be most important. One continuing use for finger counting is for people who speak different languages to communicate prices in the marketplace.

Cognitive Theorists and Constructivists

Constructivists believe that students may construct knowledge by themselves. In other words, students are actively engaged in the construction of their own knowledge. Students will assimilate and accommodate in order to build new knowledge, based on previous knowledge. Thus, in planning instruction based on constructivism, a teacher would focus on grouping designs, environment, problem-solving tasks, and inclusion of multiple representations. The goal in such a classroom would be for students to construct knowledge on their own. There are different levels of constructivism, including weak constructivism and radical constructivism.

Cognitivists differ from constructivists in that they believe that active exploration is important in helping students make sense of observations and experiences. However, the students are not expected to invent or construct knowledge by themselves. They are only expected to make sense of the mathematics. In planning instruction based on cognitivism, a teacher would employ similar methods to those discussed above, with the focus on active exploration. Students would do a lot of comparisons of mathematical methods in making sense of ideas.

Constructivism

Three types of constructivism are weak constructivism, social constructivism, and radical constructivism. **Weak constructivists** believe that students construct their own knowledge, but also accept certain preconceived notions or facts. **Social constructivists** believe that students construct knowledge by interacting with one another and holding discussions and conversations. **Radical constructivists** believe that all interpretations of knowledge are subjective, based on the individual learner. In other words, there is no real truth; it is all subjective. Classroom instructional planning based on a weak constructivist viewpoint might involve incorporation of some accepted theorems and definitions, while continuing to plan active explorations and discussions. Planning based on a social constructivist viewpoint might involve group activities, debates, discussion forums, etc. Planning based on a radical constructivist viewpoint would involve activities that are open-ended, where there is more than one correct answer. The problems would invite more than one correct answer.

Project-Based Learning

Project-based learning is learning that centers on the solving of a problem. Students learn many different ideas by solving one "big" problem. For example, for a unit on sine and cosine functions, a teacher may design a problem whereby the students are asked to model a real-world phenomenon using both types of functions. Students must investigate the effects of changes in amplitude, period, shifts, etc., on the graphs of the functions. Students will also be able to make connections between the types of functions when modeling the same phenomenon. Such a problem will induce high-level thinking.

Project-based learning is derived from constructivist theory, which contends that students learn by doing and constructing their own knowledge.

COOPERATIVE LEARNING

Cooperative learning simply means that students will learn by cooperating with one another. Students will be placed into groups of a size determined by the teacher. With such an approach, students work together to succeed in learning. Students may work together to learn a topic, complete an assignment, or compete with other groups.

Examples of cooperative learning include Think-Pair-Share and Jigsaw. **Think-Pair-Share** is a cooperative learning strategy that involves thinking about some given topic, sharing ideas, thoughts, or questions with a partner, and then sharing the partner discussion with the whole group. For example, in the mathematics classroom, a teacher may ask the class to think about the meaning of a proportional relationship. Each student would think for a set period of time, share ideas with a partner, and then each partner group would share their ideas regarding the meaning of proportionality. **Jigsaw** is another cooperative learning strategy that involves dividing among each group member reading material or ideas to be learned. Each student will then read his or her information, summarize it, and share the findings or ideas with the group. In mathematics, students might be given information on modeling with cosine and sine functions. Students could then share what they learned about real-world phenomena modeled by each. Different students may also be assigned to read in-depth material on amplitude, period, shifts, etc.

CONTROL STRATEGIES

"**Control strategies**" is another name for "metacognitive learning strategies," which indicate any strategy that promotes a learner's awareness of his or her level of learning. With such strategies, the student will work to determine what he or she knows and does not know regarding a subject. Possible control strategies are thinking, self-regulation, and discussing ideas with peers.

Example:

> A student may discover his or her level of "knowing" about functions by keeping a journal of any questions he or she might have regarding the topic. The student may list everything that he or she understands, as well as aspects not understood. As the student progresses through the course, he or she may go back and reconfirm any correct knowledge and monitor progress on any previous misconceptions.

MEMORIZATION AND ELABORATION STRATEGIES

Memorization is simply a technique whereby rote repetition is used to learn information. **Elaboration** strategies involve the connection of new information to some previously learned information. In mathematics, for example, students may use elaboration strategies when learning how to calculate the volume of a cone, based on their understood approach for calculating the volume of a cylinder. The student would be making connections in his or her mind between this new skill and other previously acquired skills. A memorization technique would simply involve memorization of the volume of a cone formula, as well as ways to evaluate the formula.

PRIOR KNOWLEDGE

Three ways of activating students' prior knowledge are concept mapping, visual imagery, and comparing and contrasting. With **concept mapping**, a student would detail and connect all known aspects of a mathematics topic. Ideas would be grouped into subgroups. Such an approach would allow a student to see what he or she does not know, prompting the activation of any prior knowledge on the subject. **Visual imagery** is simply the use of any pictures or diagrams to promote activation of prior knowledge. For example, giving a picture of Pascal's triangle would likely activate students' prior knowledge regarding the binomial theorem. **Comparing and contrasting** means that the student will compare and contrast ideas or approaches. For example, a student might be given a mapping of an inverse function. He or she could then compare and contrast this mapping to a known mapping of a function, in order to decide how they are the same and different. This would activate a student's prior understanding of functions and the definition thereof.

Three methods for ascertaining, or assessing, students' prior knowledge are portfolios, pre-tests, and self-inventories. **Portfolios** are simply a compilation of prior student activity related to mathematics topics. For example, a portfolio might show a student's work with transforming functions. **Pre-tests** are designed to measure a student's understanding of mathematics topics that will be taught in the course during the year. **Self-inventories** are just what the name implies: inventories that ask the students to name, list, describe, and explain information understood about various mathematics topics.

Once a teacher has assessed students' level of prior knowledge regarding some mathematics topic, he or she may use that information to scaffold the instruction. In other words, the teacher may decide to further break down the mathematics material into more integral parts. Exact processes or steps may be shown, including justification for using certain properties or theorems. More examples may be shown, while including examples of many different variations of problems, in order to ensure that students are not simply memorizing one approach that will be incorrectly applied to any problem of that sort. The teacher may also decide that more group work, peer cooperation, and discussion are needed.

For example, suppose a teacher determines that students have very little understanding of logic and valid arguments. The teacher may decide to re-teach the creation of truth tables, including truth values for intersections and "if p, then q" statements. The teacher may also decide to re-teach how a truth table may be used to show if an argument is valid. Students may be placed into groups and asked to determine the validity of several simple arguments. Once students understand the concept, they may move on to more rigorous arguments, including equivalence relations.

Concept Whereby Usage of Manipulatives Would Increase Conceptual Understanding

Understanding of how to solve one-variable equations would certainly be enhanced by using rods and counters. With this manipulative, the rod would represent the variable, or x, while the counters would represent the constants on each side of the equation. A sample diagram of the equation, $x + 4 = 8$, is shown below. Note that the vertical line represents the equals sign.

In order to solve the equation (and isolate x), four counters may be removed from each side of the mat. This process is shown below:

Now, the final illustration is:

Thus, the solution is $x = 4$. The manipulative helps students understand the meaning of the subtraction property of equality in action, without simply memorizing its meaning.

Piaget's Cognitive Development Theory

Piaget's cognitive development theory is aligned with **constructivism**. In fact, constructivism is built on his ideas. Piaget's cognitive development theory indicates that students actively participate in the construction of their own knowledge via assimilation and accommodation. Current cognitive theorists do not believe that students have to construct their own knowledge, but instead that they only have to make sense of what they are observing.

The four stages of learning, as developed by Piaget, are sensorimotor, preoperational, concrete operational, and formal operational. The defined stages show the progression from concrete thinking to abstract thinking. In other words, a child would need an object to understand properties, in the first stage. By the fourth stage, the child would be able to think abstractly, without some concrete form. In mathematics, this idea might be illustrated by first working with diagrams and manipulatives of numbers and then later writing symbolic forms of the numbers, including the numerals. This would illustrate the progression from 0 to 7 years. In the years of 11 to adulthood, much deeper abstraction is utilized. For example, people would be able to discuss functions and general properties, without looking at any concrete graphs or representations.

Review Video: Piaget's Cognitive Development Theory
Visit mometrix.com/academy and enter code: 100376

Progression That a Student Undergoes as He or She Learns Mathematics

When learning mathematics, students begin with concrete representations and ideas. Later, students are able to abstract meaning and make generalizations. Students will also be asked to apply abstract ideas from one topic to another mathematics topic. In other words, students would move from concrete representations, ideas, and facts to symbolic representations and generalizations. Piaget outlined such a progression in his general four stages of cognitive learning. For example, a student may first learn about solving equations by using a balance scale. After the student understands the process, he or she can solve alone, using the symbolic equations. He or she would also be able to describe the process for solving any equation.

Direct Instruction Versus Student-Centered Instruction

Direct instruction is instruction whereby the teacher delivers all content knowledge to be learned, and students, more or less, passively listen. The teacher employs a step-by-step instruction method for learning content. Student-centered instruction is learning whereby the teacher serves as a facilitator of learning and students actively participate in their own learning. Research has shown that students show a higher level of procedural and conceptual understanding when learning in a student-centered approach. Direct instruction might be more appropriate when teaching basic or fundamental theorems. Student-centered learning might be more appropriate when helping students make connections or develop higher-level thinking regarding a topic.

Cooperative Learning Task Versus Traditional Task

Think-Pair-Share is an activity whereby a topic is first given for consideration on an individual basis. Next, the students are arranged in pairs and asked to discuss the topic (e.g., any questions, comments, generalizations, etc.). Finally, each pair will contribute to a whole-class discussion on the topic.

In mathematics, students would likely develop a higher level of understanding by using such an activity as Think-Pair-Share when learning about trigonometric functions. For example, students might be asked to consider different real-world situations that may be modeled with sine and cosine functions. Students could individually make a list and then share with a partner. Each partner group could then contribute to a whole class list. This list could be used as a reference sheet.

Implementing Technology in Classroom Instruction

Technology may be implemented in the mathematics classroom in many ways. For example, Excel may be used to perform regressions, calculate lines of best fit, calculate correlation coefficients, plot residuals, show convergence or divergence of a sequence, etc. Calculators may be used to evaluate and graph functions, find area under the normal curve, calculate combinations and permutations, perform statistical tests, etc. Graphing software, such as GeoGebra, may be used to graph and explore many shapes and functions. Students may also use it to graph reflections, rotations, translations, and dilations.

Modifying Instruction to Accommodate English-Language Learners

In mathematics specifically, instruction may be modified to include illustrations of ideas, in addition to given words. Audio may also be included for problem tasks. English-language learners may also be grouped with other fluent English-speaking students in order to assist with learning of the mathematics topic. Students will be able to hear the conversation, in addition to seeing the topic in print. In addition, problems may be broken down into smaller pieces, which can help the student focus on one step at a time. Further, additional one-on-one time with the teacher may be needed, whereby the teacher reads aloud and illustrates examples to be learned.

Effective Learning Environment for ELL Students

Characteristics of an effective learning environment for ELL students include creation of a low threshold for anxiety, use of pictures to teach vocabulary and mathematics ideas, implementation of graphic organizers, explicit teaching of vocabulary words, and use of active learning strategies. The latter two are extremely important, since ELL students need to learn exact terms and exact definitions while also engaging with fellow students, as opposed to sitting alone at a desk. Research completed by professors at the University of Houston and University of California list collaborative learning, use of multiple representations, and technology integration as important facets of an effective learning environment for ELL students (Waxman & Tellez, 2002).

Closed-Ended Mathematics Question and Then Rewritten in an Open-Ended Manner

Closed-Ended:

- Look at the graph of $y = x^2 + 2$. Decide if the graph represents a function.

Open-Ended:

- Provide an example of an equation that represents a function. Provide an example of an equation that does not represent a function. Explain how the graphs of the two equations compare to one another.

The first question will elicit a simple, straightforward response, or "Yes, it is a function."

The second question prompts the student to come up with two equations and then describe how the graphs of the two equations would compare. There is more than one possible answer, and the student has to make a comparison as well.

Good Questioning Response Techniques

A few good questioning response techniques are:

- Make sure the wait time is sufficient;
- Do not include leading prompts within questions;
- Ask more questions based on student answers;
- Confirm or restate correct student comments.

The key to good questioning response techniques is to show the student that his or her comments are important and to connect those comments to other student comments. The student should feel that he or she has made a contribution to the community of learners. A teacher should always ask a meaningful, thought-provoking question and provide sufficient time for the student to provide a meaningful and well-thought-out response. Student answers should lead to more questions and ideas and not serve as an endpoint.

NCTM Categories of Questions That Teachers Should Ask

The professional standards describe five categories of questions that teachers should ask. These categories are: 1) working together to make sense of problems; 2) individually making sense of problems; 3) reasoning about mathematics; 4) providing conjectures about mathematics; and 5) making connections within and outside of mathematics. Sample questions include "What does this mean?," "How can you prove that?," and "What does this relate to?". Categories 4 and 5 are high level and include questions that prompt students to invent ideas and make meaningful connections.

Accountants and Mathematical Modeling

Accountants use mathematical modeling in a variety of ways. For example, an accountant models the future value of a certificate of deposit (CD) using the compound interest formula. An accountant also may fit a regression line to a client's overall savings over x years. An accountant may model tax payments with residual plots. Accountants may use past income tax returns to predict future tax expenses. Accountants may compare rates of return when investing in different mutual funds, by fitting and comparing regression lines.

Scientists and Functions

Scientists use functions to model real-world phenomena. For example, scientists use quadratic functions to model the height of an object tossed into the air or dropped from a certain height. Scientists use sine and cosine functions to model real-world occurrences such as the depth of water at various times of the day, the movement of a pendulum, etc. Scientists use exponential functions to analyze and predict the number of bacteria present after x amount of time. Scientists also use functions when analyzing the time it takes a rocket to reach a destination.

Making Mathematics Relevant to Students' Lives

Teachers can make mathematics relevant to students, using a variety of strategies. Teachers may include items relevant and pertinent to students within question stems, such as including "iPad," "apps," and video game names. Teachers should pose questions that are similar to what students may have asked themselves, such as, "If I invest this much money in an account and save for x years, after how many years will I have y dollars?" Teachers should include real-world problems to solve, and not simply include rote solving of equations. Students should know what sorts of scenarios may be modeled with rational expressions. Many researchers believe that curricula should be centered on the "real world," with all facets of mathematics learning spawning from that center. In other words, students often know how to convert a decimal to a percentage, but when reading *The Wall Street Journal*, they may not be able to interpret a percentage yield.

Assessment

Assessment Tool

A **mathematics assessment tool** is used to assess a student's prior knowledge, current knowledge, skill set, procedural knowledge, conceptual understanding, depth of understanding, and ability to make abstractions and generalizations. Perhaps the most important purpose of such a tool is to help the student develop and modify instruction. A teacher may determine that students are ready to surpass the current lesson or need it to be much more scaffolded. A teacher may also use the assessment to track students' progress. For example, a portfolio might show students' initial understanding of functions and end with their work with function modeling.

When a teacher needs to decide on an appropriate assessment tool, he or she needs to consider the purpose of the assessment. For example, if the purpose of an assessment is to direct the instruction, a pre-test may be a good assessment to use. If the purpose of the assessment is to determine the level of student understanding, then a whole-class discussion may be desired. If the purpose of an assessment is to assess student understanding of a unit of material, then an exam would be appropriate. If a teacher wishes to analyze student understanding and ability to abstract knowledge, then a performance assessment may be used. If a teacher wishes to check off skills mastered by students, then a checklist would be appropriate.

Valid Test

A test is valid if it tests what it is supposed to test. In other words, a test is valid if it appropriately covers the material it is supposed to cover. For example, a topic not taught in class should not be included on a valid test. In order to construct a valid test, a teacher should make a list of all standards covered during that time period. The teacher should also closely mirror the design of problems examined in class, for homework, and in group discussions. Finally, the teacher should make sure that there is an even balance of questions to cover all of the material.

Valid Exam

In order to select a **valid exam**, a teacher should make sure that the test aligns with the objectives and standards covered in the unit. The teacher should also make sure that the test problems are similar to those covered during class time. The teacher should make sure the percentages of questions devoted to each objective are balanced. In order for a test to be valid, it must be reliable, meaning that it produces similar results with different groups. A teacher may wish to check the validity and reliability results of an exam.

In general, an exam is considered **invalid** if it does not measure what it is supposed to measure. The exam may include questions from another unit. It may include questions with different wording techniques, making it much more difficult. The exam may include representations different from those covered in class. An invalid exam would not be reliable, meaning the results would not be consistent with different administrations of the exam. Biased questions and wording may also make an exam invalid.

Assessing Students' Understanding of What Has Been Taught

In order to assess thought processes, **open-ended questions** are needed. The teacher may wish to have students write an essay, write entries in a mathematics journal, undergo a performance task, or participate in a debate or discussion. The teacher may also design a pre-test that includes all constructed response questions. In particular, a performance task requires students to justify solutions, which provide the teacher with insight into students' understanding and reasoning. In general, the assessment should include questions that ask students to make abstractions and justify their thinking.

Testing Issue

Example: A student claims that an exam is more difficult and includes more content than what was presented in class. How might a teacher determine if the student's claim is true?

The teacher would need to make a list of all objectives and standards covered during the time period. The teacher would also need to compile all problems and examples covered in class and as homework. Finally, the teacher would need to do a careful analysis of the wording of the problems covered in class and as homework. If any of these items are not aligned to the exam, the teacher would need to go back and re-teach the material, using the created test as a guide for instruction.

Performance Task

A **performance task** allows the teacher to assess process as well as product, meaning that a teacher can assess students' thought processes as well as their final answer. The level of student learning will be much clearer when reviewing a performance task. A performance task goes beyond a multiple-choice format, allowing for oral and tactile-kinesthetic performances. Furthermore, a performance task may combine several mathematics concepts into one assessment instrument. This type of assessment often includes real-world problems, which helps the student connect mathematics to the outside world.

Formative and Summative Assessments

Formative assessments are those given during the learning process. Formative assessments provide the teacher with information related to a student's progress at various stages throughout a time period. Formative assessments are used to modify instruction as needed. In other words, formative assessments inform instruction. Summative assessments are those given at the end of a learning period. Summative assessments serve to measure the cumulative knowledge gained. Examples of formative assessments include quizzes, checklists, observations, and discussion. Examples of summative assessments include exams, portfolios, performance tasks, and standardized tests.

Four formative assessments include quizzes, checklists, observations, and discussion. **Quizzes** are often short assessments that may include multiple-choice items, short response items, or essay items. Quizzes are often administered following presentation of a portion of a mathematics unit. **Checklists** include a list of skills or concepts that should be mastered or understood. A teacher will check off all items mastered by a student. **Observations** are informal means of assessing students' understanding of a topic. A teacher may observe students' questions, engagement, and performance on projects. **Discussion** is another informal formative assessment. Discussions, both in groups and whole-class formats, allow the teacher to analyze students' thinking.

Four summative assessments include exams, portfolios, performance tasks, and standardized tests. **Exams** may include closed-ended or open-ended questions. Exams may be administered after each unit, semester, or at the end of the year. **Portfolios** include tasks created by a student and may include writing pieces and other large projects. Although the portfolio contains formative work, the tool itself may be used as a summative assessment piece. **Performance tasks** are large-scale problems that include many different components that relate to some big idea. For example, a student may be asked to formulate a plan for modeling a real-world phenomenon with a sine function. The student may be asked to explain how the function would change, given changes to the amplitude, period, shifts, etc. The student may then explain how these components would need to change to fit a new function. **Standardized tests** are tests that compare a student's performance to that of other students. They are often given at the end of the school year.

Review Video: Formative and Summative Assessments
Visit mometrix.com/academy and enter code: 804991

Review Video: Assessment Reliability and Validity
Visit mometrix.com/academy and enter code: 424680

Scoring Rubric

A **strong rubric** will include unique performance criteria for each bullet. In other words, a portion of one criteria statement should not be included in a portion of another criteria statement. Each criteria statement should be clearly delineated, describing exactly what the student must be able to do. Furthermore, a strong rubric will often have scoring options, ranging from 0 to 4. When designing the rubric, it is helpful to create a model student response that will warrant each rubric score. It is also helpful to provide a space to provide feedback to students.

Enhancing Student Understanding

In order for an assessment to enhance student understanding, it should provide an opportunity for the student to learn something. The assessment should be a learning opportunity for the student. It should prompt the student to think deeper about a mathematics topic. In other words, the student should think, "Okay. I understand this. I wonder how the process/solution would change if I did this." The assessment might prompt the student to ask deeper questions in the next class session or complete research on a certain topic. In order to create such an assessment, open-ended and challenging questions should be included on the exam. The exam should not consist of simple, lower-level, one-answer questions.

Testing Mathematical Misconceptions

In order to design such an assessment, the teacher should include mathematical error-type problems, whereby the student must look at a solution process or conjecture and determine if he or she agrees, of if and where an error occurred. The student would need to identify the error, correct it, and explain why it was erroneous. The assessment should include a variety of mathematical misconceptions. One solution process may include more than one error. A teacher may also simply ask students to participate in a collaborative learning activity, whereby the students must share ideas and thoughts regarding a new mathematical topic.

Assessing Prior Knowledge

Such a pre-test must not include any leading prompts. It should include open-ended and constructed-response items as well. A pre-test with solely multiple-choice items will not be sufficient, since a student has the option of guessing. The test should include higher-level questions that require connections within the field of mathematics. In other words, the questions should not all be mutually exclusive. They should build on one another. Finally, the test might include student error problems as well.

Assessing Both Procedural Knowledge and Conceptual Understanding

The assessment should include rote, algorithmic-type problems, as well as those that ask the student to utilize higher-level thinking, abstractions, and generalizations. The test should include open-ended, constructed-response-type problems. A performance task is an excellent assessment for assessing a student's ability to solve a problem, while also examining the student's thought processes, rationales, etc. In order to assess both types of understanding, the assessment will need to ask students to justify and explain solutions. In other words, the assessments should include questions at both ends of Bloom's Taxonomy.

Pre-Test and Post-Test

A **post-test** should be exactly the same as an administered pre-test. If the teacher is to compare the results of a post-test to a pre-test, then the test and testing conditions should be identical. The **pre-test** assesses students' prior knowledge, while a post-test assesses students post knowledge. Comparing the results, side by side, allows the teacher to track student progress. The teacher may wish to add additional questions to the post-test, but the original questions should remain.

Assessment That Will Show What Students Do and Do Not Know

The teacher should include questions that are straightforward, involve errors, require justification, and require shown work. A student self-assessment is one such tool that would show misconceptions, understood material, and advanced knowledge. The assessment should include more than multiple-choice questions. Designing a performance assessment with scaffolded questions, whereby only one solution may be found based on a previous answer, will also show students' exact level of understanding. A debate format is one type of assessment whereby the teacher will be able to see a student's level of understanding, as he or she seeks to respond with a rebuttal.

Assessment to Hone in on Any Error Patterns Evident in Students' Work

A **portfolio** would be an excellent assessment for monitoring any student error patterns. The teacher would be able to track student errors as the course progressed. The teacher would be given insight into how, and if, errors improved, or if some knowledge was acquired but other knowledge was still incorrect. The portfolio might include a series of similar questions related to a certain topic. For example, a portfolio may include function transformation questions. A student's ability to transform functions may be tracked, starting with simple linear functions and ending with complex sine functions.

Components That Must Be Present in an Assessment That Supports Student Learning

The assessment must require students to **think deeper** than what they have covered in class. It should prompt them to make connections between topics. It should invite different ways of thinking about problem solving. In other words, the student may think, "Okay. I have seen a similar version in class. This problem is slightly different, in that the parabola is shifted left. This is the opposite of shifting right, so I will add the constant to the x-term." The assessment will thus solidify the student's understanding of how to shift any function.

Using Assessment Results from ELL Learners in Order to Modify Instruction

The teacher would be able to see if language itself is a barrier in learning. In other words, if the group of ELL students, as a whole, show difficulty with a mathematics topic, the teacher may deduce that the content was not clear due to minimal supporting pictures, diagrams, and auditory support. The teacher may decide to reteach the lesson, using more visual cues, verbal pronunciations, explicit vocabulary usage, and peer-group placement. Collaborative learning may be employed.

A Teacher's Questions Regarding the Results of an Administered Exam

The teacher may ask the following:

- Did I cover the content in an explicit manner?
- Did I show plenty of examples?
- Did I use multiple representations when teaching the concepts?
- Did I design instruction such as to accommodate all modes of learning?
- Was the test valid?
- Did students have an adequate amount of time to complete the test?
- Why did some groups of students score lower or higher?
- Did any biased questions affect the results?

Effects of Focus on Career and College Readiness

The focus on college and career-readiness standards prompts publishers and teachers to utilize more real-world problems in instruction and assessments. The focus in mathematics classrooms is shifting to more real-world, cumulative problems that require understanding of many different mathematics concepts in order to solve. Problems are related to science, finance, medicine, etc. The focus includes the ability to apply the algorithms to many different career situations. In summary, the recent focus shifts the instructional design to an application-based status.

Role of Assessment in a Classroom Focused on Cognitive Instruction

A cognitively guided classroom would be similar to a constructivist classroom, in that **active participation** would be present. However, in a cognitive classroom (as advocated by current cognitive theorists), students are not required to invent their own knowledge. Instead, they must simply make sense of what they are observing and experiencing. They may be assisted by the teacher. Thus, the role of an assessment in such a classroom is to ascertain student thought processes. Such an assessment would ask students to describe thinking and perhaps make connections to other mathematics topics. The assessment must ascertain students' reasoning abilities.

Instructional Cycle Described by a Learning Theorist

The **5E Learning Model** is based on the thinking of Jean Piaget. It is a constructivist learning model. Piaget believed that students construct their own knowledge via active participation and experiences. Problem solving is integral to student learning. The cycle is listed as engagement, exploration, explanation, elaboration, and evaluation. Thus, with active engagement and exploration, the student is able to develop his or her own explanation, use assimilation and accommodation to make sense of the information, and then evaluate the material and make conjectures, etc.

TExES Practice Test #1

Want to take this practice test in an online interactive format?
Check out the online resources page, which includes interactive practice questions and much more: **mometrix.com/resources719/texesmath4-8**

1. Quinn deposits $250 from each quarterly paycheck into a savings account. How much will he have deposited in the account after 5 years?

a. $4,800
b. $5,000
c. $5,200
d. $5,400

2. What is the value of x, shown in the diagram below?

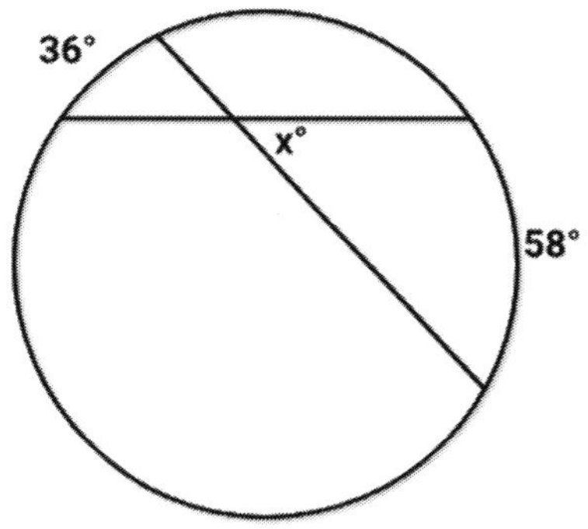

a. 11
b. 47
c. 51
d. 94

3. Amelia made an array of cubes that is 10 cubes by 10 cubes. Ms. Becker asked her to make the array 10 cubes by 15 cubes. Amelia picks up 15 more cubes. Which of the following statements best describes Amelia's error?

a. Amelia does not yet know number facts above 100
b. Amelia does not fully understand how changes to dimension affect measures of area and volume
c. Amelia does not fully understand the commutative property of multiplication
d. Amelia does not yet understand how to interpret mathematical models

4. The figure on the graph below represents a triangular walking path, beginning and ending at point x. If each unit represents 0.25 miles, which of the following best represents the total distance of the path?

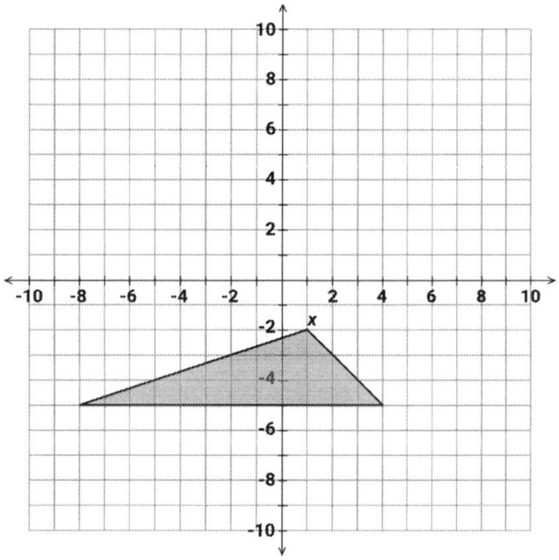

a. 6.4 miles
b. 12.2 miles
c. 15.8 miles
d. 25.7 miles

5. What is the interquartile range of the data below?

$$\{2, 4, 6, 8, 10, 12, 14, 16, 18, 20\}$$

a. 10
b. 11
c. 12
d. 13

6. In addition to math, in which other area of life do we tend to see patterns and relationships?

a. Works of art
b. Pieces of music
c. Articles of clothing
d. In all of these areas

7. Ms. Cho's students are solving multiplication and division word problems without using manipulatives. They read the following prompt:

> "Daniel is feeding his neighbor's 4 dogs. Each dog gets 3 scoops of food daily. How many scoops of food will Daniel use each day?"

What question would Ms. Cho ask first in order to help her students express the word problem algebraically?

a. "How many scoops does Daniel need each day?"
b. "How can we calculate the total number of scoops?"
c. "Are we going to multiply or divide in this problem?"
d. "How many groups of 3 scoops will Daniel need?"

8. Jake rolls a standard six-sided die. What is the probability he rolls a number less than or equal to 5?

a. $\frac{5}{6}$
b. $\frac{1}{5}$
c. $\frac{3}{4}$
d. $\frac{1}{3}$

9. Which of the following statements is NOT true?

a. In a negatively skewed distribution, the tail is on the left.
b. In a positively skewed distribution, the median is greater than the mode.
c. In a normal distribution, the mean is at the peak.
d. In a positively skewed distribution, the median is closer to the third quartile than the first.

10. What is the converse of the statement below?

If it is Saturday, Joe buys a donut.

a. If it is not Saturday, Joe does not buy a donut.
b. If it is Saturday, Joe buys a donut.
c. If Joe buys a donut, it is Saturday.
d. If Joe does not buy a donut, it is not Saturday.

11. Which of the following accurately describes the set of integers?

a. The set of counting numbers
b. The set of counting numbers, plus zero
c. The set of numbers that may be written as the ratio of $\frac{a}{b}$, where $b \neq 0$
d. The set of counting numbers, zero, and the negations of the counting numbers

12. A car is accelerating. Which of the following accurately describes the appearance of the position-time graph?

a. It is a line with a positive slope.
b. It is a line with a negative slope.
c. It is a curve with an increasing slope.
d. It is a curve with a decreasing slope.

13. A convex three-dimensional figure has 9 edges and 6 vertices. How many faces does it have?

a. 4
b. 5
c. 6
d. 8

14. Ms. Dulik wants to introduce her students to the concept that a representation of data could be misleading. Which of the following pairs of data representation would best accomplish her goal? Select all that apply.

a. Two charts that contain different data sets
b. Two bar graphs that use different scales on the y-axis
c. Two drawings of a floor plan, with one marked "Not to scale"

15. Which of the following equations may be used to convert $0.\overline{4}$ to a fraction?

a. $10x - x = 4.\overline{4} - 0.\overline{4}$
b. $100x - x = 4.\overline{4} - 0.\overline{4}$
c. $10x - x = 44.\overline{4} - 4.\overline{4}$
d. $100x - 10x = 4.\overline{4} - 0.\overline{4}$

16. Which of the following measurements is the best approximation of 1,982 square centimeters?

a. 307 in^2
b. 865 in^2
c. 7,463 in^2
d. 12,787 in^2

17. What is the converse of the statement below?

If I go skiing, then it is winter.

a. If it is not winter, then I do not go skiing.
b. If it is winter, then I go skiing.
c. If it is not winter, then I go skiing.
d. If I go skiing, then it is not winter.

18. For which of the following data sets would the mean be an appropriate measure of center to use?

a. 7, 15, 20, 24, 27, 28, 31, 36, 41, 50
b. 6, 7, 8, 8, 9, 9, 10, 20, 34, 50
c. 5, 18, 30, 42, 43, 44, 46, 48, 49, 50
d. 8, 10, 12, 13, 14, 16, 20, 22, 24, 2200

19. Erika must choose her outfit from 4 pairs of jeans, 6 tops, and 5 pairs of shoes. How many possible outfits may she create with one item from each category?

a. 12
b. 24
c. 60
d. 120

20. Which of the following represents the net of a triangular prism?

a. 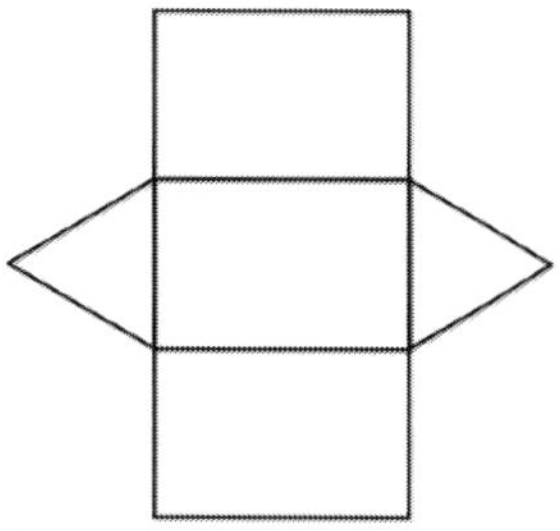

b. 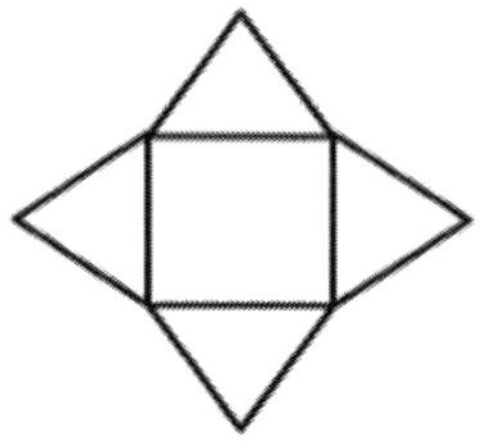

c. 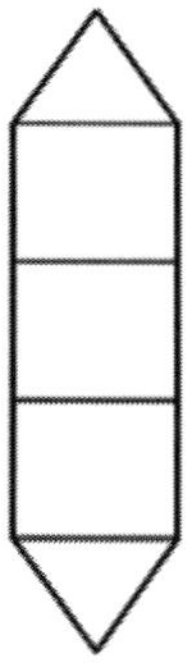

d. 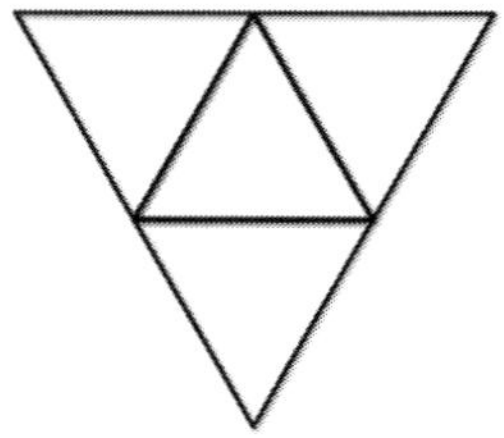

21. Which of these approaches to mathematics instruction is generally recognized as being the most effective?

a. Students need to memorize formulas and follow standard procedures for problem solving.
b. The use of mental math to solve complex problems should be discouraged.
c. Pencil-and-paper drills should be the primary focus of math class.
d. Students should be encouraged to solve problems in ways that make sense to them.

22. The table below shows the average amount of rainfall Houston receives during the summer and autumn months.

Month	Rainfall (in inches)
June	5.35
July	3.18
August	3.83
September	4.33
October	4.5
November	4.19

What percentage of rainfall in this timeframe occurs during October?

a. 13.5%
b. 15.1%
c. 16.9%
d. 17.7%

23. Which of the following graphs does NOT represent a function?

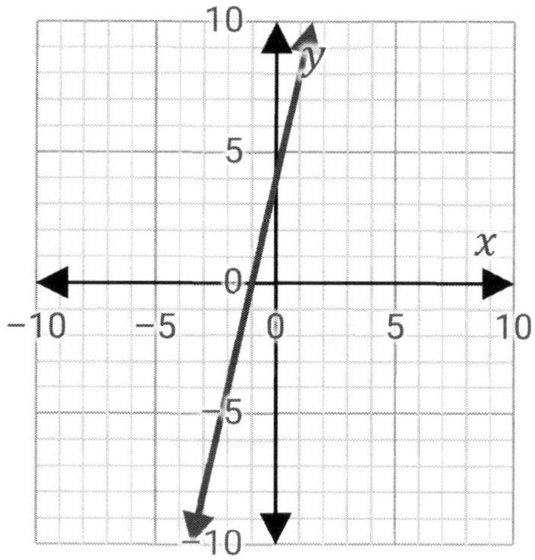

a.

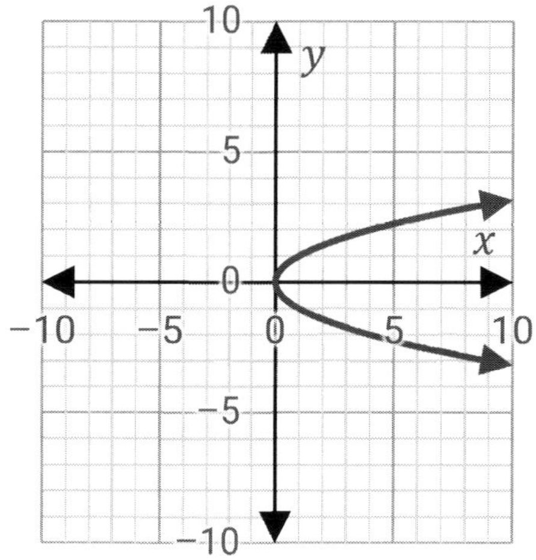

b.

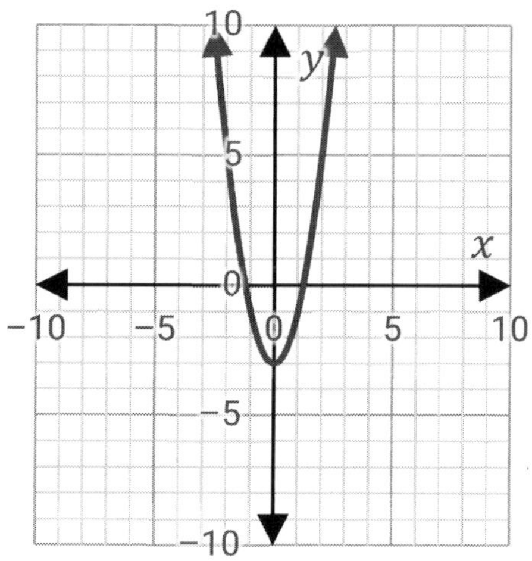

c.

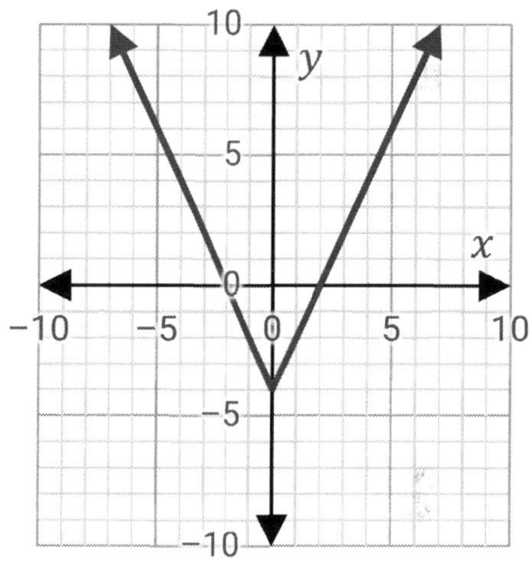

d.

24. What is the area of the figure graphed below?

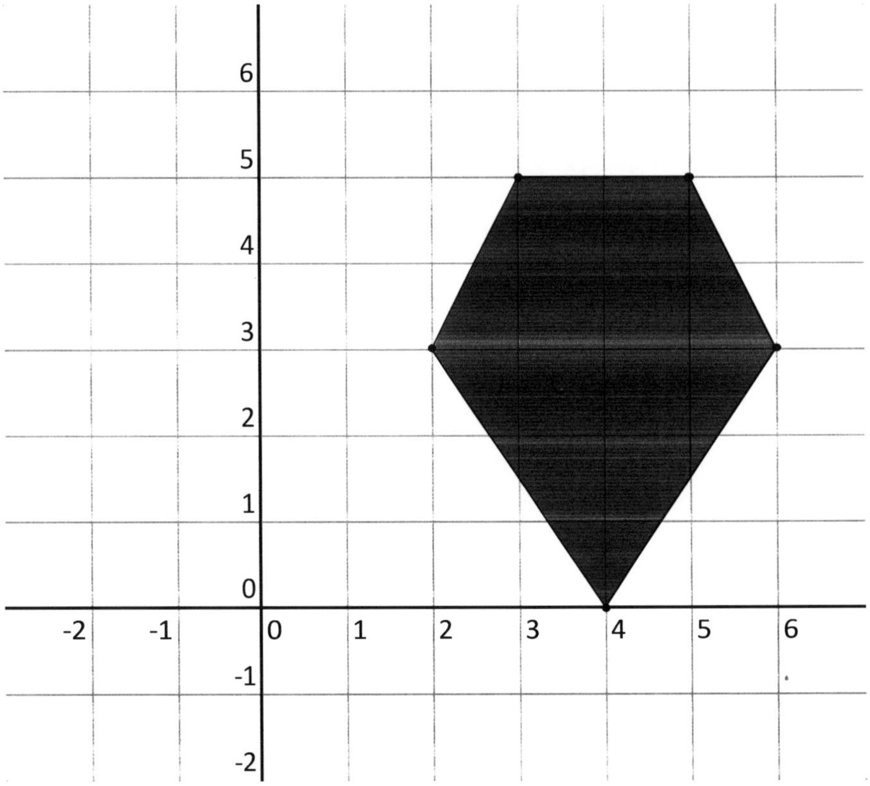

a. 11 $units^2$
b. 11.5 $units^2$
c. 12 $units^2$
d. 12.5 $units^2$

25. Tomas held out both hands, clearly showing ten digits – eight fingers and two thumbs – and proclaimed "I actually have nine fingers!" His friend Jerzy replied "No, you only have eight fingers!". To prove that he had nine fingers Tomas counted backward on one hand "$8 - 7 - 6 - 5$", then said "and 4 on this hand makes 9 fingers". This logic is incorrect because:

a. Tomas counted his thumb as one of the fingers
b. Tomas was mixing ordinal and cardinal numbers
c. Tomas began counting from the left instead of the right
d. Tomas began counting from the right instead of the left

26. Which of the following represents a function?

a. $\{(2,1), (3,-2), (6,8), (-1,-4), (4,-1)\}$
b. $\{(8,5), (7,9), (3,1), (4,7), (3,6)\}$
c. $\{(-4,6), (2,3), (4,-2), (3,6), (-4,2)\}$
d. $\{(2,6), (6,1), (5,8), (2,-1), (-3,1)\}$

27. Eric's dietary plan consists of 4 different entrées, 5 different appetizers, and 3 different desserts. How many possible meals can he create that contain one entrée, one appetizer, and one dessert?

a. 12
b. 24
c. 60
d. 120

28. A bag contains 5 red marbles, 4 green marbles, and 3 yellow marbles. What is the probability that Fran pulls a red marble, keeps that marble in her possession, and then pulls a green marble?

a. $\frac{5}{36}$
b. $\frac{1}{6}$
c. $\frac{7}{132}$
d. $\frac{5}{33}$

29. On the first day of a new unit in math, a teacher gives students a pretest of the unit with 10 questions. All students score at least 80 percent on the pretest. If anything, what should the teacher do differently after seeing the pretest results?

a. Continue with the theme of the unit, but teach more advanced questions to further challenge students.
b. Move on to the next unit since students have mastered this one.
c. Reteach the questions that students missed on the pretest so that all students can score 100 percent.
d. Do not change instruction for the unit because the teacher is doing a good job already.

30. $g(x) = \frac{x}{x+3}$. What is the equation of the horizontal asymptote?

a. $y = 0$
b. $y = 0.5$
c. $y = 1$
d. $y = 3$

31. Marlon pays $45 for a jacket that has been marked down 25%. What was the original cost of the jacket?

a. $80
b. $75
c. $65
d. $60

32. Which type of function is represented by the table of values below?

x	y
−2	8
−1	2
0	0
1	2
2	8

a. Linear
b. Quadratic
c. Cubic
d. Exponential

33. On the first day of school, a teacher asks her students to create a list of tasks they feel they do well. What is the primary way in which this activity can help the teacher throughout the year?

a. It is a way for the teacher to informally assess her students' abilities and learn about their interests.
b. It serves as a tool the teacher can use to assess each student's background knowledge.
c. It will help the teacher know which students to pair in groups based on their skills.
d. It helps the students feel confident about what they already know.

34. A 4th-grade teacher introduces the math topic of decimals to the class. Together they preview their textbook chapter on decimals. The teacher assigns small groups of students to generate questions to which they want answers. Which of the following examples is the least helpful question to guide them at this stage of their learning?

a. "How are decimals important to us in our everyday lives?"
b. "How can decimals be whole numbers and also fractions?"
c. "In the number 467.912, which digit is in the hundredths?"
d. "Can we make fractions decimals, and decimals fractions?"

35. Alicia rolls a standard six-sided die. What is the probability she rolls a number greater than or equal to 3?

a. $\frac{5}{6}$
b. $\frac{3}{5}$
c. $\frac{3}{4}$
d. $\frac{2}{3}$

36. During February, the sixth-grade teachers at an elementary school decide to work together to teach a unit about the heart. The English teacher will have the students write essays about how the heart functions. The science teacher will teach the basic parts of the heart. The art teacher will have the students build models of the heart. The math teacher will have the students determine the amount of blood that flows through the heart in everyday units of capacity. Which of the following concepts are the teachers implementing?

a. Differentiated instruction
b. Formative assessment
c. Thematic units
d. Collaborative learning

37. Lilia needs to buy envelopes and stamps. Each box of envelopes costs $2.50. Each book of stamps costs $6.00. She intends to spend no more than $30. Which of the following graphs represents the possible combinations of stamps and envelopes that she may purchase, if the *y*-axis represents books of stamps and the *x*-axis represents boxes of envelopes?

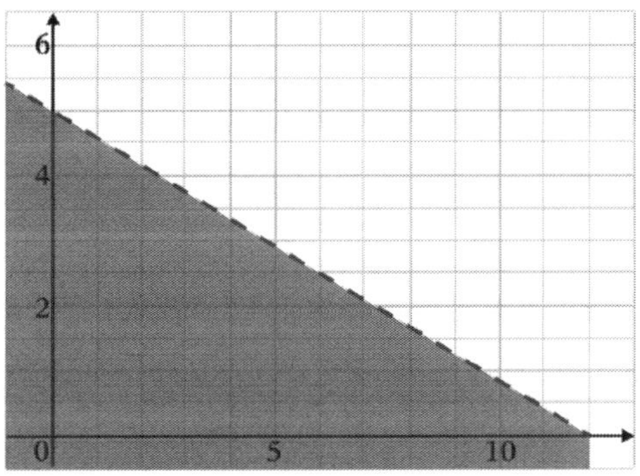

a.

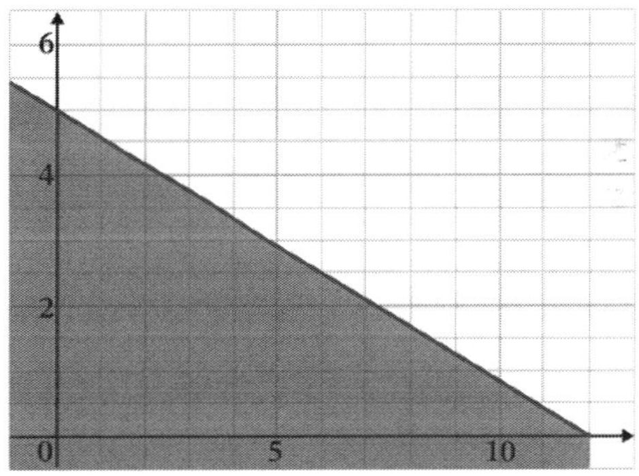

b.

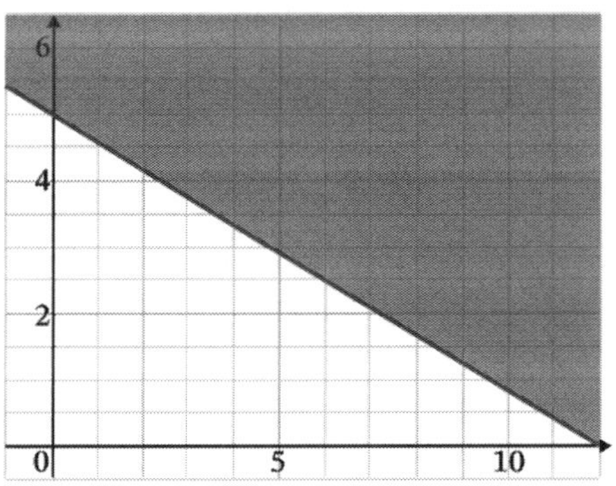

c.

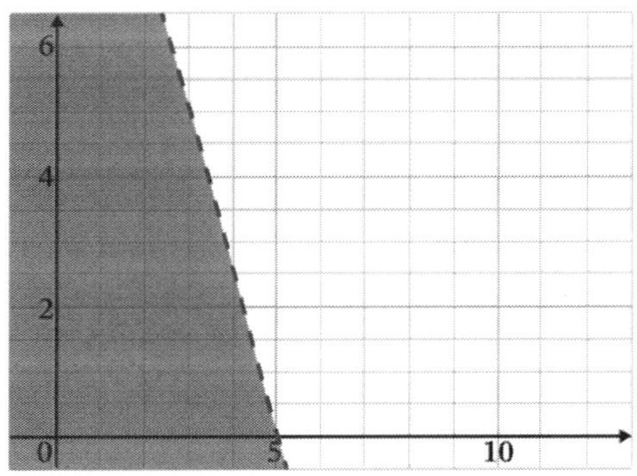

d.

38. The table below shows Marc's electricity bill during the summer and autumn months.

Month	Electricity bill
June	$143.79
July	$156.82
August	$160.91
September	$149.28
October	$127.56
November	$138.20

What percentage of Marc's total electricity costs were incurred during the month of October?

a. 13.5%
b. 14.6%
c. 15.9%
d. 17.2%

39. $g(x) = \frac{2x-3}{3-x}$**. What is the equation of the horizontal asymptote?**

a. $y = -2$
b. $y = -1$
c. $y = \frac{2}{3}$
d. $y = 3$

40. Kayla rolls a die and tosses a coin. What is the probability she gets an even number and heads?

a. $\frac{1}{6}$
b. $\frac{1}{4}$
c. $\frac{1}{3}$
d. 1

41. What is the interquartile range of the data below?

$$\{4, 7, 7, 9, 11, 14, 17, 18, 18, 23\}$$

a. 10
b. 11
c. 12
d. 13

42. Which of the following transformations has been applied to the triangle in Quadrant I?

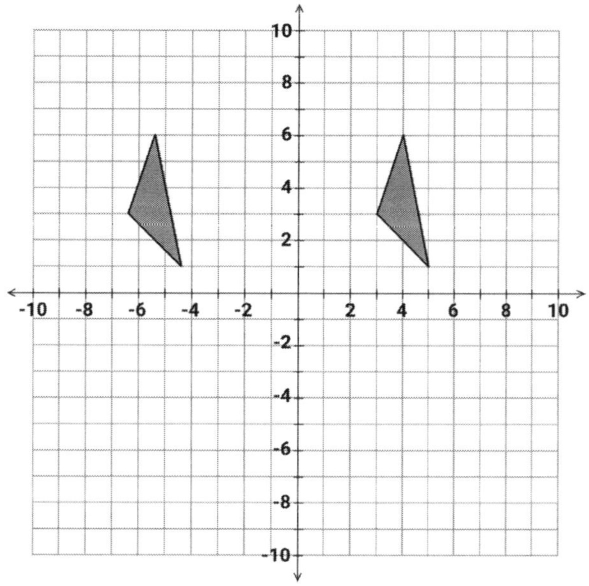

a. Translation
b. Rotation of 90 degrees
c. Reflection
d. Dilation

43. A city is at an elevation of 6,700 feet. Which of the following best represents the elevation in miles?

a. 0.77 miles
b. 1.27 miles
c. 1.56 miles
d. 1.89 miles

44. The table below shows the amount that Kelli spent on gas in the last six months.

Month	Gas expense
January	$78.85
February	$69.49
March	$97.48
April	$82.37
May	$72.86
June	$77.91

What percentage of the total gas costs for the six months was spent in March?

a. 17.5%
b. 18.1%
c. 19.9%
d. 20.4%

45. How many square inches of paper would it take to wrap a ball with a radius of 0.8 feet?

a. 8.04
b. 59.72
c. 437.96
d. 1,157.76

46. Which of the following formulas may be used to represent the sequence 9, 27, 81, 243, ...?

a. $y = 3x + 6$
b. $y = x + 9$
c. $y = 3^{x+1}$
d. $y = (x + 1)^3$

47. Mr. Abbas is teaching a lesson on calculating perimeter and area of two-dimensional shapes. He wants the lesson to engage his students in the practice of using appropriate tools strategically. Which of the following activities is best aligned with Mr. Abbas' objective?

a. Give each student a piece of yarn, a ruler, and a worksheet with pictures of various shapes. Ask students to use the tools to determine the perimeters and areas of the shapes.
b. Give each student a worksheet with pictures of various objects. Ask them to calculate the perimeter and area, showing their work.
c. Give each student a ruler or yardstick and a worksheet naming various objects in the classroom. Ask students to find the area of those objects.
d. Give each student a set of interlocking cubes and a worksheet naming various objects in the classroom. Ask students to estimate the area of those objects.

48. The two prisms shown below are similar. What is the measurement of x?

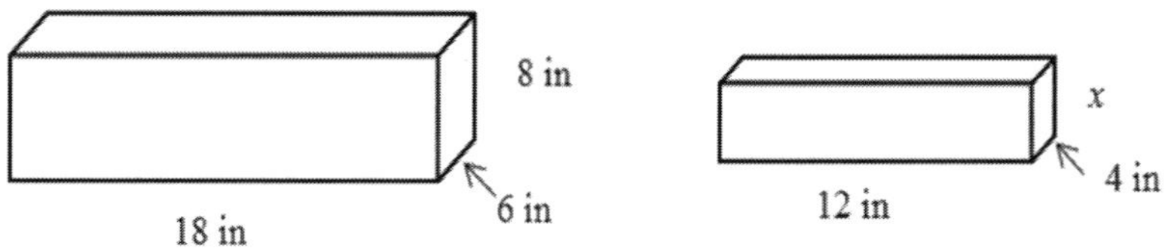

a. $4\frac{3}{4}$ in
b. $5\frac{1}{3}$ in
c. $5\frac{2}{3}$ in
d. $5\frac{3}{4}$ in

49. During a unit on integers, a math teacher administers a quiz to assess her students. A large proportion of students receive a failing grade. What is the best strategy the teacher should implement to correct this issue?

a. The teacher should individually conference with each student who failed to ask what they did to prepare for the quiz
b. The teacher should look at the quizzes to see what common mistakes were made, and work on reteaching the material to the students
c. The teacher should increase homework and encourage students to study at home
d. The teacher should ask students for input on what they still need to learn to be successful

50. What is the sum of the first 40 positive multiples of 3?

a. 615
b. 1,230
c. 2,460
d. 4,920

51. Jamal is placing an order for ink cartridges and reams of paper. Each ink cartridge costs \$7.50. Each ream of paper costs \$3. He intends to spend less than \$45. Which of the following graphs represents the possible combinations of paper and ink that he may purchase, if the x-axis represents ink cartridges and the y-axis represents reams of paper?

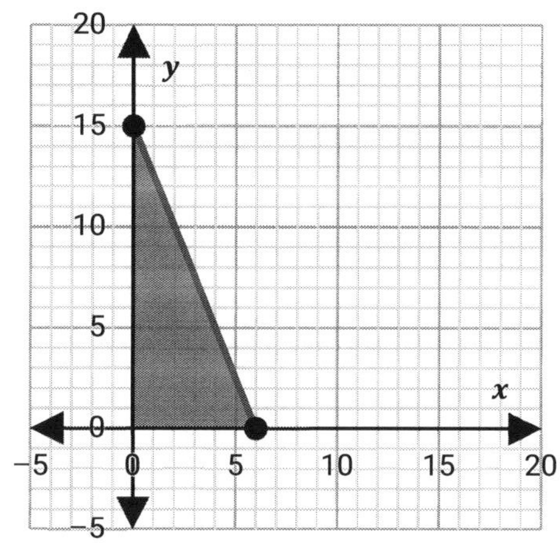

a.

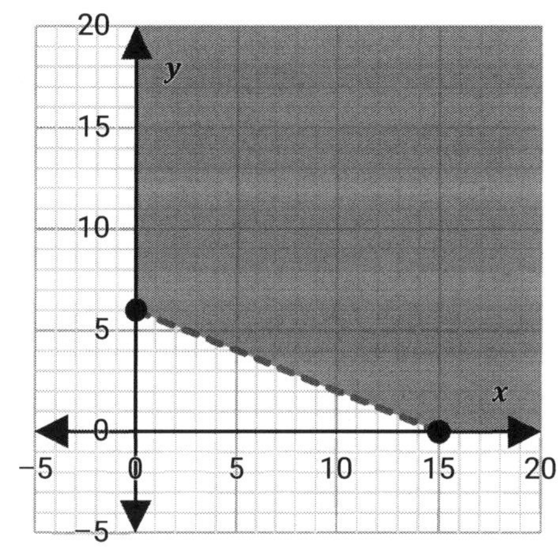

c.

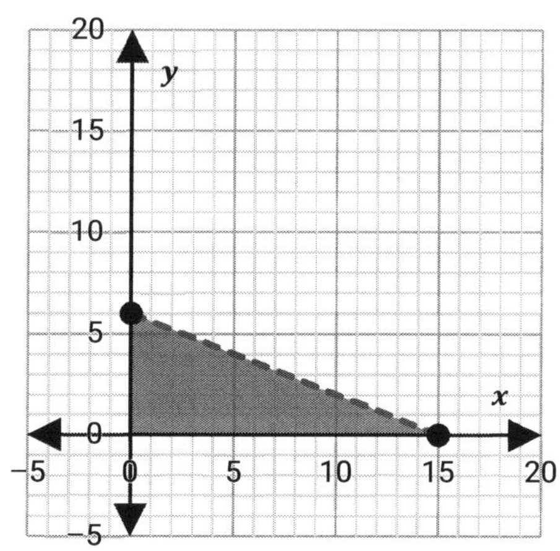

b.

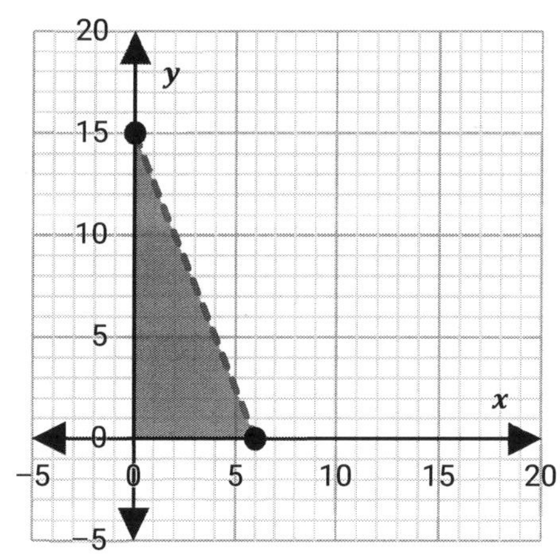

d.

52. **Which expression is represented by the diagram below?**

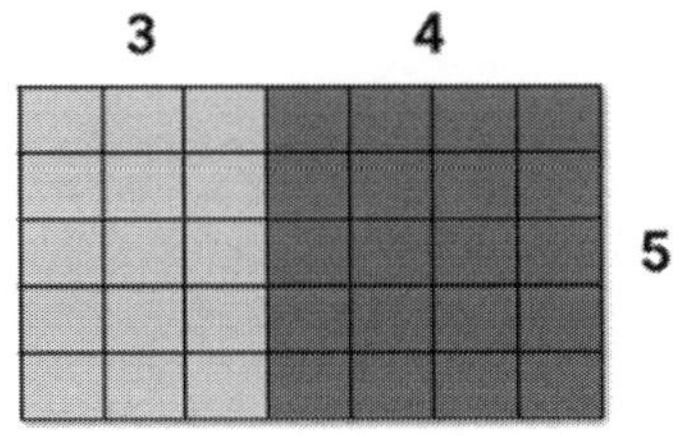

a. $5 + (3 + 4)$
b. $5 \times (3 \times 4)$
c. $5 + (3 \times 4)$
d. $5 \times (3 + 4)$

53. **Which of the following functions has a limit of 0?**

a. $f(x) = 6x^2 - 6$
b. $f(x) = \frac{4x}{x}$
c. $f(x) = \frac{3}{x+3}$
d. $f(x) = \frac{x+1}{x}$

54. **A coin is tossed 300 times. How many of those tosses can you expect to show heads?**

a. 50
b. 100
c. 150
d. 200

55. **Josué is skip-counting by twos while looking at a page with the numbers 1–40 on a number line. His teacher overhears him say the following: "6, 8, 10, 12, 14, 16, 18, 20, 21, 22." Why might Josué skip-count accurately to a point and then begin to have trouble? Choose all that apply.**

a. He is not able to use the concept of a number line.
b. He does not understand that the ones digits will follow the same patterns in numbers larger than 20 as they did in numbers 0–19.
c. He has good fluency counting by ones in numbers 0–20 but does not have the same fluency in numbers larger than 20.

56. Given the diagram below, which of the following theorems may be used to verify that lines *a* and *b* are parallel?

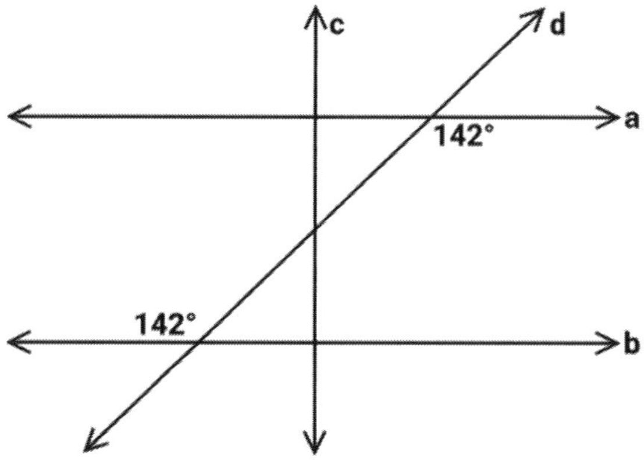

a. Alternate interior angles converse theorem
b. Alternate exterior angles converse theorem
c. Consecutive interior angles converse theorem
d. Corresponding angles converse theorem

57. Miss Wise asks her students to work in pairs to construct Venn diagrams which classify rational numbers, irrational numbers, real numbers, and integers. As she walks around the room to observe their progress, which of the following criterion could she use to assess the students' understanding of these sets of numbers?

a. The set of integers should include the other three sets.
b. The set of rational numbers should include the other three sets.
c. The set of irrational numbers should include the other three sets.
d. The set of real numbers should include the other three sets.

58. What is the approximate area of the shaded region in the figure shown below?

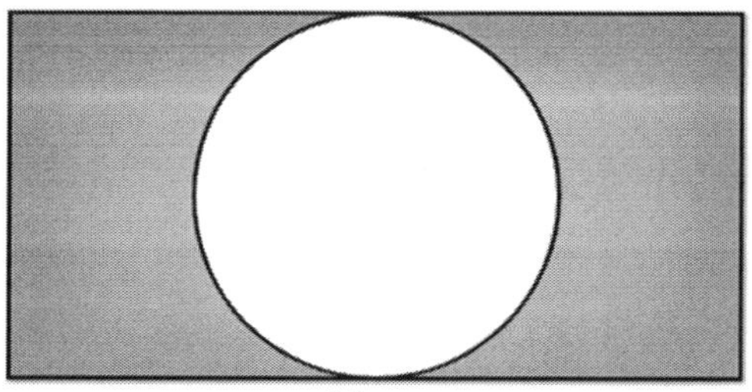

a. 122 cm^2
b. 144 cm^2
c. 176 cm^2
d. 193 cm^2

59. The initial term of a sequence is 7. Each term in the sequence is $\frac{8}{9}$ the amount of the previous term. What is the sum of the terms, as *n* approaches infinity?

a. 8
b. 28.25
c. 56
d. 63

60. An English language learner (ELL) student demonstrates a particular aptitude for mathematics in general, including arithmetic and algebra. The student's L1 is Arabic. The teacher incorporates vocabulary from the student's primary language into lessons in these subjects for the class and into assignments for the student. What is accurate about this practice?

a. It is appropriate for the student's content-area abilities but is not culturally or linguistically related.
b. It is culturally responsive and suits student content-area abilities but is not linguistically relevant.
c. It is culturally responsive, linguistically accessible, and meets the student's content-area abilities.
d. It is not culturally or linguistically meaningful and does not address student content-area abilities.

61. Which of the following accurately describes the set of rational numbers?

a. The set of whole numbers
b. The set of integers plus the roots of positive numbers
c. The set of numbers that may be written as the ratio of $\frac{a}{b}$, where $b \neq 0$
d. The set of counting numbers, zero, and the negations of the counting numbers

62. Given the two-way frequency table below, which of the following *best* represents *P*(bowl or chicken soup)?

	Chicken Soup	Vegetable Soup	Total
Cup	329	248	577
Bowl	642	591	1,233
Total	971	839	1,810

a. 70%
b. 75%
c. 80%
d. 85%

63. Amy saves $450 every 3 months. How much does she save after 3 years?

a. $4,800
b. $5,200
c. $5,400
d. $5,800

64. Which of the following correctly compares the sets of rational numbers and integers?

a. The sets of rational numbers and integers are equal.
b. The sets of rational numbers and integers are disjoint.
c. The set of integers is a subset of the set of rational numbers.
d. The set of rational numbers is a subset of the set of integers.

65. Of the following, which is an advantage of using analytical checklists for assessment?

a. They allow for differences in assessing individual tasks across students.
b. They require additional notes to identify other notable feats observed.
c. They save time and effort by listing tasks, skills, or behaviors in advance.
d. They sometimes constrain assessment to Yes/No without quality levels.

66. Which of the following tables contains points in an exponential function?

a.

x	y
−4	12
−1	−3
0	0
3	9
6	18

b.

x	y
−4	16
−1	2
0	1
2	$\frac{1}{4}$
5	$\frac{1}{32}$

c.

x	y
−3	9
−1	−3
0	0
2	6
5	15

d.

x	y
−4	−7
2	5
4	9
5	11
7	15

67. A seventh-grade math teacher considers how to use scaffolding to support her students in learning how to create a graph using a table. What is the first step she should take in scaffolding?

a. The teacher completes the task with student input.
b. The teacher models how to complete the task to students.
c. Both the teacher and student share the task duties.
d. Students try to complete the task on their own without support.

68. Which of the following best represents the measurement of x, shown in the right triangle below?

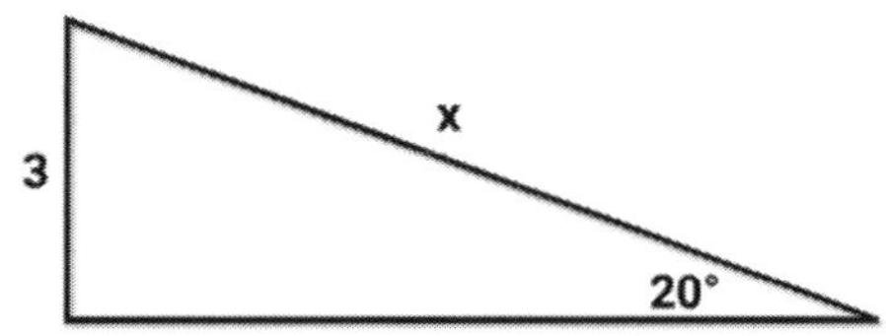

a. 8.8
b. 9.9
c. 10.1
d. 11.2

69. Which approach to assessment offers the strongest chance of quantifying what a student has learned?

a. Multiple choice tests
b. Essay questions
c. Combining several methods
d. Tests using a simple question-and-answer format

70. A missing object problem like the one below is one way of helping students learn what concept?

Truck car bike train truck car bike ______ truck car bike train

a. Counting
b. Problem solving
c. Manipulation of objects
d. Basic addition

71. A tree with a height of 15 feet casts a shadow that is 5 feet in length. A man standing at the base of the shadow formed by the tree is 6 feet tall. How long is the shadow cast by the man?

a. 1.5 feet
b. 2 feet
c. 2.5 feet
d. 3 feet

72. Jackson can decorate a cake in 3 hours. Eli can decorate the same cake in 2 hours. If they work together, how long will it take them to decorate the cake?

a. 0.8 hours
b. 1.2 hours
c. 1.5 hours
d. 1.8 hours

73. A math teacher spends a week teaching her advanced students a new concept. After giving a quiz, she notices that four students in her class are still having difficulty mastering the subject. What should this teacher's next step be in helping these students learn the material?

a. Assign the other students an enrichment activity while using targeted instruction with the group of four.
b. Allow the struggling students the opportunity to retake assessments to see if they improve.
c. Assign each of the four students a peer tutor in the classroom to assist them with their work.
d. Assign the students extra homework to see if their work improves in class.

74. Kendra uses the pie chart below to represent the allocation of her annual income. Her annual income is $40,000.

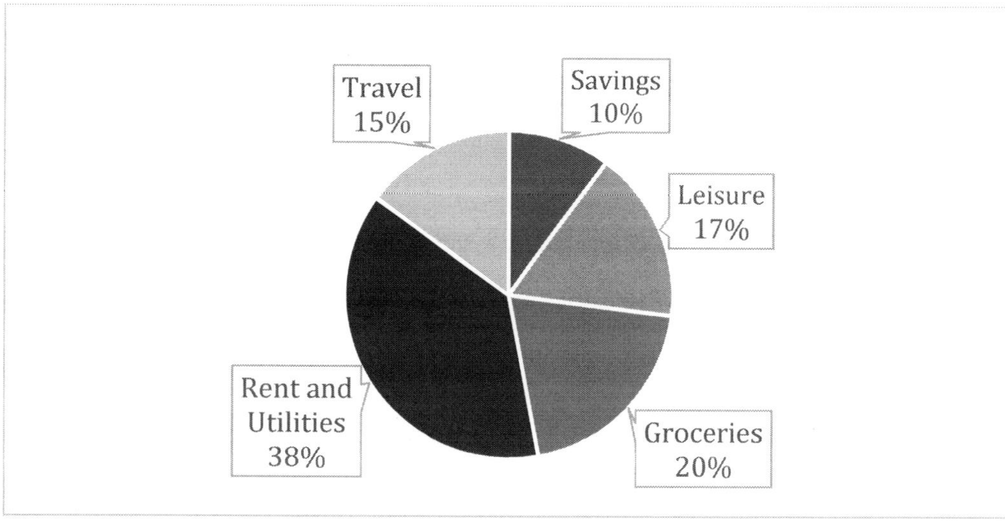

Which of the following statements is true?

a. The amount of money she spends on travel and savings is more than $11,000.
b. The amount of money she spends on rent and utilities is approximately $15,000.
c. The amount of money she spends on groceries and savings is more than $13,000.
d. The amount of money she spends on leisure is less than $5,000.

75. Which of the following statements is NOT true?

a. In a skewed distribution, the mean, median, and mode are all different.
b. In a positively skewed distribution, the mean will be to the right of the median.
c. In a positively skewed distribution, the mode is greater than the median.
d. The area under a normal curve is 1.

76. Each base of a triangular prism has a base length of 13 cm and a height of 15 cm. The height of the prism is 19 cm. What is the volume of the prism?

a. 1,572 cm^3
b. 1,684.75 cm^3
c. 1,775 cm^3
d. 1,852.5 cm^3

77. Given the diagram below, what is the measure of $\widehat{AC}$?

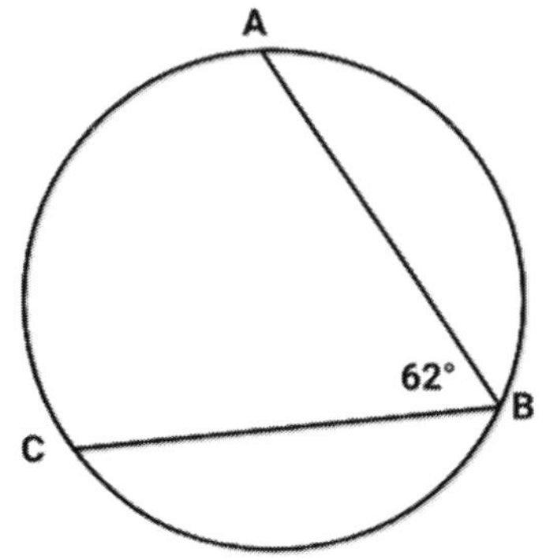

a. 31°
b. 62°
c. 124°
d. 208°

78. Mr. Fields wants to design an assessment method for his sixth grade math class that will help his students learn from their assignments and motivate them to improve. Which of the following approaches is most likely to accomplish this objective?

a. Assigning ungraded homework problems and having weekly tests
b. Assigning nightly homework problems that are peer-graded in class the next day, and going over the answers after the assignment is graded
c. Assigning homework problems that are graded by the teacher and returned on the day before the unit test
d. Assigning nightly homework problems which are graded and returned with a correct answer key within three days

79. Eloisa's monthly car payment is $400. She is trading her car in for a newer model with a monthly payment of $525. What is the percent increase in her monthly payment?

a. 25%
b. 31.25%
c. 35%
d. 42.75%

80. Which of the following is an advantage of using anecdotal notes to assess student work?

a. Teachers can use these to collect information both during assessment and outside of it.
b. Unless a teacher adds norms or criteria for comparison, these notes lack standardization.
c. Teachers cannot record observations of individual student behaviors as with most tools.
d. Writing anecdotal notes can yield valuable insights but often lacks any supporting context.

81. A trough is in the shape of an inverted square pyramid. If the base has a side length of 9 feet and the height of the container is 2.5 feet, how many cubic feet of water can the trough hold?

a. 67.5 ft^3
b. 75 ft^3
c. 88.5 ft^3
d. 102 ft^3

82. Given that the two horizontal lines in the diagram below are parallel, which pair of angles is congruent?

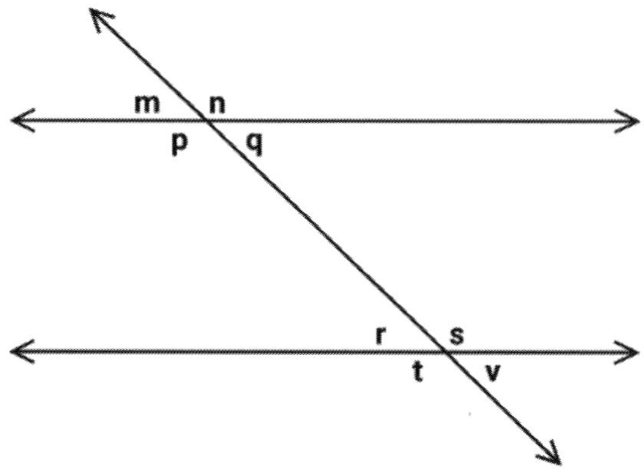

a. $\angle n$ and $\angle s$
b. $\angle m$ and $\angle p$
c. $\angle q$ and $\angle s$
d. $\angle s$ and $\angle v$

83. Eliza rolls a die. What is the probability she gets a 6 or an even number?

a. $\frac{1}{4}$
b. $\frac{1}{2}$
c. $\frac{2}{3}$
d. $\frac{3}{4}$

84. Which of the following graphs does NOT represent a function?

a. 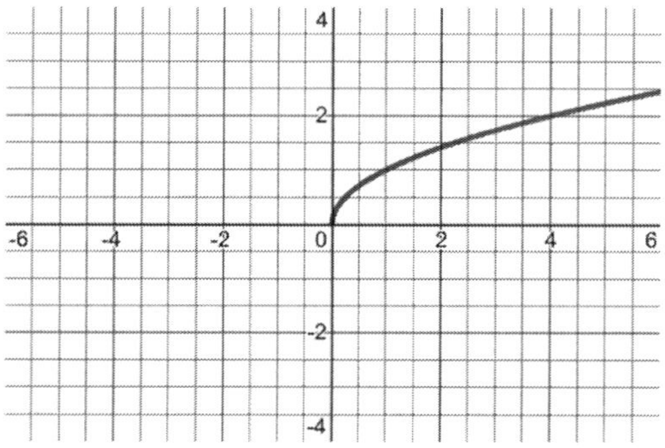

b. 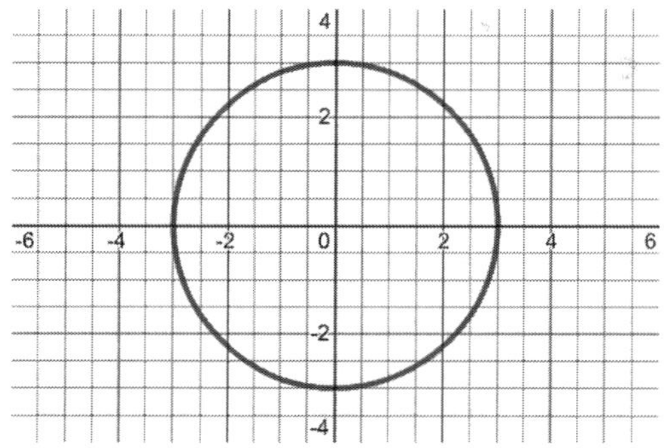

c. 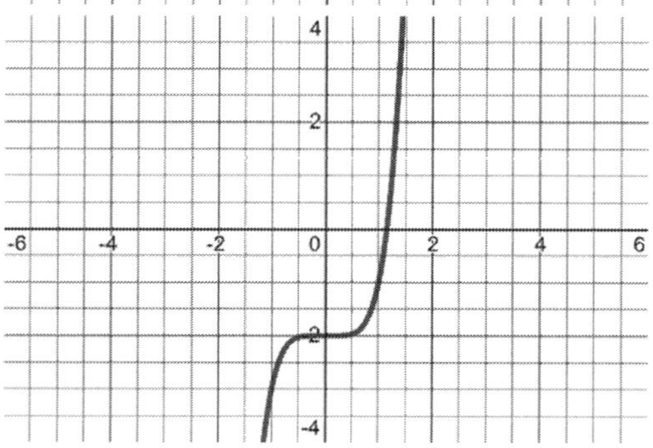

d. 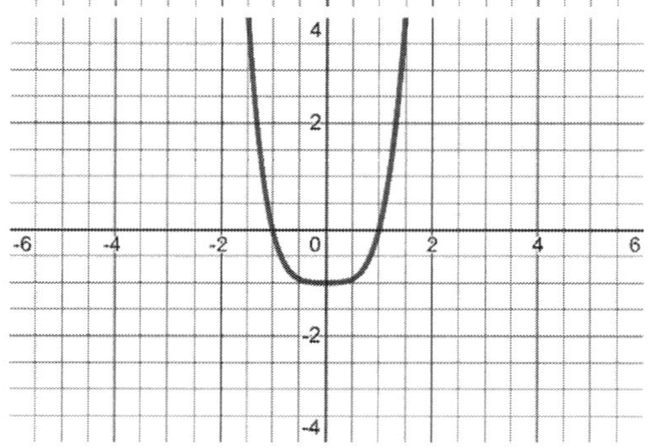

85. Zac eats $\frac{1}{9}$ of a bowl of chocolates. If the bowl contains $8\frac{4}{7}$ ounces of chocolate, how much chocolate does he eat?

a. $\frac{59}{60}$ ounces
b. $\frac{79}{80}$ ounces
c. $\frac{20}{21}$ ounces
d. $\frac{62}{63}$ ounces

86. A ball has a radius of 2.75 inches. Which of the following best represents the volume of the ball?

a. 79.9 in^3
b. 87.1 in^3
c. 96.5 in^3
d. 104.3 in^3

87. Lewis rolls a die and tosses a coin. What is the probability he gets a number less than 3 and heads?

a. $\frac{1}{6}$
b. $\frac{1}{4}$
c. $\frac{1}{3}$
d. 1

88. Which of the following best represents the value of x, shown in the triangle below?

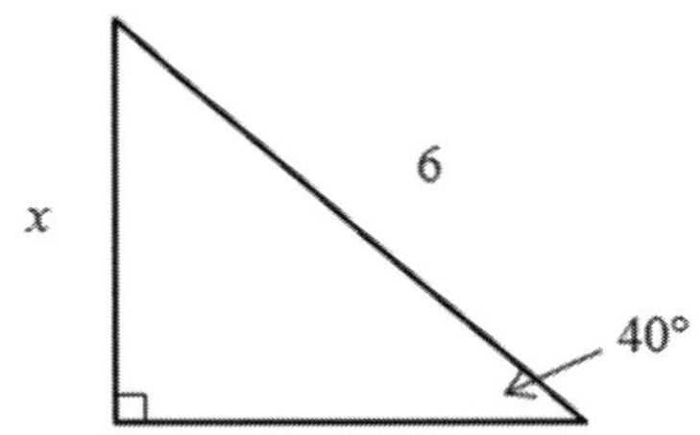

a. 2.6
b. 3.1
c. 3.9
d. 4.4

89. What is the midpoint of the line segment below?

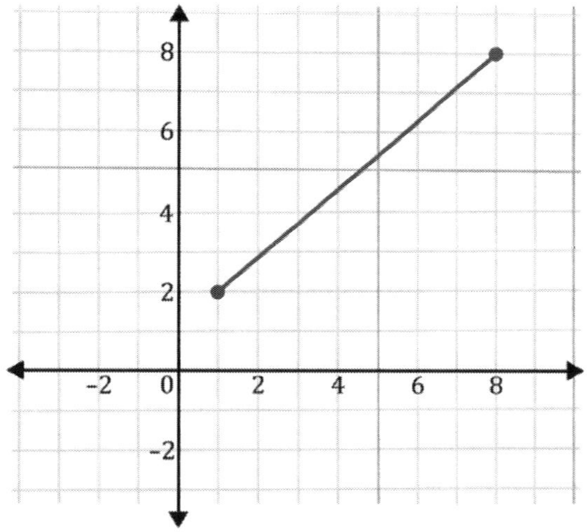

a. (3.5,4)
b. (4,4)
c. (4.5,5)
d. (5,5)

90. 225 students are surveyed. 95 of the students like only coffee. 30 of the students like only tea. 55 of the students like both coffee and tea. How many students like neither coffee nor tea?

a. 25
b. 35
c. 45
d. 55

91. Which of the following statements is true?

a. The set of rational numbers is a subset of the set of natural numbers.
b. The set of integers is a subset of the set of whole numbers.
c. The set of natural numbers is a subset of the set of whole numbers.
d. The set of complex numbers is a subset of natural numbers.

92. Which of the following statements is NOT true?

a. In most cases of a skewed distribution, the mean is pulled towards the longer tail.
b. In most cases of a skewed distribution, the mean is pulled towards the area with a higher frequency of scores.
c. In a normal distribution, the mean, median, and mode are the same value.
d. The area under a normal curve is 1.

93. The expression $2x^2 - 4x - 30$ is equal to the product of $(x - 5)$ and which other factor?

a. $(2x - 10)$
b. $(2x + 25)$
c. $(2x + 7)$
d. $(2x + 6)$

94. A third-grade student's continuous inability to do which of the following may indicate the potential need for further evaluation?

a. Multiply three-digit whole numbers
b. Compare and order fractions
c. Divide two-digit whole numbers
d. Add and subtract whole numbers within 100

95. What is $\lim_{x \to -4} \left(2x^3 - \frac{1}{2}x^2 - 1\right)$?

a. -137
b. -121
c. 4
d. 119

96. Mike is ordering a new polo shirt for each of his 12 employees, spending at least $150. Which of the following inequalities represents the possible costs?

a. $150 < 12p$
b. $150 > 12p$
c. $150 \leq 12p$
d. $150 \geq 12p$

97. Ms. King has taught rounding to her students by showing them to round to the nearest hundredth. She now wants her students to correctly identify situations in which this skill will be useful. She plans to present the students with two situations and ask them to choose the one that calls for rounding to the nearest hundredth. Which pair of situations would best match her objective?

a. Dividing a cookie equally between friends or buying enough cookies for 6 friends when the cookies come in packs of 4
b. Calculating sales tax on a pack of 4 cookies that costs $2.25 or dividing a cookie equally between friends
c. Calculating sales tax on a pack of 4 cookies that costs $2.25 or calculating the cost per cookie in a pack of 4 cookies that costs $2.25
d. Buying enough cookies for 6 friends when the cookies come in packs of 4 or calculating the cost of buying enough cookies for 6 friends when the cookies come in packs of 4 and cost $2.25

98. $g(x) = \frac{4-x}{x+6}$. What is the equation of the horizontal asymptote?

a. $y = 0$
b. $y = \frac{2}{3}$
c. $y = -1$
d. $y = -\frac{1}{6}$

99. Given the diagram below, what is the measure of the inscribed angle?

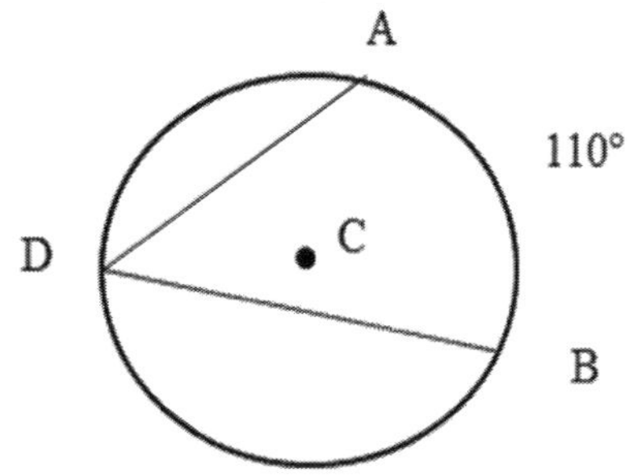

a. 37°
b. 45°
c. 55°
d. 57°

100. Raquel pays $12 per ticket to the fair, plus an $8 parking fee. Let x represent the number of tickets she buys. Which of the following equations represents her total cost y?

a. $y = 8x + 12$
b. $y = 20x$
c. $y = 12x + 8$
d. $y = 12x + 20$

Answer Key and Explanations for Test #1

1. B: There are 60 months in 5 years. Since a quarter is 3 months, the following proportion may be written.

$$\frac{250}{3} = \frac{x}{60}$$

We solve by first cross-multiplying.

$$3x = 15{,}000$$

Then, divide both sides of the equation by 3.

$$x = 5{,}000$$

Therefore, Quinn will have deposited $5,000 into the account after 5 years.

2. B: The measure of an angle formed by intersecting chords inside a circle is equal to one-half of the sum of the measures of the intercepted arcs. Thus, $x = \frac{1}{2}(36° + 58°)$, or 47°.

3. B: Amelia underestimated how many more cubes she would need to fill an area when provided with a change in dimension. Choice C would also be correct if it referred to the distributive property rather than the commutative property of multiplication Amelia could have chosen the correct number of cubes if she understood that $10(15) = 10(10) + 10(5)$.

4. A: The perimeter of the triangle is equal to the sum of the side lengths. The length of the longer diagonal side may be represented as $d = \sqrt{(1 - -8)^2 + (-2 - -5)^2}$, which simplifies to $d = \sqrt{90}$. The length of the shorter diagonal side may be represented as $d = \sqrt{(4 - 1)^2 + (-2 - -5)^2}$, which simplifies to $d = \sqrt{18}$. The base length is 12 units. Thus, the perimeter is equal to $12 + \sqrt{90} + \sqrt{18}$, which is approximately 25.73 units. Since each unit represents 0.25 miles, the total distance of the path is equal to the product of 25.73 and 0.25, or approximately 6.4 miles.

5. A: The median of the lower half of the scores is 6. The median of the upper half of the scores is 16. The interquartile range is the difference between the first and third quartiles: $16 - 6 = 10$.

6. D: We tend not only to see or impose patterns and relationships where they do not objectively exist (like seeing animal, human, and object shapes in the clouds); we also deliberately create patterns and relationships in the works of art (A), pieces of music (B), and articles of clothing (C) we produce. We also notice and appreciate the patterns and relationships in these products that others have created.

7. B: The question in choice B prompts the students to begin thinking about what operations are needed to find the quantity the question is asking for. Choice A simply restates the question asked in the word problem. Choices C and D are clarifying questions that Ms. Cho could ask after students have begun thinking about how to calculate the total amount of food that Daniel needs.

8. A: The number of outcomes for the event is 5 (rolling a 1, 2, 3, 4, or 5), and the sample space is 6 (numbers 1–6). Thus, the probability may be written as $\frac{5}{6}$.

9. D: In a positively skewed distribution, the median is closer to the first quartile than the third.

10. C: If the statement is written in the form $p \to q$, then the converse is represented as $q \to p$. Thus, the converse should read, "If Joe buys a donut, it is Saturday."

11. D: The set of integers is represented as $\{\dots, -3, -2, -1, 0, 1, 2, 3, \dots\}$. The numbers 1, 2, 3, ... are counting numbers, or natural numbers. Thus, the set contains the counting numbers, zero, and the negations of the counting numbers.

12. C: The position of an accelerating car is changing according to a non-constant speed. Thus, the graph will show a curve with an increasing slope. The slope is increasing since it represents the velocity, and the velocity is increasing.

13. B: The relationship between number of faces, edges, and vertices is represented by Euler's Formula, $E = F + V - 2$. Substituting 9 for E and 6 for V gives: $9 = F + 6 - 2$, which simplifies to $9 = F + 4$. Thus, $F = 5$.

14. B, C: Both choice B and choice C require careful reading of scale and labels in order to properly interpret the visual data representation.

15. A: The repeating decimal may be converted to a fraction by writing:

$$\begin{array}{r} 10x = 4.\overline{4} \\ -\quad x = 0.\overline{4} \\ \hline \end{array}$$

which simplifies as $10x - x = 4.\overline{4} - 0.\overline{4}$.

16. A: Because 1 inch is 2.54 centimeters, the following proportion may be written and solved for x: $\frac{2.54^2}{1} = \frac{1{,}982}{x}$. So $(2.54)(2.54)x = 1{,}982$. Dividing both sides of the equation by 6.4516 gives $x \approx 307.21$. Thus, 1,982 square centimeters is approximately equal to 307 square inches.

17. B: If the statement is written in the form $p \to q$, then the converse is represented as $q \to p$. Thus, the converse should read, "If it is winter, then I go skiing."

18. A: Data sets B and C are asymmetrical: data set B is skewed toward lower values, and data set C is skewed toward higher values. This makes the mean a poor measure of center. Data set D is mostly symmetrical but has a large outlier. The mean is very sensitive to outliers and is not an appropriate measure of center for data sets that include them. Data set A is roughly symmetrical and has no outliers; the mean would be an appropriate measure of center here.

19. D: This is a counting problem. The possible number of outfits is equal to the product of the possibilities for each category. The product of 4, 6, and 5 is 120. Thus, there are 120 outfits that she may create.

20. A: The net of a triangular prism has three rectangular faces and two triangular faces, and the rectangular faces must all be able to connect to each other directly. This is shown in choice A.

21. D: Each student is a unique individual, and different students may have different ways of conceptualizing the same problem. In the long run, allowing students to find their own ways of thinking about mathematics will make them better problem solvers. Mental math has an important role to play in everyday life. Memorization and drills also have their place, but they should not be the central focus in the classroom.

22. D: Begin by calculating the total rainfall in the summer and autumn months by adding all the values together. The total rainfall is 25.38 inches. Then, create a ratio comparing the rainfall in October to the total rainfall. The ratio $\frac{4.5}{25.38}$ represents the fraction of rainfall received during October. Convert the ratio to a percentage by dividing the numerator by the denominator and then multiplying by 100: $\frac{4.5}{25.38} \approx 0.177 = 17.7\%$. Therefore, about 17.7% of the rain fell during October.

23. B: The vertical-line test can determine whether a graph is a function. If any vertical line passes through more than one point at once, then the graph is not a function. A vertical line will cross a sideways parabola at two points anywhere beyond the vertex, so choice B is not a function.

24. C: The area of a trapezoid may be calculated using the formula, $A = \frac{1}{2}(b_1 + b_2)h$. Thus, the area of the trapezoid is represented as $A = \frac{1}{2}(4 + 2)(2)$, which simplifies to $A = 6$. The area of the triangle is represented as $A = \frac{1}{2}(4)(3)$, which also simplifies to $A = 6$. Thus, the total area is 12 square units.

25. B: When mixing ordinal and cardinal numbers the point of reference shifts by one unit. Ordinal numbering begins from 1, while cardinal numbering begins from 0.

26. A: A function is a relation in which there is not any x-value that is mapped to more than one y-value. The only relation that represents a function is $\{(2,1), (3,-2), (6,8), (-1,-4), (4,-1)\}$.

27. C: This is a counting problem. The possible number of meals is equal to the product of the possibilities for each category. The product of 4, 5, and 3 is 60. Thus, there are 60 meals that he can create.

28. D: To find the probability of Fran pulling two different marbles from the bag, we must find the probability of each event occurring individually, then multiply those probabilities together. To start, we can determine that Fran's chance of pulling a red marble is $\frac{5}{12}$ because there are 5 red marbles out of a total 12 marbles. Next, we must determine that Fran has a $\frac{4}{11}$ chance of pulling a green marble because there are 4 green marbles out of a new total 11 marbles. Notice, our total must now be reduced to 11 because Fran has one marble already in her possession. When we multiply our two events, $\frac{5}{12} \times \frac{4}{11}$, we get $\frac{20}{132}$, or $\frac{5}{33}$. The chance of Fran pulling a red marble followed by a green marble is $\frac{5}{33}$.

29. A: When students show mastery at the beginning of a unit, teachers should still work to teach material on the same topic, but teach more advanced concepts at a higher level. This helps challenge students and keeps them engaged in the material, and it helps students become more proficient at the easier questions while also allowing them to work towards answering the more challenging questions. While the teacher could shorten the unit to move on to harder units, it probably is best that they continue teaching the unit so that students can reinforce their skills to build on their pre-existing knowledge for the next unit. It is important to allow students a chance to learn more advanced material when the planned material may be too simple for them, as it will help increase their confidence and allow students a chance to improve on what they know.

30. C: The horizontal asymptote is equal to the ratio of the coefficients of x, or $\frac{1}{1}$, which equals 1.

31. D: The original cost may be represented by the equation $45 = x - 0.25x$ or $45 = 0.75x$. Dividing both sides of the equation by 0.75 gives $x = 60$.

32. B: The points in the table represent a symmetrical curve mirrored across the y-axis. This is a parabola, or a quadratic equation.

33. A: Asking students to create lists of what skills they feel they are strong in allows the teacher to informally assess what students know as well as learn about the students' interests. This should allow the teacher to use their strengths and interests to better plan instruction and activities in the classroom. Asking students to create a list of strengths is not a formal assessment and should not be used as an all-inclusive tool to assess the background knowledge of a student. While the teacher may be able to use the list of tasks as a way of gauging what students know, self-reported strengths on the first day of school are insufficient to make grouping decisions. Although creating a list of tasks that students can perform may increase student confidence temporarily, it is not the ultimate purpose of this activity and is instead a secondary benefit.

34. C: Question A is good for meeting the standard of applying mathematics to real life. Question B is good for students to learn the conceptual relationship of decimals and fractions as different yet equivalent ways of expressing parts of a whole. Question D is good for students to learn how to convert fractions to decimals and vice versa. Question C is better asked by the teacher than by students—and not at this stage of their learning, but only after they understand place value.

35. D: The number of outcomes in the event is 4 (rolling a 3, 4, 5, or 6), and the sample space is 6 (numbers 1–6). Thus, the probability may be written as $\frac{4}{6}$, which simplifies to $\frac{2}{3}$.

36. C: Since all of the teachers are implementing a theme about the heart, this is a thematic unit. Collaborative learning typically involves students working in groups. Formative assessments are ways teachers assess learning while working on a unit. Differentiated instruction is the use of multiple methods when teaching a unit. Therefore, the correct answer is choice C.

37. B: The situation may be modeled by the inequality $2.5x + 6y \leq 30$. Isolating the y-term gives $6y \leq -2.5x + 30$. Solving for y gives $y \leq -\frac{5}{12}x + 5$. Thus, the line's y-intercept is 5, and the slope is $-\frac{5}{12}$. Since she wants to spend \$30 or less, the shading should be below the line. Because she can choose to spend exactly \$30 (i.e., ≤ 30 rather than < 30), the line should be solid, not dashed.

38. B: The total electricity cost is \$876.56. Thus, the ratio $\frac{127.56}{876.56}$ represents the percentage of electricity cost incurred during October. $\frac{127.56}{876.56} \approx 0.146$ or 14.6%.

39. A: The horizontal asymptote is equal to the ratio of the two coefficients of x, or $\frac{2}{-1}$, which equals -2.

40. B: The probability may be written as $P(E \text{ and } H) = P(E) \times P(H)$. The probability of rolling an even number on a die is $E = \frac{3}{6} = \frac{1}{2}$. The probability of a coin landing on heads is $H = \frac{1}{2}$. Substituting the probability of each event gives $P(E \text{ and } H) = \frac{1}{2} \times \frac{1}{2} = \frac{1}{4}$.

41. B: The median of the lower half of the scores (the first quartile) is 7. The median of the upper half of the scores (the third quartile) is 18. The interquartile range equals the difference between the first and third quartiles: $18 - 7 = 11$.

42. A: The triangle was translated across the y-axis. In translation, each point is moved the same distance and direction.

43. B: The following proportion may be written and solved for x: $\frac{5{,}280}{1} = \frac{6{,}700}{x}$. Thus, $x \approx 1.27$.

44. D: The total gas cost is \$478.96. Thus, the ratio $\frac{97.48}{478.96}$ represents the percentage of gas cost spent in March. $\frac{97.48}{478.96} \approx 0.204$ or 20.4%.

45. D: The surface area of a sphere may be calculated using the formula $SA = 4\pi r^2$. Substituting 0.8 for r gives $SA = 4\pi(0.8)^2$, which simplifies to $SA \approx 8.04$. The surface area of the ball is approximately 8.04 square feet. There are twelve inches in a foot, so there are $12^2 = 144$ square inches in a square foot. In order to convert this measurement to square inches, then, the following proportion may be written and solved for x: $\frac{144}{1} = \frac{x}{8.04}$. This means $x \approx 1{,}157.76$. It would take approximately 1,157.76 square inches of wrapping paper to wrap the ball.

46. C: The ratio between successive terms is constant (3), so this is a geometric sequence. A geometric sequence is represented by an exponential function.

47. A: The teacher is looking to teach about perimeter and area, a skill which applies only to two-dimensional shapes. The activity the teacher wants to use focuses on "using appropriate tools strategically," which means that the students should have an assortment of tools to use.

A good activity for teaching those skills is to provide students with shapes to find the area of. Shapes can include straight-edged shapes like squares and triangles, but they can also include circles or other shapes with rounded edges. The activity that is chosen needs to accommodate a variety of shapes, which is why the students would need yarn to trace curved edges and a ruler to measure the yarn or straight edges. The teacher should also be interested in having all students do the same activity to help make grading fair and possible, so using worksheets is probably a good idea but not the only option.

Choices B, C, and D all refer to "objects," which are three-dimensional. Surface area and volume are skills that build on area and perimeter, so a teacher would want to be careful about selecting a task that can be easily followed by the students. Choice B focuses on calculation and not on using appropriate tools. Choice C provides only one tool for the job, and may not accommodate curved shapes. Choice D also only provides the students with one tool to use, and it is a tool that is not typically used in the real world. Choice A is the best option because it requires the students to think strategically about what tools to use to obtain a measurement and calculate both perimeter and area. Keep in mind that an activity does not need to target all objectives at once, so it is okay if the teacher decided to have the students calculate only perimeter or only area.

48. B: Since the figures are similar, the following proportion may be written and solved for x.

$$\frac{6}{4} = \frac{8}{x}$$
$$6x = 4 \times 8$$
$$6x = 32$$
$$x = \frac{32}{6} = 5\frac{2}{6} = 5\frac{1}{3}$$

Therefore, the measure of x is $5\frac{1}{3}$ in.

49. B: When a large portion of students receive a failing grade on an assessment, the teacher should take the time to look at common mistakes made on the assessment. The teacher then should work on reteaching the material to the students and administer another assessment to gauge student progress. If most students did not perform well on an assessment, instead of individually conferencing with students to see what they did to prepare, the teacher should first self-reflect to see what they did to get the students prepared for the assessment. While encouraging students to study at home is a good practice for improving student performance, increasing the amount of homework does not guarantee better performance. In fact, it may do the opposite if students' stress levels increase due to the increase in amount of work. Although asking students for input on what they need is something teachers should do, it is not the requirement of the student to know what they need to be successful within a classroom.

50. C: The value of the 40th term may be found using the formula $a_n = a_1 + (n-1)d$. Substituting the number of terms for n, the initial value of 3 for a, and the common difference of 3 for d gives: $a_{40} = 3 + (40-1)(3)$, which simplifies to $a_{40} = 120$. Now, the value of the 40th term may be substituted into the formula, $S_n = \frac{n(a_1+a_n)}{2}$, which gives: $S_{40} = \frac{40(3+120)}{2}$, which simplifies to $S_{40} = 2{,}460$.

51. D: The situation may be modeled by the inequality $7.5x + 3y < 45$. Isolating the y-term gives $3y < -7.5x + 45$. Solving for y gives $y < -2.5x + 15$. Thus, the y-intercept will be 15, the line will be dotted, and a test point of (0,0) indicates the shading should occur below the line.

52. D: The rectangular array represents the product of the side lengths of 5 and $(3 + 4)$.

53. C: As the denominator approaches infinity, the value of the function will get smaller and smaller and converge to 0.

54. C: The probability of tossing a coin and getting heads is $\frac{1}{2}$. Multiply the probability by the number of coin tosses: $\frac{1}{2} \times 300 = 150$. You would expect to get heads about 150 times.

55. B, C: Choices B and C each explain a possible reason that the student only begins to make mistakes after a certain number. If choice A were correct, we could expect him to make mistakes more consistently. It is common for a young student to have better fluency with and understanding of smaller numbers that they use more frequently and can easily represent visually or concretely.

56. A: The alternate interior angles have congruent angle measures, each measuring 142°. According to the alternate interior angles converse theorem, two lines are parallel if a transversal, intersecting the lines, forms congruent alternate interior angles.

57. D: Real numbers include all rational and irrational numbers. Rational numbers include all integers. The set of real numbers include the other three sets.

58. A: The area of the rectangle is equal to $10 \times (20)$, or 200 square centimeters. The area of the circle is equal to $\pi(5)^2$, or approximately 78.5 square centimeters. The area of the shaded region is equal to the difference of the area of the rectangle and the area of the circle, or $200\text{ cm}^2 - 78.5\text{ cm}^2$, which equals 121.5 cm^2. So the area of the shaded region is about 122 cm^2.

59. D: The sum of an infinite geometric series may be modeled by the formula $S = \frac{a}{1-r}$, where a represents the initial value and r represents the common ratio. Substituting the initial value of 7 and common ratio of $\frac{8}{9}$ into the formula gives $S = \frac{7}{1-\frac{8}{9}}$, which simplifies to $S = \frac{7}{\frac{1}{9}}$ or 63.

60. C: This practice is culturally responsive and linguistically accessible because the Arab culture significantly contributed to the development of arithmetic and algebra, and the Arabic language is the origin of many arithmetic concepts and algebraic terms. It is also appropriate to the student's content-area abilities because the student displays a particular aptitude for arithmetic and algebra. Incorporating Arabic into lessons as well as assignments can also inform other students about the origins of arithmetic, algebra, and their concepts and terminology. Therefore (A), (B), and (D) are all incorrect.

61. C: The set of rational numbers includes any number that can be written as a fraction of two integers, where the denominator is not zero.

62. D: Let $P(B)$ represent the probability of choosing a bowl, and let $P(CS)$ represent the probability of choosing chicken soup. Then $P(B \text{ or } CS) = P(B) + P(CS) - P(B \text{ and } CS)$. Substituting values from the table, we find: $P(B \text{ or } CS) = \frac{1{,}233}{1{,}810} + \frac{971}{1{,}810} - \frac{642}{1{,}810} = \frac{1{,}562}{1{,}810} = 0.8629834254 \ldots \approx 85\%$.

63. C: There are 36 months in 3 years. Since Amy saves \$450 every 3 months, the following proportion can be written to find the amount she saves in 36 months: $\frac{450}{3} = \frac{x}{36}$. Cross multiplying gives you the equation $3x = 16{,}200$, which can be solved for x. Dividing both sides of the equation by 3 gives $x = 5{,}400$.

64. C: The set of integers is represented as $\{\ldots -3, -2, -1, 0, 1, 2, 3, \ldots\}$. The set of rational numbers includes all of these as well as any number that can be represented as a fraction of two integers, where the denominator is not zero. So the set of integers is a subset of the set of rational numbers.

65. C: Using analytical checklists as assessment tools has the advantage of saving time and effort by listing the tasks, skills, or behaviors to be performed and assessed in advance. They also have the advantage of making assessment uniform across students relative to tasks and/or their components, making choice A incorrect. They do require additional notes for teachers to identify other notable feats that teachers observe students accomplishing beyond the designated tasks (B), but this is a disadvantage. Although some checklists include performance levels similarly to rubrics, others constrain assessment to Yes/No responses (D), another disadvantage.

66. B: The table represents part of a geometric sequence, with a common ratio of $\frac{1}{2}$, so it also represents points of an exponential function.

67. B: When considering scaffolding, teachers should first begin with modeling the task that they would like students to be able to accomplish independently. Students observe how the teacher completes the task. The next step is to then have the teacher complete the task with student input, with the teacher primarily completing the task. After that, teachers release responsibility to the students with guided support. Finally, the teacher allows the students to complete the task independently.

68. A: The following equation may be written and solved for x: $\frac{\sin 20°}{1} = \frac{3}{x}$. Cross-multiplying gives: $x = \frac{3}{\sin 20°}$, or $x \approx 8.8$.

69. C: Some students perform better on tests, while others do better with papers or other projects. Just as students learn in a variety of ways, their talents for expressing what they have learned also varies widely. A teacher that evaluates students based on a wide variety of tasks will come away with a much more complete picture of each student's strengths and weaknesses.

70. B: Problem solving. Because an item is missing in the middle of the pattern, the process asked for cannot be counting or addition. Solving this puzzle does not involve manipulation of objects.

71. B: The following proportion may be written and solved for x: $\frac{15 \text{ ft}}{5 \text{ ft}} = \frac{6 \text{ ft}}{x \text{ ft}}$. Cross multiplying results in $15x = 30$. Dividing by 15 gives $x = 2$. Thus, the shadow cast by the man is 2 feet in length.

72. B: The situation may be modeled with the equation $\frac{1}{3} + \frac{1}{2} = \frac{1}{t}$, which simplifies to $\frac{5}{6} = \frac{1}{t}$. Thus, $t = \frac{6}{5} = 1.2$. If working together, it will take them 1.2 hours to decorate the cake.

73. A: When a small group of students have trouble understanding a new concept, a teacher should attempt to help remediate those students. One of the best ways to handle this during class time is to provide an enrichment activity to the students who have mastered the concept while providing additional instruction to the students still working on mastery. Retaking assessments can also be utilized, but material should be retaught before having students retake assessments. Taking the time to try to help students understand concepts is particularly important in math classrooms because concepts tend to build upon each other, and teachers should try to incorporate this into their lesson plans when students are struggling.

74. B: The amount she spends on rent and utilities is equal to 0.38($40,000), or $15,200, which is approximately $15,000.

75. C: The median is always greater than the mode in a positively skewed distribution.

76. D: The volume of a prism may be calculated using the formula $V = Bh$, where B represents the area of the base and h represents the height of the prism. The area of each triangular base is represented by $A = \frac{1}{2}(13)(15)$, so the area of each base is equal to 97.5 square centimeters. Substituting 97.5 for the area of the base and 19 for the height of the prism gives $V = (97.5)(19)$ or $V = 1{,}852.5$. The volume of the prism is 1,852.5 cm^3.

77. C: The measure of the inscribed angle is half of the measure of the intercepted arc. Since the inscribed angle measures 62°, the intercepted arc is equal to (62°)(2) or 124°.

78. B: Mr. Fields is most likely to achieve his objective by assigning nightly homework problems that are peer-graded in class the next day, and going over the answers after the assignment is graded. This method offers two advantages: first, students receive immediate feedback on their performance that they can begin to apply to future assignments and tests; second, students have the opportunity to find out why they arrived at wrong answers when the teacher goes over the problems. This makes assessment a positive experience that helps students perform better in the future, rather than making it a negative experience that de-motivates students by making them feel powerless to improve their performance.

79. B: The percent increase is represented as $\frac{525-400}{400}$, which equals 0.3125 or 31.25%.

80. A: One advantage of writing anecdotal notes as an assessment tool is that teachers can collect information about student skills and behaviors outside of assessment activities as well as during them; this can help teachers realize valuable insights into student learning and behavior. The fact that such notes are not standardized unless the teacher incorporates norms or criteria for comparison (B) is a disadvantage. An advantage of anecdotal notes is that teachers *can* record observations of individual student behaviors, which standard test instruments, checklists, and most other tools do *not* allow (C). The fact that anecdotal notes often lack any supporting context (D) is a disadvantage.

81. A: The volume of a pyramid may be calculated using the formula $V = \frac{1}{3}Bh$, where B represents the area of the base and h represents the height of the pyramid. Since the base is a square, the area of the base is equal to 9^2, or 81 square feet. Substituting 81 for B and 2.5 for h gives $V = \frac{1}{3}(81)(2.5)$, which simplifies to $V = 67.5$ ft³.

82. A: Since $\angle n$ and $\angle s$ are corresponding angles, they are congruent.

83. B: Since they are not mutually exclusive events, the probability may be written as $P(6 \text{ or } E) = P(6) + P(E) - P(6 \text{ and } E)$. Substituting the probability of each event gives $(6\ or\ E) = \frac{1}{6} + \frac{1}{2} - \frac{1}{6}$, or $\frac{1}{2}$.

84. B: A vertical line will cross the graph at more than one point. Thus, it is not a function.

85. C: The amount Zac eats may be written as $\frac{1}{9} \times \frac{60}{7}$, which equals $\frac{60}{63}$ or $\frac{20}{21}$. Thus, he eats $\frac{20}{21}$ ounces of chocolate.

86. B: The volume of a sphere may be calculated using the formula $V = \frac{4}{3}\pi r^3$, where r represents the radius. Substituting 2.75 for r gives $V = \frac{4}{3}\pi(2.75)^3$, which simplifies to $V \approx 87.1$.

87. A: The probability may be written as $P(N \text{ and } H) = P(N) \times P(H)$. Substituting the probability of each event gives $(N \text{ and } H) = \frac{1}{3} \times \frac{1}{2}$, which simplifies to $\frac{1}{6}$.

88. C: The following equation may be written and solved for x: $\sin 40° = \frac{x}{6}$. Multiplying both sides of the equation by 6 gives: $6 \cdot \sin 40° = x$, or $x \approx 3.9$.

89. C: A line segment with endpoints (x_1, y_1) and (x_2, y_2) has the midpoint $\left(\frac{x_1+x_2}{2}, \frac{y_1+y_2}{2}\right)$. The line segment shown has endpoints (1,2) and (8,8), so its midpoint is $\left(\frac{1+8}{2}, \frac{2+8}{2}\right)$, or (4.5,5).

90. C: A Venn diagram may be drawn to assist in finding the answer.

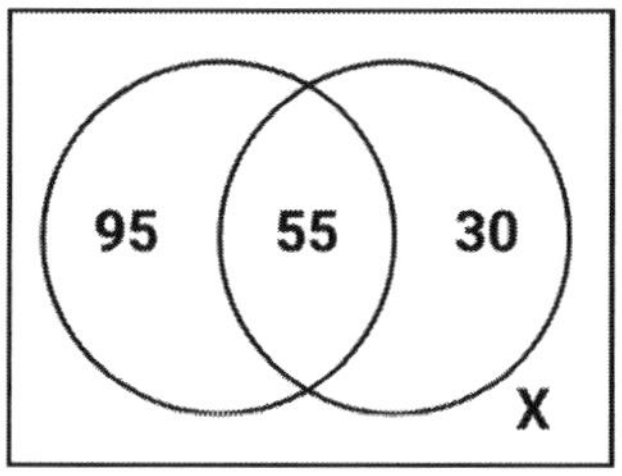

Since the set contains 225 total people, the solution is equal to $225 - (95 + 55 + 30)$, or 45 people

91. C: The set of natural numbers is contained within the set of whole numbers, and is hence a subset. Whole numbers include all positive integers plus zero, while natural numbers include all positive integers but not zero.

92. B: The mean is pulled towards the longer tail of a skewed distribution in most cases. It is not pulled towards the area with the higher frequency of scores. When outliers are added to an otherwise symmetric distribution, the mean shifts towards those outliers. For example, if a runner typically finishes a race in about 5 minutes and has one bad day in which she takes 20 minutes, that single outlier could significantly increase her mean time.

93. D: To factor an expression, find two expressions that multiply together to get the original expression. Since one factor is already known, we need to use the reverse FOIL method to find the other factor.

$$(x - 5)(?)$$

To find the first term of the second expression, divide $2x^2$ by x.

$$2x^2 \div x = 2x$$

$$(x - 5)(2x + ?)$$

To find the second term of the expression, we need to divide -30 by -5.

$$-30 \div -5 = 6$$

Therefore, the factored form of this expression is $(x - 5)(2x + 6)$. The FOIL method can be applied to multiply these two factors together and get the original expression, so the two factors are $(x - 5)$ and $(2x + 6)$.

94. D: While individual students will progress mathematically at varying rates, it is important that teachers are aware of the general expectations for typical skill development associated with each grade level. This is necessary for teachers to identify areas of individual student need so that they can differentiate and incorporate appropriate supports into instruction as well as recognize the signs of a developmental delay or learning disability. By third grade, students should have acquired a degree of fluency in adding and subtracting whole numbers within 100. If a student is continuously struggling to do so despite the implementation of academic supports, it may indicate a learning disability or delay and would require further evaluation to determine the need for special education services.

95. A: Evaluation of the expression for an x-value of -4 gives: $\left(2(-4)^3 - \frac{1}{2}(-4)^2 - 1\right)$, which equals -137.

96. C: Since he spends at least \$150, the relation of the number of polo shirts to the minimum cost may be written as $12p \geq 150$. Alternatively, the inequality may be written as $150 \leq 12p$.

97. B: This is the only choice that presents one real-world situation where students would apply rounding to the nearest hundredth (calculating sales tax). Choices A and D do not contain a real-world situation using rounding to the nearest hundredth. Both situations in choice C involve rounding to the nearest hundredth and therefore does not fit the teacher's objective for the activity.

98. C: The horizontal asymptote is equal to the ratio of the two coefficients of x, or $\frac{-1}{1}$, which equals -1.

99. C: The measure of the inscribed angle is half of the measure of the intercepted arc. Since the intercepted arc measures 110°, the inscribed angle is equal to $\frac{110°}{2}$ or 55°.

100. C: Raquel's total cost y equals \$12 times the number of tickets x, plus \$8. In other words, $y = 12x + 8$.

TExES Practice Test #2

1. Which of the following represents the net of a square pyramid?

a. 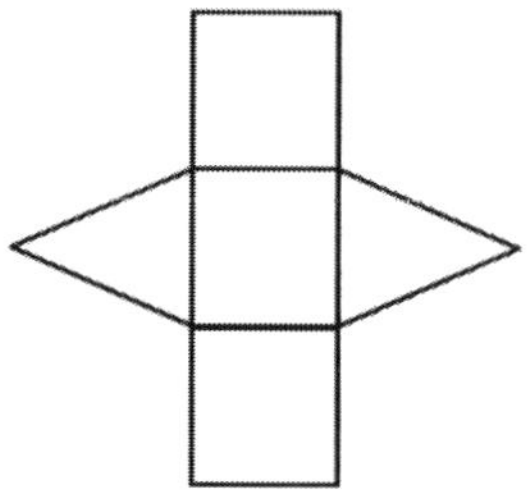

b. 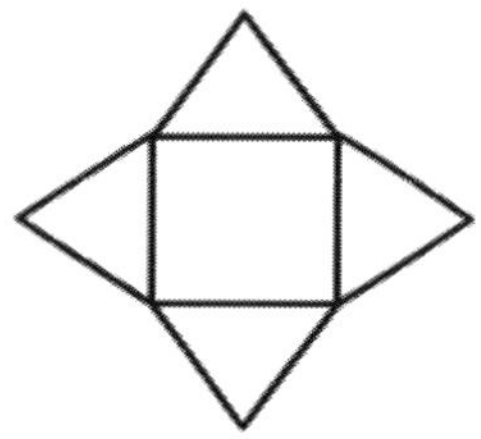

c. 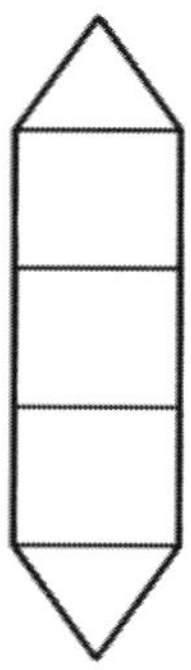

d. 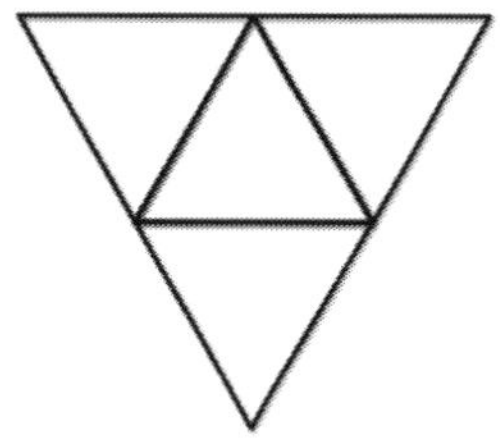

2. A man standing on a flat, level surface casts a shadow that is 6.2 ft in length. The man is 5.8 ft tall. Which of the following best represents the distance from the top of his head to the end of the shadow?

a. 7 ft
b. 7.5 ft
c. 8 ft
d. 8.5 ft

3. A dress is marked down 45%. The cost, after taxes, is $39.95. If the tax rate is 8.75%, what was the original price of the dress?

a. $45.74
b. $58.61
c. $66.79
d. $72.31

4. What is the size of the sample space for tossing four coins?

a. 8
b. 12
c. 16
d. 20

5. A coin is tossed three times. What is the size of the resulting sample space?

a. 8
b. 12
c. 16
d. 20

6. A fifth-grade teacher assigns her students a new math problem to be solved by the end of the day. Which of these is the most effective method of assessing students' work?

a. Administering a standardized test
b. Classroom observation
c. Portfolio assessment
d. Small group discussion

7. Which of the following describes a sampling technique that will likely increase the sampling error?

a. Choosing every 4th person from a list
b. Decreasing the sample size
c. Grouping a sample according to age and then choosing every 7th person from the list
d. Assigning numbers to a sample and then using a random number generator to choose numbers

8. Which of the following equations represents a line perpendicular to the one graphed below and passing through the point $(1, -2)$?

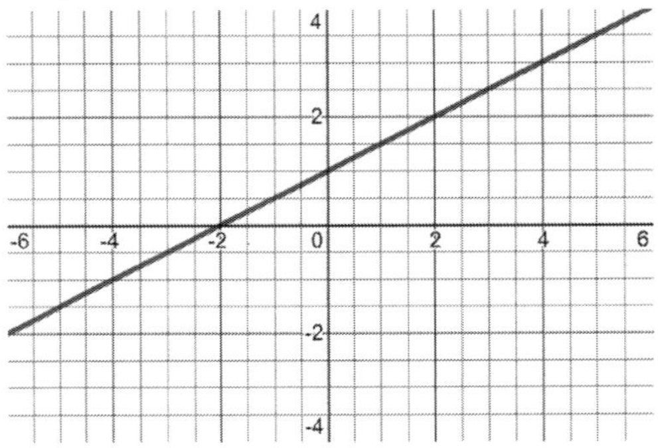

a. $y = \frac{1}{2}x + 1$
b. $y = \frac{1}{2}x - 1$
c. $y = -2x + \frac{1}{2}$
d. $y = -2x$

9. Nikki buys a used book that is marked down 35% from the original price. She pays 8.25% sales tax. Her total cost is $9.14. What was the original price of the book?

a. $11.99
b. $12.49
c. $12.99
d. $13.49

10. 320 students are surveyed. 120 of the students like only Dallas. 150 of the students like only Houston. 48 of the students like neither city. How many students like Dallas *and* Houston?

a. 2
b. 3
c. 4
d. 5

11. The variables x and y are in a linear relationship. The table below shows a few sample values. Which of the following graphs correctly represents the linear equation relating x and y?

x	y
−2	2
−1	1.5
0	1
1	0.5
2	0

a. 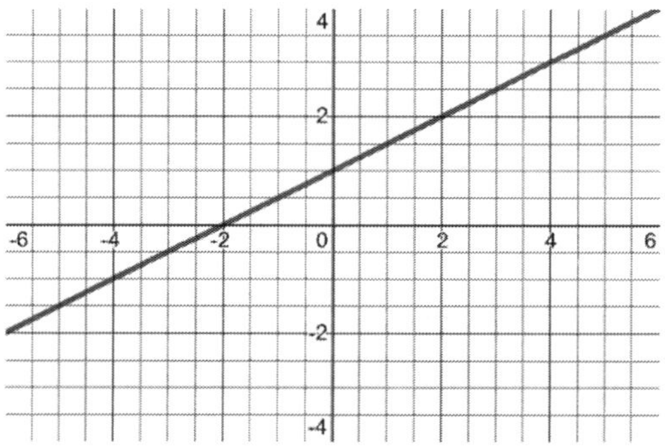

b. 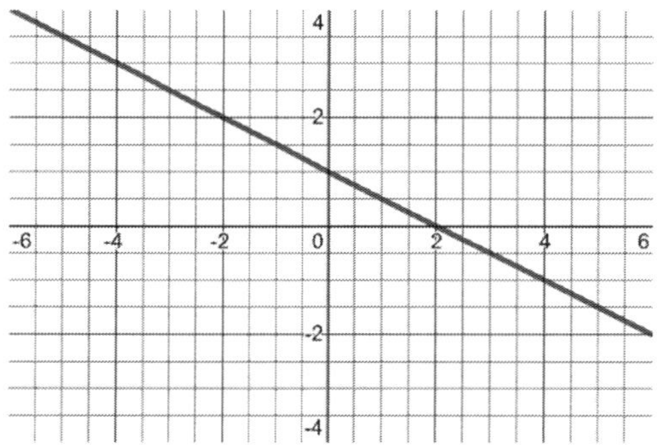

c. 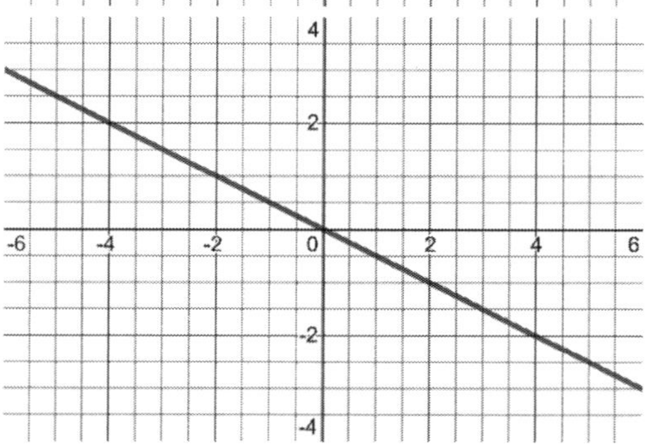

d. 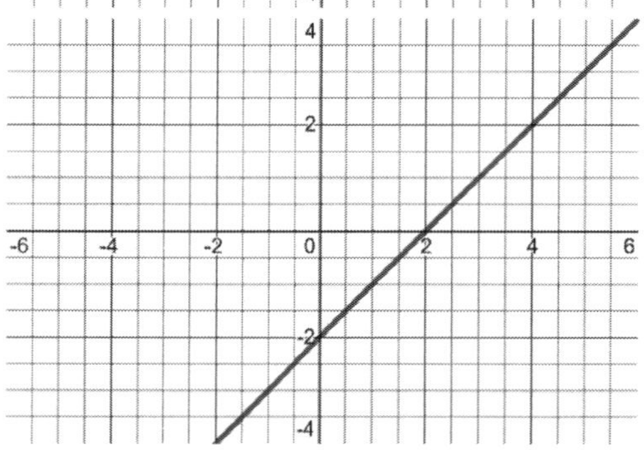

12. Which of the following activities would students be able to complete successfully BEFORE they can identify the relationship between counting and the concept of larger and smaller numbers?

a. Assign the correct number to a group of objects.
b. Choose which of two groups of objects contains more, is greater, or is larger.
c. Both (a) and (b)
d. Neither (a) nor (b)

13. Which of the following word problems is worded best to help students apply the distributive property?

a. Mikey is counting his art supplies. He has 2 boxes of crayons with 12 crayons in each box, 5 glue sticks, 3 sets of markers with 8 markers in each set, and one case of colored pencils that contains 16 pencils. Excluding the pencil box, how many items does Mikey have altogether?
b. Mikey is counting his art supplies. He has 2 pencil boxes. Each pencil box has 5 colored pencils and 8 markers. How many items does Mikey have altogether?
c. Mikey is counting his art supplies. He has 2 pencil boxes. Each pencil box has 5 colored pencils and 8 markers. How many markers does Mikey have? How many colored pencils does he have?
d. Mikey is counting his art supplies. He has 2 boxes of crayons with 12 crayons in each box, 5 glue sticks, 3 sets of markers with 8 markers in each set, and one case of colored pencils that contains 16 pencils. How many crayons does Mikey have?

14. Kyra sets aside $\frac{1}{3}$ of her income to pay rent and utilities at her apartment. If the monthly cost of rent and utilities is \$1,050, what is her monthly salary?

a. \$3,150
b. \$3,225
c. \$3,750
d. \$4,050

15. What is the constant of proportionality represented by the table below?

x	y
−10	−5
−6	−3
−2	−1
0	0
4	2

a. -2
b. $-\frac{1}{2}$
c. 2
d. $\frac{1}{2}$

16. Which of the following is an irrational number?

a. $3.\overline{13}$
b. $\sqrt{25}$
c. $\frac{\pi}{2}$
d. $\frac{37}{5}$

17. The expression $5x^2 - 3x - 14$ is equal to the product of $(x - 2)$ and which other factor?

a. $(5x - 14)$
b. $(5x - 3)$
c. $(5x + 7)$
d. $(5x + 14)$

18. Before the start of the school year, a seventh-grade math teacher plans out how much time she will spend on each unit during the school year. She considers the English Language Development (ELD) standards that will be covered along with each content standard. What is this approach known as?

a. Backwards lesson planning
b. Differentiating lessons
c. Curriculum mapping
d. Holistic assessments

19. Given the diagram below, which of the following theorems may be used to verify that lines *a* and *b* are parallel?

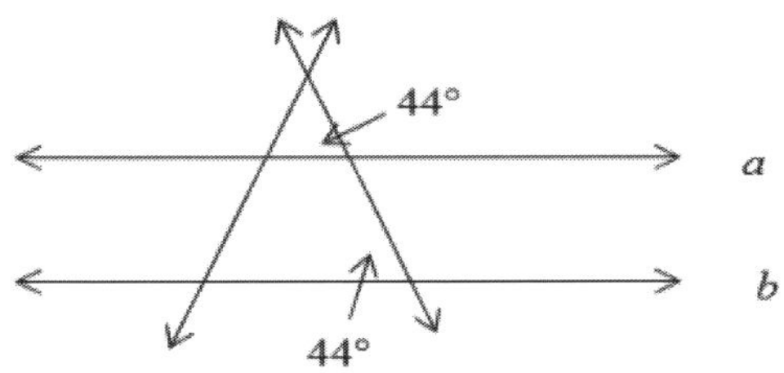

a. Alternate Interior Angles Converse Theorem
b. Alternate Exterior Angles Converse Theorem
c. Consecutive Interior Angles Converse Theorem
d. Corresponding Angles Converse Theorem

20. What is the constant of proportionality represented by the table below?

x	y
2	−8
5	−20
7	−28
10	−40
11	−44

a. -12
b. -8
c. -6
d. -4

21. Which of the following represents an inversely proportional relationship?

a. $y = 3x$
b. $y = \frac{1}{3}x$
c. $y = \frac{3}{x}$
d. $y = 3x^2$

22. What is the sum of the first 35 odd, positive integers?

a. 1,225
b. 1,435
c. 1,850
d. 2,250

23. $f(x) = \frac{3x-5}{2x}$**. What is the equation of the horizontal asymptote?**

a. $y = -\frac{5}{2}$
b. $y = \frac{1}{2}$
c. $y = 0$
d. $y = \frac{3}{2}$

24. Which of the following best represents the measurement of x, shown in the right triangle below?

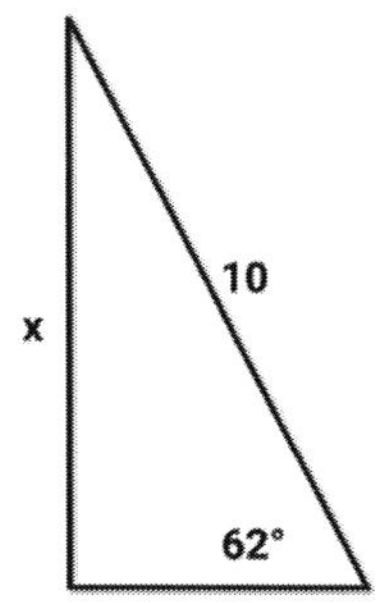

a. 5.6
b. 6.4
c. 7.9
d. 8.8

25. What is the solution to the system of linear equations below?

$$2x - 3y = 24$$
$$5x + 6y = -21$$

a. $(-6,3)$
b. $(-3,-10)$
c. $(3,-6)$
d. $(6,-4)$

26. The two prisms shown below are similar (units are inches). What is the measure of x?

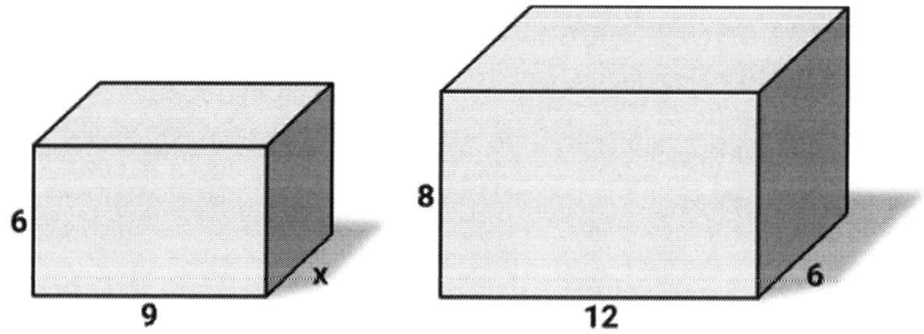

a. $4\frac{1}{2}$ in
b. $4\frac{3}{4}$ in
c. 5 in
d. $5\frac{1}{4}$ in

27. What is the contrapositive of the statement below?

If I get paid, then I go to the beach.

a. If I get paid, then I do not go to the beach.
b. If I go to the beach, then I get paid.
c. If I do not get paid, then I go to the beach.
d. If I do not go to the beach, then I do not get paid.

28. Which of the following correctly compares the sets of rational and irrational numbers?

a. The set of rational numbers is a subset of the set of irrational numbers.
b. The set of irrational numbers is a subset of the set of rational numbers.
c. The sets of irrational and rational numbers are disjoint.
d. The sets of irrational and rational numbers are equal.

29. What is the solution to the system of linear equations below?

$$4x - 2y = -38$$
$$2x + 3y = 17$$

a. $(-5,9)$
b. $(-2,11)$
c. $(-3,7)$
d. $(-4,11)$

30. Which of the following is an irrational number?

a. $4.\overline{2}$
b. $\sqrt{2}$
c. $\frac{4}{5}$
d. $\frac{21}{5}$

31. You wish to determine the area of a regular pentagon, and all you know is the length of one side. What additional information is sufficient for you to be able to compute the area?

a. The length of all the other sides
b. The width of the pentagon
c. The length of the apothem
d. No other information needed

32. What is the value of x, shown in the diagram below?

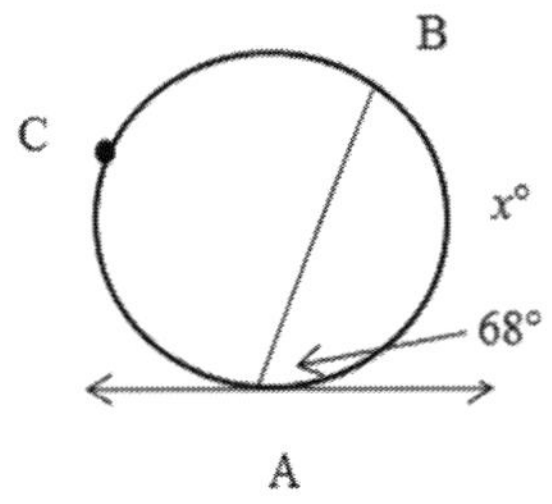

a. 68°
b. 76°
c. 128°
d. 136°

33. For how long at a time should a teacher initially plan to hold open class discussions of subject matter at the middle school/junior high school level?

a. 3-5 minutes
b. 10-15 minutes
c. 30-45 minutes
d. For an entire class period

34. Which of the following represents a discretionary expense?

a. Textbook
b. Rent
c. DVD
d. Groceries

35. Which of the following describes a sampling technique that will likely increase the sampling error?

a. choosing every 5th person from a list
b. grouping a sample according to gender and then choosing every 10th person from a list
c. using an intact group
d. assigning numbers to a sample and then using a random number generator to choose numbers

36. Given the diagram below, which of the following theorems may be used to verify that lines *a* and *b* are parallel?

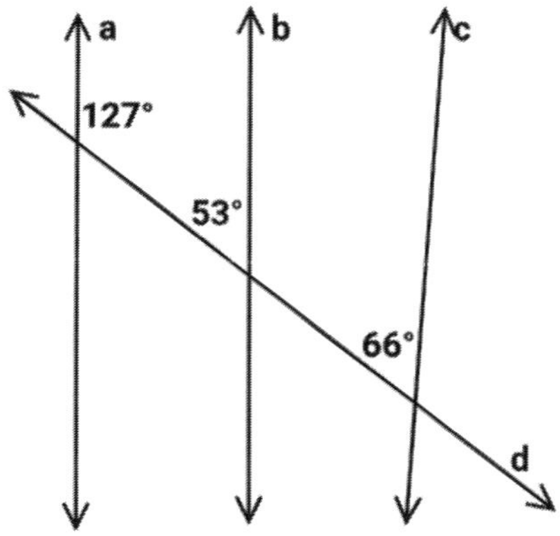

a. Alternate Interior Angles Converse Theorem
b. Alternate Exterior Angles Converse Theorem
c. Consecutive Interior Angles Converse Theorem
d. Corresponding Angles Converse Theorem

37. A teacher has concerns that a standardized test she is required to give does not accurately measure what it is designed to measure. The test claims to measure students' abilities to make inferences, yet there are no questions that directly address this skill. The teacher has concerns with which aspect of the standardized test?

a. Validity
b. Reliability
c. Bias
d. Objectivity

38. In screening and assessment instruments, what is an example of test sensitivity?

a. How often a test over-identifies or under-identifies target problems
b. How much potential a test has to offend or harm the test-taker
c. How often a test accurately rules out a problem it is meant to test
d. How often a test accurately identifies a problem it is meant to test

39. Olivia receives her weekly paycheck and calculates that she will spend $\frac{1}{4}$ of it on groceries. If the groceries cost \$120, what is the amount of her paycheck?

a. \$360
b. \$425
c. \$480
d. \$600

40. Each base of a triangular prism has a base length of 7.5 cm and a height of 10 cm. The height of the prism is 12 cm. What is the volume of the prism?

a. 375 cm^3
b. 450 cm^3
c. 525 cm^3
d. 600 cm^3

41. A 6th grade math teacher is introducing the concept of positive and negative numbers to a group of students. Which of the following models would be the most effective when introducing this concept?

a. Fraction strips
b. Venn diagrams
c. Shaded regions
d. Number lines

42. A ball has a diameter of 7 inches. Which of the following best represents the volume?

a. 165.7 in^3
b. 179.6 in^3
c. 184.5 in^3
d. 192.3 in^3

43. The graph of the parent function $y = x^2$ is shifted 5 units to the left and 4 units down. Which of the following equations represents the transformed function?

a. $y = (x - 5)^2 - 4$
b. $y = (x + 5)^2 - 4$
c. $y = (x - 5)^2 + 4$
d. $y = (x + 5)^2 + 4$

44. Julia drops a ball from a second-story window. The height of the ball is modeled by the function $f(x) = -2.5x^2 + 2x + 9$, where $f(x)$ represents the height of the ball and x represents the number of seconds. Which of the following best represents the number of seconds that will pass before the ball reaches the ground?

a. 2.1
b. 2.3
c. 2.5
d. 2.8

45. What is the converse of the statement below?

If I see a robin, it is spring.

a. If it is not spring, I do not see a robin.
b. If it is spring, I do not see a robin.
c. If I do not see a robin, it is not spring.
d. If it is spring, I see a robin.

46. When given the equation $8B + 11 = 43$, a student found $B = 6.75$. What mistake did the student most likely make?

a. When isolating the like terms, the student divided incorrectly by 8.
b. When isolating like terms, the student added instead of subtracting 11 from the right side.
c. The student used the wrong order of operations.
d. The student forgot to isolate like terms.

47. A fourth-grade teacher is planning direct instruction for a unit on decimals and calculating simple percentages. Which of the following additional activities could this teacher implement to foster students' real-world connections to these concepts?

a. Creating a budget for a grocery shopping trip
b. Preparing and acting out a scene from a restaurant
c. Listing the ingredients from a favorite recipe
d. Solving word problems that include decimals and percentages

48. Kevin saves $3 during Month 1. During each subsequent month, he plans to save 4 more dollars than he saved during the previous month. Which of the following equations represents the amount he will save during the *n*th month?

a. $a_n = 3n - 1$
b. $a_n = 3n + 4$
c. $a_n = 4n + 3$
d. $a_n = 4n - 1$

49. Which of the following best represents the standard deviation of the data below?

3, 4, 4, 5, 6, 12, 12, 15

a. 2.9
b. 3.4
c. 4.1
d. 4.6

50. Which of the following statements is true?

a. The set of whole numbers is a subset of the set of natural numbers.
b. The set of integers is a subset of the set of natural numbers.
c. The set of integers is a subset of the set of rational numbers.
d. The set of rational numbers is a subset of the set of integers.

51. What is the constant of proportionality represented by the table below?

x	y
-3	9
0	0
2	-6
7	-21
12	-36

a. −12
b. −9
c. −3
d. 3

52. Which of the following characteristics accurately describes authentic assessment techniques?

a. They are norm-referenced
b. They are designed to build higher-order thinking skills
c. They allow students to choose from a set of teacher-prepared responses
d. They measure students' performance at a specific point in time

53. Mr. James wants his students to draw a square based on specific attributes he says aloud. Which of the following is the most precise definition he could give his students?

a. "This shape has 4 sides. The opposite sides are parallel to each other."
b. "This shape has 4 sides that are all the same length. The opposite sides are parallel to each other."
c. "This shape has 4 sides that are all the same length. Each side is at a 90° angle to the other sides it touches."
d. "This shape has 4 sides. Each side is at a 90° angle to the other sides it touches."

54. Which of the following formulas represents the sequence 8, 12, 16, 20, 24, ...?

a. $a_n = 8n + 4; n \in \mathbb{N}$
b. $a_n = 4n + 4; n \in \mathbb{N}$
c. $a_n = n + 8; n \in \mathbb{N}$
d. $a_n = 8n; n \in \mathbb{N}$

55. Which of the following graphs represents the solution to the system of inequalities below?

$$-2x + 3y \leq 3$$
$$-8x + 6y \geq -3$$

a.

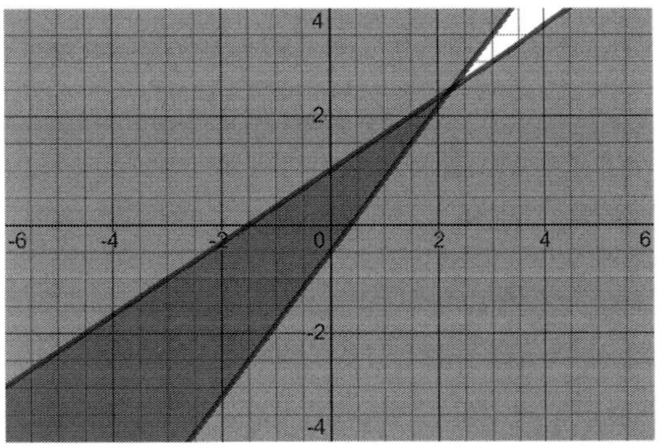

b.

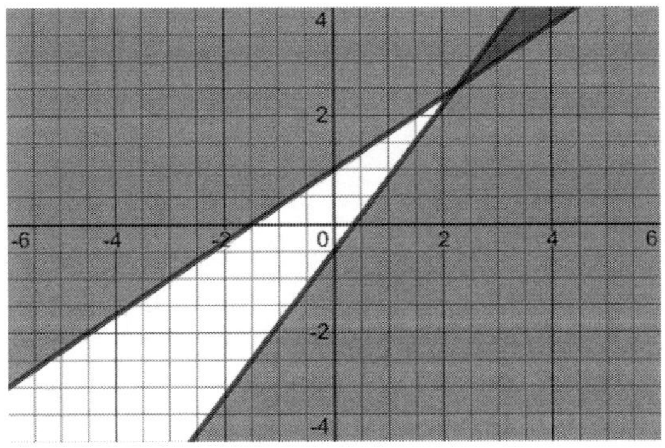

c.

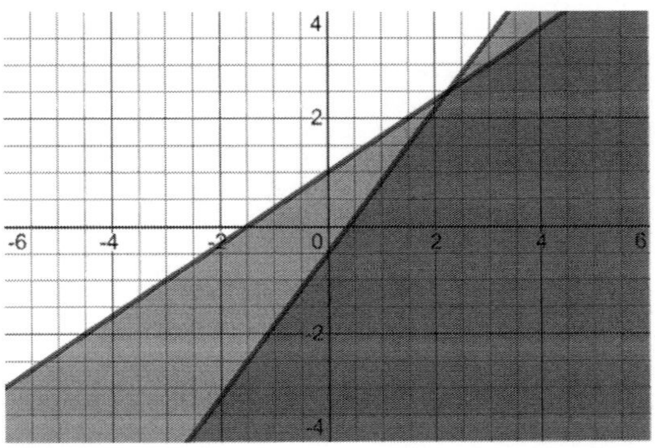

d.

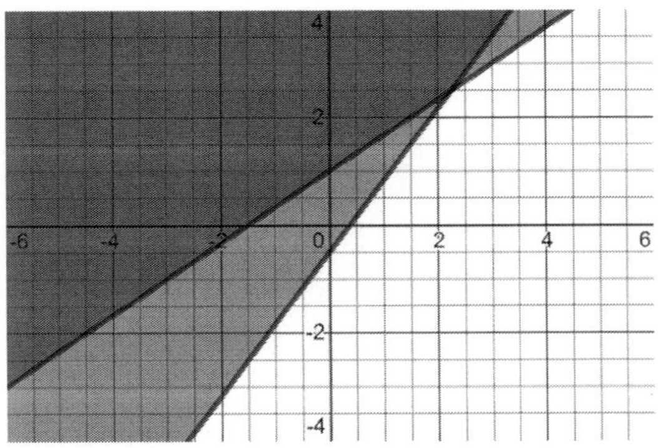

56. The values below represent a sample taken from a larger population. Which of the following best represents the standard deviation of the larger population?

$$\{8, 10, 11, 13, 13, 16, 17, 20\}$$

a. 2.9
b. 3.4
c. 4.0
d. 4.6

57. Sofia is learning to match equivalent fractions. Her homework question asks: "Circle the fraction(s) equivalent to $\frac{1}{2}$." The options given are: $\frac{2}{3}, \frac{2}{4}, \frac{3}{4}$, and $\frac{3}{6}$. Sofia circles $\frac{2}{3}$ and $\frac{3}{4}$. When her teacher asks her to explain her reasoning, what might Sofia say?

a. "I multiplied the top and the bottom of the fraction by the same numbers."
b. "I added the same numbers to the top and the bottom of the fraction."
c. "I drew a pie and split the $\frac{1}{2}$ into two pieces and into two more pieces."
d. "I drew three pies and split one into thirds, one into fourths, and one into sixths. Then I colored in the pies to match the fractions and circled the ones where I had colored in one half of the pie."

58. A city is at an elevation of 4,900 feet. Which of the following best represents the elevation in miles?

a. 0.93 miles
b. 0.98 miles
c. 1.08 miles
d. 1.21 miles

59. Which of the following describes a sampling technique that will likely increase the sampling error?

a. Alphabetizing names on a list and choosing every other name
b. Using a larger sample size
c. Replicating the study with new groups
d. Grouping a sample according to age and choosing the first 50 people

60. A 12-foot-tall tree casts a shadow that is 9.8 ft in length. Which of the following best represents the distance from the top of the tree to the end of the shadow?

a. 6.9 ft
b. 12.8 ft
c. 15.5 ft
d. 18.5 ft

61. Andrew rolls a die. What is the probability he gets a 4 or an even number?

a. $\frac{1}{4}$
b. $\frac{1}{2}$
c. $\frac{2}{3}$
d. $\frac{3}{4}$

62. A group of teachers are given a day to plan interdisciplinary units collaboratively prior to the beginning of a school year. What should these teachers do first to ensure that they plan effectively?

a. Create an outline of key concepts in each unit to see which concepts overlap between subjects.
b. Have each teacher discuss what they want to accomplish in the interdisciplinary unit.
c. Work together to create a detailed summative assessment for the unit that will assess each subject being taught.
d. Construct a list of what information they want students to learn from this unit.

63. Jeni buys a phone charger for $28. If it had been marked down 30%, what was the original cost?

a. $30
b. $32
c. $35
d. $40

64. The x-axis in the scatter plot below represents the number of miles Cyndi drives. The y-axis represents the gallons of gas left in her car's tank. About how many gallons will remain when she has driven 250 miles? Choose the best estimate.

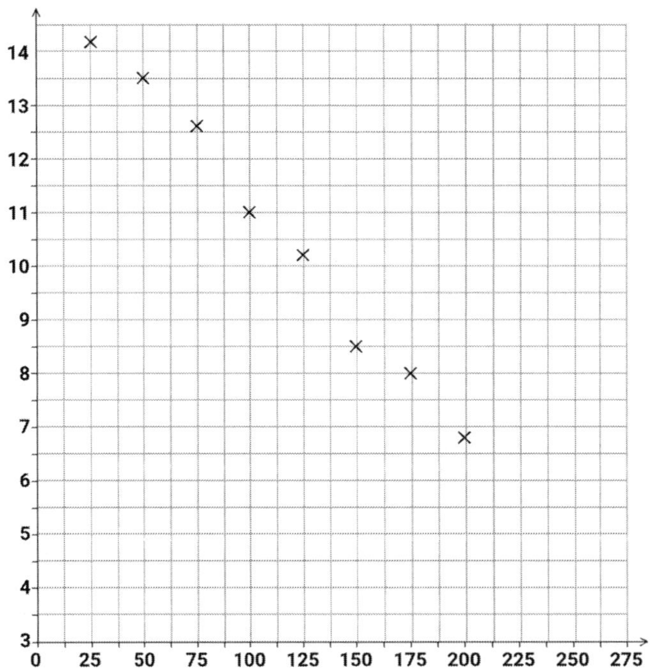

a. 3.5 gallons
b. 4.5 gallons
c. 5.5 gallons
d. 6.5 gallons

65. Given that the two horizontal lines in the diagram below are parallel, which of the following statements is correct?

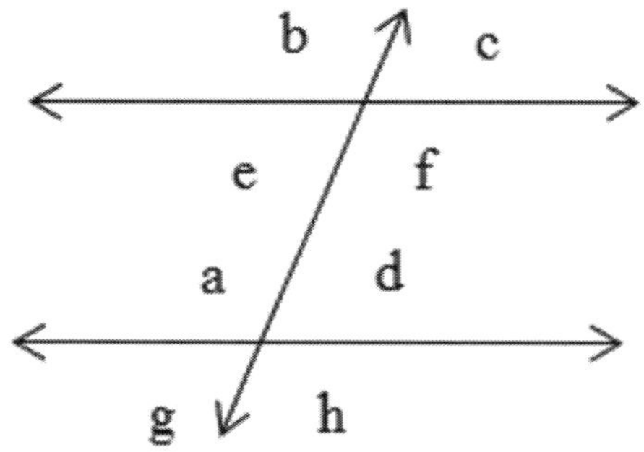

a. Angles b and g are complementary.
b. Angles d and c are supplementary.
c. Angles a and e are supplementary.
d. Angles e and h are congruent.

66. What is the length of the hypotenuse in the right triangle shown below?

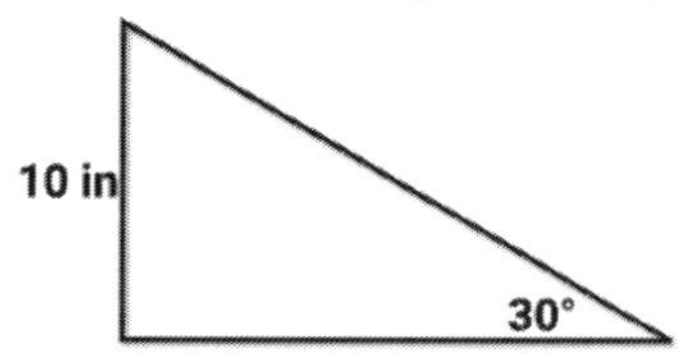

a. $\frac{20}{3}\sqrt{3}$ in
b. $10\sqrt{3}$ in
c. 20 in
d. $20\sqrt{3}$ in

67. Which of these is true about having an awareness of patterns and relationships in the real world?

a. It does not inform our understanding of the basic structure of things.
b. It helps us understand series of events, but not predict future ones.
c. It is unrelated to our basic feeling of confidence in the environment.
d. It increases our self-efficacy about interacting with our environment.

68. Which of the following pairs of equations represents the lines of symmetry in the figure below?

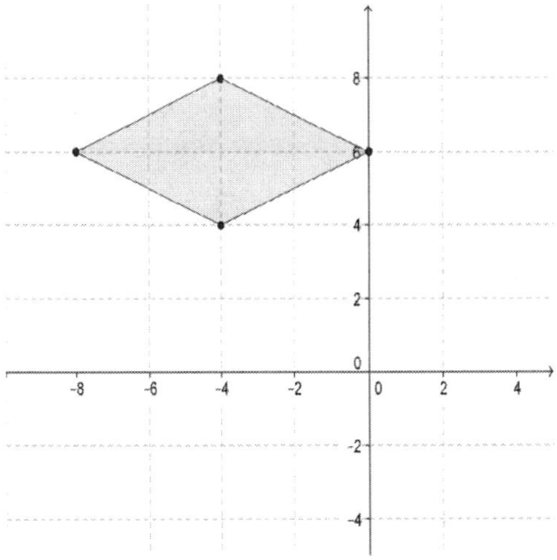

a. $x = -4, y = 6$
b. $x = 4, y = 6$
c. $y = -4, x = 6$
d. $y = 4, x = -6$

69. Which of these is/are most representative of using statistics in everyday life to predict probabilities?

a. An actuarial table in an insurance company
b. A weather forecast for the chances of rain
c. A chart comparing results of interventions
d. Answers (A) and (B) represent probability

70. Mark's nightstand currently holds 6 books, 12 pencils, and 1 highlighter. If he must place one item from each category into his backpack, how many possible selections are there?

a. 19
b. 72
c. 144
d. 180

71. Which of the following pairs of equations represents the lines of symmetry in the figure below?

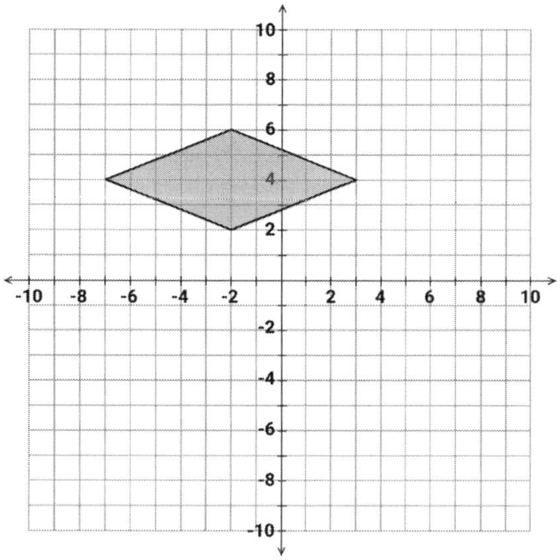

a. $x = -2, y = 4$
b. $x = 2, y = 4$
c. $y = -2, x = 4$
d. $y = 2, x = 4$

72. Ms. Byrne stresses the importance of daily math homework with her sixth- and seventh-grade students. She states that the consistent practice will help students solidify their understanding of mathematical principles. Ms. Byrne also reviews this homework on a daily basis to help her understand what the students understand and to guide her instruction. This practice is an example of:

a. Summative assessment
b. Diversity in assignments
c. Formative assessment
d. Standards set forth for middle-grade mathematics

73. Which of the following functions has a limit of 0?

a. $f(x) = 2x$
b. $f(x) = \frac{4}{x}$
c. $f(x) = \frac{x}{8}$
d. $f(x) = \frac{3x+1}{x}$

74. Which of the following is the best representation of 30,490 in scientific notation?

a. 3.049×10^{-4}
b. 3.049×10^{3}
c. 30.490×10^{3}
d. 3.049×10^{4}

75. For which of the following data sets would the mean be an appropriate measure of center to use?

a. 7, 7, 9, 10, 10, 11, 13, 14, 46, 50
b. 6, 8, 11, 15, 17, 17, 21, 22, 25, 25
c. 4, 9, 36, 41, 43, 44, 48, 48, 49, 50
d. 2, 91, 92, 96, 96, 98, 100, 102, 104, 105

76. What is the limit of the series below?

$$1 + \frac{2}{3} + \frac{4}{9} + \frac{8}{27} + \frac{16}{81} + \cdots$$

a. 2
b. $2\frac{1}{3}$
c. $2\frac{2}{3}$
d. 3

77. Mrs. Miller is teaching a unit on numbers and operations with her sixth-grade class. At the beginning of class, she asks the students to work in groups to sketch a Venn diagram to classify whole numbers, integers, and rational numbers on a white board. Which of the following types of assessments has the teacher used?

a. Summative assessment
b. Formative assessment
c. Formal assessment
d. Informal assessment

78. Adam rolls a standard six-sided die. What is the probability he rolls a number greater than or equal to 5?

a. $\frac{1}{6}$
b. $\frac{1}{5}$
c. $\frac{1}{4}$
d. $\frac{1}{3}$

79. What is the slope of the leg marked x in the triangle graphed below?

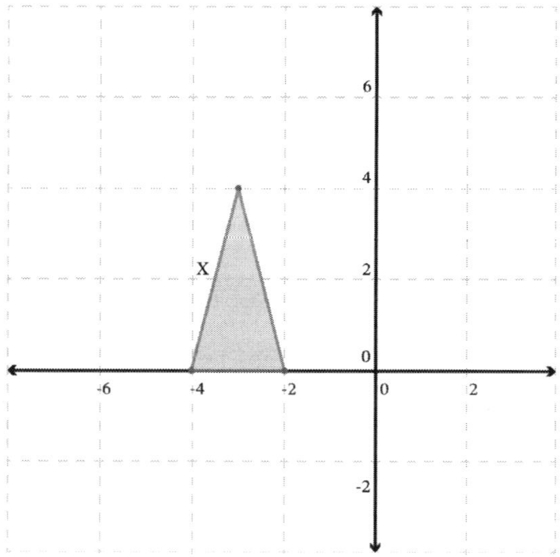

a. 2
b. 3.5
c. 4
d. 4.5

80. Laura buys 6 pens and 2 notebooks for $7.20. Julio buys 15 pens and 1 notebook for $12.60. How much does one notebook cost?

a. $0.50
b. $0.75
c. $1.35
d. $1.50

81. How many ways can you arrange the letters below, if order does NOT matter?

STATISTICS

a. 12,600
b. 25,200
c. 50,400
d. 100,800

Refer to the following for question 82:

> The administrators at a middle school are considering implementing a team teaching model for sixth-grade classes in the upcoming school year. The administrators, including the principal and vice-principal, have convened a staff meeting to discuss this possibility with the sixth-grade teachers.

82. At the end of the year, the teachers decide that they want to evaluate the effectiveness of the team teaching model for their sixth-grade students. Which of the following research strategies would provide them with the best assessment of the model?

a. The teachers should compare this group of students' performance on standardized tests in previous years with their performance in sixth grade at the end of the year.
b. The teachers should compare the students' performance in classes that are part of the team teaching model (math, science, language arts, social studies) with their performance in classes that are not team-taught (health, physical education, art).
c. The teachers should compare their students' performance in sixth grade to the performance of sixth-grade students at schools that do not use team teaching.
d. The teachers should compare their sixth-grade students' performance this year with the performance of sixth-grade students in previous years where team teaching was not used; they should also consider the performance history of this particular group of sixth graders relative to previous groups.

83. You are asked to vote on the #1 and #2 performers from a list of 5 candidates. How many possible selections could you make?

a. 120
b. 100
c. 20
d. 10

84. When planning a unit on linear equations, a teacher would most likely include discussion on which of the following topics?

a. Conjugating to remove irrational denominators
b. Slope of a straight line
c. Order of operations
d. Characteristics of the diagonals of various quadrilaterals

85. The most effective way to structure a math session for the benefit of primary students is to:

a. Check all homework assignments and be sure that all workbook pages are completed
b. Focus almost entirely on computation skills
c. Focus almost entirely on the application of math skills to real-life situations
d. Divide class time evenly between computation skills and real-life applications

86. A car moves at a constant velocity. Which of the following accurately describes the appearance of the position-time graph?

a. It is a line with a positive slope.
b. It is a line with a negative slope.
c. It is a curve with an increasing slope.
d. It is a curve with a decreasing slope.

87. Which of the following represents an inversely proportional relationship?

a. $y = \frac{1}{x}$
b. $y = \frac{1}{2}x$
c. $y = x$
d. $y = x^2$

88. Danielle pays a fee of 0.1% of her paycheck for direct deposit into her bank account. If her monthly paycheck is $3,200, what will her fee be each month?

a. $0.32
b. $3.20
c. $32
d. $320

89. What is the approximate area of the shaded region between the circle and the square in the figure shown below? Use 3.14 for π.

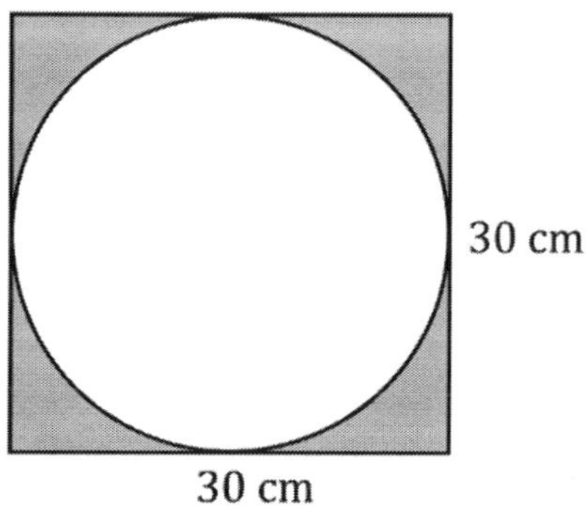

a. 177 cm^2
b. 181 cm^2
c. 187 cm^2
d. 193 cm^2

90. Meg buys a used car for $6,375. The original price had been marked down by 15%. What was the original price of the car?

a. $7,150
b. $7,375
c. $7,500
d. $7,775

91. By the end of what grade level should a student be able to use algebraic principles to analyze both proportional and non-proportional linear relationships?

a. 5th grade
b. 6th grade
c. 7th grade
d. 8th grade

92. What is $\lim_{n\to\infty} \frac{n^3-n^2}{n}$?

a. 0
b. 1
c. 2
d. There is no limit.

93. Maria uses the pie chart below to represent the allocation of her time on an average 24-hour school day.

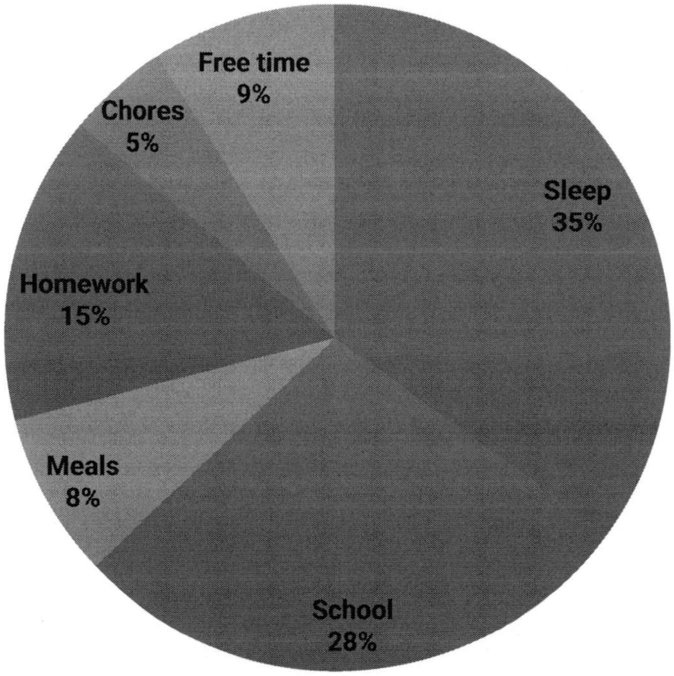

Which of the following statements is true?

a. The amount of time she spends on sleep is less than 8 hours per night.
b. The amount of time she spends on chores and free time is approximately 4 hours per day.
c. The amount of time she spends on meals and homework is more than 5 hours per day.
d. The amount of time she spends on school is more than 7 hours per day.

94. Andrea must administer $\frac{1}{12}$ of a medicine bottle to a patient. If the bottle contains $3\frac{4}{10}$ fluid ounces of medicine, how much medicine should be administered?

a. $\frac{17}{60}$ fluid ounces
b. $\frac{15}{62}$ fluid ounces
c. $\frac{3}{19}$ fluid ounces
d. $\frac{17}{67}$ fluid ounces

95. Given that the two horizontal lines in the diagram below are parallel, which of the following statements is correct?

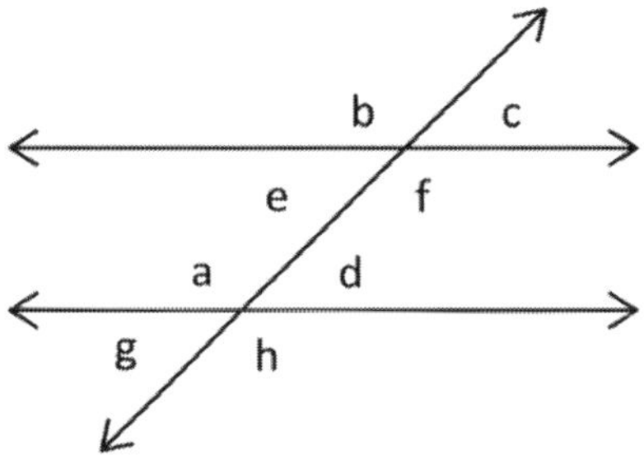

a. $\angle c$ and $\angle g$ are complementary.
b. $\angle c$ and $\angle h$ are supplementary.
c. $\angle a$ and $\angle f$ are supplementary.
d. $\angle g$ and $\angle h$ are congruent.

96. Kevin uses the pie chart below to represent how he spends his allowance. His monthly allowance is $50.

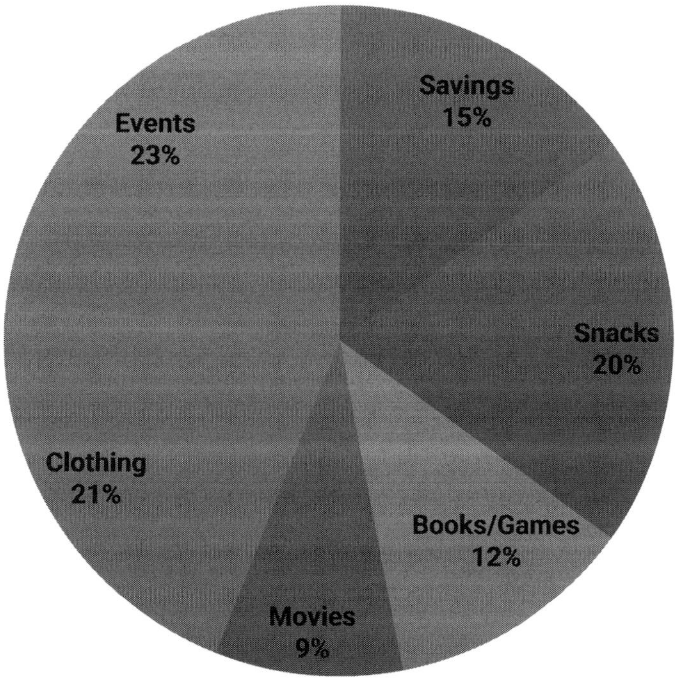

Which of the following statements is true?

a. The amount of money he spends on snacks is more than $10.
b. The amount of money he spends on movies, books, and games is more than $10.
c. The amount of money he spends on savings is less than $7.
d. The amount of money he spends on clothing and events is less than $10.

97. 75 students are surveyed. 36 of the students like only pepperoni pizza. 22 of the students like only supreme pizza. 12 of the students like neither kind of pizza. How many students like pepperoni *and* supreme pizza?

a. 2
b. 3
c. 4
d. 5

98. Dan rolls a standard six-sided die and tosses a coin. What is the probability he gets a non-prime number or tails?

a. $\frac{1}{2}$
b. $\frac{2}{3}$
c. $\frac{3}{4}$
d. $\frac{5}{6}$

99. Which of the following shapes is NOT a possible cross-section of a triangular prism?

a. Circle
b. Rectangle
c. Trapezoid
d. Triangle

100. Which of the following equations represents a line parallel to the one graphed below and passing through the point $(-1, 4)$?

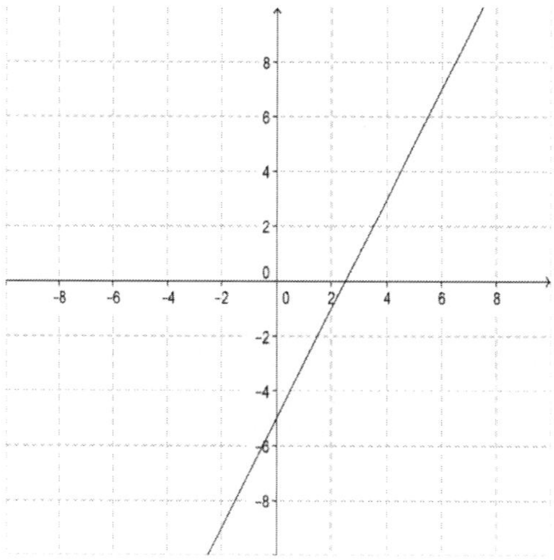

a. $y = 2x - 2$
b. $y = 3x + 6$
c. $y = 3x - 4$
d. $y = 2x + 6$

Answer Key and Explanations for Test #2

1. B: The net of a square pyramid has a square base and four triangular faces. So only choice B can be folded into a square pyramid. Choice A creates a triangular prism. Choice C does not create a proper 3D figure because the triangle sides overlap. Choice D creates a triangular pyramid.

2. D: The Pythagorean theorem may be used to find the diagonal distance from the top of his head to the base of the shadow. Using the following equation, we can determine this distance, c: $5.8^2 + 6.2^2 = c^2$. Thus, $c \approx 8.5$. The distance is approximately 8.5 ft.

3. C. The original price may be modeled by the equation:

$$(x - 0.45x) + 0.0875(x - 0.45x) = \$39.95$$

This simplifies to $0.598125x = \$39.95$. Dividing each side of the equation by the coefficient of x gives $x \approx \$66.79$.

4. C: The number in the sample space is equal to the number of possible outcomes for one coin toss, 2, raised to the power of the number of coin tosses, or 4. $2^4 = 16$.

5. A: The size of the sample space equals the number of possible outcomes for one coin toss, 2, raised to the power of the number of coin tosses, 3. So the sample space for tossing a coin three times is $2^3 = 8$.

6. C: Students should submit written samples of their work for the teacher to review on a daily basis. Standardized tests would not be appropriate for assessing the student's understanding of the given task. As students are likely to work on the problems at different times, classroom observation would not be practical, and group discussions would not necessarily be useful for assessment purposes.

7. B: Decreasing the sample size will likely increase the sampling error by increasing the likelihood of deviations from the true population. The other techniques utilize random sampling.

8. D: The slope of the graphed line is $\frac{1}{2}$. A line perpendicular to this one will have a slope of –2. Substituting the slope and the x- and y-values from the point $(1, -2)$ into the slope-intercept form of an equation gives: $-2 = -2(1) + b$, which simplifies to $-2 = -2 + b$. Adding 2 to each side of the equation gives $b = 0$; therefore, the equation of a line perpendicular to this one and passing through the point $(1, -2)$ is $y = -2x$.

9. C: The original price x may be modeled by the equation $(x - 0.35x) \times 1.0825 = 9.14$, which simplifies to $0.703625x = 9.14$. Dividing each side of the equation by the coefficient of x gives $x \approx 12.99$. The book was originally \$12.99.

10. A: A Venn diagram such as the one shown below may be drawn to assist in finding the answer.

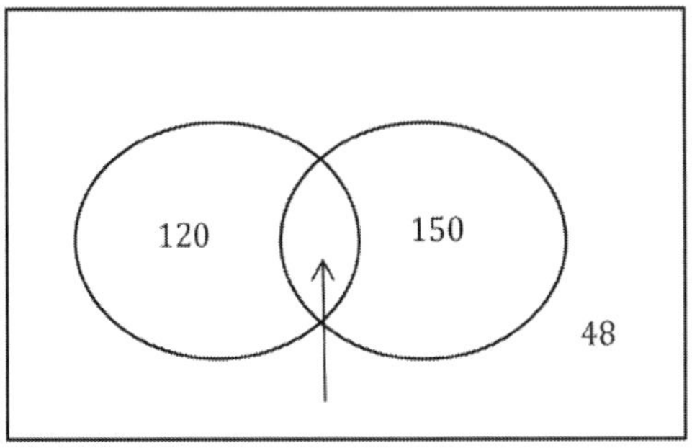

Since the set contains 320 total people, the solution is equal to $320 - (120 + 150 + 48)$ or 2 people.

11. B: The table shows the y-intercept to be 1. The slope is equal to the ratio of change in y-values to change in corresponding x-values. As each x-value increases by 1, each y-value decreases by 0.5. Thus, the slope is $\frac{-0.5}{1}$, or $-\frac{1}{2}$. This graph represents the equation $y = -\frac{1}{2}x + 1$.

12. C: In order for students to identify the relationship between counting and the concept of larger and smaller numbers, they must first understand that numbers represent objects and be able to accurately match the amount of objects to the corresponding number. However, this is not sufficient, as they must also understand the concept of larger and smaller. Some groups of objects have more items than other groups of objects. Once they can use numbers to represent amounts and determine which groups of objects are larger or smaller, then they can identify the relationship between these two concepts.

13. B: The distributive property of multiplication over addition is $a(b + c) = ab + ac$. Option B best prompts the usage of $2(5 + 8) = 2(5) + 2(8)$ by requiring students to find the total number of items by multiplying both the number of colored pencils and markers and adding them together. Choice A would test students' ability to apply order of operations to a word problem. Choice B asks students to answer two separate problems, which only require basic multiplication. Choice D would test students' ability to find the pertinent information in solving a word problem.

14. A: Kyra's monthly salary may be modeled as $\frac{1}{3}x = 1{,}050$. Multiplying both sides of the equation by 3 gives $x = 3{,}150$.

15. D: The constant of proportionality is equal to the slope. Using the points, (0,0) and (4,2), the slope may be written as $\frac{2-0}{4-0}$, which equals $\frac{1}{2}$.

16. C: The decimal expansion of an irrational number does not terminate or repeat. The number π is considered irrational because it does not terminate or repeat.

17. C: The product of $(x - 2)(5x + 7)$ equals $5x^2 + 7x - 10x - 14$, which simplifies to $5x^2 - 3x - 14$.

18. C: The strategy of planning which standards will be taught over the course of the school year and allocating the amount of time each topic will be taught is known as curriculum mapping. Backwards planning is when lessons are intentionally developed with a specific standard in mind. The assessment aligns closely to the standard being taught, and then the activities that would best support the standard are selected. Differentiation occurs when a teacher considers the needs of the students and incorporates choice into process, product, and content. Holistic assessment refers to evaluating a student globally through multiple data points.

19. D: The corresponding angles have congruent angle measures, each measuring 44°. According to the Corresponding Angles Converse Theorem, two lines are parallel if a transversal, intersecting the lines, forms congruent corresponding angles.

20. D: The constant of proportionality is equal to the slope. Using the points, $(2, -8)$ and $(5, -20)$, the slope may be written as $\frac{-20-(-8)}{5-2}$, which equals -4.

21. C: An inversely proportional relationship is written in the form $y = \frac{k}{x}$; thus, the equation $y = \frac{3}{x}$ shows that y is inversely proportional to x.

22. A: The value of the 35th term may be found using the formula $a_n = a_1 + (n-1)d$. Substituting the number of terms for n, the initial value of 1 for a, and the common difference of 2 for d gives: $a_{35} = 1 + (35-1)(2)$, which simplifies to $a_{35} = 69$. Now, the value of the 35th term may be substituted into the formula, $S_n = \frac{n(a_1+a_n)}{2}$, which gives: $S_{50} = \frac{35(1+69)}{2}$, which simplifies to $S_{35} = 1{,}225$.

23. D: The horizontal asymptote is equal to the ratio of the coefficient of $3x$ to the coefficient of $2x$, or $\frac{3}{2}$.

24. D: The following equation may be written and solved for x: $\sin 62° = \frac{x}{10}$. Multiplying both sides of the equation by 10 gives: $10 \times \sin 62° = x$, or $x \approx 8.8$.

25. C: Given the coefficients of the equations, the simplest procedure will be to use the elimination method, multiplying the first equation by two and summing them:

$$\begin{array}{c} 4x - 6y = 48 \\ \underline{5x + 6y = -21} \\ 9x + 0y = 27 \end{array}$$

Solve for x:

$$x = \frac{27}{9} = 3$$

Plug the value for x into one of the original equations:

$$2(3) - 3y = 24$$

$$3y = 6 - 24 = -18$$

$$y = -\frac{18}{3} = -6$$

Thus, the solution to the system of equations is $(3, -6)$.

26. A: Since the figures are similar, the following proportion may be written and solved for x: $\frac{8}{6} = \frac{6}{x}$. Thus, $x = \frac{36}{8}$ or $4\frac{1}{2}$.

27. D: If the statement is written in the form $p \to q$, then the contrapositive is represented as $\neg q \to \neg p$. Thus, the contrapositive should read, "If I do not go to the beach, then I do not get paid."

28. C: The set of irrational numbers is separate from the set of rational numbers. A rational number cannot be irrational, and an irrational number cannot be rational.

29. A: Given the coefficients of the equations, the simplest procedure will be to use the elimination method, multiplying the second equation by negative two and summing them:

$$\begin{array}{r} 4x - 2y = -38 \\ \underline{-4x - 6y = -34} \\ 0x - 8y = -72 \end{array}$$

Solve for y:

$$y = \frac{-72}{-8} = 9$$

Plug the value for y into one of the original equations:

$$4x - 2(9) = -38$$

$$4x - 18 = -38$$

$$4x = -20$$

$$x = -\frac{20}{4} = -5$$

Thus, the solution to the system of equations is $(-5,9)$.

30. B: The decimal expansion of an irrational number does not terminate or repeat. The decimal expansion of $\sqrt{2}$ does not terminate or repeat.

31. D: Since the pentagon is regular, all the sides are equal, and the shape is convex. Because of this, there are enough constraints to determine the area as a function of the side length of the pentagon.

32. D: The measure of the angle formed by the chord and the tangent is equal to one-half of the measure of the intercepted arc. Since the measure of the angle is 68°, the measure of the intercepted arc may be found by writing $68° = \frac{1}{2}x$. Dividing both sides of the equation by $\frac{1}{2}$ gives $x = 136°$. The measure of the intercepted arc may also be found by multiplying 68° by 2. Thus, the value of x is 136°.

33. B: At this level, it can often be difficult to sustain a productive discussion for longer than 15 minutes or so. After that, students will tend to lose interest or veer the discussion off topic.

34. C: Purchasing a DVD is a discretionary expense because it is based on personal desire rather than need. In other words, it is an expense made at the discretion of the consumer. Discretionary expenses are those over which a consumer has the most control. A comprehensive budget must include discretionary expenses as well as fixed and variable expenses. Fixed expenses, such as rent, are the same every month. Variable expenses, including groceries, school supplies, and heating oil, are always present but vary in amount over the course of a year.

35. C: Use of an intact group is called a convenience sample. Such a sample increases sampling error, since randomization was not employed. The other described techniques utilize random sampling.

36. C: The consecutive interior angles have supplementary angle measures, as 127° and 53° add up to 180°. According to the Consecutive Interior Angles Converse Theorem, two lines are parallel if a transversal, intersecting the lines, forms consecutive interior angles that are supplementary.

37. A: A test is valid if it measures what it is designed to measure. If a test claims to measure a student's ability to make inferences, then the questions on the test should require students to use this skill. Reliability refers to ensuring that there is consistency in test results over time and between participants. Bias refers to ensuring that the test does not put any participants at a disadvantage. Objectivity refers to ensuring that all tests are scored in the same manner without being affected by any outside influences or bias.

38. D: The definition of sensitivity in a test instrument is how often (typically measured in percentages) it accurately identifies a specific problem or disorder that it is designed to identify, e.g., a mental health disorder, a developmental delay, or a learning disability. If tests either over-identify or under-identify problems that are its targets (A), these are measurement errors rather than levels of sensitivity. Sensitivity in screening does not refer to adverse effects of a test on the person being tested (B), though this is a separate ethical concern if the test is harmful to the test cases. Sensitivity does not mean ruling out (C) a targeted condition. How often a test rules out a problem is often referred to as specificity.

39. C: Olivia's paycheck x may be modeled by $\frac{1}{4}x = 120$. Multiplying both sides of the equation by 4 gives $x = 480$. Her paycheck is \$480.

40. B: The volume of a prism may be calculated using the formula $V = Bh$, where B represents the area of the base and h represents the height of the prism. The area of each triangular base is represented by $A = \frac{1}{2}(7.5)(10)$. So, the area of each base is equal to 37.5 square centimeters. Substituting 37.5 for the area of the base and 12 for the height of the prism gives $V = (37.5)(12)$ or $V = 450$. The volume of the prism is 450 cm^3.

41. D: Number lines can help students understand the concepts of positive and negative numbers. Fraction strips are most commonly used with fractions. Venn diagrams are commonly used when comparing groups. Shaded regions are commonly used with fractions or percentages.

42. B: The volume of a sphere may be calculated using the formula $V = \frac{4}{3}\pi r^3$, where r represents the radius. Substituting 3.5 for r gives $V = \frac{4}{3}\pi(3.5)^3$, which simplifies to $V \approx 179.6\ \text{in}^3$.

43. B: Inside the squared term, the sign of the constant is positive for a shift to the left and negative for a shift to the right. Thus, a movement of 5 units left is indicated by $y = (x + 5)^2$. A shift of 4 units down is indicated by subtracting 4 units from the squared term, giving $y = (x + 5)^2 - 4$.

44. B: A graph of the function shows the positive x-intercept to occur at approximately (2.3,0). Thus, the ball will reach the ground after approximately 2.3 seconds.

45. D: If the statement is written in the form $p \rightarrow q$, then the converse is represented as $q \rightarrow p$. Thus, the converse should read, "If it is spring, I see a robin."

46. B: When learning to solve algebraic equations, it is necessary to treat the two sides of an equation equally. In order to isolate the variable, the first step is to subtract the constant from both sides. In this case, the constant is 11. By reworking the problem using the suggestion found in choice B, it is possible to arrive at the student's incorrect answer. The best method to solving this question is to use a trial and error method, determining which answer yields the incorrect answer.

47. B: As many mathematical concepts are abstract in nature, implementing concrete learning opportunities is beneficial in providing students with a real-world context to strengthen understanding. Doing so demonstrates the applications of math in everyday life, thus helping students build personal connections to learning that make the overall experience more relevant and meaningful. An assignment in which students prepare and act out a skit from a restaurant requires them to apply knowledge of decimals when selecting items from the menu and calculating their bill and use percentages when determining the tax and tip. Such an activity illustrates the real-world applications of these concepts by placing them in a familiar setting. Further, incorporating dramatic play into math instruction allows young students to process, organize, and ultimately internalize new information for greater retention.

48. D: This situation may be modeled by an arithmetic sequence, with a common difference of 4 and an initial value of 3. Substituting the common difference and initial value into the formula, $a_n = a_1 + (n-1)d$, gives $a_n = 3 + (n-1)(4)$, which simplifies to $a_n = 4n - 1$.

49. D: The standard deviation is equal to the square root of the ratio of the sum of the squares of the deviation of each score from the mean to the square root of the difference of n and 1. The mean of the data set is 7.625. The deviations are −4.625, −3.625, −3.625, −2.625, −1.625, 4.375, 4.375, and 7.375. The sum of the squares of the deviations may be written as:

$$21.39 + 13.14 + 13.14 + 6.89 + 2.64 + 19.14 + 19.14 + 54.39 = 149.87$$

Division of this sum by $n - 1 = 7$ gives 21.41. The square root of this quotient is approximately 4.6.

50. C: The set of integers is contained within the set of rational numbers and is therefore a subset of the rational numbers. A rational number may be written as the ratio, $\frac{a}{b}$, where a and b are integers and $b \neq 0$.

51. C: The constant of proportionality is equal to the slope. Using the points $(-3,9)$ and $(0,0)$, the slope may be written as $\frac{0-9}{0-(-3)}$, which equals −3.

52. B: Authentic assessment techniques are designed to build higher-order thinking skills because they require students to construct their own answers instead of choosing from preselected answers. They also allow for the possibility that multiple "correct" answers are possible because students bring different perspectives and prior experiences to the material. They typically measure student performance over an extended period of time and are graded on a criterion-referenced basis (e.g., students are compared to an objective standard, rather than being directly compared to one another).

53. C: Choice A could be any parallelogram. Choice B could be any rhombus, and choice D could be any rectangle. Choice C best matches the mathematical definition of a square (a plane figure with four equal sides and four right (90°) angles).

54. B: The sum of 4 and the product of each term number and 4 equals the term value. For example, for term number 3, the value is equal to $4(3) + 4$, or 16.

55. A: The test point of (0,0) indicates that shading should occur above the line with the steeper slope. The same test point indicates that shading should occur below the other line. The overlapped shading occurs between these two lines, in the lower left.

56. C: For a data sample with n values x_1 to x_n, with mean value $\bar{x}$, the formula for standard deviation is:

$$s = \sqrt{\frac{\sum_{i=1}^{n}(x_i - \bar{x})^2}{n-1}}$$

The mean of this data sample is $\bar{x} = 13.5$. The values for $(x_i - 13.5)$ are –5.5, –3.5, –2.5, –0.5, –0.5, 2.5, 3.5, and 6.5. The sum of the squares of these terms is:

$$\sum_{k=1}^{8}(x_k - 13.5)^2 = 30.25 + 12.25 + 6.25 + 0.25 + 0.25 + 6.25 + 12.25 + 42.25 = 110$$

Substituting this value into the original formula, we get:

$$s = \sqrt{\frac{110}{8-1}} \approx 4.0$$

57. B: If Sofia had correctly used the techniques described in choice A or choice D, she would have arrived at the correct answers, $\frac{2}{4}$ and $\frac{3}{6}$. Choice C would have shown her that $\frac{2}{4}$ and $\frac{4}{8}$ are equivalent fractions of $\frac{1}{2}$. By adding equal numbers to the numerator and denominator of $\frac{1}{2}$, Sophia concluded that $\frac{2}{3}$ and $\frac{3}{4}$ were equivalent fractions.

58. A: The following proportion may be written and solved for x: $\frac{5{,}280}{1} = \frac{4{,}900}{x}$. Thus, $x \approx 0.93$.

59. D: Choosing either the 50 youngest or 50 oldest people in a group is likely to increase sampling error, since randomization was not employed. The other described techniques utilize random sampling or other methods of decreasing sampling error.

60. C: The Pythagorean theorem may be used to find the diagonal distance from the top of the tree to the base of the shadow. Using the following equation, we can determine this distance, c: $12^2 + 9.8^2 = c^2$. Thus, $c \approx 15.5$. The distance is approximately 15.5 ft.

61. B: Since they are not mutually exclusive events, $P(4 \text{ or } E) = P(4) + P(E) - P(4 \text{ and } E)$. Substituting the probability of each event gives $P(4 \text{ or } E) = \frac{1}{6} + \frac{1}{2} - \frac{1}{6} = \frac{1}{2}$.

62. A: Creating an outline of key concepts to see which ones overlap between subjects is the first step teachers should take when planning interdisciplinary units. This will allow the teachers to see which skills overlap that they can target in instruction. While teachers should be able to discuss what they want to individually accomplish in the unit, this should not be the first step. Creating a summative assessment should be one of the first steps for planning the unit, but they should first identify which concepts they want students to learn before planning the assessment. Likewise, constructing a list of what information they want students to learn is helpful, but this needs to happen after outlining the key concepts from each subject in the interdisciplinary unit.

63. D: The original cost may be represented by the equation $28 = x - 0.3x$ or $28 = 0.7x$. Dividing both sides of the equation by 0.7 gives $x = 40$.

64. B: The points may be entered into a graphing calculator to find the least-squares regression line. This line is approximately $y = -0.044x + 15.59$. Substituting 250 for x gives $y = -0.044(250) + 15.59 = 4.59$. Thus, 4.5 gallons is a good estimate for the amount of gas that will be left after 250 miles.

Alternatively, if you visually predict a line of best fit using any two points, for example, the points (25,14.2) and (100,11), the slope between those points is approximately –0.043, and the line passes through the y-axis around $y = 15$. Using slope-intercept form ($y = mx + b$, where m is the slope and b is the y-intercept), we get the equation $y = -0.043x + 15$. At $x = 250$ we get $y = -0.043(250) + 15 = 4.25$. Thus, another good estimate would be 4.25 gallons, which is also close to 4.5.

65. C: When two parallel lines are cut by a transversal, the consecutive angles formed inside the lines are supplementary.

66. C: The triangle is a 30-60-90 right triangle. Thus, if the short leg is represented by x, the hypotenuse is represented by $2x$, and the long leg is represented by $x\sqrt{3}$. Thus, the hypotenuse is equal to 20 inches.

67. D: Being aware that patterns (regular repetitions) and relationships (associations between/among things) exist in the world affords us greater self-efficacy about our interacting with the environment, as well as increases our sense of confidence in the environment itself (C). This awareness not only helps us to understand sequences of events; it moreover enables us to predict the next event in the series before it occurs (B). Having an awareness of patterns and relationships in things also informs our understanding of the basic structure of those things (A).

68. A: The vertical line of symmetry is represented by an equation of the form $x = a$. The horizontal line of symmetry is represented by an equation of the form $y = b$. One line of symmetry occurs at $x = -4$. The other line of symmetry occurs at $y = 6$.

69. D: Both an insurance company's actuarial table (A) and a weather forecast for the chances of rain (B) predict the probability or likelihood of something happening—for an individual's illness, injury, or death by a given age (A), or for precipitation to occur in a given day or week (B). A chart comparing the results of different interventions (C) organizes and allows people to interpret data related to which method was more or less effective with certain populations rather than predicting the likelihood of any occurrence.

70. B: This is a counting problem. The number of possible selections equals the product of the possibilities for each category: $6 \times 12 \times 1 = 72$. There are 72 ways for Mark to fill his backpack.

71. A: The vertical line of symmetry is represented by an equation of the form $x = a$. The horizontal line of symmetry is represented by an equation of the form $y = a$. One line of symmetry occurs at $x = -2$. The other line of symmetry occurs at $y = 4$.

72. C: Formative assessment refers to any kind of evaluation by a teacher that helps guide her instruction. In mathematics instruction, teachers need to know exactly what the students have mastered in order to teach them appropriately because so many principles must be taught consecutively and in appropriate order. Conversations, class work and homework are all examples of formative assessments. These practices help teachers know where students might need more help and where instruction should be focused.

73. B: As the denominator approaches infinity, the value of the function will get smaller and smaller and converge to 0.

74. D: In scientific notation, only one digit should remain to the left of the decimal. In the original number, the decimal point is four places to the right of the first digit, 3. Therefore, $30{,}490 = 3.049 \times 10^4$ is the correct answer. Choice C, 30.490×10^3 is equal to the correct value, but it incorrectly places two digits to the left of the decimal point.

75. B: Data sets A and C are asymmetrical. Data set A is skewed toward lower values, and data set C is skewed toward higher values. This makes the mean a poor measure of center. Data set D is mostly symmetrical but has a small outlier. The mean is very sensitive to outliers and is not an appropriate measure of center for data sets that include them. Data set B is roughly symmetrical and has no outliers. The mean would be an appropriate measure of center here.

76. D: The series is an infinite geometric series. The sum may be calculated using the formula $S = \frac{a}{1-r}$, where a represents the value of the first term and r represents the common ratio. Substituting 1 for a and $\frac{2}{3}$ for r gives $S = \frac{1}{1-\frac{2}{3}}$ or 3.

77. B: This is a formative assessment because she is assessing students while she is still teaching the unit. Summative assessments are given at the end of the unit. Formal assessments are usually quizzes or tests. Informal assessments include asking individual students questions. Therefore, the correct choice is (B).

78. D: The number of outcomes in the event is 2 (rolling a 5 or 6), and the sample space is 6 (numbers 1 to 6). Thus, the probability may be written as $\frac{2}{6}$, which simplifies to $\frac{1}{3}$.

79. C: The slope may be written as $m = \frac{4-0}{-3-(-4)}$, which simplifies to $m = 4$.

80. C: The situation may be modeled by the system $\begin{cases} 6x + 2y = 7.20 \\ 15x + y = 12.60 \end{cases}$. One way to solve this system is to multiply the bottom equation by −2.

$$\begin{cases} 6x + 2y = 7.20 \\ -30x - 2y = -25.20 \end{cases}$$

Then, add the two equations and solve for x.

$$-24x = -18$$
$$x = 0.75$$

Thus, one pen costs \$0.75. We can plug this value back into the second equation and solve for y to find the price of one notebook.

$$15(0.75) + y = 12.60$$
$$11.25 + y = 12.60$$
$$y = 1.35$$

Therefore, one notebook costs $1.35.

81. C: The number of ways the letters can be arranged may be represented as $\frac{10!}{3!3!2!1!1!}$, which equals 50,400.

82. D: In order to assess the effectiveness of the team teaching model, the teachers should compare their sixth-grade students' performance this year with the performance of sixth-grade students in previous years where team teaching was not used. This will eliminate the possibility of differences among schools that would be present if they compared their students to students in other schools (C). Comparing their performance on standardized testing to the previous year (A) would not be a good measure of the success of the team teaching model, as students are expected to progress between grades. Comparing their performance in team teaching classes to their performance in other classes (B) also would not be a good assessment, as these classes require different skills and test different areas.

83. C: This situation describes a permutation, since order matters. The number of permutations of length r from a set of n elements is $P(n,r) = \frac{n!}{(n-r)!}$. This situation may be represented as $P(5,2) = \frac{5!}{(5-2)!} = \frac{5\times4\times3!}{3!} = 5 \times 4 = 20$. Therefore, there are 20 ways to rank the top 2 performers from a group of 5 candidates.

84. B: The slope of a straight line is a vital concept to understanding linear equations.

85. D: Students need to learn and practice computation skills, but they also need to learn that the mathematical skills they acquire in the classroom have practical value in their lives outside of school.

86. A: The position of the car is changing according to a constant speed. Thus, the graph will show a straight line with a positive but constant slope.

87. A: An inversely proportional relationship is written in the form $y = \frac{k}{x}$, thus the equation $y = \frac{1}{x}$ shows that y is inversely proportional to x.

88. B: The amount she pays is equal to 0.001(3,200). Thus, she pays $3.20.

89. D: The area of the square is $A = s^2 = (30 \text{ cm})^2 = 900 \text{ cm}^2$. The area of the circle is $A = \pi r^2 = (3.14)(15 \text{ cm})^2 \approx 707 \text{ cm}^2$. The area of the shaded region is equal to the difference between the area of the square and the area of the circle, or $900 \text{ cm}^2 - 707 \text{ cm}^2$, which equals 193 cm^2.

90. C: The original price may be represented by the equation $6{,}375 = x - 0.15x$ or $6{,}375 = 0.85x$. Dividing both sides of the equation by 0.85 gives $x = 7{,}500$.

91. D: Students in 8th grade should be able to use basic algebraic concepts to analyze both proportional and non-proportional linear relationships. Remember that in a proportional relationship between x and y, the ratio between the two variables is constant. In a non-proportional relationship, the ratio is varied; in other words, the graph of the ratio between x and y will not be a straight line. Algebraic concepts are introduced in previous grades, but this standard is not expected to be used consistently until 8th grade.

92. D: We first factor the numerator: $n^2(n-1)$. We can then write the expression as $\frac{n^2(n-1)}{n}$, which reduces to $n(n-1)$. As the limit approaches infinity, both n and $n-1$ increase without bound, so the expression has no limit.

93. C: The amount of time she spends on meals and homework is equal to 0.23(24), or 5.52, which is more than 5.

94. A: The amount to be administered may be written as $\frac{1}{12} \times \frac{34}{10}$, which equals $\frac{17}{60}$. Thus, she should administer $\frac{17}{60}$ fluid ounces of medicine.

95. B: When two parallel lines are cut by a transversal, the consecutive angles formed inside the lines are supplementary.

96. B: The amount he spends on movies, books, and games is equal to 0.21(50), or \$10.50, which is more than \$10.

97. D: A Venn diagram may be drawn to assist in finding the answer.

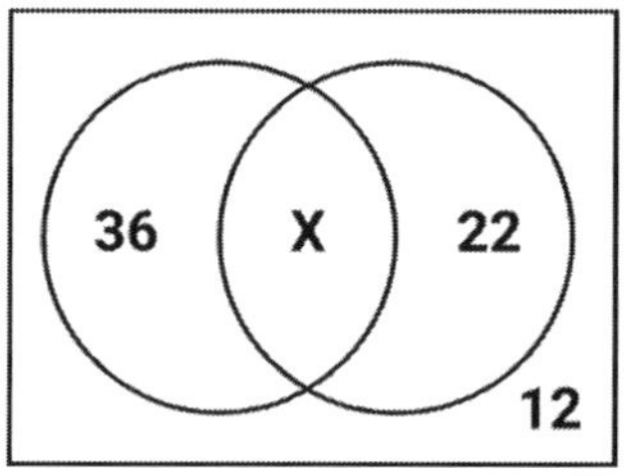

Since the set contains 75 total people, the solution is equal to $75 - (36 + 22 + 12)$ or 5 people.

98. C: Since they are not mutually exclusive events, the probability may be written as $P(N \text{ or } T) = P(N) + P(T) - P(N \text{ and } T)$. Because the events are independent, $P(N \text{ and } T) = P(N) \times P(T)$. Substituting the probability of each event gives $(N \text{ or } T) = \frac{1}{2} + \frac{1}{2} - \left(\frac{1}{2} \times \frac{1}{2}\right)$, or $\frac{3}{4}$.

99. A: The cross-section of a triangular prism will never be a circle. The cross-section of a polyhedron, such as a triangular prism, is always a polygon.

100. D: The slope of the graphed line is 2. A line parallel to this one will also have a slope of 2. Substituting the slope and the x- and y-values from the point $(-1,4)$ into the slope-intercept form of an equation gives $4 = 2(-1) + b$, which simplifies to $4 = -2 + b$. Adding 2 to both sides of the equation gives $b = 6$. So, the equation of a line parallel to this one and passing through the point $(-1,4)$ is $y = 2x + 6$.

TExES Practice Test #3

1. Myles has a $60 budget to purchase a team lunch. He plans to buy sandwiches and salads. He needs to purchase a minimum of 15 items to make sure everyone has food. Each sandwich costs $3 and each salad costs $5. Which of the following graphs correctly shows the possible combinations of sandwiches and salads that he may buy, assuming that the x-axis represents sandwiches and the y-axis represents salads?

a.

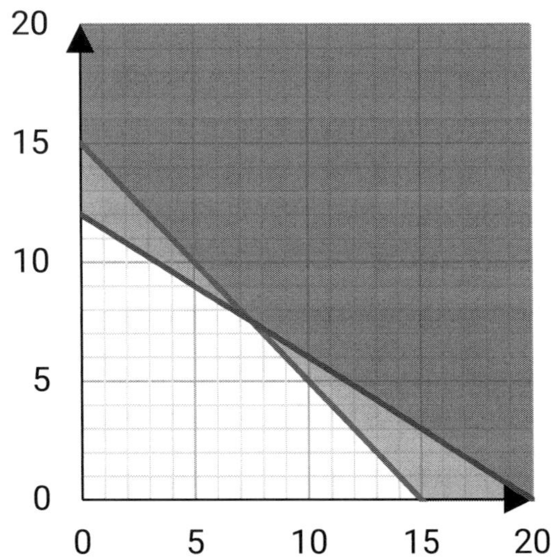

b.

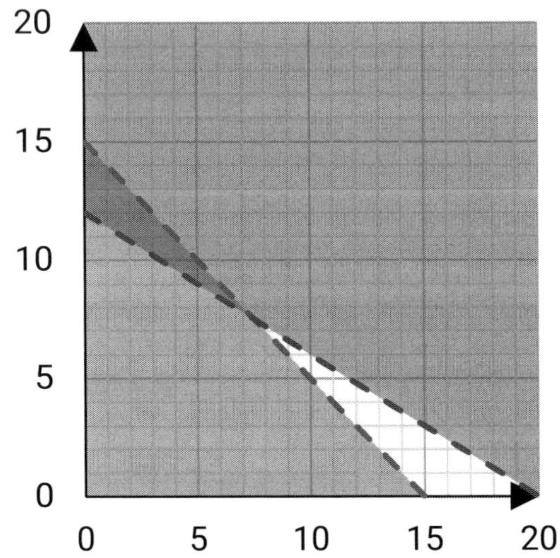

c.

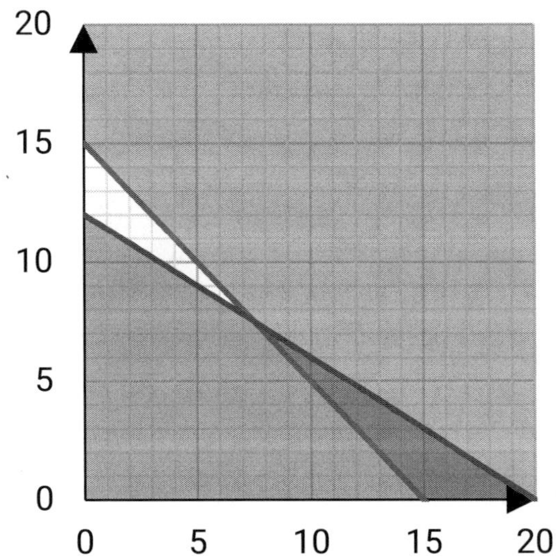

d.

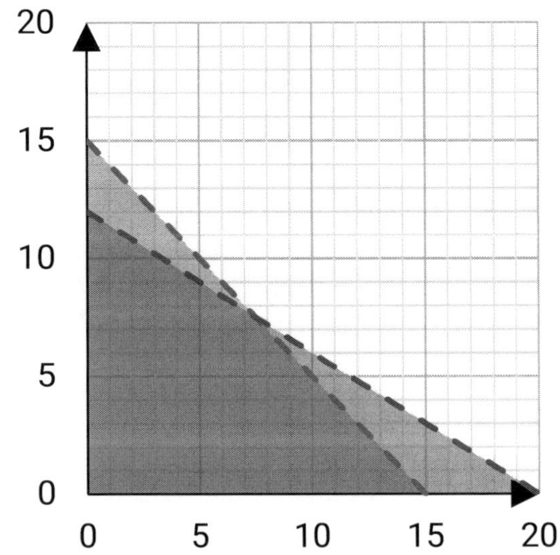

2. Mrs. Vories, a fifth-grade teacher, asks her class to use compatible numbers to help her determine approximately how many chicken nuggets she needs to buy for a school-wide party. The school has 589 students and each student will be served nine nuggets. Which student correctly applied the concept of compatible numbers?

a. Madison estimates: $500 \times 10 = 5{,}000$ nuggets
b. Audrey estimates: $600 \times 5 = 3{,}000$ nuggets
c. Ian estimates: $600 \times 10 = 6{,}000$ nuggets
d. Andrew estimates: $500 \times 5 = 2{,}500$ nuggets

3. What is the length of the hypotenuse in the right triangle shown below?

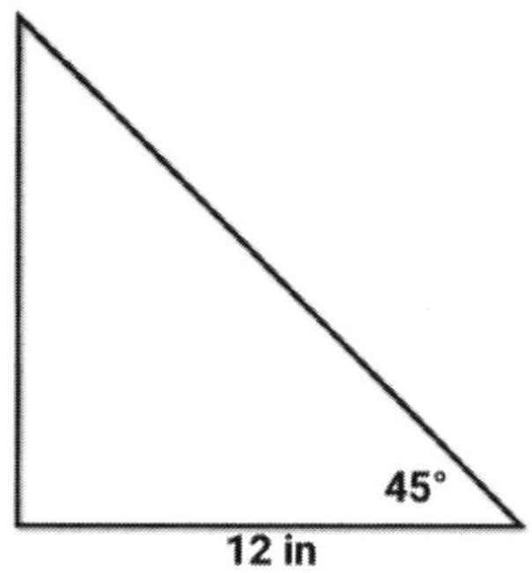

a. 15 in
b. $12\sqrt{3}$ in
c. 18 in
d. $12\sqrt{2}$ in

4. What is the midpoint of the line segment below?

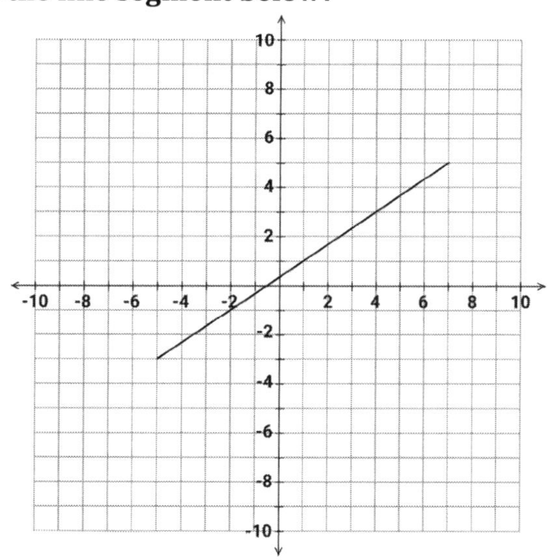

a. (−0.5,2)
b. (1,1)
c. (1.5,3)
d. (2,1.5)

5. A building is 44 feet tall and casts a shadow that is 59.2 ft in length. Which of the following best represents the distance from the top of the building to the end of the shadow?

a. 39.6 ft
b. 45.5 ft
c. 61.9 ft
d. 73.8 ft

6. Which of the following postulates may be used to prove the similarity of ΔABC and ΔADE?

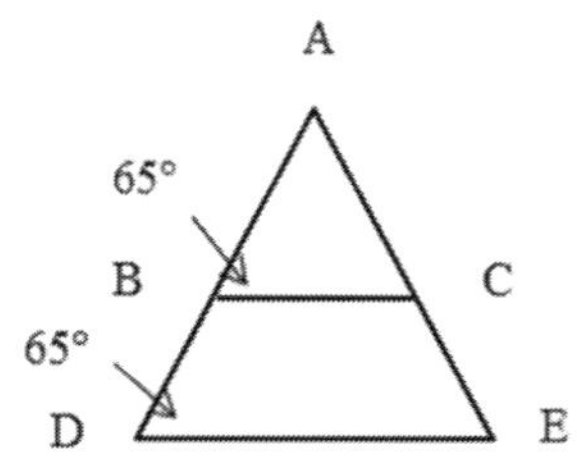

a. ASA
b. AA
c. SAS
d. SSS

7. Students are given the following algebra problem: $2x + 5 = 20$. One student comes up with an answer of $x = 12.5$. Is the student correct? If not, what has the student most likely done wrong?

a. Yes, the student's answer is correct.
b. No, the student has not rounded up to 13.
c. No, the student has probably not divided both sides by 2.
d. No, the student has most likely added 5 to both sides rather than subtracting.

8. Kim's current monthly rent is $800. She is moving to another apartment complex, where the monthly rent will be $1,100. What is the percent increase in her monthly rent amount?

a. 25.5%
b. 27%
c. 35%
d. 37.5%

9. Which of the following represents the graph of $y = (x + 2)^2 - 3$?

a. 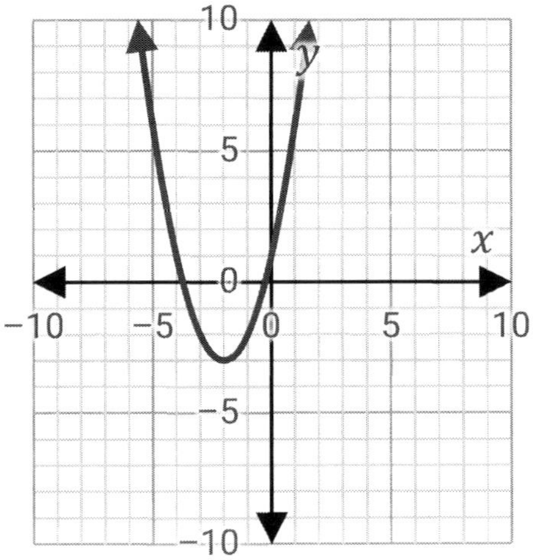

b. 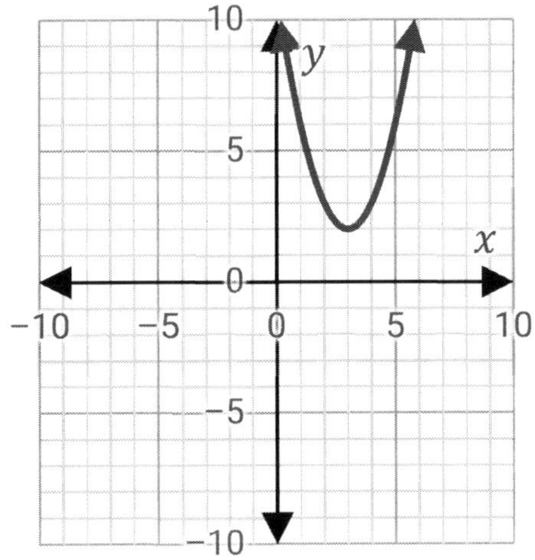

c. 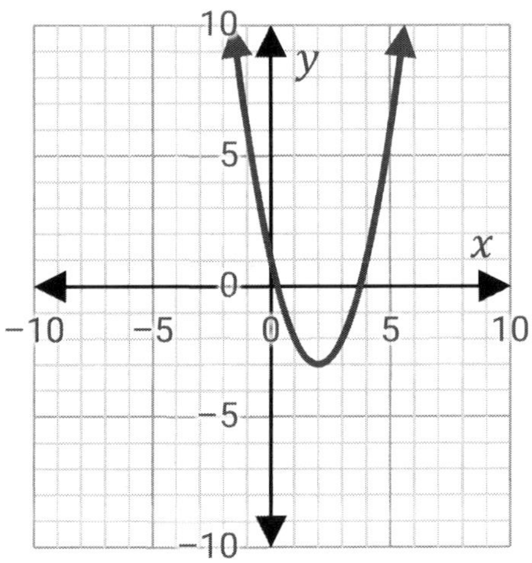

d. 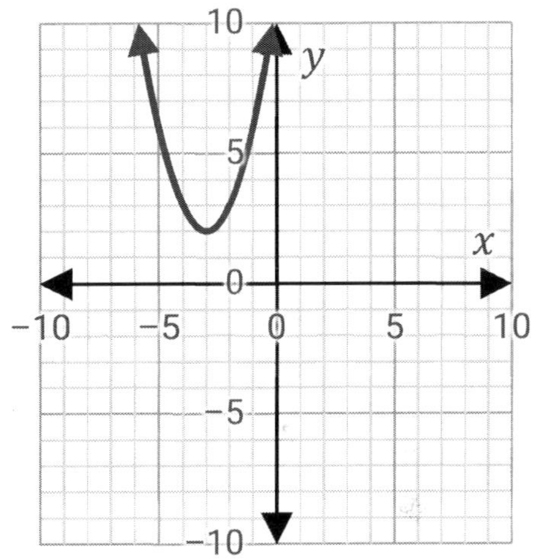

10. Becca needs to order 8 sandwiches for her team lunch, and she knows they will cost at least $40. Which of the following inequalities represents the possible costs?

a. $40 \geq 8s$
b. $40 < 8s$
c. $40 > 8s$
d. $40 \leq 8s$

11. What is $\lim_{n \to \infty} \frac{n-1}{n^2}$?

a. 0
b. 1
c. 2
d. There is no limit.

12. A convex three-dimensional figure has 12 edges and 8 vertices. How many faces does it have?

a. 4
b. 5
c. 6
d. 8

13. Which of the following learning goals is most appropriate for a fourth-grade unit on geometry and measurement?

a. The students will be able to use a protractor to determine the approximate measures of angles in degrees to the nearest whole number.
b. The students will be able to describe the process for graphing ordered pairs of numbers in the first quadrant of the coordinate plane.
c. The students will be able to determine the volume of a rectangular prism with whole number side lengths in problems related to the number of layers times the number of unit cubes in the area of the base.
d. The students will be able to classify two-dimensional figures in a hierarchy of sets and subsets using graphic organizers based on their attributes and properties.

14. The expression $3x^2 + 3x - 18$ is equal to the product of $(x + 3)$ and which other factor?

a. $(3x - 4)$
b. $(3x - 6)$
c. $(3x + 4)$
d. $(3x + 6)$

15. Which of the following represents 2,417?

a. 2.417×10^{-3}
b. 2.417×10^{3}
c. 24.17×10^{3}
d. 2.417×10^{4}

16. Anne rolls a die and tosses a coin. What is the probability she gets a prime number greater than 2 or heads?

a. $\frac{1}{2}$
b. $\frac{2}{3}$
c. $\frac{3}{4}$
d. $\frac{5}{6}$

17. What is the contrapositive of the statement below?

If Lucy wears a scarf, it is winter.

a. If Lucy wears a scarf, it is not winter.
b. If Lucy does not wear a scarf, it is not winter.
c. If it is not winter, Lucy does not wear a scarf.
d. If it is winter, Lucy does not wear a scarf.

18. Mrs. Thomas recently taught her fifth grade students a new math concept that they seemed to understand clearly. However, when she administered a unit test of the material, more than half of the students failed. Mrs. Thomas' first reaction should be to:

a. Give the students another chance to learn the material by re-teaching it the same way as she did the first time
b. Analyze the test and the results to determine whether the assessment was well-designed and fairly administered
c. Review the test results to discover exactly which aspect of the material the students had trouble with
d. Compare her students' test results with the performance of last year's fifth grade class on the same test to see if there is a discrepancy

19. Given the boxplots below, which of the following statements is correct?

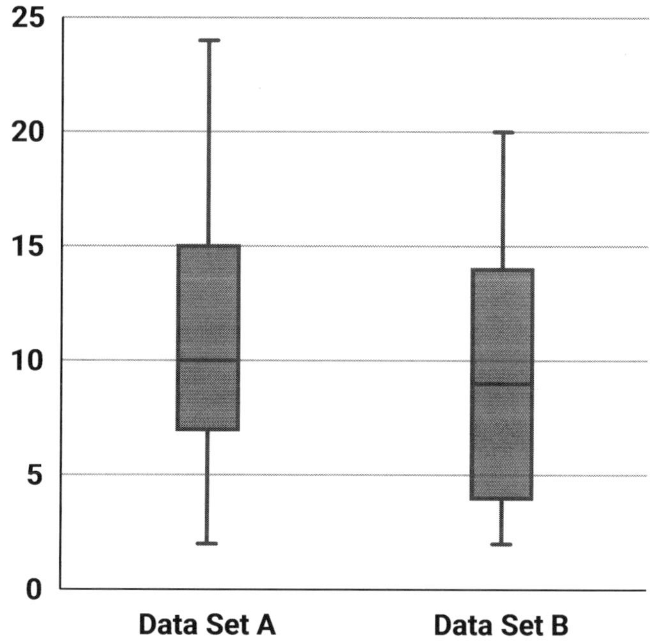

a. Data Set A has a larger range and a larger median.
b. Data Set A has a smaller range and a larger median.
c. Data Set A has a larger range and a smaller median.
d. Data Set A has a smaller range and a smaller median.

20. Which of the following measurements is the best approximation of 2,012 square inches?

a. 11.85 ft^2
b. 12.28 ft^2
c. 13.97 ft^2
d. 15.29 ft^2

TExES Practice Test #3

21. What scale factor was applied to the smaller triangle to obtain the larger triangle below?

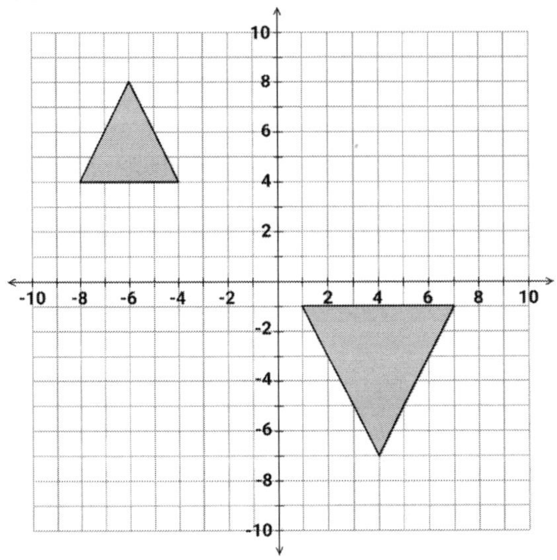

a. $\frac{1}{2}$
b. $\frac{2}{3}$
c. $\frac{3}{2}$
d. $\frac{5}{4}$

22. What is the length of the hypotenuse in the triangle shown below?

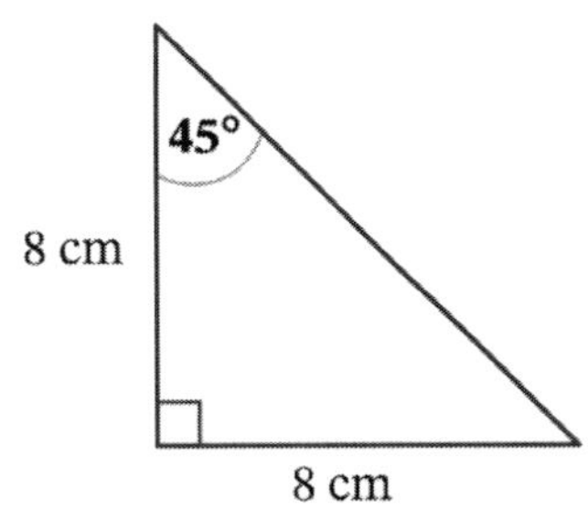

a. 4 cm
b. $8\sqrt{3}$ cm
c. 16 cm
d. $8\sqrt{2}$ cm

23. Which of the following equations represents a line perpendicular to the one graphed below and passing through the point $(3, 2)$?

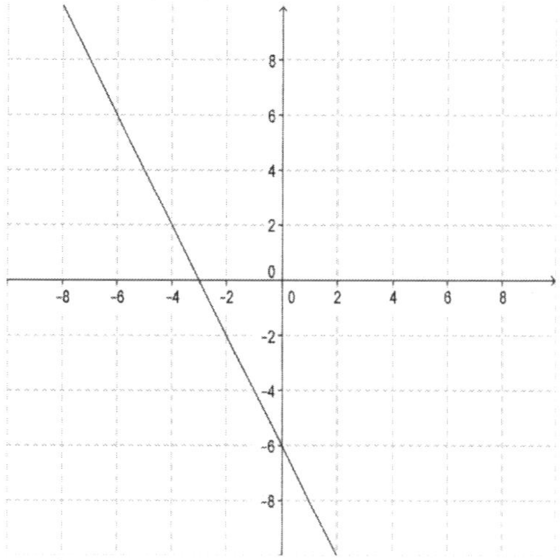

a. $y = \frac{1}{2}x + 2$
b. $y = \frac{1}{2}x + \frac{1}{2}$
c. $y = \frac{3}{2}x + \frac{1}{2}$
d. $y = 2x + 2$

24. Which of the following correctly compares the sets of whole numbers and counting numbers?

a. The sets of whole and counting numbers are equal.
b. The sets of whole and counting numbers are disjoint.
c. The set of whole numbers is a subset of the set of counting numbers.
d. The set of counting numbers is a subset of the set of whole numbers.

25. The total amount Carlos has spent on his rent is represented by the graph below. The x-axis represents the number of months since he began his lease, and the y-axis represents the total cost ($500 deposit plus $750 per month). What is the relationship between the total cost and the number of months?

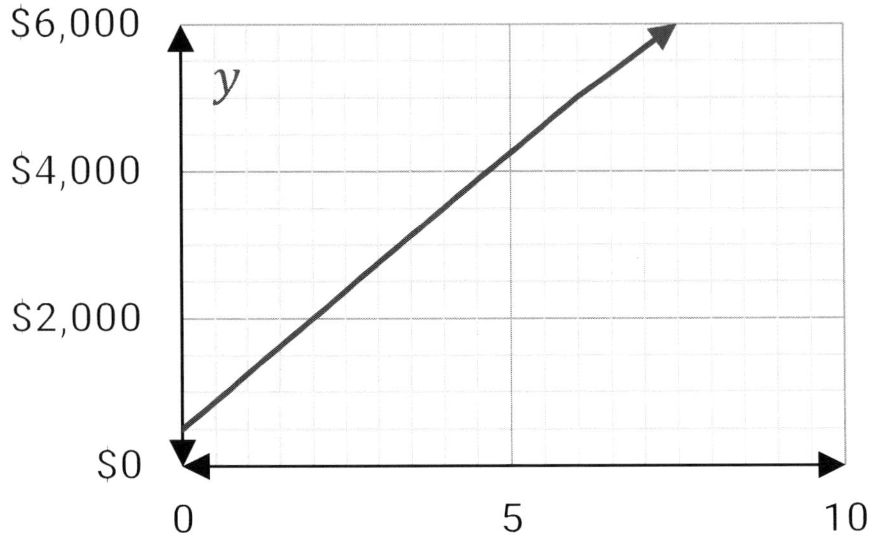

a. The cost is linear, but not proportional.
b. The cost is linear and proportional.
c. The cost is proportional, but not linear.
d. The cost represents an inverse proportional relationship.

26. Which of the following assessment methods is most likely to be used in a learner-centered classroom?

a. A method that provides different alternatives for students to demonstrate their knowledge
b. A method that allows students to complete the assessment in groups
c. A structured method that allows students' mastery to be compared with that of other students
d. A multiple-choice test which students help to construct and grade

27. Which of the following represents a function?

a. $\{(2,9), (3,5), (6,8), (-1,-6), (3,-2)\}$
b. $\{(8,8), (7,9), (2,1), (8,3), (3,6)\}$
c. $\{(-4,6), (2,4), (-4,-2), (3,5), (9,2)\}$
d. $\{(2,6), (6,5), (5,9), (1,0), (-3,1)\}$

28. Which of the following steps were applied to ΔABC?

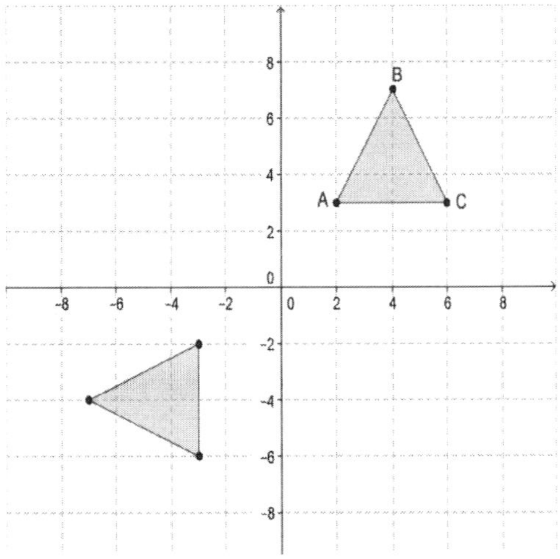

a. Reflection across the x-axis and counterclockwise rotation of 90 degrees about the origin
b. Reflection across the x-axis and counterclockwise rotation of 180 degrees about the origin
c. Reflection across the x-axis and counterclockwise rotation of 270 degrees about the origin
d. Reflection across the y-axis and counterclockwise rotation of 180 degrees about the origin

29. Which of the following pairs of shapes may tessellate a plane?

a. Equilateral triangles and squares
b. Regular pentagons and equilateral triangles
c. Regular pentagons and squares
d. Regular octagons and equilateral triangles

30. Gillian works out for 15 minutes a day for the first month. During each subsequent month, she plans to exercise an additional 5 minutes per day compared to the previous month. Which of the following equations represents the amount she will work out each day during the nth month?

a. $a_n = 15n - 5$
b. $a_n = 15n + 1$
c. $a_n = 5n + 10$
d. $a_n = 5n + 15$

31. Mario makes an offer of $158,400 on a home. This is a markdown of 12% from the asking price. What was the asking price?

a. $175,000
b. $175,550
c. $178,500
d. $180,000

32. Of the following, which use of math skills for everyday situations is most related to a student's application of math for an English class?

a. To determine the value of an unknown number
b. To determine scores needed to get from B to A
c. To determine the area of the school auditorium
d. To determine supplies needed for PTA meeting

33. The best time to introduce a student to subtraction with two-digit numerals is:

a. Before the student reaches the fourth grade
b. When the student has proved proficient in adding long columns of numbers
c. When the student has achieved automatic response to subtraction facts
d. When the student expresses an interest in advancing his or her subtraction skills

34. What is the main purpose of formative assessments?

a. To establish the background knowledge of students prior to beginning a unit
b. To assess students partway through a unit to establish which content is mastered and which needs to be retaught
c. To compare data to other teachers and assess the effectiveness of the teacher
d. To assess students at the conclusion of a unit of study

35. Matt rolls a standard six-sided die. What is the probability he rolls a prime number?

a. $\frac{1}{4}$
b. $\frac{1}{2}$
c. $\frac{2}{3}$
d. $\frac{3}{4}$

36. According to the scatter plot below, which of the following is the *best* estimate for the earnings received for 20 hours of work?

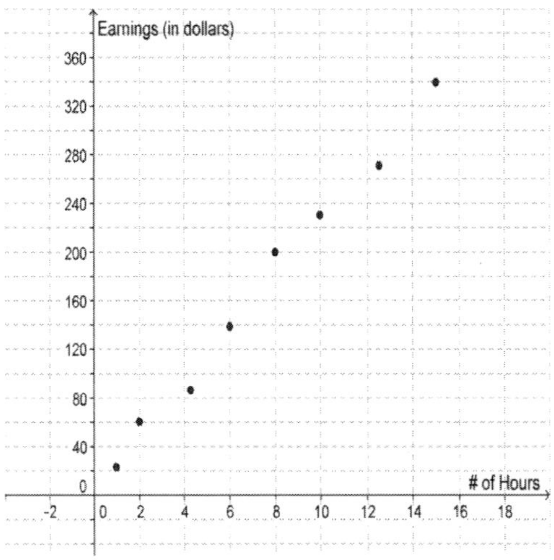

a. $342
b. $446
c. $528
d. $602

37. What is $\lim_{n \to \infty} \frac{n^2+1}{n}$?

a. 0
b. 1
c. 2
d. There is no limit.

38. What is $\lim_{x \to -2} (3x^3 - 6x^2 + 4)$?

a. −44
b. −42
c. 4
d. 52

39. Which of the following pairs of shapes may tessellate a plane?

a. Regular pentagons and squares
b. Regular pentagons and equilateral triangles
c. Equilateral triangles and regular hexagons
d. Regular octagons and equilateral triangles

40. A class is multiplying whole numbers by fractions. Four of the students correctly responded that $10 \times \frac{3}{5} = 6$. Their teacher asks each student to give his or her reasoning. The students' responses show that each student arrived at his or her answer in a different way. Read the following student explanations and indicate which explanations demonstrate mathematically valid reasoning. Select all that apply.

Student responses	Valid	Invalid
A: "I made $\frac{3}{5}$ into the decimal 0.3 and then multiplied it by 10 and multiplied that by 2."		
B: "I divided 10 by 5, which is 2, and then multiplied it by 3."		
C: "I multiplied 10 by 3, which is 30, and then divided it by 5."		
D: "I drew 10 rectangles and split them all into fifths and colored three fifths in all of them and then regrouped the colored ones to see how many I had."		

TExES Practice Test #3

41. Mel is purchasing gifts for her students. She wants to buy stickers and notepads. She may purchase a maximum of 25 items and plans to spend at least $60. Each sheet of stickers costs $2, and each notepad costs $3. Which of the following graphs correctly shows the possible combinations of stickers and notepads that she may buy, assuming that the x-axis represents sheets of stickers and the y-axis represents notepads?

a. 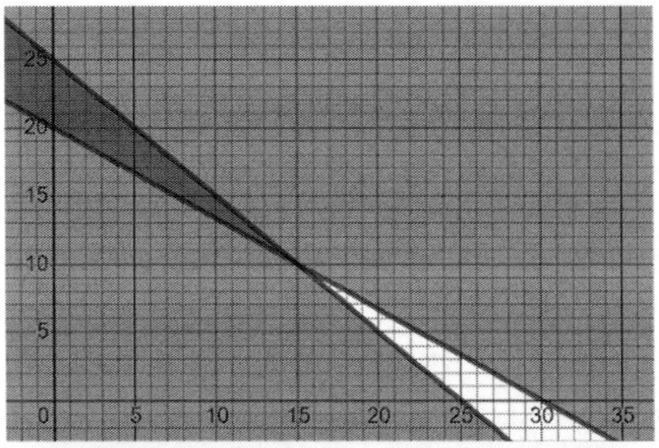

b. 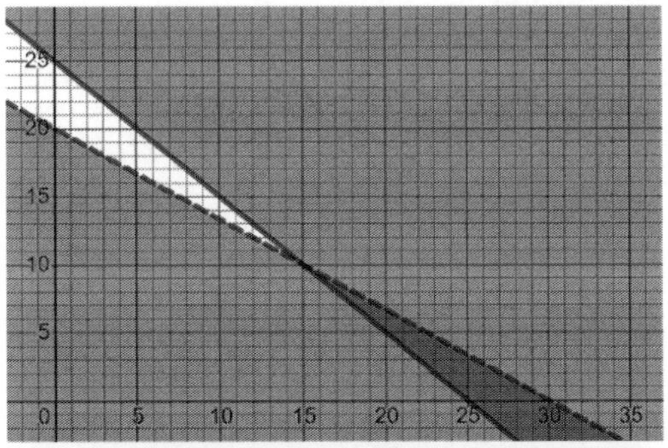

c. 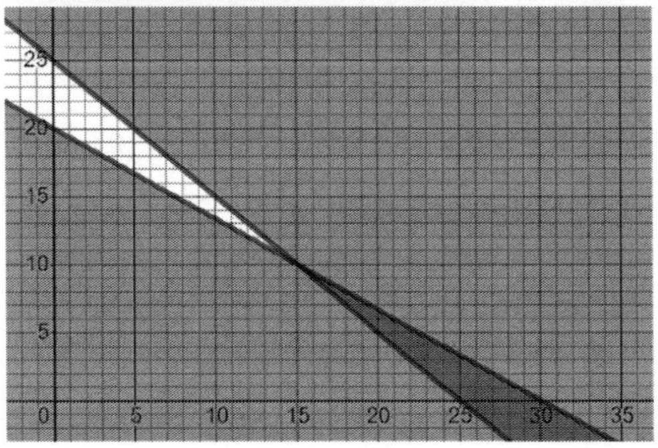

d. 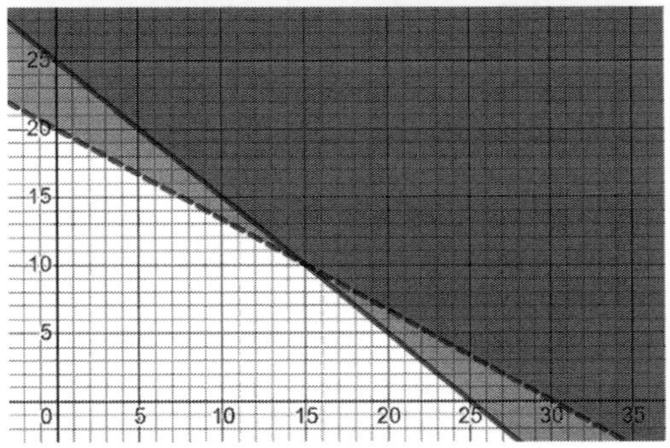

42. Keisha is solving a problem asking her to mix lemonade from a powder mix:

> The instructions on the lemonade label say "To make 8 cups of lemonade, mix 1 cup powder with 8 cups of water". You need 24 cups of lemonade. How much powder should you use?

Keisha writes that she will need 17 cups of lemonade powder. Which teacher prompt best addresses Keisha's error and helps her find the correct answer?

a. "It looks like you multiplied 8 by 2 instead of 3. Let's try multiplying by 3."
b. "It looks like you added 16 cups to both the lemonade powder and the water. Could you instead tell me how many batches of 8 cups you will need to make in order to get 24 cups?"
c. Both (a) and (b)
d. Neither (a) nor (b)

43. Which of the following transformations has been applied to ΔABC?

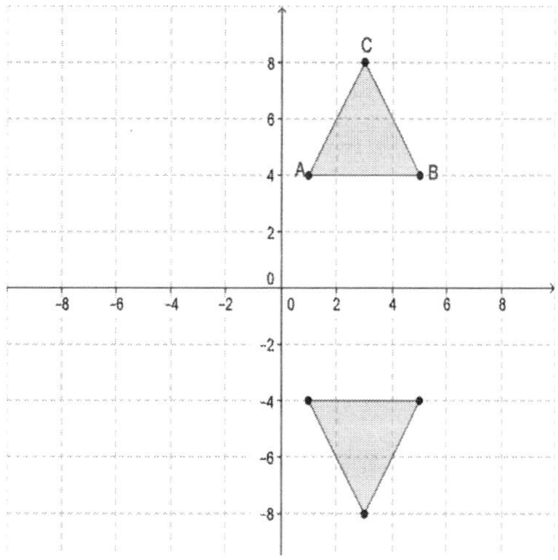

a. Translation
b. Rotation of 90 degrees
c. Reflection
d. Dilation

44. Which of the following correctly represents the expanded form of 0.158?

a. $1 \times \frac{1}{10^0} + 5 \times \frac{1}{10^1} + 8 \times \frac{1}{10^2}$
b. $1 \times \frac{1}{10^1} + 5 \times \frac{1}{10^2} + 8 \times \frac{1}{10^3}$
c. $1 \times \frac{1}{10^3} + 5 \times \frac{1}{10^2} + 8 \times \frac{1}{10^1}$
d. $1 \times \frac{1}{10^2} + 5 \times \frac{1}{10^3} + 8 \times \frac{1}{10^4}$

45. Given the two-way frequency table below, which of the following best represents P(Blue or Felt tip)?

	Felt tip	Ballpoint	Total
Black	3,114	5,283	8,397
Blue	1,756	2,459	4,215
Total	4,870	7,742	12,612

a. 55%
b. 60%
c. 65%
d. 70%

46. Which of the following is an irrational number?

a. $0.\overline{5}$
b. $e + 3$
c. $\frac{41}{3}$
d. $(\sqrt{3})^2$

47. Mr. Martinez is explaining to his students how they can tell if a fraction is less than one, equal to one, or greater than one. Which of the following math vocabulary terms must his students know in order to be able to understand and apply his explanation?

a. Mixed and equivalent
b. Like and unlike
c. Proper and improper
d. Numerator and denominator

48. The first thing students should be encouraged to do when attempting to solve a mathematical word problem is to:

a. Write the appropriate equation
b. List the steps needed to solve the problem
c. Think about what information the problem is asking them to find
d. Compare the problem to similar problems they have solved in the past

49. What is the perimeter of the trapezoid graphed below?

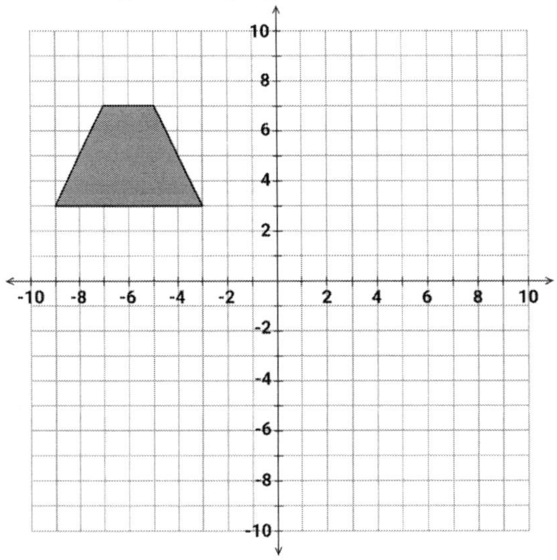

a. $6 + \sqrt{10}$
b. $8 + 4\sqrt{5}$
c. $8 + 2\sqrt{5}$
d. $7 + 2\sqrt{10}$

50. If $f(x) = \frac{2x^3 - 10x + 6}{3x}$, what is $f(3)$?

a. $\frac{10}{3}$
b. 10
c. $\frac{10}{9}$
d. 2

51. For which of the following data sets would the mean be an appropriate measure of center to use?

a. 7, 7, 7, 10, 12, 13, 16, 17, 41, 42
b. 6, 12, 52, 52, 54, 57, 57, 59, 61, 65
c. 5, 8, 9, 9, 13, 16, 18, 19, 21, 21
d. 27, 28, 30, 30, 35, 38, 41, 41, 42, 1786

52. A ball has a diameter of 5 inches. Which of the following best represents the volume?

a. 65.4 in^3
b. 69.6 in^3
c. 72.5 in^3
d. 78.3 in^3

53. Given the boxplots below, which of the following statements is correct? (Note that the boxes are not drawn to scale with one another.)

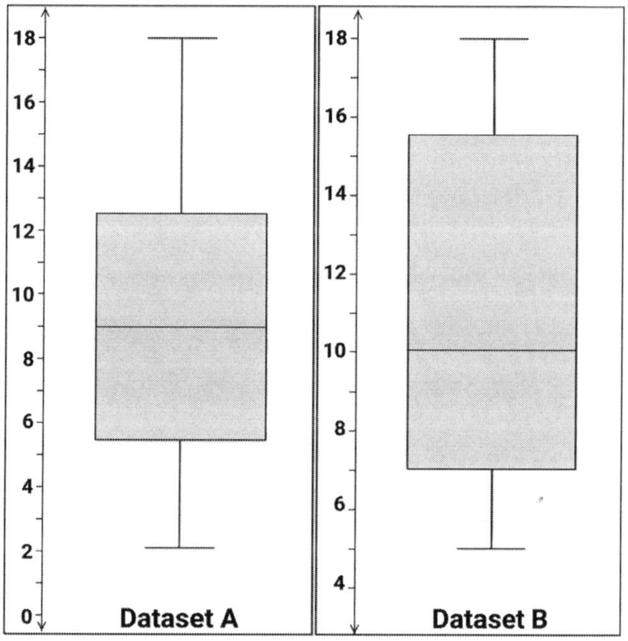

a. Dataset A has a larger range and a larger median.
b. Dataset A has a smaller range and a larger median.
c. Dataset A has a larger range and a smaller median.
d. Dataset A has a smaller range and a smaller median.

54. Which of the following skills do students need in order to solve word problems involving mean and median?

a. Counting, ordering, adding, subtracting, and dividing
b. Counting, adding, and dividing
c. Counting, ordering, adding, and dividing
d. Ordering, adding, and dividing

55. Eric has a beach ball with a radius of 9 inches. He is planning to wrap the ball with wrapping paper. Which of the following is the best estimate for the number of square feet of wrapping paper he will need? Use 3.14 for π.

a. 4.08
b. 5.12
c. 7.07
d. 8.14

56. A gift box has a length of 14 inches, a height of 8 inches, and a width of 6 inches. How many square inches of wrapping paper are needed to wrap the box?

a. 56
b. 244
c. 488
d. 672

57. Regarding the relationship of cognitive problem-solving skills to mathematics, which of these is true?

a. Problem-solving skills inform mathematical thinking but not social skills.
b. Developing problem-solving skills aids math rather than language skills.
c. Students apply logical reasoning to solve every day and novel problems.
d. Children must be taught to have interest in solving everyday problems.

58. What is $\lim_{x \to -\infty} \frac{x}{x^2-4}$?

a. 1
b. $-\frac{1}{4}$
c. 0
d. There is no limit.

59. Which of the following functions converges?

a. $f(x) = \frac{3x^2}{2x}$
b. $f(x) = 12 - \frac{7x^2}{x^2}$
c. $f(x) = 7x$
d. $f(x) = \frac{x^2+2}{x}$

60. Which type of function is represented by the table of values below?

x	y
−2	-4
−1	-0.5
0	0
1	0.5
2	4

a. Linear
b. Quadratic
c. Cubic
d. Exponential

61. Which of the following formulas may be used to represent the sequence 1, 2, 4, 8, 16, ...?

a. $y = 2x$
b. $y = x + 2$
c. $y = 2^{x-1}$
d. $y = x^2$

62. Natasha designs a square pyramidal tent for her children. Each of the sides of the square base measures x ft, and the tent's height is h feet. If Natasha were to increase by 1 ft the length of each side of the base, how much more interior space would the tent have?

a. $\frac{x^2h+2xh+h}{3}$ ft^3
b. $\frac{2xh+h}{3}$ ft^3
c. $\frac{x^2h+3}{3}$ ft^3
d. 1 ft^3

63. Which of the following correctly represents the expanded form of 0.593?

a. $5 \times \frac{1}{10^0} + 9 \times \frac{1}{10^1} + 3 \times \frac{1}{10^2}$
b. $5 \times \frac{1}{10^2} + 9 \times \frac{1}{10^3} + 3 \times \frac{1}{10^4}$
c. $5 \times \frac{1}{10^3} + 9 \times \frac{1}{10^2} + 3 \times \frac{1}{10^1}$
d. $5 \times \frac{1}{10^1} + 9 \times \frac{1}{10^2} + 3 \times \frac{1}{10^3}$

64. A box has a length of 22 centimeters, a height of 5 centimeters, and a width of 8 centimeters. How many square centimeters of plastic are needed to shrink-wrap the box?

a. 560
b. 652
c. 748
d. 880

65. Julia rolls a standard six-sided die 300 times. How many times can she expect to roll a 6?

a. 50
b. 75
c. 100
d. 125

66. Ms. Grimes knows that her 4th-grade students will be taking standardized tests next month and hopes to prepare them well. She notices during practice testing that the students are struggling with money concepts, particularly the concept of making change. This is not a complete surprise to her, based upon the students' class work. What would be the best way to approach this scenario?

a. Review each question on the practice tests carefully and walk the students through the proper way to do each problem. Deliver the practice test again a few days later to determine if the students' skills have improved.
b. Use test questions and answers from last year's test to practice and memorize
c. Set up a miniature grocery store with real items and packages labeled with prices; allow the students to practice purchasing items at the "store" and making change. Monitor and review practice test questions.
d. Give more lessons on, and review about, adding and subtracting decimals in order to help the students solidify their procedural knowledge. Explain that money concepts are simply word problems that involve decimals.

67. Mr. Tollison has noticed that many of his eighth grade math students are not completing their homework assignments at all, are partially completing them or are completing the wrong problems. Mr. Tollison's first response should be to:

a. Call the students' parents if they fail to turn in more than one assignment
b. Grade whatever problems the students do turn in, even if they are not the right ones
c. Develop a system to ensure that all students correctly record the homework assignment
d. Walk the students through a few of the homework problems before they leave class

68. In a probability unit in eighth grade, a teacher assigns multiple word problems nightly for the students' homework. The students complain that the word problems are boring and that they do not want to do them. What can the teacher do to help the students become more engaged in the probability unit?

a. Excuse the students from homework and only do math problems in class for the remainder of the unit.
b. Teach a lesson on the importance of word problems and how they will relate to everyday life.
c. Ask teachers of other subjects for word problems that can be used in her classroom.
d. Create word problems that better relate to real-world experiences for the students.

69. Students in a second-grade class have just completed an end-of-chapter test on basic multiplication facts. While scoring the assessments, the teacher noticed that many students did not perform well. Therefore, she is planning instruction to reteach foundational skills. Which of the following strategies would be helpful for this teacher to review to develop students' understanding of this concept?

a. Place value
b. Decomposing numbers
c. Counting on
d. Skip counting

70. What is the slope of the hypotenuse in the triangle graphed below?

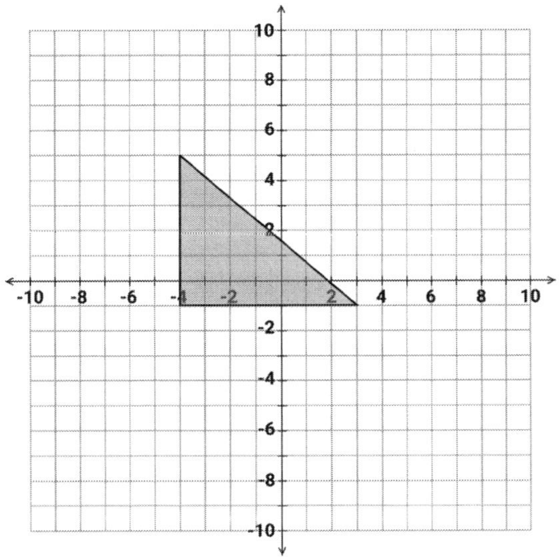

a. $-\frac{6}{7}$
b. $-\frac{7}{6}$
c. $\frac{6}{7}$
d. $\frac{7}{6}$

71. Elijah pays a $30 park entrance fee plus $4 for every ticket he buys. Which of the following equations correctly represents his total cost y in terms of the number of tickets x?

a. $y = 30x + 4$
b. $y = 34x$
c. $y = 4x + 30$
d. $y = 34x + 30$

72. Which of the following best represents the standard deviation of the data below?

23, 24, 26, 28, 31, 32, 35, 35

a. 3.9
b. 4.3
c. 4.7
d. 5.1

TExES Practice Test #3

73. What linear equation includes the data in the table below?

x	y
−3	1
1	−11
3	−17
5	−23
9	−35

a. $y = -3x - 11$
b. $y = -6x - 8$
c. $y = -3x - 8$
d. $y = -12x - 11$

74. What is the interquartile range of the data below?

$$\{1,2,4,8,11,14,14,18,19,23\}$$

a. 8
b. 10
c. 12
d. 14

75. What is the best way that a teacher can utilize the data from standardized tests from the previous year?

a. Seat students with similar deficiencies together in class to make it easier to facilitate learning
b. Identify the highest and the lowest achievers and enact a plan for the highest achievers to assist the lowest achievers
c. Identify the achievement gaps of each student and create a plan that addresses the largest gaps
d. Compare data with other teachers in the grade level to evaluate the best methods for instruction

76. How many ways can the 1st–4th place finishers be selected from 7 competitors?

a. 120
b. 360
c. 720
d. 840

77. The initial term of a sequence is 5. Each term in the sequence is $\frac{3}{5}$ the amount of the previous term. What is the sum of the terms, as n approaches infinity?

a. 5
b. 8
c. 12.5
d. 15.75

78. Javier finds a laptop on sale for \$450. If it had been marked down 40%, what was the original cost?

a. \$800
b. \$750
c. \$650
d. \$600

79. Which of the following correctly represents the expanded form of 0.867?

a. $8 \times \frac{1}{10^0} + 6 \times \frac{1}{10^1} + 7 \times \frac{1}{10^2}$
b. $8 \times \frac{1}{10^2} + 6 \times \frac{1}{10^3} + 7 \times \frac{1}{10^4}$
c. $8 \times \frac{1}{10^3} + 6 \times \frac{1}{10^2} + 7 \times \frac{1}{10^1}$
d. $8 \times \frac{1}{10^1} + 6 \times \frac{1}{10^2} + 7 \times \frac{1}{10^3}$

80. Which expression is represented by the diagram below?

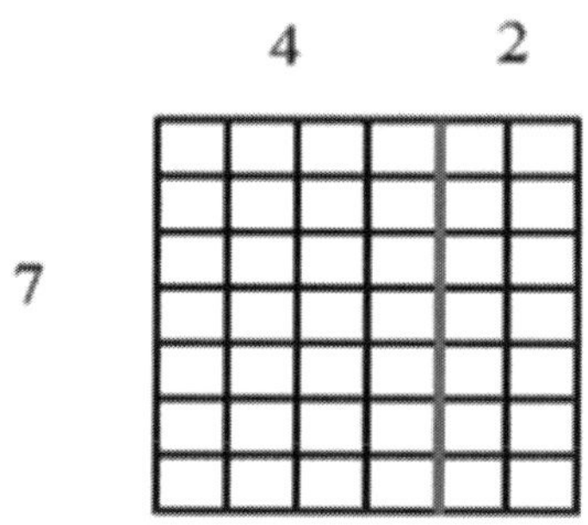

a. $7 + (4 + 2)$
b. $7 \times (4 \times 2)$
c. $7 + (4 \times 2)$
d. $7 \times (4 + 2)$

81. Given the two-way frequency table below, which of the following best represents *P*(male or graduate)?

	Undergraduate	Graduate	Total
Male	2,940	2,045	4,985
Female	3,026	2,068	5,094
Total	5,966	4,113	10,079

a. 55%
b. 60%
c. 70%
d. 75%

82. Megan rolls a standard six-sided die and tosses a coin. What is the probability she gets a number greater than 5 and tails?

a. $\frac{1}{6}$
b. $\frac{1}{4}$
c. $\frac{1}{8}$
d. $\frac{1}{12}$

83. Which of the following equations represents a line that is parallel to the one graphed below and that passes through the point $(-2, 2)$?

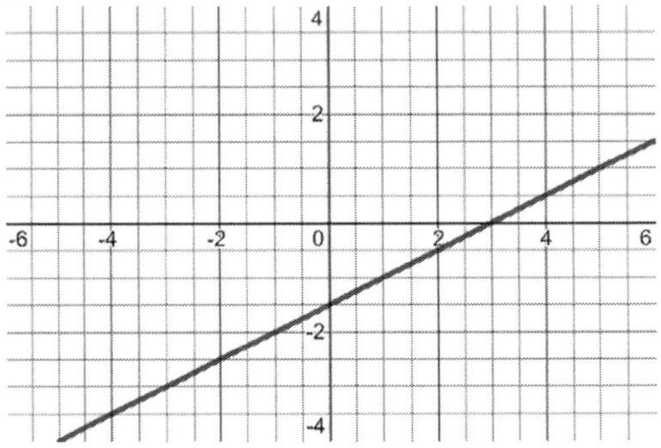

a. $y = \frac{1}{2}x + 3$
b. $y = \frac{1}{2}x - \frac{3}{2}$
c. $y = -2x - 2$
d. $y = -2x - \frac{3}{2}$

84. Four students all love animals equally, but express it differently and have different individual talents. As an example of helping them make informed educational and career decisions, which one should educators encourage to explore pursuing a career as a veterinarian?

a. The student who excels at gentle handling and beautifying but hates math and science
b. The student who excels at and enjoys all subjects in mathematics and in the sciences
c. The student who excels at rescuing and nursing animals and is average in math/science
d. The student who excels at conservation, protecting species, and captive habitat work

85. Will tosses a coin 250 times. How many times can he expect to get tails?

a. 75
b. 100
c. 125
d. 150

86. Which of the following graphs represents the solution to $y \geq 3x - 6$?

a. 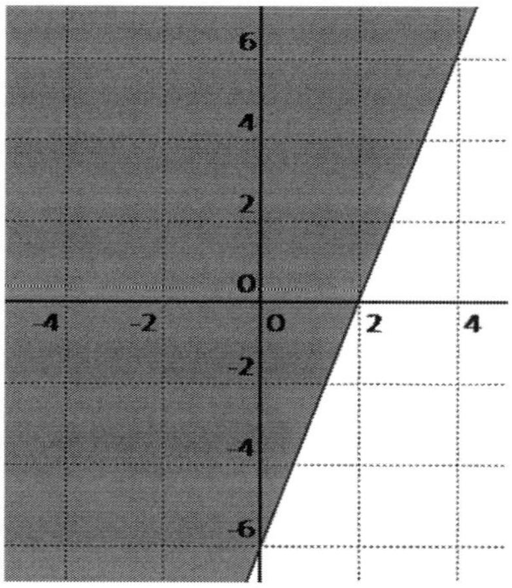

b. 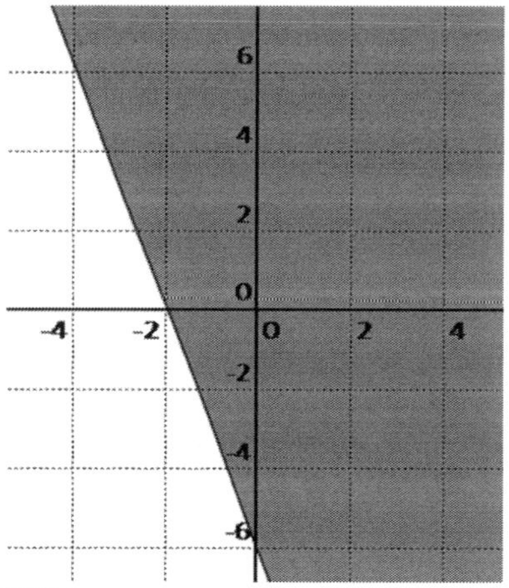

c. 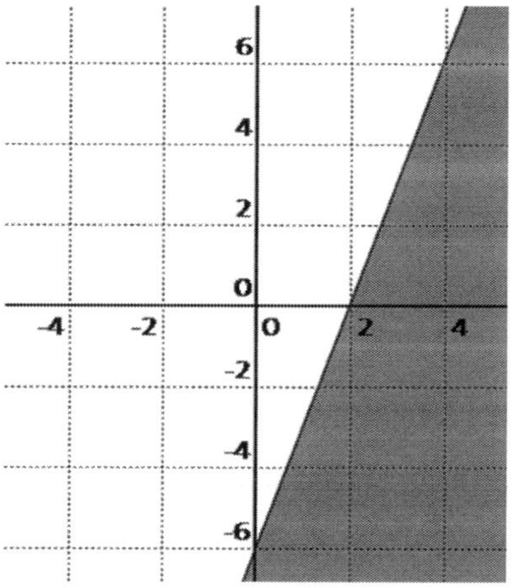

d. 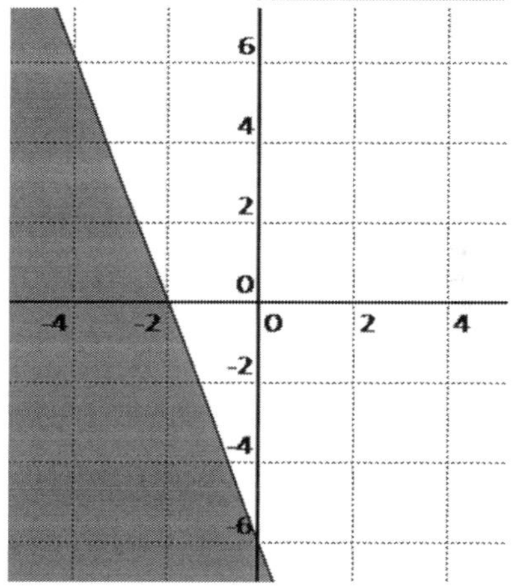

87. Ms. Brooks, a math specialist, is observing a first-year teacher whose learning objective is "Students will use proportional relationships to make an accurate scale model of a backyard." She hears the teacher gives the following explanation:

> "Let's say that the backyard is 60 feet by 30 feet. Obviously we don't have a piece of paper big enough to draw the back yard exactly the size that it is. So, what we are going to do is choose a smaller measurement to represent a foot. If we use an inch to be that smaller measurement, then we need a piece of paper that is 60 inches by 30 inches. But our paper is only 30 inches by 20 inches. Does anyone have a suggestion for what smaller measurement we should use?"

In order for the teacher to meet the learning objective, what should she change about her explanation?

a. Find a different size of paper for the students to use
b. Explain the difference between linear feet and square feet
c. Represent inches as a fraction of a foot
d. Show students the way to write the chosen scale mathematically

88. Robert needs to buy milk and bread. Each gallon of milk costs \$3. Each loaf of bread costs \$2. He intends to spend at least \$20. Which of the following graphs represents the possible combinations of gallons of milk and loaves of bread that he may purchase?

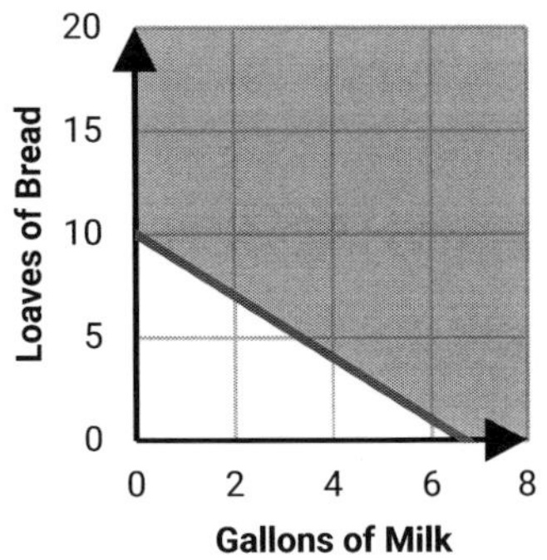

a.

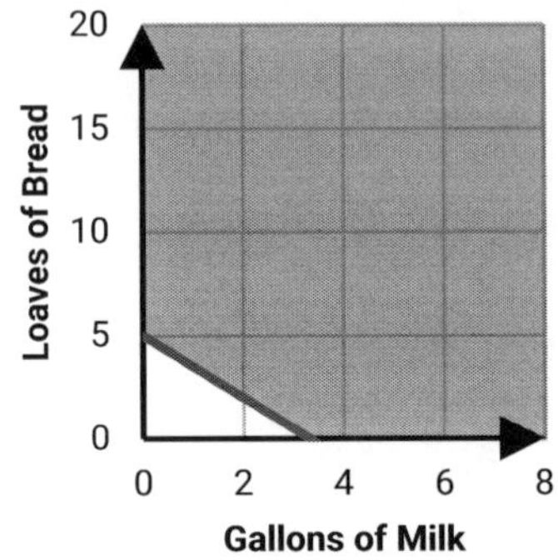

b.

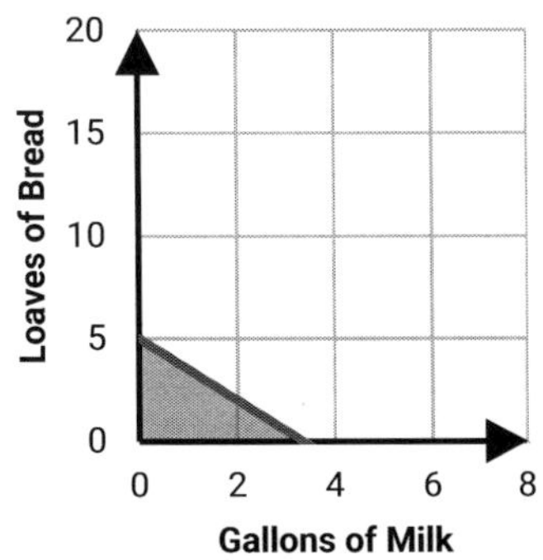

c.

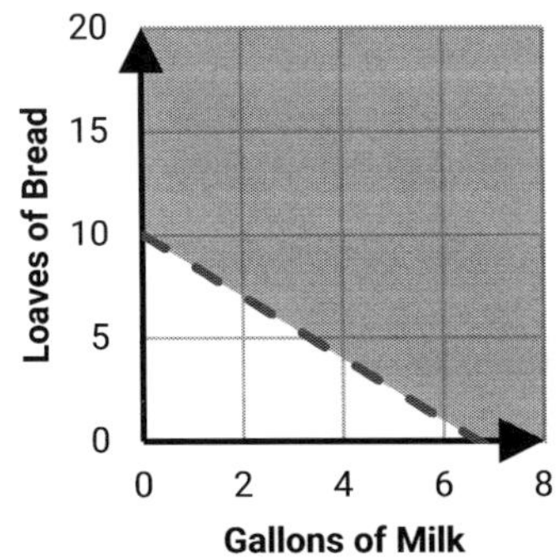

d.

89. Ben's current monthly rent is \$750. He is moving to another apartment complex, where the monthly rent will be \$900. What is the percent increase in his monthly rent amount?

a. 15%
b. 17.5%
c. 19.25%
d. 20%

90. How many ways can you arrange the letters below, if order does NOT matter?

PIZZA

a. 30
b. 60
c. 90
d. 120

91. Quentin sets aside 10% of his monthly salary to save for a car. If his monthly salary is \$2,450, how much will he set aside each month?

a. \$2.45
b. \$24.50
c. \$245
d. \$2,450

92. What scale factor was applied to the larger triangle to obtain the smaller triangle below?

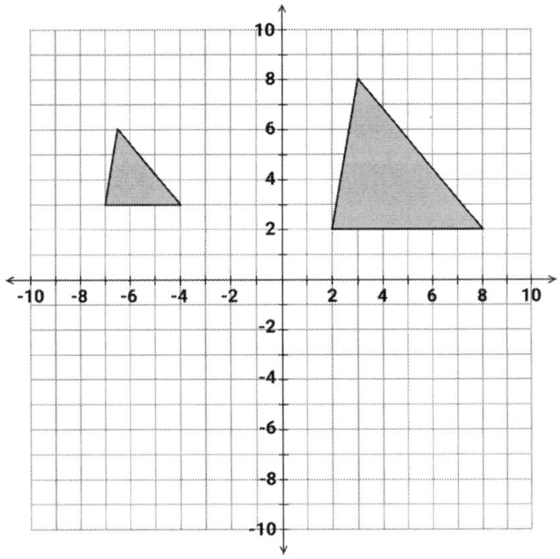

a. $\frac{1}{4}$
b. $\frac{1}{3}$
c. $\frac{1}{2}$
d. $\frac{2}{3}$

93. What is the size of the sample space for flipping a coin five times?

a. 8
b. 16
c. 32
d. 64

94. If the x-axis in the scatter plot below represents the number of items sold and the y-axis represents the total profit in dollars, which of the following is the best estimate for the profit received for selling 15 items?

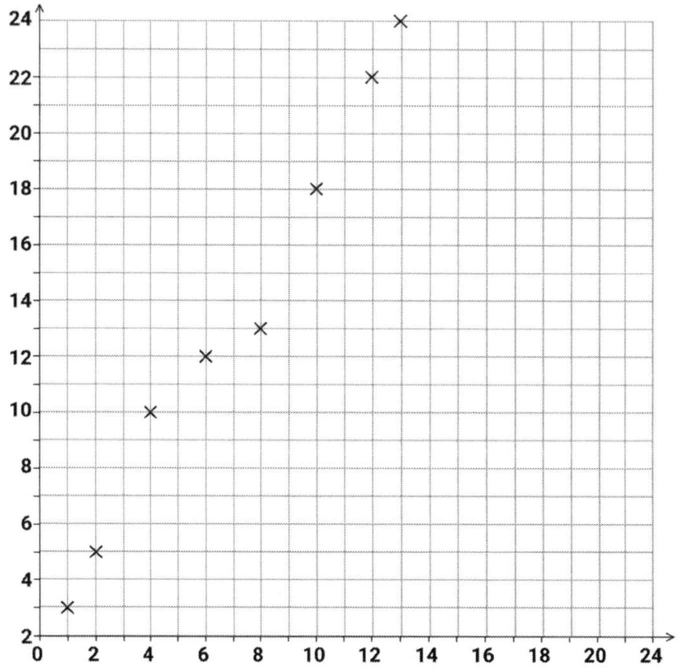

a. $24
b. $27
c. $30
d. $33

95. What is the contrapositive of the statement below?

If Bryan eats peanuts, he has an allergic reaction.

a. If Bryan eats peanuts, he does not have an allergic reaction.
b. If Bryan does not have an allergic reaction, he does not eat peanuts.
c. If Bryan does not eat peanuts, he does not have an allergic reaction.
d. If Bryan does not eat peanuts, he has an allergic reaction.

96. A teacher is working on improving organizational skills with her students. She allows five minutes of time at the end of every class for students to record what they were working on carefully into their notebooks and update their student planners with any homework or test information. What is the primary function of this strategy?

a. It conveys her expectations that students will be held accountable while in her classroom.
b. It helps to make students aware of which skills need more improvement.
c. It helps teach important life skills that will hopefully lead to increased academic success.
d. It demonstrates to her students that her classroom is a place where they should feel safe to learn.

97. Robert buys a car for $24,210. The price of the car has been marked down by 10%. What was the original price of the car?

a. $25,900
b. $26,300
c. $26,900
d. $27,300

98. Eli rolls a six-sided die and tosses a coin. What is the probability that he gets a prime number or tails?

a. $\frac{1}{4}$
b. $\frac{1}{3}$
c. $\frac{1}{2}$
d. $\frac{3}{4}$

99. Which of the following illustrates the additive inverse property?

a. The sum of a and 0 is a.
b. The sum of a and $-a$ is 0.
c. The sum of a and a is $2a$.
d. The sum of a and any variable x is $a + x$.

100. What is the slope of the leg marked x in the triangle graphed below?

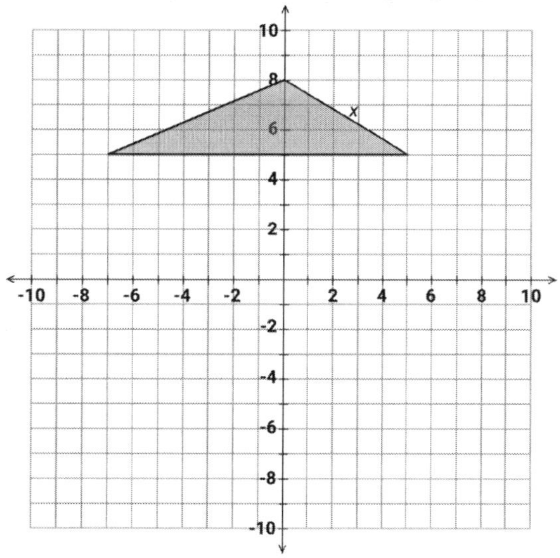

a. -3
b. $-\frac{3}{5}$
c. $\frac{3}{5}$
d. 3

Answer Key and Explanations for Test #3

1. C: Myles needs to purchase a combined total of at least 15 sandwiches and salads, so $x + y \geq 15$. Each sandwich costs \$3, each salad costs \$5, and he has a budget of \$60, so $3x + 5y \leq 60$. Therefore, the system of inequalities is:

$$\begin{cases} x + y \geq 15 \\ 3x + 5y \leq 60 \end{cases}$$

Graph the two lines. They should both be solid lines since both expressions allow equality (i.e., we have $\geq$ and $\leq$ rather than $>$ or $<$). The first inequality should be shaded above the line because he needs to buy 15 or more items, and the second inequality should be shaded below the line because he needs to spend \$60 or less. The overlapping shading occurs in the lower-right portion between the lines, which matches graph C.

2. C: The number 589 can be estimated to be 600. The number 9 can be estimated to be 10. The number of chicken nuggets is approximately 600×10, which is 6,000 nuggets. Therefore, the correct choice is (C).

3. D: The triangle is a 45-45-90 right triangle. If each leg is represented by x, the hypotenuse is then represented by $x\sqrt{2}$. Thus, the hypotenuse is equal to $12\sqrt{2}$ in.

4. B: The midpoint may be calculated by using the formula $m = \left(\frac{x_1+x_2}{2}, \frac{y_1+y_2}{2}\right)$. Thus, the midpoint of the line segment shown may be written as $m = \left(\frac{-5+7}{2}, \frac{-3+5}{2}\right)$, which simplifies to $m = (1, 1)$.

5. D: The Pythagorean theorem may be used to find the diagonal distance from the top of the building to the base of the shadow. The following equation may be written and solved for c: $44^2 + 59.2^2 = c^2$. Thus, $c \approx 73.8$. The distance is approximately 73.8 ft.

6. B: The two triangles are similar because they each have an angle measuring 65°, and the measurement of $\angle A$ is the same for both triangles, due to the Reflexive Property. So the two triangles are similar according to the AA (Angle-Angle) Similarity Postulate.

7. D: The student's answer is incorrect, most likely because the student has added rather than subtracted 5 to both sides. When solving a simple algebraic equation of this type, the goal is to isolate the variable on one side. This is done by eliminating the other terms and coefficients one by one. The most common first step in this problem would be to eliminate the 5 by subtracting an equal amount from both sides of the equation. This would leave $2x = 15$, which leads to the correct solution $x = 7.5$. If 5 was added, however, the resulting equation would be $2x = 25$, which would lead to the student's incorrect answer.

8. D: This problem can be solved using the percent change formula: $\%\ change = \frac{new-old}{old} \times 100\%$. Thus, the percentage increase is represented as $\%\ change = \frac{1{,}100-800}{800} \times 100\% = 37.5\%$.

9. A: Compare the equation $y = (x + 2)^2 - 3$ with its parent function, $y = x^2$. Replacing x with $(x + 2)$ moves the parent function 2 units to the left. Subtracting 3 moves the function 3 units down. Graph A is shifted 2 units left and 3 units down.

10. D: Since she spends at least \$40, the relation of the number of sandwiches to the minimum cost may be written as $8s \geq 40$. Alternatively, the inequality may be written as $40 \leq 8s$.

11. A: If we divide both terms in the numerator by n^2, the expression reduces to $\frac{1}{n} - \frac{1}{n^2}$. Both $\frac{1}{n}$ and $\frac{1}{n^2}$ converge to 0, so the expression can be written as $0 - 0 = 0$. Thus, the limit is 0.

12. C: The relationship between number of faces, edges, and vertices is represented by Euler's Formula, $E = F + V - 2$. Substituting 12 for E and 8 for V gives: $12 = F + 8 - 2$, which simplifies to $12 = F + 6$. Thus, $F = 6$.

13. A: Choice (A) is correct because standards for fourth grade state that students will be able to use a protractor to determine the approximate measures of angles in degrees to the nearest whole number. Choices (B), (C), and (D) are stated in the standards for fifth grade.

14. B: The product of $(x + 3)(3x - 6)$ equals $3x^2 - 6x + 9x - 18$, which simplifies to $3x^2 + 3x - 18$.

15. B: The decimal point is 3 places to the right of the first digit, 2. Thus, $2{,}417 = 2.417 \times 10^3$.

16. B: Since they are not mutually exclusive events, the probability may be written as $P(P \text{ or } H) = P(P) + P(H) - P(P \text{ and } H)$. Because the events are independent, $P(P \text{ and } H) = P(P) \times P(H)$. Substituting the probability of each event gives $(P \text{ or } H) = \frac{1}{3} + \frac{1}{2} - \left(\frac{1}{3} \times \frac{1}{2}\right)$, or $\frac{2}{3}$.

17. C: If the statement is written in the form $p \to q$, then the contrapositive is represented as $\neg q \to \neg p$. Thus, the contrapositive should read, "If it is not winter, Lucy does not wear a scarf."

18. B: In order to identify and resolve the problem, Mrs. Thomas' first step should be to consider whether there may be a problem with the assessment itself. Perhaps the assessment did not directly test the material that was covered, or perhaps the students were not given adequate time to complete the assessment. Only if Mrs. Thomas finds no problems with the test itself should she analyze the results to find out exactly which aspects of the material the students struggled with.

19. A: The ends of Data Set A are farther apart, indicating a larger range. The horizontal line in the middle of a boxplot represents the median, so Data Set A also has a larger median.

20. C: Since there are 144 square inches in 1 square foot, the following proportion may be written and solved for x: $\frac{144}{1} = \frac{2{,}012}{x}$. $144x = 2{,}012$. Dividing both sides of the equation by 144 gives $x \approx 13.97$. Thus, 2,012 square inches is approximately equal to 13.97 square feet.

21. C: The smaller triangle has a base length of 4 units and a height of 4 units. The larger triangle has a base length of 6 units and a height of 6 units. Using the base lengths, the dimensions of the smaller triangle were multiplied by a scale factor of $\frac{6}{4}$, which reduces to $\frac{3}{2}$.

22. D: The triangle is a 45-45-90 right triangle. Thus, if each leg is represented by x, the hypotenuse is represented by $x\sqrt{2}$. Thus, the hypotenuse is equal to $8\sqrt{2}$ cm.

23. B: The slope of the graphed line is −2. A line perpendicular to this one will have a slope of $\frac{1}{2}$. Substituting the slope and the x- and y-values from the point (3,2), into the slope-intercept form of an equation gives: $2 = \frac{1}{2}(3) + b$, which simplifies to $2 = \frac{3}{2} + b$. Subtracting $\frac{3}{2}$ from each side of the equation gives $b = \frac{1}{2}$. So, the equation of a line perpendicular to this one and passing through the point (3,2) is $y = \frac{1}{2}x + \frac{1}{2}$.

24. D: The set of whole numbers is represented as $\{0, 1, 2, 3, \dots\}$. The set of counting numbers is represented as $\{1, 2, 3, \dots\}$. Thus, the set of whole numbers includes all counting numbers plus zero, so the set of counting numbers is a subset of the set of whole numbers.

25. A: The graph is a straight line, so it is linear. If there were no deposit, the total cost would also be proportional to the number of months ($750 per month). But because the total cost is increased by the one-time $500 deposit, it is not proportional to the number of months.

26. A: Learner-centered assessment provides alternatives that allow different students to be assessed differently. Although student participation in assessment creation (D) is also an important part of learner-centered assessment, a multiple choice test does not reflect the goals of learner-centered assessment because it does not provide an authentic assessment experience.

27. D: Relation D is the only one in which there is not any x-value that is mapped to more than one y-value. Thus, this relation represents a function.

28. C: A reflection across the x-axis will result in a triangle with vertices at $(2, -3)$, $(4, -7)$, and $(6, -3)$. A rotation of 270 degrees counterclockwise is denoted by the following: $(x, y) \rightarrow (y, -x)$. Thus, a rotation of the reflected triangle by 270 degrees will result in a figure with vertices at $(-3, -2)$, $(-7, -4)$, and $(-3, -6)$. The transformed triangle indeed has these coordinates as its vertices.

29. A: Equilateral triangles and squares may tessellate a plane. Each triangle may be attached to each side of a square, leaving no gaps in the plane.

30. C: This situation may be modeled by an arithmetic sequence, with a common difference of 5 and an initial value of 15. Substituting the common difference and initial value into the formula, $a_n = a_1 + (n - 1)d$, gives $a_n = 15 + (n - 1)5$, which simplifies to $a_n = 5n + 10$.

31. D: The original price may be represented by the equation $158{,}400 = x - 0.12x$ or $158{,}400 = 0.88x$. Dividing both sides of the equation by 0.88 gives $x = 180{,}000$.

32. B: A student could apply math to choice (A) most for an algebra class, or any other situation wherein some numbers are known but one is not. For an English class, a student could apply math most to determine what scores are needed to raise a "B" grade to an "A." A student could apply math to choice (C) most for planning attendance at a school play, assembly, or other event using the auditorium space; and to choice (D) for planning to furnish refreshments, seating, forms/paper, pens, etc. at a PTA meeting.

33. C: A student is not ready to solve more complex subtraction problems until he or she has mastered all the single-digit subtraction facts. Grade level, proficiency in addition, and the desire to move ahead are not sufficient indications of the student's readiness.

34. B: The purpose of formative assessments is to assess students partway through a unit to see which parts of the units the students have mastered, as well as which parts of the unit may need to be retaught. These learning checks give the teacher a chance to see how the class is doing and how each student is doing individually. Formative assessments can be given in a variety of manners, including quizzes, tickets out the door, short essays or paragraphs explaining what was learned, as well as multiple other methods.

35. B: The probability of rolling a prime number (2, 3, or 5), denoted $P(Q)$, may be written as $P(Q) = \frac{1}{6} + \frac{1}{6} + \frac{1}{6} = \frac{1}{2}$.

36. B: The points may be entered into a graphing calculator or Excel spreadsheet to find the least-squares regression line. This line is approximately $y = 22x + 6$. Substituting 20 for x gives $y = 22(20) + 6$, or $y = 446$. Thus, \$446 is a good estimate for the earnings received after 20 hours of work. If a line of best fit is predicted visually, the slope between points near that line is around 20, and the line passes near the origin. Thus, another good estimate would be \$400. The estimate of \$446 is closer to \$400 than any of the other choices.

37. D: If we divide both terms in the numerator by n, the expression reduces to $n + \frac{1}{n}$. Although $\frac{1}{n}$ converges to 0, n increases without bound. The expression therefore has no limit.

38. A: Evaluation of the expression for an x-value of −2 gives: $(3(-2)^3 - 6(-2)^2 + 4)$, which equals −44.

39. C: Equilateral triangles and regular hexagons may tessellate a plane. Each triangle may be attached to each side of a hexagon, leaving no gaps in the plane.

40. B, C, D: Choices B and C both use correct order of operations to solve the problem. Choice D is an accurate visual representation of the problem. In choice A, the student inaccurately converted $\frac{3}{5}$ to the decimal 0.3 and did not explain why he or she multiplied by 2 at the end.

41. A: The situation may be modeled by the following system of inequalities: $\begin{cases} 2x + 3y \geq 60 \\ x + y \leq 25 \end{cases}$. A test point of (0,0) indicates shading should occur above the line for the top equation and below the line for the bottom equation. The overlapped shading occurs in the upper left portion between the lines. Thus, choice A represents the correct combinations of items that Mel may buy.

42. B: This prompt would help Keisha think of how to keep the ratio the same while still making the right amount of lemonade.

43. C: The original triangle was reflected across the x-axis. When reflecting across the x-axis, the x-values of each point remain the same, but the y-values of the points will be opposites.

$$(1,4) \rightarrow (1,-4) \quad (5,4) \rightarrow (5,-4) \quad (3,8) \rightarrow (3,-8)$$

44. B: The 1 is in the tenths place, the 5 in the hundredths place, and the 8 in the thousandths place. Thus, 0.158 is equal to the sum of the product of 1 and $\frac{1}{10}$, the product of 5 and $\frac{1}{100}$, and the product of 8 and $\frac{1}{1{,}000}$.

45. B: The probability may be written as $P(Blue \text{ or } FT) = P(Blue) + P(FT) - P(Blue \text{ and } FT)$. Substituting the probabilities, the following may be written: $P(Blue \text{ or } FT) = \frac{4{,}215}{12{,}612} + \frac{4{,}870}{12{,}612} - \frac{1{,}756}{12{,}612}$, which simplifies to $P(Blue \text{ or } FT) = \frac{7{,}329}{12{,}612}$, or approximately 60%.

Answer Key and Explanations #3

46. B: A rational number is any number that can be expressed as a ratio (or fraction) of two integers. A number is rational if and only if its decimal form either terminates or repeats infinitely. Choice A, $0.\overline{5} = 0.555 \ldots$, repeats infinitely, so it is rational. Choice C, $\frac{41}{3}$, is the ratio of the integers 41 and 3, so it is rational. Choice D, $(\sqrt{3})^2 = 3$, has a decimal form that terminates, so it is rational.

However, in choice B, the number $e = 2.71828 \ldots$ is known to be irrational. And $e + 3 = 5.71828 \ldots$ will likewise have infinite, nonrepeating decimal digits, so it must be irrational as well.

47. D: The characteristics of these three groups of fractions depend on how their numerator (the number on the top) and their denominator (the number on the bottom) compare. If the denominator is greater than the numerator, then the fraction is less than 1 (e.g., $\frac{5}{7}$). If the numerator and the denominator are the same, the number is equal to 1 (e.g., $\frac{5}{5}$). If the numerator is greater than the denominator, the number is greater than 1 (e.g., $\frac{7}{5}$).

48. C: The student needs to determine what she is being asked to find out before she can decide what equations or steps are needed to solve the problem. Comparing the problem to others like it may be useful, but it is not the first step in solving the problem.

49. B: The perimeter is equal to the sum of the lengths of the two bases, 6 and 2 units, and the diagonal distances of the other two sides. Using the distance formula, each side length may be represented as $d = \sqrt{2^2 + 4^2} = \sqrt{20} = 2\sqrt{5}$. Thus, the sum of the two sides is equal to $2\sqrt{20}$, or $4\sqrt{5}$. The whole perimeter is equal to $8 + 4\sqrt{5}$.

50. A: Substituting 3 for each x-value gives $f(3) = \frac{2(3)^3 - 10(3) + 6}{3(3)} = \frac{54 - 30 + 6}{9} = \frac{30}{9} = \frac{10}{3}$.

51. C: Data sets A and B are asymmetrical: data set A is skewed toward lower values, and data set B is skewed toward higher values. This makes the mean a poor measure of center. Data set D is mostly symmetrical, but has a large outlier. The mean is very sensitive to outliers, and is not an appropriate measure of center for data sets that include them. Data set C is roughly symmetrical and has no outliers; the mean would be an appropriate measure of center here.

52. A: The volume of a sphere may be calculated using the formula $V = \frac{4}{3}\pi r^3$, where r represents the radius. Substituting 2.5 for r gives $V = \frac{4}{3}\pi(2.5)^3$, which simplifies to $V \approx 65.4$.

53. C: The ends of Dataset A are farther apart (from 2 to 18 instead of 5 to 18), indicating a larger range. The horizontal line in the middle of a boxplot represents the median, so Dataset A has a smaller median (9 instead of 10).

54. C: To find a mean, students must be able to add the data points, count the number of data points, and divide the sum of the data points by the number of data points. To find a median, students must be able to order the data points, count the number of data points, and divide the number of data points by two in order to find the midpoint.

55. C: The surface area of a sphere may be calculated using the formula $SA = 4\pi r^2$. Substituting 9 for r and 3.14 for π gives $SA = 4(3.14)(9)^2$, which simplifies to $SA = 1{,}017.36$. So, the surface area of the ball is approximately 1,017.36 square inches. There are twelve inches in a foot, so there are $12^2 = 144$ square inches in a square foot. In order to convert this measurement to square feet, the following proportion may be written and solved for x: $\frac{1}{144} = \frac{x}{1{,}017.36}$. So $x = 7.07$. He needs approximately 7.07 square feet of wrapping paper.

56. C: The surface area of a rectangular prism may be calculated using the formula $SA = 2lw + 2wh + 2hl$. Substituting the dimensions of 14 inches, 6 inches, and 8 inches gives $SA = 2(14)(6) + 2(6)(8) + 2(8)(14)$. Thus, the surface area is 488 square inches.

57. C: Students apply logical reasoning to solve both usual, everyday problems and unusual, novel problems they encounter. Developing problem-solving skills not only helps students to think mathematically; it also develops their social skills (A) and language skills (B) when they collaborate to solve problems in math questions, in other school subjects, and in real life; and when they communicate, compare, and discuss their solutions. Children are naturally curious about how everyday problems can be solved: rather than having to teach them this interest (D), teachers can take advantage of this naturally existing motivation by asking them to propose problems; to propose solutions to problems and explain how they reached them; and asking questions about problems and solutions.

58. C: As x goes to positive or negative infinity, only the leading term of a polynomial function of x matters. Therefore, we can ignore the "−4" in the denominator; $\lim_{x\to-\infty} \frac{x}{x^2-4} = \lim_{x\to-\infty} \frac{x}{x^2} = \lim_{x\to-\infty} \frac{1}{x}$. As x goes to negative infinity, $\frac{1}{x}$ approaches zero. The limit is therefore 0.

59. B: The limit of the expression $\frac{7x^2}{x^2}$, is 7, so the limit of the entire function is $12 - 7 = 5$. The function converges.

60. C: The points in table represent a nonlinear curve that rises toward the origin, levels off as it crosses, and then rises again. This is a cubic function.

61. C: The ratio between successive terms is constant (2), so this is a geometric sequence. A geometric sequence is represented by an exponential function. The y-value in this formula represents the value shown in the sequence. The x-value in this formula represents the position of the value in the sequence. For example, the value 4 is the third term in the sequence. Therefore, the x-value is equal to 3. $y = 2^{(3-1)} = 2^2 = 4$. This is the only formula shown that can be applied to the sequence given. Answer choice A is not correct since it represents a linear pattern. If this pattern was used, the first value in the sequence would be 2 instead of 1, since $2(1) = 2$. Answer choice B also represents a linear pattern. If this pattern was used, the first value in the sequence would be 3 instead of 1, since $(1) + 2 = 3$. Thus, choice B is not correct. Answer choice D does represent an exponential function, but the values do not match the pattern in the sequence given. If this pattern was used, the first values match, but the second value would be 4 instead of 2, since $2^2 = 4$. Therefore, answer choice D is also incorrect.

62. B: The volume of Natasha's tent can be found by using the volume formula for a square pyramid, $V = \frac{1}{3}Bh = \frac{1}{3}s^2h$, where B is the area of the base, s is the side length of the square base, and h is the height of the pyramid. Therefore, the volume of her tent is $\frac{x^2h}{3}$. If she were to increase the length of each side of the square base by 1 ft, the tent's volume would be $\frac{(x+1)^2h}{3} = \frac{(x^2+2x+1)(h)}{3} = \frac{x^2h+2xh+h}{3} = \frac{x^2h}{3} + \frac{2xh+h}{3}$. Notice this is the volume of Natasha's tent, $\frac{x^2h}{3}$, increased by $\frac{2xh+h}{3}$.

63. D: The 5 is in the tenths place, the 9 in the hundredths place, and the 3 in the thousandths place. Thus, 0.593 is equal to the sum of the product of 5 and $\frac{1}{10}$, the product of 9 and $\frac{1}{100}$, and the product of 3 and $\frac{1}{1,000}$.

64. B: The surface area of a rectangular prism may be calculated using the formula $SA = 2lw + 2wh + 2hl$. Substituting the dimensions of 22 centimeters, 5 centimeters, and 8 centimeters gives $SA = 2(22)(8) + 2(8)(5) + 2(5)(22)$. Thus, the surface area is 652 square inches.

65. A: The theoretical probability is $\frac{1}{6}$, and $\frac{1}{6}(300) = 50$.

66. C: Students often struggle with money, even though it is a familiar and real-world concept, because there are multiple aspects to consider. In order to do these problems accurately, students must be able to add and subtract decimals. However, they must also understand the practical applications of this concept in their lives. Choices A and B both use test material that will improve this skill without addressing the concept itself. Students need to understand how to make change in the "real world," as well as how to complete a word problem on a test. Choice C addresses the money on a conceptual level in a fun way, combined with monitoring test practice to make sure the students are translating this knowledge to this context. Choice D only addresses one aspect of this issue, without connecting the interrelated skills in a meaningful way.

67. C: Before punishing the students or assuming that they don't understand the material, Mr. Tollison should ensure that all of the students know what the homework assignment is and correctly record it before leaving the classroom. Students may not complete the assignment correctly if they fail to write it down, especially if the assigned problems are shouted out hastily at the end of class.

68. D: When students continually show that they are not engaged in their assignments, teachers should make every effort possible to make the content more relevant to the students. A good way to do this is to create problems and assignments that better relate to the real world the students are experiencing. If they can personally connect to the material, they are more likely to see the value in the assignment. Excusing students from homework for the unit is not a realistic scenario, and teaching a lesson about the importance of word problems is not likely to be an engaging lesson that the students will connect with. While getting other teachers' input can be helpful when designing lessons and problems, the most direct way to improve engagement is to make the word problems relate to the real-world experiences of the students.

69. D: Summative assessments are administered at the end of an instructional unit to evaluate students' mastery of learning objectives. In mathematics instruction, these assessments provide teachers with feedback regarding areas of individual or whole-class need to plan future instruction and determine the need for reteaching specific skills. In this situation, the fact that many students in the class did not perform well on a summative assessment focused on basic multiplication facts indicates the need for whole-class reteaching of foundational skills. One such skill that would be beneficial to review includes skip counting. Skip counting refers to a strategy for counting in ascending order in specific intervals, such as by twos, fives, or tens. Reteaching this concept promotes students' ability to quickly count equal sets of numbers, thus establishing the foundation of understanding necessary to solve basic multiplication problems.

70. A: The slope may be written as $m = \frac{5-(-1)}{-4-3}$, which simplifies to $m = -\frac{6}{7}$.

71. C: Elijah's total cost is \$30 plus \$4 times the number of tickets. Rewriting this in mathematical notation (using y for total cost and x for the number of tickets) gives $y = 30 + 4x$, which is equivalent to choice C.

72. C: The standard deviation is equal to the square root of the ratio of the sum of the squares of the deviation of each score from the mean to the square root of the difference of n and 1. The mean of the data set is 29.25. The deviations are −6.25, −5.25, −3.25, −1.25, 1.75, 2.75, 5.75, and 5.75. The sum of the squares of the deviations may be written as:

$$39.0625 + 27.5625 + 10.5625 + 1.5625 + 3.0625 + 7.5625 + 33.0625 + 33.0625 = 155.5$$

Division of this sum by $n - 1 = 7$ gives 22.21. The square root of this quotient is approximately 4.7.

73. C: Using the points $(-3,1)$ and $(1,-11)$, the slope may be written as $m = \frac{-11-1}{1-(-3)}$ or $m = -3$. Substituting the slope of −3 and the x- and y-values from the point $(-3,1)$, into the slope-intercept form of an equation gives $1 = -3(-3) + b$, which simplifies to $1 = 9 + b$. Subtracting 9 from both sides of the equation gives $b = -8$. Thus, the linear equation that includes the data in the table is $y = -3x - 8$.

74. D: The median of the lower half of the scores is 4. The median of the upper half of the scores is 18. The interquartile range is the difference between the first and third quartiles: $18 - 4 = 14$.

75. C: The best way that a teacher could use standardized test data in her classroom is to use it to analyze gaps in learning that her students may have. They could potentially identify common gaps among the students and identify which students struggled more on specific standards than other students. It allows for the teacher to have an opportunity to plan out what she wants her students to improve upon in the upcoming year and enact a plan to see them achieve.

76. D: This situation describes a permutation, since order matters. The formula for calculating a combination is $P(n,r) = \frac{n!}{(n-r)!}$. This situation may be represented as $P(7,4) = \frac{7!}{(7-4)!}$, which equals 840.

77. C: The sum of an infinite geometric series may be modeled by the formula $S = \frac{a}{1-r}$, where a represents the initial value and r represents the common ratio. Substituting the initial value of 5 and common ratio of $\frac{3}{5}$ into the formula gives $S = \frac{5}{1-\frac{3}{5}}$, which simplifies to $S = \frac{5}{\frac{2}{5}}$ or $\frac{25}{2}$. This can be written as 12.5.

78. B: The original cost may be represented by the equation $\$450 = x - 0.4x$ or $\$450 = 0.6x$. Dividing both sides of the equation by 0.6 gives $x = \$750$.

79. D: The 8 is in the tenths place, the 6 in the hundredths place, and the 7 in the thousandths place. Thus, 0.867 is equal to the sum of the product of 8 and $\frac{1}{10}$, the product of 6 and $\frac{1}{100}$, and the product of 7 and $\frac{1}{1,000}$.

80. D: The rectangular array represents the product of the side lengths of 7 and $(4 + 2)$, resulting in the expression $7 \times (4 + 2)$.

81. C: The probability may be written as $P(M \text{ or } G) = P(M) + P(G) - P(M \text{ and } G)$. Substituting the probabilities yields $P(M \text{ or } G) = \frac{4{,}985}{10{,}079} + \frac{4{,}113}{10{,}079} - \frac{2{,}045}{10{,}079}$, which simplifies to $P(M \text{ or } G) = \frac{7{,}053}{10{,}079}$, or approximately 70%.

82. D: The probability may be written as $P(N \text{ and } T) = P(N) \times P(T)$. Substituting the probability of each event gives $(N \text{ and } T) = \frac{1}{6} \times \frac{1}{2}$, which simplifies to $\frac{1}{12}$.

83. A: The slope of the graphed line is $\frac{1}{2}$. A line parallel to this one will also have a slope of $\frac{1}{2}$. Substituting the slope and the x- and y-values from the point $(-2,2)$ into the slope-intercept form of an equation gives: $2 = \frac{1}{2}(-2) + b$, which simplifies to $2 = -1 + b$. Adding 1 to both sides of the equation gives $b = 3$; therefore, the equation of a line that is parallel to this one and that passes through the point $(-2,2)$ is $y = \frac{1}{2}x + 3$.

84. B: Educators can encourage the student who both loves animals and excels in mathematics and sciences to consider a career as a veterinarian, a medical doctor requiring more education and training than physicians treating humans; the student who hates these subjects but excels at gentle handling and beautification (a) to consider a professional pet groomer career; the average math and science student who excels at rescuing and nursing animals (c) to consider working as a veterinary technician or in an animal rescue organization; the student concerned with wildlife conservation, protecting endangered species, and working to improve captive animal habitats (d) to consider becoming a wildlife biologist or zoo curator. Students may share a common interest, but need educator help relating it to different individual higher education and career decisions.

85. C: The theoretical probability is $\frac{1}{2}$, and $\frac{1}{2}(250) = 125$.

86. A: This graph shows a slope of 3, a y-intercept of −6, and the correct shading above the line. Using the test point (0,0), the equation $0 \geq 0 - 6$ may be written. Since $0 \geq -6$, the solution is the shaded area above the line, which contains the point (0,0).

87. D: If the learning objective states that students should use proportional relationships, it would be important for them to be able to express the proportion they are using. The teacher suggested 1 foot : 1 inch (or 1 : 12) but did not express it mathematically.

88. A: The situation may be modeled by the inequality $3x + 2y \geq 20$. Isolating the y-term gives $2y \geq -3x + 20$. Solving for y gives $y \geq -\frac{3}{2}x + 10$. Thus, the y-intercept will be 10, the line will be solid, the slope will be $-\frac{3}{2}$, and the shading should occur above the line because y is greater than or equal to the expression on the other side of the inequality.

89. D: The percent change can be found using the following formula.

$$\% \text{ Change} = \frac{\text{new} - \text{old}}{\text{old}} \times 100$$

The old value is his current rent (750), and the new value is his new monthly rent (900).

$$\% \text{ Change} = \frac{900 - 750}{750} \times 100$$
$$\% \text{ Change} = \frac{150}{750} \times 100$$
$$\% \text{ Change} = \frac{1}{5} \times 100$$
$$\% \text{ Change} = 20$$

Since the percent change is positive, this represents a percent increase of 20%.

90. B: The number of ways the letters can be arranged may be represented as $\frac{5!}{2!1!1!1!}$, which equals 60.

91. C: The amount he saves is equal to $0.1 \times \$2{,}450$. Thus, he saves \$245.

92. C: The larger triangle has a base length of 6 units and a height of 6 units. The smaller triangle has a base length of 3 units and a height of 3 units. Thus, the dimensions of the larger triangle were multiplied by a scale factor of $\frac{1}{2}$.

93. C: The size of the sample space is the number of possible outcomes for one coin toss, 2, raised to the power of the number of coin tosses, 5. There are $2^5 = 32$ possible outcomes.

94. B: The points may be entered into a graphing calculator or Excel spreadsheet to find the least-squares regression line. This line is approximately $y = 1.67x + 1.74$. Substituting 15 for x gives $y = 1.67(15) + 1.74$, or $y = 26.79$. Thus, \$27 is a good estimate for the profit received for selling 15 items. If a line of best fit is predicted visually, the slope between points near that line is approximately $1\frac{3}{4}$, and the line passes near the origin. This gives an estimate of \$27.75, which is closer to \$27 than any of the other choices.

95. B: If the statement is written in the form $p \rightarrow q$, then the contrapositive is represented as $\neg q \rightarrow \neg p$. Thus, the contrapositive should read, "If Bryan does not have an allergic reaction, he does not eat peanuts."

96. C: Allowing students time at the end of class to organize and secure their belongings is a great way to teach and model proper organizational skills for students. By allowing time at the end of class to secure their belongings and update their planners with important information, this teacher is emphasizing to her students how important it is to both organize and keep track of dates and responsibilities. This should help set a good foundation for the students to implement these skills in other classes so that they have the tools to be successful in school.

97. C: The original price may be represented by the equation $24{,}210 = x - 0.10x$ or $24{,}210 = 0.9x$. Dividing both sides of the equation by 0.9 gives $x = 26{,}900$.

98. D: Let $P(T)$ represent the probability of getting tails on the coin toss. We can see that $P(T) = \frac{1}{2}$. Let $P(P)$ be the chance of getting a prime number on the die. Of the possible outcomes (1 through 6), three are prime (2, 3, and 5), so $P(P) = \frac{3}{6} = \frac{1}{2}$.

Since $P(P)$ and $P(T)$ are not mutually exclusive, $P(P \text{ or } T) = P(P) + P(T) - P(P \text{ and } T)$. Because the events are independent, $P(P \text{ and } T) = P(P) \times P(T)$. Substituting the probability of each event gives $P(P \text{ or } T) = \frac{1}{2} + \frac{1}{2} - \left(\frac{1}{2} \times \frac{1}{2}\right) = \frac{1}{2} + \frac{1}{2} - \frac{1}{4} = \frac{3}{4}$.

99. B: The additive inverse property states that the sum of a number and its negative value is 0.

100. B: The slope may be written as $m = \frac{8-5}{0-5}$, which simplifies to $m = -\frac{3}{5}$.

How to Overcome Test Anxiety

Just the thought of taking a test is enough to make most people a little nervous. A test is an important event that can have a long-term impact on your future, so it's important to take it seriously and it's natural to feel anxious about performing well. But just because anxiety is normal, that doesn't mean that it's helpful in test taking, or that you should simply accept it as part of your life. Anxiety can have a variety of effects. These effects can be mild, like making you feel slightly nervous, or severe, like blocking your ability to focus or remember even a simple detail.

If you experience test anxiety—whether severe or mild—it's important to know how to beat it. To discover this, first you need to understand what causes test anxiety.

Causes of Test Anxiety

While we often think of anxiety as an uncontrollable emotional state, it can actually be caused by simple, practical things. One of the most common causes of test anxiety is that a person does not feel adequately prepared for their test. This feeling can be the result of many different issues such as poor study habits or lack of organization, but the most common culprit is time management. Starting to study too late, failing to organize your study time to cover all of the material, or being distracted while you study will mean that you're not well prepared for the test. This may lead to cramming the night before, which will cause you to be physically and mentally exhausted for the test. Poor time management also contributes to feelings of stress, fear, and hopelessness as you realize you are not well prepared but don't know what to do about it.

Other times, test anxiety is not related to your preparation for the test but comes from unresolved fear. This may be a past failure on a test, or poor performance on tests in general. It may come from comparing yourself to others who seem to be performing better or from the stress of living up to expectations. Anxiety may be driven by fears of the future—how failure on this test would affect your educational and career goals. These fears are often completely irrational, but they can still negatively impact your test performance.

Elements of Test Anxiety

As mentioned earlier, test anxiety is considered to be an emotional state, but it has physical and mental components as well. Sometimes you may not even realize that you are suffering from test anxiety until you notice the physical symptoms. These can include trembling hands, rapid heartbeat, sweating, nausea, and tense muscles. Extreme anxiety may lead to fainting or vomiting. Obviously, any of these symptoms can have a negative impact on testing. It is important to recognize them as soon as they begin to occur so that you can address the problem before it damages your performance.

The mental components of test anxiety include trouble focusing and inability to remember learned information. During a test, your mind is on high alert, which can help you recall information and stay focused for an extended period of time. However, anxiety interferes with your mind's natural processes, causing you to blank out, even on the questions you know well. The strain of testing during anxiety makes it difficult to stay focused, especially on a test that may take several hours. Extreme anxiety can take a huge mental toll, making it difficult not only to recall test information but even to understand the test questions or pull your thoughts together.

Effects of Test Anxiety

Test anxiety is like a disease—if left untreated, it will get progressively worse. Anxiety leads to poor performance, and this reinforces the feelings of fear and failure, which in turn lead to poor performances on subsequent tests. It can grow from a mild nervousness to a crippling condition. If allowed to progress, test anxiety can have a big impact on your schooling, and consequently on your future.

Test anxiety can spread to other parts of your life. Anxiety on tests can become anxiety in any stressful situation, and blanking on a test can turn into panicking in a job situation. But fortunately, you don't have to let anxiety rule your testing and determine your grades. There are a number of relatively simple steps you can take to move past anxiety and function normally on a test and in the rest of life.

Physical Steps for Beating Test Anxiety

While test anxiety is a serious problem, the good news is that it can be overcome. It doesn't have to control your ability to think and remember information. While it may take time, you can begin taking steps today to beat anxiety.

Just as your first hint that you may be struggling with anxiety comes from the physical symptoms, the first step to treating it is also physical. Rest is crucial for having a clear, strong mind. If you are tired, it is much easier to give in to anxiety. But if you establish good sleep habits, your body and mind will be ready to perform optimally, without the strain of exhaustion. Additionally, sleeping well helps you to retain information better, so you're more likely to recall the answers when you see the test questions.

Getting good sleep means more than going to bed on time. It's important to allow your brain time to relax. Take study breaks from time to time so it doesn't get overworked, and don't study right before bed. Take time to rest your mind before trying to rest your body, or you may find it difficult to fall asleep.

Along with sleep, other aspects of physical health are important in preparing for a test. Good nutrition is vital for good brain function. Sugary foods and drinks may give a burst of energy but this burst is followed by a crash, both physically and emotionally. Instead, fuel your body with protein and vitamin-rich foods.

Also, drink plenty of water. Dehydration can lead to headaches and exhaustion, especially if your brain is already under stress from the rigors of the test. Particularly if your test is a long one, drink water during the breaks. And if possible, take an energy-boosting snack to eat between sections.

Along with sleep and diet, a third important part of physical health is exercise. Maintaining a steady workout schedule is helpful, but even taking 5-minute study breaks to walk can help get your blood pumping faster and clear your head. Exercise also releases endorphins, which contribute to a positive feeling and can help combat test anxiety.

When you nurture your physical health, you are also contributing to your mental health. If your body is healthy, your mind is much more likely to be healthy as well. So take time to rest, nourish your body with healthy food and water, and get moving as much as possible. Taking these physical steps will make you stronger and more able to take the mental steps necessary to overcome test anxiety.

Mental Steps for Beating Test Anxiety

Working on the mental side of test anxiety can be more challenging, but as with the physical side, there are clear steps you can take to overcome it. As mentioned earlier, test anxiety often stems from lack of preparation, so the obvious solution is to prepare for the test. Effective studying may be the most important weapon you have for beating test anxiety, but you can and should employ several other mental tools to combat fear.

First, boost your confidence by reminding yourself of past success—tests or projects that you aced. If you're putting as much effort into preparing for this test as you did for those, there's no reason you should expect to fail here. Work hard to prepare; then trust your preparation.

Second, surround yourself with encouraging people. It can be helpful to find a study group, but be sure that the people you're around will encourage a positive attitude. If you spend time with others who are anxious or cynical, this will only contribute to your own anxiety. Look for others who are motivated to study hard from a desire to succeed, not from a fear of failure.

Third, reward yourself. A test is physically and mentally tiring, even without anxiety, and it can be helpful to have something to look forward to. Plan an activity following the test, regardless of the outcome, such as going to a movie or getting ice cream.

When you are taking the test, if you find yourself beginning to feel anxious, remind yourself that you know the material. Visualize successfully completing the test. Then take a few deep, relaxing breaths and return to it. Work through the questions carefully but with confidence, knowing that you are capable of succeeding.

Developing a healthy mental approach to test taking will also aid in other areas of life. Test anxiety affects more than just the actual test—it can be damaging to your mental health and even contribute to depression. It's important to beat test anxiety before it becomes a problem for more than testing.

Study Strategy

Being prepared for the test is necessary to combat anxiety, but what does being prepared look like? You may study for hours on end and still not feel prepared. What you need is a strategy for test prep. The next few pages outline our recommended steps to help you plan out and conquer the challenge of preparation.

Step 1: Scope Out the Test

Learn everything you can about the format (multiple choice, essay, etc.) and what will be on the test. Gather any study materials, course outlines, or sample exams that may be available. Not only will this help you to prepare, but knowing what to expect can help to alleviate test anxiety.

Step 2: Map Out the Material

Look through the textbook or study guide and make note of how many chapters or sections it has. Then divide these over the time you have. For example, if a book has 15 chapters and you have five days to study, you need to cover three chapters each day. Even better, if you have the time, leave an extra day at the end for overall review after you have gone through the material in depth.

If time is limited, you may need to prioritize the material. Look through it and make note of which sections you think you already have a good grasp on, and which need review. While you are studying, skim quickly through the familiar sections and take more time on the challenging parts.

Write out your plan so you don't get lost as you go. Having a written plan also helps you feel more in control of the study, so anxiety is less likely to arise from feeling overwhelmed at the amount to cover.

Step 3: Gather Your Tools

Decide what study method works best for you. Do you prefer to highlight in the book as you study and then go back over the highlighted portions? Or do you type out notes of the important information? Or is it helpful to make flashcards that you can carry with you? Assemble the pens, index cards, highlighters, post-it notes, and any other materials you may need so you won't be distracted by getting up to find things while you study.

If you're having a hard time retaining the information or organizing your notes, experiment with different methods. For example, try color-coding by subject with colored pens, highlighters, or post-it notes. If you learn better by hearing, try recording yourself reading your notes so you can listen while in the car, working out, or simply sitting at your desk. Ask a friend to quiz you from your flashcards, or try teaching someone the material to solidify it in your mind.

Step 4: Create Your Environment

It's important to avoid distractions while you study. This includes both the obvious distractions like visitors and the subtle distractions like an uncomfortable chair (or a too-comfortable couch that makes you want to fall asleep). Set up the best study environment possible: good lighting and a comfortable work area. If background music helps you focus, you may want to turn it on, but otherwise keep the room quiet. If you are using a computer to take notes, be sure you don't have any other windows open, especially applications like social media, games, or anything else that could distract you. Silence your phone and turn off notifications. Be sure to keep water close by so you stay hydrated while you study (but avoid unhealthy drinks and snacks).

Also, take into account the best time of day to study. Are you freshest first thing in the morning? Try to set aside some time then to work through the material. Is your mind clearer in the afternoon or evening? Schedule your study session then. Another method is to study at the same time of day that you will take the test, so that your brain gets used to working on the material at that time and will be ready to focus at test time.

Step 5: Study!

Once you have done all the study preparation, it's time to settle into the actual studying. Sit down, take a few moments to settle your mind so you can focus, and begin to follow your study plan. Don't give in to distractions or let yourself procrastinate. This is your time to prepare so you'll be ready to fearlessly approach the test. Make the most of the time and stay focused.

Of course, you don't want to burn out. If you study too long you may find that you're not retaining the information very well. Take regular study breaks. For example, taking five minutes out of every hour to walk briskly, breathing deeply and swinging your arms, can help your mind stay fresh.

As you get to the end of each chapter or section, it's a good idea to do a quick review. Remind yourself of what you learned and work on any difficult parts. When you feel that you've mastered the material, move on to the next part. At the end of your study session, briefly skim through your notes again.

But while review is helpful, cramming last minute is NOT. If at all possible, work ahead so that you won't need to fit all your study into the last day. Cramming overloads your brain with more information than it can process and retain, and your tired mind may struggle to recall even previously learned information when it is overwhelmed with last-minute study. Also, the urgent nature of cramming and the stress placed on your brain contribute to anxiety. You'll be more likely to go to the test feeling unprepared and having trouble thinking clearly.

So don't cram, and don't stay up late before the test, even just to review your notes at a leisurely pace. Your brain needs rest more than it needs to go over the information again. In fact, plan to finish your studies by noon or early afternoon the day before the test. Give your brain the rest of the day to relax or focus on other things, and get a good night's sleep. Then you will be fresh for the test and better able to recall what you've studied.

Step 6: Take a Practice Test

Many courses offer sample tests, either online or in the study materials. This is an excellent resource to check whether you have mastered the material, as well as to prepare for the test format and environment.

Check the test format ahead of time: the number of questions, the type (multiple choice, free response, etc.), and the time limit. Then create a plan for working through them. For example, if you have 30 minutes to take a 60-question test, your limit is 30 seconds per question. Spend less time on the questions you know well so that you can take more time on the difficult ones.

If you have time to take several practice tests, take the first one open book, with no time limit. Work through the questions at your own pace and make sure you fully understand them. Gradually work up to taking a test under test conditions: sit at a desk with all study materials put away and set a timer. Pace yourself to make sure you finish the test with time to spare and go back to check your answers if you have time.

After each test, check your answers. On the questions you missed, be sure you understand why you missed them. Did you misread the question (tests can use tricky wording)? Did you forget the information? Or was it something you hadn't learned? Go back and study any shaky areas that the practice tests reveal.

Taking these tests not only helps with your grade, but also aids in combating test anxiety. If you're already used to the test conditions, you're less likely to worry about it, and working through tests until you're scoring well gives you a confidence boost. Go through the practice tests until you feel comfortable, and then you can go into the test knowing that you're ready for it.

Test Tips

On test day, you should be confident, knowing that you've prepared well and are ready to answer the questions. But aside from preparation, there are several test day strategies you can employ to maximize your performance.

First, as stated before, get a good night's sleep the night before the test (and for several nights before that, if possible). Go into the test with a fresh, alert mind rather than staying up late to study.

Try not to change too much about your normal routine on the day of the test. It's important to eat a nutritious breakfast, but if you normally don't eat breakfast at all, consider eating just a protein bar. If you're a coffee drinker, go ahead and have your normal coffee. Just make sure you time it so that the caffeine doesn't wear off right in the middle of your test. Avoid sugary beverages, and drink enough water to stay hydrated but not so much that you need a restroom break 10 minutes into the test. If your test isn't first thing in the morning, consider going for a walk or doing a light workout before the test to get your blood flowing.

Allow yourself enough time to get ready, and leave for the test with plenty of time to spare so you won't have the anxiety of scrambling to arrive in time. Another reason to be early is to select a good seat. It's helpful to sit away from doors and windows, which can be distracting. Find a good seat, get out your supplies, and settle your mind before the test begins.

When the test begins, start by going over the instructions carefully, even if you already know what to expect. Make sure you avoid any careless mistakes by following the directions.

Then begin working through the questions, pacing yourself as you've practiced. If you're not sure on an answer, don't spend too much time on it, and don't let it shake your confidence. Either skip it and come back later, or eliminate as many wrong answers as possible and guess among the remaining ones. Don't dwell on these questions as you continue—put them out of your mind and focus on what lies ahead.

Be sure to read all of the answer choices, even if you're sure the first one is the right answer. Sometimes you'll find a better one if you keep reading. But don't second-guess yourself if you do immediately know the answer. Your gut instinct is usually right. Don't let test anxiety rob you of the information you know.

If you have time at the end of the test (and if the test format allows), go back and review your answers. Be cautious about changing any, since your first instinct tends to be correct, but make sure you didn't misread any of the questions or accidentally mark the wrong answer choice. Look over any you skipped and make an educated guess.

At the end, leave the test feeling confident. You've done your best, so don't waste time worrying about your performance or wishing you could change anything. Instead, celebrate the successful completion of this test. And finally, use this test to learn how to deal with anxiety even better next time.

Review Video: Test Anxiety
Visit mometrix.com/academy and enter code: 100340

Important Qualification

Not all anxiety is created equal. If your test anxiety is causing major issues in your life beyond the classroom or testing center, or if you are experiencing troubling physical symptoms related to your anxiety, it may be a sign of a serious physiological or psychological condition. If this sounds like your situation, we strongly encourage you to seek professional help.

Online Resources

Due to our efforts to try to keep this book to a manageable length, we've created a link that will give you access to all of your online resources:

mometrix.com/resources719/texesmath4-8

It's Your Moment, Let's Celebrate It!

Share your story @mometrixtestpreparation